ROYALLY WRONGED

ROYALLY WRONGED

The Royal Society of Canada and Indigenous Peoples

Edited by
Constance Backhouse, Cynthia E. Milton,
Margaret Kovach, and Adele Perry

McGill-Queen's University Press
Montreal & Kingston • London • Chicago

© McGill-Queen's University Press 2021

ISBN 978-0-2280-0902-3 (cloth)
ISBN 978-0-2280-0903-0 (paper)
ISBN 978-0-2280-0911-5 (ePDF)
ISBN 978-0-2280-0912-2 (ePUB)

Legal deposit fourth quarter 2021
Bibliothèque nationale du Québec

Printed in Canada on acid-free paper that is 100% ancient forest free (100% post-consumer recycled), processed chlorine free

This book has been published with the help of a grant from the Canadian Federation for the Humanities and Social Sciences, through the Awards to Scholarly Publications Program, using funds provided by the Social Sciences and Humanities Research Council of Canada.

Funded by the Government of Canada   Financé par le gouvernement du Canada      Canada Council for the Arts   Conseil des arts du Canada

We acknowledge the support of the Canada Council for the Arts.
Nous remercions le Conseil des arts du Canada de son soutien.

Library and Archives Canada Cataloguing in Publication

Title: Royally wronged : the Royal Society of Canada and Indigenous peoples / edited by Constance Backhouse, Cynthia E. Milton, Margaret Kovach, and Adele Perry.
Names: Backhouse, Constance, 1952– editor. | Milton, Cynthia E., editor. | Kovach, Margaret, 1964– editor. | Perry, Adele, editor.
Description: Includes bibliographical references and index.
Identifiers: Canadiana (print) 20210276827 | Canadiana (ebook) 20210278641 | ISBN 9780228009023 (hardcover) | ISBN 9780228009030 (softcover) | ISBN 9780228009115 (PDF) | ISBN 9780228009122 (ePUB)
Subjects: LCSH: Royal Society of Canada. | LCSH: Indigenous peoples Canada. | LCSH: Knowledge, Sociology of. | LCSH: Learned institutions and societies—Canada—History. | LCSH: Colonization. | LCSH: Decolonization.
Classification: LCC AS42.R67 R69 2021 | DDC 061/.1—dc23

This book was typeset in 10.5/13 Sabon.

While some are surprised when difficult truths come to light, others have tried to keep them hidden. Our difficult past must be publicly addressed. While we, the Royal Society of Canada, cannot change the errors of our past, as an organization we promise to defend the rights of all, now and in the future.

Jeremy N. McNeil, CM, FRSC, President,
Royal Society of Canada (2018–2022)

Contents

Figures xi

Foreword xiii
Cindy Blackstock

Introduction: The Royal Society of Canada and the Marginalization of Indigenous Knowledge 3
Constance Backhouse and Cynthia E. Milton

PART ONE: THE ROYAL SOCIETY OF CANADA'S HISTORIC ROLE

1 Rather of Promise than of Performance: Tracing Networks of Knowledge and Power Through the *Proceedings and Transactions of the Royal Society of Canada*, 1882–1922 21
Ian Wereley

2 Duncan Campbell Scott and the Royal Society of Canada: The Legitimation of Knowledge 59
Constance Backhouse

3 "Perhaps the white man's God has willed it so": Reconsidering the "Indian" Poems of Pauline Johnson and Duncan Campbell Scott 88
Carole Gerson

4 "Sooner or later they will be given the privelage [sic] asked for": Duncan Campbell Scott and the Dispossession of Shoal Lake 40, 1913–14 111
Adele Perry

PART TWO: THE ROYAL SOCIETY OF CANADA AND ACADEMIC WRITINGS

5 Three Fellows in Mi'kma'ki: The Power of the Avocational   131
   John G. Reid

6 "Not a little disappointment": Forging Postcolonial Academies from Emulation and Exclusion   152
   Cynthia E. Milton

7 Nostra Culpa? Reflections on "The Indian in Canadian Historical Writing"   179
   James W. St G. Walker

PART THREE: RETHINKING ACADEMIA AND INDIGENEITY

8 Forensic Anthropology and Archaeology as Tools for Reconciliation in Investigations into Unmarked Graves at Indian Residential Schools   203
   Katherine L. Nichols, Eldon Yellowhorn, Deanna Reder, Emily Holland, Dongya Yang, John Albanese, Darian Kennedy, Elton Taylor, and Hugo F.V. Cardoso

9 Confronting "Cognitive Imperialism": What Reconstituting a Contracts Law School Course is Teaching Me about Law   230
   Jane Bailey

10 Murder They Wrote: Unknown Knowns and Windsor Law's Statement Regarding *R. v. Stanley*   250
   Reem Bahdi

11 History in the Public Interest: Teaching Decolonisation through the RSC Archive   276
   Jennifer Evans, Meagan Breault, Ellis Buschek, Brittany Long, Sabrina Schoch, and David Siebert

12 Cause and Effect: The Invisible Barriers of the Royal Society of Canada   298
   Joanna R. Quinn

PART FOUR: FUTURE DIRECTIONS

13 Memorandum to the Royal Society of Canada (2019) 319
    *Marie Battiste and James Sákéj Youngblood Henderson,
    endorsed by John Borrows, Margaret Kovach, Kiera Ladner,
    Vianne Timmons, and Jacqueline Ottmann*

14 Golden Eagle Rising: A Conversation on Indigenous
    Knowledge and the Royal Society of Canada 326
    Shain Jackson and Cynthia E. Milton

Afterword: Closing Circle Words 335
Margaret Kovach

Contributors 345

Index 353

Figures

1.1 List of RSC Council and Officers, Inaugural Meeting, 1882. Photograph by Darren Gilmour. Courtesy of the Royal Society of Canada. 25

1.2 Copies of Proceedings and Transactions, Walter House, Ottawa. Photographed by Ian Wereley with the permission of the Royal Society of Canada. 32

1.3 RSC Archives in Roderick A. Macdonald Room, Walter House, Ottawa. Photographed by Ian Wereley with the permission of the Royal Society of Canada. 45

2.1 Duncan Campbell Scott, 1915. Photograph by M.O. Hammond. Thomas Fisher Rare Book Library, University of Toronto. Duncan Campbell Scott Papers, MS Coll 00013, box 1B, folder 5. 60

2.2 Duncan Campbell Scott, undated. Reproduced from K.P. Stich, ed., *The Duncan Campbell Scott Symposium* (Ottawa: University of Ottawa Press, 1980), vi. Photograph credited as courtesy of John G. Aylen. 67

2.3 Duncan Campbell Scott at piano. Photograph by Yousuf Karsh, 1942. Reproduced from Robert L. McDougall, ed., *The Poet and the Critic* (Ottawa: Carleton University Press, 1983), iii. 72

2.4 Residence of Reverend William Scott, 108 Lisgar Street, September 1890. Photographed by William James Topley. Topley Studio, Library and Archives Canada. PA-027209. 74

3.1 *Proceedings and Transactions*, 1897. Section II, 79. Courtesy of the Royal Society of Canada. 93

Figures

3.2   Publicity photographs of Pauline Johnson, circa 1892. Photograph by Cochran. Vancouver Public Library, VPL_9430. 95
6.1   Excerpt from the "Vocabulary of about Seven Hundred Words from the Kwakiool Language." George M. Dawson, "Notes and Observations on the Kwakiool People of the Northern Part of Vancouver Island and Adjacent Coasts, Made During the Summer of 1885." RSC, *Proceedings and Transactions,* 1888, Section II, 92. 161
6.2   Meeting of the French Section of the Royal Society of Canada, 18 November 1945. Photograph by Roger Bédard. Fonds d'archives du Centre de recherche en civilisation canadienne-française, University of Ottawa. 170
7.1   Reproduction of the first page of James W. St G. Walker's 1971 article "The Indian in Canadian Historical Writing." Historical Papers, Communications Historiques 1971 (Canadian Historical Association: 1971), 21. 182
8.1   Students, Brandon Residential School. United Church Archives MBNWO, Winnipeg, Manitoba (Leonore Kirk Fonds_06). 208
8.2   New students arrive at Brandon Residential School. United Church Archives MBNWO, Winnipeg, Manitoba (Coulter Fonds_020). 209
8.3   Boys with piglets. United Church Archives MBNWO, Winnipeg, Manitoba (Leonore Kirk Fonds_16). 210
8.4   Brandon Girl Guides at the Brandon Residential School's First Cemetery in Curran Park. Photographer unknown, courtesy of B. Jolly. 212
8.5   Brandon Residential School's First Cemetery, circa 2004. Photograph by Robert and Diane Haglund, courtesy of the photographers. 213
8.6   Brandon Residential School's Second Cemetery, 2013. Photograph by author. 214
10.1 Exhibit at the Biggar Museum, Saskatchewan. https://www.biggarmuseum.com/collectionsexhibits.htm 252
14.1 Shain Jackson, *Double-Headed Golden Eagle (Ch' ask-in) Rising.* Photograph by Shain Jackson. 324

FOREWORD

The Royal Society of Canada and Colonialism: The Legacy of Duncan Campbell Scott

Cindy Blackstock

It was a landmark decision. In 2016, the Canadian Human Rights Tribunal confirmed what First Nations had known for decades: the federal government's inequitable provision of public services was discriminatory on the grounds of race and national ethnic origin.[1] The Canadian government welcomed the ruling publicly but continued its longstanding pattern of inadequate measures, resulting in nineteen non-compliance and procedural orders and counting.[2] One of the latest found Canada's discrimination to be "wilful and reckless" in a "worst case-scenario" contributing to the deaths of some children and the unnecessary family separations of many others.[3] The Tribunal awarded the children and families victimized by Canada's conduct the maximum amount of compensation allowable under the *Canadian Human Rights Act*, $40,000 per victim. Canada filed for a judicial review of the Tribunal's decision, arguing that victims of systemic discrimination are not owed individual compensation and the funds required to compensate victims would amount to irreparable harm for Canada.[4]

Canada's discrimination is deeply rooted in its history, its academia, and, indeed, in the Royal Society of Canada (RSC) itself. In his 1922 RSC presidential address, Duncan Campbell Scott lauded the organization's promotion of French and English scholarship. According to Scott, these would be the "first civilized languages heard by the natives of this country,"[5] before he went on to say, "[T]he former story-telling function of History and the needless re-weaving of that tissue of tradition which surrounded and obscured the life of a people has given place to a higher conception of the duty of the

Historian and the obligation to accept no statement without the support of documentary evidence."[6] Yet, even as he delivered this address, Scott's historical footprint was being whitewashed by the very organization that ought to have held him accountable to the truth.

Scott achieved his RSC fellowship in 1899, eventually climbing to the stations of honorary secretary then president at the Royal Society (1921–22), owing to his poetic prowess. Despite this, the legacy of his role as superintendent of the Indian Department continues to overshadow his literary career.

Ambitious by nature, Scott's plans to become a physician were thwarted by his family's modest means, so his father, William Scott, found Scott a job in the public service. On 14 November 1879, family friend John A. Macdonald appointed Scott to a clerk position, from which he quickly rose through the ranks to become the longest-serving and highest-placed bureaucrat on the residential school file.[7] In 1922, the same year Scott was serving as president of the Royal Society of Canada, Dr Peter Henderson Bryce, MD, former medical health officer for the Indian Department, was busy circulating a pamphlet around Ottawa entitled, "The Story of a National Crime: An Appeal for Justice to the Indians of Canada."[8] Bryce recounted his 1907 research, which found that children in residential schools were dying from tuberculosis at a rate of 24 per cent owing to inequitable health services, poor health practices, and unsanitary conditions. The report pointed to Scott's repeated efforts to foil the reforms needed to save the children's lives. Scott's misdeeds were hardly a secret. In 1908, the front page of the *Ottawa Evening Citizen* featured the headline, "*Schools Aid White Plague: Startling Death Rolls Revealed.*"[9] The article recounted Bryce's report and noted the "absolute inattention to bare necessities of health," causing the schools to become "veritable hotbeds of disease."[10] Samuel Hume Blake, a lawyer and later a judge, spoke out saying "in that Canada fails to obviate the preventable causes of death it brings itself into unpleasant nearness with the charge of manslaughter."[11]

However, Blake was atypical of the demure academic response and, to my knowledge, there was no mention of Bryce's report in Royal Society records. Similar headlines appeared in papers across the country in 1922 with Bryce's release of "A National Crime,"[12] and yet, the Annual Report for the Royal Society of Canada says nothing of the complicity of its president in the deaths of countless children. Indeed, instead of investigating Scott when his wrongdoing became public, the RSC continued to promote him within its ranks and awarded him the prestigious Lorne Pierce Medal for literature.

In 2015, the Truth and Reconciliation Commission estimated that at least four thousand to six thousand children died in the schools due to maltreatment and the rampant tuberculosis epidemic Bryce had tried to prevent. The TRC concluded that residential schools amounted to "cultural genocide."

One hundred years after Bryce published his original report documenting the preventable deaths of children in residential schools and urging reform, national headlines reported that the First Nations Child and Family Caring Society and the Assembly of First Nations had filed a human rights complaint against Canada alleging that its inequitable provision of First Nations child welfare and other children's services amounted to racial discrimination. While there was a mild increase in the number of academics paying attention and helping these children, the overall response was one of academic slumber.

The highly educated have littered colonialism across the country while many others remained silent in the face of the obvious human tragedy of residential schools and discriminatory child welfare. Lawyers wrote and implemented colonial laws while discounting Indigenous law,[13] social workers promoted assimilation,[14] medical professionals and researchers conducted nutritional experiments on Indigenous children in residential schools,[15] and highly educated bureaucrats designed and implemented colonial policies to harm Indigenous families and communities.[16] The highly educated in Canadian society were not just bystanders – they deployed their knowledge and skills to abet colonialism and, in too many cases, continue to do so today.

As a result, I stumbled into academia as a matter of practicality. I needed to learn more so I could better help tackle the inequalities that had been piling up on the hopes and dreams of First Nations children since confederation. I selected my academic fields based on what I needed to know to do a better job for these children, which landed me in four different disciplines at four different universities.

To say I am not a typical academic is an understatement, which is why I was so honoured and surprised to receive an invitation from the Royal Society to address their annual meeting in 2016. Then the worry set in. I knew of Scott's history with the Royal Society and decided that it was time to give life to Scott's 1922 address and give "place to a higher conception of the duty of the Historian and the obligation to accept no statement without the support of documentary evidence."[17] This volume represents the RSC's initial response to the invitation to dive deep into its own history so as to learn why academia was more often an aid to colonialism than a force against it. The ultimate goal is to raise a generation of academics who are not as tempted to ignore evidence, even when it raises serious questions about academics, academic institutions, and assumptions of what counts as academia. All of this and more is required for individual academics, fields of study, and the RSC to move meaningfully toward reconciliation in the way envisioned by the Truth and Reconciliation Commission of Canada.[18]

NOTES

1 *First Nations Child and Family Caring Society et al. v. Attorney General of Canada*, 2016, Canadian Human Rights Tribunal (hereafter CHRT) 2. These documents are available at https://fncaringsociety.com/chrt-orders.
2 *First Nations Child and Family Caring Society et al. v. Attorney General of Canada*, 2016 CHRT 10, 2016 CHRT 16, 2017 CHRT 7; 2017 CHRT 14, 2018 CHRT 4, 2019 CHRT 1; 2019 CHRT 7; 2019 CHRT 39.
3 *First Nations Child and Family Caring Society et al. v. Attorney General of Canada*, 2019 CHRT 39.
4 *Attorney General of Canada v. First Nations Child and Family Caring Society et al.*, FC: T-162-19.
5 D.C. Scott, Appendix A: *Presidential address: poetry and progress* (Ottawa: Royal Society of Canada, 1922).
6 Ibid., LI.
7 P Edgar, "Duncan Campbell Scott," *The Dalhousie Review*, (1926): 38–46.
8 P.H. Bryce, *The Story of a National Crime: An Appeal for Justice to the Indians of Canada* (Ottawa: James Hope and Sons, 1922).
9 "Schools Aid White Plague: Startling Death Rolls Revealed," *Evening Citizen*, 15 November 1908.
10 Ibid.
11 John Milloy, *A National Crime: The Canadian Government and the Residential School System, 1879–1986* (Winnipeg: University of Manitoba Press, 1999).
12 Ibid.

13 John Borrows, "With or Without You: First Nations Law (in Canada)," *McGill Law Journal* 41, (1996): 629–664.
14 Cindy Blackstock, "The Occasional Evil of Angels: Learning from Social Work's Experiences with Aboriginal Peoples," *First Peoples Child and Family Review* 14, no.1 (2019):137–152.
15 Ian Mosby, "Administering Colonial Science: Nutrition Research and Human Biomedical Experimentation in Aboriginal Communities and Residential Schools, 1942–1952," *Histoire sociale–Social History* XLVI, no.91 (Mai–May 2013):145–172.
16 Truth and Reconciliation Commission of Canada, *Honouring the Truth, Reconciling for the Future: Summary of the Final Report of the Truth and Reconciliation Commission of Canada* (Winnipeg: Truth and Reconciliation Commission, 2015).
17 Ibid., 6.
18 Ibid., 16.

ROYALLY WRONGED

INTRODUCTION

The Royal Society of Canada and the Marginalization of Indigenous Knowledge

Constance Backhouse and Cynthia E. Milton

In September 2015, then president of the Royal Society of Canada (RSC), Dr Graham Bell, received a letter from University of Alberta professor Dr Cindy Blackstock, member of the Gitxsan First Nation, a leading advocate for Indigenous children in Canada, and an honorary witness for the Truth and Reconciliation Commission of Canada. When there was no reply, Dr Blackstock sent a second letter to the chief executive officer of the RSC in November 2015. Just months prior, the Truth and Reconciliation Commission of Canada (TRC) had issued its powerful *Calls to Action*, a series of ninety-four instructions to the Canadian government, organizations, and communities to guide reconciliation.[1]

Dr Blackstock's objecives were twofold: to set in motion the institutional reforms called for in the *Calls to Action* and to prod the RSC to reckon with historic and ongoing marginalization of Indigenous knowledge and knowledge keepers. This was not some passive or indirect exclusion or harm, she argued. The RSC had been directly involved in the multigenerational violence. Among the RSC's illustrious past members, it had inducted Duncan Campbell Scott, deputy superintendent of Indian Affairs and the primary architect of residential schools, as a fellow in 1899 and given him several honours, including voting him RSC president from 1921 to 1922. His deep ties to the RSC, Blackstock noted, constituted "an important historical link to the residential school era." In her generously worded letter, Dr Blackstock did not set out to publicly shame the RSC. Rather she wished to make the current RSC president and council aware of this past so that they might consider how best to move forward.[2]

The RSC lists on its website the mandate to serve Canada and Canadians by "recognizing Canada's leading intellectuals, scholars, researchers and artists and, by mobilizing them in open discussion and debate, advancing knowledge, encouraging integrated interdisciplinary understandings and addressing issues that are critical to Canada and Canadians."[3] Today's fellows are nearly 2,500 in number, divided between three academies: the Academy of Arts and Humanities, the Academy of Social Sciences, and the Academy of Science. Established in 2014, the RSC's College of New Scholars, Artists and Scientists has since added over four hundred members.

Although membership in the RSC is understood as something like a "seal" of acknowledgment, and a recognition of intellectual and artistic excellence, the knowledge produced and celebrated inside the organization has taken place within a context of colonialism. Scholarly experts have played a significant role in shaping the knowledge required to build and implement policies that have proven catastrophic for Indigenous communities. Academics have been involved in ethnographic research and studies on political, economic, and legal structures affecting Indigenous communities. The direct impact of this research has been broad and profound from medical care, policing, and social conditions within Indigenous societies. Scholars from a wide range of disciplines have helped to construct the scaffolding upon which Euro-Canadian and Indigenous relationships were forged.

This was the history and current situation which Dr Cindy Blackstock wished to draw to the attention of the RSC president: Canada's long history of discrimination against First Nations, Métis, and Inuit peoples, the role of the RSC in the marginalization of Indigenous knowledge, and the consequent harms that followed. In her keynote address at the RSC's Annual General Meeting in Kingston in 2016, on the occasion of her becoming a fellow of the RSC, Dr Blackstock reminded the audience that the majority of the 4,500 children who died in residential schools did so during Scott's tenure at the Department of Indian Affairs. She emphasized that it was Duncan Campbell Scott who requisitioned a warrant from the Department of Justice in 1895 to allow for the forcible removal of "Indian" children from their families.

Her call to action was compelling. She stated, "the Royal Society's leadership role promoting leadership and research aligns with the Truth and Reconciliation Commission's requirement for truth-telling and call for active engagement in reconciliation by all Canadians and organizations. As an act of reconciliation, I would recommend that the Society educate your members and others in your circle about Duncan Campbell Scott and his role in the Royal Society and actively engage in the implementation of the TRC recommendations as a matter of priority."[4]

In addition to pointing to the need to look internally within the RSC and ways to promote awareness and recognition as necessary for reconciliation, Dr. Blackstock also addressed the harmful role of academia on Indigenous peoples and knowledge systems. Academia's harms were at least threefold: complicity with the colonial regime even in the face of evidence of harms viewed by some people of the period to be immoral, if not criminal; ignoring of the situation of First Nations, Métis, and Inuit peoples; and direct engagement with colonial harms via experiments on children in the schools, legal efforts intended to strip Indigenous rights, and creation of conditions for the perpetuation of colonialism and discrimination in public policy.[5]

In 2017, in response to Dr Blackstock's letter and the TRC's *Calls to Action*, the RSC created a Truth and Reconciliation Task Force, with participation open to all RSC fellows and members of the RSC College. Dr Blackstock agreed to assist the Task Force in an advisory capacity. At the time of writing, this Task Forc is composed of more than sixty members, Indigenous and settler, from all the academies. Its objectives are to:

1 address the recommendations made by the Canadian Truth and Reconciliation Commission;
2 examine the RSC's historical role in the Indian residential school system and academia's larger role in the marginalization of Indigenous knowledge and dispossession of Indigenous peoples;
3 make proposals as to how the RSC can engage in more meaningful inclusion of First Nations, Métis, and Inuit communities.

This volume of interdisciplinary essays emerged from an open call for papers that the Task Force issued to all members of the RSC. The call requested papers that would explore the historical contribution of the RSC and of Canadian scholars to the production of ideas and policies that underpin the disastrous interaction of settlers, especially white ones, with Indigenous peoples. It also sought papers about newly emerging scholarly directions that attempt to create significant change. The authors who responded to the call chose to focus predominantly upon scholarship from anglophone RSC members from the social sciences, arts, and humanities. Although the chapters that follow profile a few francophone and scientist members of the RSC, the records of RSC scientists and francophones need significantly more study. This leaves promising vistas for further exploration into the impact of the Academy of Science and the francophone members of the RSC on Indigenous communities and Indigenous knowledge. We would like to make an explicit invitation to scientific and francophone scholars within the RSC to consider further research that would expand upon the work in this volume.[6]

In response to Dr Blackstock's call to action, this collection of essays begins with the origins of the RSC and centres upon the involvement of Duncan Campbell Scott. A complete assessment of the role of the RSC and its legacy within academia more generally would take many books and articles. We offer this volume as a modest first step, an undertaking begun here mainly by current RSC fellows and College members. The historical essays in the first two sections focus upon the time from the RSC's founding in 1882 up to the mid-twentieth century. The later chapters then bring the discussion forward to the present and future prospects for change.

Although the chapters in this volume chronicle the detrimental impact that RSC fellows had upon Indigenous communities and Indigenous knowledge, we are aware that some members had more varied views; as Joan Sangster noted in her 2017 Canadian Historical Address, there were "small cracks in colonialist thinking."[7] In the same vein, not all Indigenous "informants" were unwilling participants, and a few shared with certain ethnographers specific stories they wished to put into the public realm for future generations. Thus, readers may query whether it is fair to concentrate so fully upon the harmful aspects of the RSC scholars' work. This is not the goal nor intention of this book; rather the inspiration for this project came in response to Dr Blackstock's request for more information on Duncan Campbell Scott and the wider responsibility of the RSC for the marginalization of Indigenous knowledge, and a larger dialogue needed into institutional responsibilities in the propagation of systemic racism as signaled by the Canadian Truth and Reconciliation Commission's *Calls to Action*. Delving into the complexities of the intentions and motivations of RSC members is a task we have chosen to leave for future analysis.

Intentions and motivations can be mixed, of course, and change in time and context. Several contributing authors to this volume note what appears at moments to be a fascination, if not obsession, with Indigenous peoples and their cultures, by the RSC's learned members. All the while that they bemoaned the "disappearance" of Indigenous peoples, they documented and collected Indigenous material culture for their own private and national collections. Fascination can go hand in hand with marginalization and the voices of the other can be appropriated by the scholarly community.

The essays in part I examine the Royal Society's historic role in constructing the intellectual foundation that shored up white-settler privilege and erased the knowledge contributions of Indigenous peoples. Ian Wereley, a newly-minted PhD, sets the stage by reviewing the archival records of the RSC from the date of its founding in 1882 to the year of Duncan Campbell Scott's death in 1947. He explores how its intricate networks of intellectuals contributed to the shaping of Indigenous policy in Canada and the promulgation of racialized ideas that brought forth the residential school system. As an aspiring academic, full of promise and optimism, his forays into the RSC archives left him cold and concerned about his choice of guild.

RSC Fellow Constance Backhouse explores how Duncan Campbell Scott came to achieve recognition in the Royal Society in the early twentieth century, and how the RSC enhanced his reputation and celebrated his expertise. It considers what the imprimatur of the RSC did to establish Scott as a man of letters and a leader among Canada's intellectual elite, and what that came to mean for Indigenous peoples.

Carole Gerson, from the RSC Academy of Arts and Humanities, compares two influential poets from Canada's late nineteenth and early twentieth centuries: Duncan Campbell Scott and Emily Pauline Johnson. She notes that their paths crossed in person and in print quite a few times, but their literary portrayal of Indigenous peoples could not have been more different. She demonstrates how Scott's framework of the "disappearing Indian" defeated by the course of history contrasts starkly with that of Johnson, a woman of Mohawk and English heritage who asserted Indigenous agency through courageous female characters. That the former was an influential

RSC fellow and president, while the latter's contributions were scarcely recognized by the RSC, tells its own tale.

Adele Perry, a more recent fellow from the Academy of Arts and Humanities, examines the egregious process by which lands and resources were wrested out of the hands of the Shoal Lake 40 First Nation in the second decade of the twentieth century in order to provide clean water to the burgeoning settler city of Winnipeg, Manitoba. She documents the nefarious ways in which various levels of government conspired together to deny the Indigenous community its rights to reserve lands. Perry probes Duncan Campbell Scott's role as superintendent of Indian Affairs and his connections to the unjust transfer of the First Nation's lands. She queries what we need to learn from the fact that a man who bears central responsibility for the intensification and administration of Canadian colonialism was also a leader within the RSC.

The essays in part II, "The Royal Society of Canada and Academic Writings," begin to move beyond the RSC itself to assess more broadly the academic depictions of Indigenous peoples. The authors examine writings by Canadian historians and poets, some RSC fellows but others not. John Reid looks back on his former confreres by focusing on three Nova Scotia RSC fellows from the late nineteenth and early twentieth centuries: Archibald MacMechan, a literary scholar at Dalhousie University, George Patterson, Presbyterian minister and amateur archaeologist in Pictou, and Thomas Head Raddall, a historical novelist. Reid traces how all three reaffirmed a hierarchy of settler and Indigenous societies, perspectives strengthened by the weight of authority that RSC membership carried.

Cynthia Milton, from the first cohort of the RSC College and past president, examines the early years of the RSC's annual publication, the *Proceedings and Transactions*, for insight into how its leading intellectuals struggled to create their own national voice in what she considers a double postcolonial predicament: their own colonial mindset that turned to Great Britain and their inability to acknowledge Indigenous knowledge keepers. She reviews the publications of English and French RSC fellows, searching for pieces that incorporate Indigenous knowledge. She describes that while Indigenous speakers were erased from the record, their knowledge filtered into RSC scholarship. This knowledge helped make Canadian scholarship unique, though unnoticed by RSC scholars using filters based on European measurements.

James W. St G. Walker looks at how Indigenous peoples were portrayed by non-Indigenous Canadian historians in their publications and history course-lists prior to the 1970s. A fellow of the RSC, Walker offers a reconsideration of his 1971 survey of the state of Canadian historiography, "The Indian in Canadian Historical Writing," written while a graduate student, which documented an alarming body of writing based on racist stereotypes. Walker reflects upon the extent to which our scholarly research has moved beyond the earlier damaging depictions to acknowledge more accurately the historical contributions of Indigenous peoples. He concludes that despite evidence of progress, much remains still to be done. Read with Ian Wereley's chapter, we are reminded of the importance of intergenerational dialogue.

Parts III and IV move forward in time to consider present and future directions. The authors, most of them also RSC fellows and College members, responded to the RSC Task Force's call for papers to probe the ways in which the RSC's historic legacies have infiltrated our academic disciplines more generally. They also consider what some RSC scholars today are trying to do differently to repair the deleterious RSC perspectives. The essays in part III, "Rethinking Academia and Indigeneity," also suggest projects that may begin to alter destructive hierarchies. The essay by Katherine L. Nichols, Eldon Yellowhorn, Deanna Reder (RSC College), Emily Holland, Dongya Yang, John Albanese, Darian Kennedy, Elton Taylor, and Hugo F.V. Cardoso (RSC College) gives a concrete example of how scholarship can be done collaboratively, eschewing the practices of past extractive research and showing how asking questions together brings new methodologies and knowledge. Knowledge in this case is about the violent practices of residential schools and where the graves of the children in state and church care are today.

The potential of law schools not only to address past exclusive practices but to actively decolonize the classroom and the profession are the focus of the next two chapters. RSC College member Jane Bailey's essay focuses on the principles of contract within the Canadian common-law system. A law professor who has taught contract law to first-year law students for almost two decades, Bailey describes how she and several other law colleagues have begun to measure the rigid rules and processes of Euro-Canadian law against Indigenous laws and legal traditions. Reem Bahdi, another Canadian law professor and member of the RSC College, analyzes the 2018 criminal trial of Saskatchewan farmer Gerald Stanley for the killing of Colten Boushie of Red Pheasant First Nation. She examines the various ways in which Canadian criminal law failed Boushie, his family, and his community, and describes how one Canadian law school attempted to register its disgust in public and then experienced the attendant backlash.

Jennifer Evans, from the RSC College, along with her students Meagan Breault, Ellis Buschek, Brittany Long, Sabrina Schoch, and David Siebert, narrate the academic experience of a history course from Carleton University. The group worked with Library and Archives Canada to catalogue and identify the RSC networks of people and ideas that shaped how successive Canadian governments and society viewed and implemented Indigenous policy. This essay begins to explore the intellectual challenges of doing this research as settlers of a certain age and generation operating within the very academic institutions buttressed by learned societies and their professors. Guided by Indigenous critiques of white-settler knowledge formations, this university class provides a snapshot of what it discovered to serve as a primer for future research, while also thinking through the absences and gaps in the historical record and what they mean for reconciliation today.

Joanna Quinn, former president of the RSC College, considers the invisible structural barriers that organizations such as the RSC have set up that result in the almost total exclusion of Indigenous people and Indigenous knowledge. She examines the concept of "structural violence" as a lens through which to view the impediments that have kept out anyone who did not "fit," and the ultimate losses for scholarship that such barriers inflicted.

Part IV, "Future Directions," contains a memorandum written by Fellows Marie Battiste and James Sákéj Youngblood Henderson and endorsed by Indigenous members of the RSC as well as two Saskatchewan university officers, addressed to the incoming presidents of the RSC and the College of New Scholars, Artists and Scientists. It is a call to action to continue efforts to decolonize the RSC and to include Indigenous holders of Indigenous knowledge systems and languages. The Royal Society of Canada and Indigenous knowledge, and the importance of truth for justice and change, are at the heart of a conversation between settler academic Cynthia Milton and Coast Salish artist and lawyer Shain Jackson whose artwork, *Double-Headed Golden Eagle (Ch' ask-in) Rising,* graces the cover of this book. Margaret Kovach (Sākohtēw pīsimw iskwēw), a College member, offers concluding words, her overview of the project represented by this volume of essays, her call to move beyond the erasure and salvage scholarship that has caused so much injustice, and her insistence that we bring Indigenous intellectual contributions into full inclusion.

The RSC was and remains a predominantly white organization. There appear to have been no racialized fellows in the early years, and it is difficult to know with certainty when the first Indigenous and racialized members were inducted. Certainly, the RSC replicated patterns of whiteness in Canadian academic life as a whole.[8] The RSC recently began a demographic audit based on self-identification by the membership. As will be apparent, our open call for papers to include in this volume was taken up by mostly non-Indigenous authors. While we hoped to include more Indigenous authors in this volume, we thank those who have so generously participated in this project. We remain cognizant of the many risks we run as mostly white-settler researchers attempting to navigate the projects of truth and reconciliation.

Much of the historical material we quote from and discuss in the essays that follow contains words and phrases that are deeply offensive. The risk is that by delving into the hateful discourse from the past we create more pain today, and that by replicating this, we may be reproducing the violence. In tracking the devastation wreaked by RSC fellows and other non-Indigenous scholars, we recognize that this writing may be emotionally difficult for readers. We have chosen to embark upon this troubling research because we believe that it is important to document the enormity of the inhuman treatment that non-Indigenous scholars have meted out to Indigenous communities. We feel strongly that as settler scholars this is our obligation in response to the TRC *Calls to Action*. Our hope is that this may open up opportunities to learn how structural violence has been perpetuated through a system of acknowledgment and reward that venerates ideas and actions harmful to First Nations, Métis, and Inuit culture, life, and well-being. We offer these essays as a first step in taking ownership of the tragedies that non-Indigenous people have fomented against Indigenous communities.

We thank the Indigenous scholars who chose to help to guide us in this challenging venture, and in particular, we thank Dr Cindy Blackstock for showing us the initial path. We include her letter to the RSC in the fall of 2015 in its entirety, and offer this volume as a partial and preliminary response in a much-needed dialogue.

LETTER FROM DR CINDY BLACKSTOCK TO THE CEO OF THE ROYAL SOCIETY OF CANADA 9 NOVEMBER 2015

9 November 2015
Iris Almeda-Cote, CEO
Royal Society of Canada, Walter House,
282 Somerset, Ottawa, ON K2P 0J6

Dear Ms. Almeda-Cote:
I previously sent this letter to Dr Bell in September of 2015 but have not received a response so I kindly ask that you review it and respond accordingly.

As a First Nations scholar and Honorary Witness for the Truth and Reconciliation Commission, I am writing with respect to the Royal Society's role in the implementation of the Truth and Reconciliation Commission's recommendations. The Royal Society's expertise and leadership in research and scholarship positions provides an ideal platform to activate the recommendations for research and scholarship cited in the TRC *Calls to Action* enumerated at 16, 62, 64 and 65. The Royal Society also has an important historical link to the residential school era as one of the main actors in the residential school tragedy – Duncan Campbell Scott was a Fellow and President of the Royal Society. This letter enumerates Mr Scott's role before moving on to provide some suggestions on how the Royal Society can meaningfully engage in the important work of reconciliation.

Known as a Confederate Poet, Duncan Campbell Scott was elected a Society Fellow in 1899 and served as President of the Royal Society in 1921–1922. He is widely acknowledged as the primary architect of residential schools and the person who made attendance by Indian students compulsory. Scott joined Indian Affairs in 1879 when he was 17 years of age and spent his entire career there. He had regular, and eventually controlling, oversight of residential schools in his role as Deputy Superintendent-General from 1913–1932. Government of Canada documents track Scott's role in residential schools throughout his civil service career. For example, in 1895, Scott requisitioned a warrant from the Department of Justice to forcibly remove First Nations children from their families and place them in residential schools. His goal was to "eliminate the Indian problem" and the federally funded and Christian-run residential schools were a means to achieve it.

The Truth and Reconciliation Commission confirms that at least 4,500 children died at the schools and the actual number is likely much higher. In fact, so many children died at the schools that it was not unusual to find a graveyard on school grounds. The majority of the child deaths occurred during Scott's tenure. The schools were also incubators for prolific child sexual and physical abuse and Scott received regular reports of the maltreatment from Department staffers and concerned citizens. While Scott retired in 1932, the last residential school did not close until 1996. The travesty of the multi-generational impacts of the deaths and abuses of children attending the residential schools were so profound that the Prime Minister issued a formal apology to Aboriginal Peoples in 2008.

Scott's legacy should not be protected by those claiming that he was simply acting in concert with the moral character of his time. In fact, many of Scott's contemporaries forcefully and publicly called on him to implement reforms to protect the children. A notable example is Dr Peter Henderson Bryce, Chief Medical Officer for the Department of the Interior and Indian Affairs. Dr Bryce had a distinguished medical career serving as President of the American Public Health Association, founder of the Canadian Public Health Association, and Ontario's first Public Health Officer before joining Indian Affairs in 1904 as Chief Medical Health Officer. In 1907, Dr Bryce published a report surveying the health of Aboriginal children attending 18 residential schools and found the death rate to be 24 percent per year and close to 50 percent over three years. The primary cause of the deaths was tuberculosis for which medical science had effective preventative and treatment options. Bryce proposed reforms to save the children but Scott refused to take action and retaliated against Dr Bryce by pushing him out of his position. Frustrated by Scott's repeated inaction, in 1922 (at the same time Scott was serving as President of the Royal Society) Bryce took his findings to the public in a pamphlet entitled "A National Crime" which was widely circulated to

Members of Parliament and ecclesiastical leaders.
Quoting directly from Dr Bryce's 1922 report:

> Recommendations, made in this report, on much the same lines as the report of 1907, followed the examination of the 243 children; but owing to the active opposition of Mr D.C. Scott, and his advice to the then Deputy Minister, no action was taken by the Department to give effect to the recommendations. This too was in spite of the opinion of Prof. George Adami, Pathologist of McGill University, in reply to a letter of the Deputy Minister asking his opinion regarding the management and conduct of the Indian schools. Prof. Adami had with the writer examined the children in one of the largest schools and was fully informed as to the actual situation. He stated that it was only after the earnest solicitation of Mr D.C. Scott that the whole matter of Dr Bryce's report was prevented from becoming a matter of critical discussions at the annual meeting of the National Tuberculosis Association in 1910 ... (Bryce, 1922: 5).

In his book "A National Crime" (named after Dr Bryce's 1922 report) leading residential school historian John Milloy recounts the residential school policy based on a detailed review of archival government documents. Milloy points to other eminent Canadians who also spoke up about the deplorable conditions in the schools such as lawyer and Judge Samuel Hume Blake, founder of the law firm Blake, Cassels and Graydon and former Vice-Chancellor of Ontario. Remarking on Bryce's 1907 report in correspondence to Minister Frank Oliver, Blake noted that the "appalling number of deaths among younger children appeals loudly to the guardians of our Indians. In doing nothing to obviate the preventable causes of death, brings the Department within unpleasant nearness to manslaughter (Milloy, 1999: 77)." A year later, the Government, under Scott's direction, requisitioned accountant F.H. Paget to survey the condition of the schools and while a handful were found to be acceptable, the vast majority were in dire condition presenting significant fire, health and wellbeing hazards to the children. Paget also noted the poor health of the children that had gone un-remedied since Bryce's report. Bryce, Blake and Paget were joined by a persistent chorus of people from all walks of life expressing significant concern for the safety of the children in the schools. Milloy (1999: 80) recounts a letter sent by an angry taxpayer from western Canada who says:

> It's a damn shame to let the Gov't schools be run as they are. You have a College [Emmanuel College, Prince Albert] here that is a disgrace to anybody. Ignorant teachers, pigsty boarding, poor clothing, everything cheap and nasty, taxpayer's money is not paid for frauds of this kind. The whole business should be ventilated before Parliament. It should be inquired into now. There is enough boodling without allowing people to make money out of poor Indian lads.

As Dr Milloy's review of government documents show, Scott was not enthusiastic in his response to critics as the costs of saving the children's lives went against his fiscal responsibilities. While the entire cost of implementing Bryce's reforms across Canada is not known, the costs of implementing the reforms in Ontario and Quebec were between $10,000 and $15,000 (translating to approximately $350,000 in today's dollars). At times when the public evidence of abuse was inescapable, Scott would acknowledge the problem and then do little or nothing to correct it. Scott's overall approach was to protect the Department at the expense of the lives and welfare of thousands of innocent children.

Scott was the highest-ranking civil servant vested with significant influence over residential schools' operations for decades. He should not be shielded from responsibility for what his peers called immoral if not illegal behavior because others in government shared in the atrocity. Nor should historical records wrongly reflect that Scott's conduct was reflective of his time. People of Scott's time knew his behavior was wrong and told him so. To cleanse Scott of responsibility for the deaths and maltreatment of the thousands of Aboriginal children is to embolden a false telling of history that denies the suffering of the children and the courageous Aboriginal and non-Aboriginal people like Bryce, Blake, Paget, and the taxpayer who stood up for the right thing.

The Truth and Reconciliation Commission of Canada (TRC) will release its final report in December of 2015 with the aim of educating Canadians about residential schools and setting a foundation for reconciliation between Aboriginal Peoples and other Canadians that ensures just, fair and respectful relationships going forward. The Royal Society's leadership role promoting leadership and research aligns with the TRC's requirement for truth telling and call for active engagement in reconciliation by all Canadians and organizations. As an act of reconciliation, I would recommend that the Society educate your members and others in your circle about Duncan Campbell Scott and his role in the Royal Society and actively engage in the implementation of the TRC recommendations as a matter of priority.

Among my activities, I serve as a Board Member for the Federation of Humanities and Social Sciences where we have adopted and are now in the process of implementing a reconciliation framework known as the Touchstones of Hope. The Touchstones of Hope reconciliation principles and process were originally developed to re-shape child welfare but have since been applied in an array of disciplines and organizations ranging including unions and academic bodies such as the Federation.

I have attached a copy of the Touchstones of Hope Reconciliation framework to this letter for your review. I also remain available to you should you require further information about reconciliation and I look forward to your response to the important matters and recommendations raised in this letter.

Regards,
Cindy Blackstock, PhD,
Associate Professor, University of Alberta, Honorary TRC Witness and Executive Director of the First Nations Child and Family Caring Society of Canada

Introduction

NOTES

We would like to thank Christl Verduyn, Gwendolyn Davies, and Carole Gerson, as well as two anonymous readers, for their constructive insights on this manuscript. We also appreciate the support we have received from the Royal Society of Canada's executive council, administration and staff, and the deep conversations with our colleagues on the RSC Truth and Reconciliation Task Force. We also thank Mark Abley for his enthusiastic reception of this project as part of McGill-Queen's University Press publications and the rest of the team. Many others have helped us bring this book to fruition: Daphné Bérard, Helen Fallding, Matthew Averback, and Adrian Mather.

1 Truth and Reconciliation Commission of Canada, *Truth and Reconciliation Commission of Canada: Calls to Action* (Ottawa: Truth and Reconciliation Commission of Canada, 2015), www.trc.ca/assets/pdf/Calls_to_Action_English2.pdf.
2 The RSC Council Minutes for 11 September 2017 state that the letter was discussed and the RSC president would send a response ("an open letter") to Cindy Blackstock. The 5 February 2018 "Action list" states that this open letter was still not written. "Draft Minutes, Meeting of the Council," 11 September 2017, 3, 5; RSC Council Materials-Personal archives; Draft Minutes, Meeting of the Council," 23 November 2017, 2; RSC Council Materials-Personal archives; "Draft Minutes, Meeting of the Council," 5 February 2018, 10; RSC Council Materials-Personal archives.
3 The Royal Society of Canada website: www.rsc-src.ca.
4 We believe that this quotation comes from Dr Blackstock's address, Kingston, 2016.
5 Correspondence from Cindy Blackstock to Cynthia Milton, 2 October 2017.
6 Scientists played prominent and powerful roles in the dispossession of Indigenous people and the settlement of newcomers on Indigenous lands. Engineers, geographers, geologists, and botanists supported the push for the Canadian Pacific Railway to expand westward, with a focus on opening up traditional Indigenous territories to white settler habitation. Sir Sandford Fleming, a founding member of the RSC, early president, and a chancellor of Queen's, was the chief engineer (and director) for the Canadian Pacific Railway. George Monro Grant, an early RSC president, oversaw the rapid growth of scientific education while principal of Queen's. Grant's travel book *Ocean to Ocean* (1873) generated political support for the railway and

promoted settlement in the northwest. George Mercer Dawson, geologist, geographer, anthropologist, and paleontologist, was another early RSC president who published ethnological papers on "Indian" conditions while he surveyed the mineral and agricultural potential of the West and advised on railway construction. Robert Charles Wallace, geologist, RSC fellow, president of the University of Alberta and principal of Queen's, conducted resource prospecting and promoted capital investing in northern Canada, while serving as an outspoken scientific advocate of eugenics. Mario Creet, "Fleming, Sir Sandford," in *Dictionary of Canadian Biography*, vol. 14, University of Toronto–Université Laval, 2003, accessed 21 December 2020, www.biographi.ca/en/bio/fleming_sandford_14E.html; D.B. Mack, "Grant, George Monro," in *Dictionary of Canadian Biography*, vol. 13, University of Toronto–Université Laval, 2003, accessed 21 December 2020, www.biographi.ca/en/bio/grant_george_monro_13E.html; Suzanne Zeller and Gale Avrith-Wakeam, "Dawson, George Mercer," *Dictionary of Canadian Biography*, vol. 13, University of Toronto–Université Laval, 2003, accessed 21 December 2020, www.biographi.ca/en/bio/dawson_george_mercer_13E.html; Robert C. Wallace, "The Quality of the Human Stock," *Canadian Medical Association Journal* (Calgary, 1934); Félix-Antoine Savard.

7 Joan Sangster, "Confronting Our Colonial Past: Reassessing Political Alliances over Canada's Twentieth Century," *Journal of the Canadian Historical Association*, 28, no.1 (2017): 1–43.

8 Frances Henry, James Carl, Peter Li, Audrey Kobayshi, Malinda Smith, Howard Ramos, Enakshi Dua, *The Equity Myth: Racialization and Indigeneity at Canadian Universities* (Vancouver: UBC Books, 2017).

PART ONE

The Royal Society of Canada's Historic Role

1

Rather of Promise than of Performance: Tracing Networks of Knowledge and Power Through the *Proceedings and Transactions of the Royal Society of Canada*, 1882–1922

Ian Wereley

During the summer and winter of 2018, I undertook a research assistantship for a project on the historical part played by the Royal Society of Canada (RSC) in Canadian cultural and political policies that marginalized Indigenous peoples and their knowledge. The project was anchored in an exploration first of Duncan Campbell Scott (former RSC president) and then broadened to the RSC as a whole during the Society's first forty years, from 1882–1922. As a historian of the British Empire, I had conducted research on other "Royal" learned societies, and was familiar with the historical intermingling of academic, scientific, and political power during the late nineteenth and early twentieth centuries. I had very little experience, however, with the RSC, and in many ways the project started with a tabula rasa – a rare and exciting opportunity for an emerging scholar. I began my research journey guided by the following questions: What was the RSC and how did it function? Who were included (and excluded) as fellows, and what projects and initiatives did they undertake? How did the RSC strive to build legitimacy in Canada and abroad, and what networks of power were leveraged in the process? Finally, what role did the RSC play in the marginalization of Indigenous peoples and their knowledge?

To answer these questions, I chose to focus on the primary publication of the RSC, the *Proceedings and Transactions of the Royal Society of Canada*. The *Proceedings and Transactions* contain a wealth of information about the RSC and its diverse activities, offering researchers a window through which to trace the unfolding history of the society.[1] Much more than an annual record of the RSC, the volumes provide insight into a broad spectrum of social, cultural, political, and scientific developments occurring in Canada during the period of this study. Over the course of several months, I worked in the RSC's national headquarters, where the *Proceedings and Transactions* are housed (quite literally) in a well-appointed Victorian mansion, Walter House. I became a close companion to these one thousand two hundred-page annual volumes. Slowly trawling through their richly detailed pages in the sunny and often breezy Roderick A. Macdonald Room, I was able to peer into the past in fascinating and unexpected ways, uncovering information that was both enlightening and disconcerting – two themes that dominated my research journey.

In the following essay, I first examine the founding of the RSC in 1881–1882, and the initial series of meetings that took place in Montreal and Ottawa. Next, I look at the early history of the RSC, mapping and reconstructing the transnational networks of knowledge and power that undergirded the projects, initiatives, and agendas pursued by the council and fellows. This helped me understand the historical context of the role that the RSC played in the marginalization of Indigenous peoples and their knowledge. Finally, I reflect on the RSC's first forty years, decades that were defined by challenges, obstacles, and missed opportunities as the society struggled to gain momentum and achieve legitimacy, even as it claimed to be Canada's premier intellectual institution. Indeed, in 1883, the society's inaugural president, John William Dawson, observed with respect to the founding of the RSC that "our claims were rather those of promise than of performance."[2]

THE FOUNDING OF THE ROYAL SOCIETY OF CANADA

In late December 1881, the governor general of Canada, His Excellency the Marquis of Lorne, later the Duke of Argyll, convened a series of meetings in Montreal to discuss with "a few gentlemen" the idea of forming a national society for the promotion of literature and science in Canada.[3] Gathered at the private manor of geologist and McGill University Principal John William Dawson were some of the dominion's most elite residents, whose titles and scholarly interests reveal much about the nascent society's vision of Canada, its Indigenous peoples, and their shared future.[4] The scientific community was well-represented. Dawson was one of the first trained geologists in the dominion and a world-renowned expert in his field, responsible for the discovery of numerous natural resources and fossil records across North America, much of which were within traditional Indigenous territory.[5] Dawson's colleague, fellow geologist Alfred Richard Cecil Selwyn, was also in attendance that evening. As director of the Geological Survey of Canada since 1869, Selwyn had visited and surveyed vast tracts of land in central and western Canada, and was a major contributor to plans for the construction of the Canada Pacific Railway.[6] The botanist and Queen's University professor of natural history, George Lawson, had travelled from Kingston to Montreal upon Lorne's invitation. A scientist-frontiersman with extensive experience travelling through western Canada, Lawson founded the Botanical Society of Canada in 1860, partially as a mechanism for documenting, preserving, and exploiting the dominion's flora and agricultural resources.[7] Charles Carpmael, the English meteorologist and director of the Toronto Magnetic Observatory, was also in attendance.[8]

The remainder of the guests gathered at Dawson's Montreal manor had backgrounds in law, literature, the arts, and humanities. The legal scholar and professor, Pierre-Joseph-Olivier Chauveau, and the journalist, Narcisse-Henri-Édouard Faucher de Saint-Maurice, both from Quebec, represented Canada's French-language academic milieu.[9] Leading figures in contemporary debates about science and race were also present that evening, including the Scottish author and ethnologist Daniel Wilson, a collector of Indigenous cultural artifacts and an expert on cranial types and measurements. As chair of history and English literature at University College, Toronto, and later as president of the University of Toronto, Wilson built a reputation in Canada and abroad as a staunch opponent to the theory of polygenesis and the notion that racial differences could be gleaned from the size and shape of an individual's skull.[10] Others on the list of attendees that night held much more problematic views about race, culture, and the human body. The writer and ethnographer, Goldwin Smith, was openly anti-Semitic and wished to see North America unified into one nation built upon the pillars of whiteness, Christianity, and the English language. According to one of his biographers, Smith viewed Canadian nationalism as "a lost cause" and believed the Anglo-Saxon cultural community to be "a superior civilization" that would naturally overtake and erase Indigenous cultures on the continent.[11] Another guest of Lorne's, the historian, constitutional law expert, and clerk of the House of Commons John George Bourinot, also published research on Teutonic and Aryan cultural superiority during this period.[12]

Lorne himself was a complicated individual with a fraught relationship with Indigenous peoples, cultures, and ways of living. He was appointed governor general of Canada in 1878 at the age of thirty-three.[13] A patron of the arts and letters, Lorne spearheaded the establishment of the Royal Canadian Academy of Arts in 1880, which later became the nucleus of the National Gallery of Canada.[14] From August to October 1881, Lorne undertook an extensive voyage across western Canada that would come to define his tenure as governor general. While on the Prairies, he learned that natural historians and paleontologists from the US Smithsonian Institute had been surveying Indigenous sites and returning to Washington with precious artifacts, a practice that irked Lorne politically and instilled in him a desire to establish a Canadian collection in Ottawa. Later in his voyage, Lorne met with Blackfoot chiefs who told him stories of their land being stolen by European settlers, of the disappearance of buffalo herds, and of widespread starvation among the Blackfoot people. According to one of his biographers, Lorne's response to an impassioned plea for assistance from Chief Crowfoot was to suggest Indigenous people abandon their traditional ways of living and take up modern methods of farming.[15] Lorne was enlightened by the beauty of the western Canadian landscape, perceiving the vast territory as a seemingly endless terra incognita ripe for imperial expansion. But he was also disconcerted about the inter-cultural strife that was fomenting across the region, and believed that First Nations and Métis resistance to European settlement would be a major obstacle to fulfilling Canada's trans-continental destiny. Lorne's advice to Prime Minister Macdonald sheds light on the extent to which the concepts of race and imperialism coloured the governor general's views of Indigenous peoples and their knowledge: establish federally funded elementary schools and industrial training centres on Indigenous reserves, and strengthen the North-West Mounted Police.[16]

Over two days of meetings at Dawson's manor, this group of elite intellectuals produced a framework for what would become the

THE ROYAL SOCIETY OF CANADA.

OFFICERS FOR 1882-83.

HONORARY PRESIDENT AND PATRON:
HIS EXCELLENCY THE RIGHT HONORABLE THE MARQUIS OF LORNE, K.T., G.C.M.G., P.C., etc., etc.,
GOVERNOR-GENERAL OF CANADA.

PRESIDENT - - - - J. W. DAWSON, C.M.G., LL.D., F.R.S.
VICE-PRESIDENT - HON. P. J. O. CHAUVEAU, LL.D., Docteur ès Lettres.

OFFICERS OF SECTIONS.

SECT. I.—French Literature, History and Allied Subjects.

PRESIDENT - - - J. M. LeMOINE.
VICE-PRESIDENT - - FAUCHER DE ST. MAURICE.
SECRETARY - - BENJAMIN SULTE.

SECT. II.—English Literature, History and Allied Subjects.

PRESIDENT - - - DANIEL WILSON, LL.D., F.R.S.E.
VICE-PRESIDENT - - GOLDWIN SMITH, D.C.L.
SECRETARY - - GEO. STEWART, JR.

SECT. III.—Mathematical, Physical and Chemical Sciences.

PRESIDENT - - - T. STERRY HUNT, LL.D., F.R.S.
VICE-PRESIDENT - - CHARLES CARPMAEL, M.A.
SECRETARY - - J. B. CHERRIMAN, M.A.

SECT. IV.—Geological and Biological Sciences.

PRESIDENT - - - A. R. C. SELWYN, LL.D., F.R.S.
VICE-PRESIDENT - - GEORGE LAWSON, PH.D., LL.D.
SECRETARY - - J. F. WHITEAVES, F.G.S.

HONORARY SECRETARY - - - - J. G. BOURINOT, B.A., F.S.S.
HONORARY TREASURER - - - - J. A. GRANT, M.D., F.G.S.

The Council for 1882-83 comprises the President and Vice-President, the Presidents and Vice-Presidents of Sections, the Honorary Secretary and the Honorary Treasurer.

Figure 1.1 List of RSC Council and Officers, Inaugural Meeting, 1882.

Royal Society of Canada.[17] The Marquis of Lorne was named patron and honorary president, and an executive council was formed, consisting of John William Dawson as president, Pierre-Joseph-Olivier Chauveau as vice-president, and John George Bourinot as honorary secretary. It was decided that the headquarters of the RSC would be located in Ottawa, and that an annual meeting of fellows would be held in that city in May. At the conclusion of these proceedings, Lorne and the RSC Council drafted a letter to Queen Victoria, requesting permission to use the title "Royal."[18]

The first annual meeting of the RSC took place from 25–27 May 1882. The proceedings began in the Senate Chamber of Parliament, where the council, fellows, and a "large number of ladies and gentlemen of the City of Ottawa" gathered to hear speeches from the governor general and RSC president.[19] The Marquis of Lorne delivered the inaugural address, offering a confident, optimistic, and ambitious vision of the RSC's future. The fledgling society had been established "for the benefit and honour of Canada," he asserted, and would bring together for the first time the best minds in the country, from the "citizens of the republic of letters ... to the students of the free world of nature."[20] The governor general stressed the unique bilingualism of the RSC, and the benefits of collaboration between descendants of the "stock of old France" and "English men of letters."[21] One day, he prophesized, the society would become an intellectual "centre around which to rally," and its fellows contributors to the "heritage of mankind."[22]

President Dawson was next to address the audience. Dawson was also cautiously optimistic about the future of the RSC, envisioning it as a body that held the potential to become "akin to those great national societies which in Great Britain and elsewhere have borne so important a part in the advancement of science and letters."[23] Despite concerns that the RSC had "still much to do to place us on a level with most other countries," Dawson believed that Canada was entering into a "new era [of] progress," in which science and the arts would flourish under "different and happier conditions" than ever before.[24] Improved networks of communication and transportation were leading to "political consolidation" in Canada, "welding together our formerly scattered provinces" and creating the conditions necessary for a national institution like the RSC. Critics could argue that the country was not yet ready for such an ambitious project, Dawson conceded, fearing "that in a country situated as this is, nearly everything is in some sense premature.... In Canada at present, whether in science, in literature, in art or in education, we look around in vain for anything that is fully ripe."[25] The Dominion of Canada was undergoing a grand nation-building experiment, and the RSC was to play a central part in its unfolding. "We have the freedom and freshness of a youthful nationality," Dawson concluded his address. "We can trace out new paths which must be followed by our successors, we have the right to plant wherever we please the trees under whose shade they will sit."[26] It is clear that Dawson, like Lorne, viewed Canada's northern and western frontiers as empty spaces on a map, poised for settlement and exploitation. Under his imperialist gaze, they became the landscapes on which to build a nation.

On the morning of 25 May 1882, the RSC gathered in the Railway Committee Room in the Centre Block of Parliament for its first annual general assembly.[27] Over the course of several hours, the fellows approved a slate of RSC bylaws, rules, and regulations, and determined the objects of the society, the duties of members and the council, and the procedures for electing officers and fellows. The structure of the RSC membership was also established. Four equal sections were created to organize the RSC's body of eighty fellows:

Section I: French literature, history, and allied subjects;
Section II: English literature, history, and allied subjects;
Section III: mathematical, physical, and chemical sciences;
Section IV: geological and biological sciences.

Each section was to elect a president and vice-president annually.[28] The RSC council was mandated to hold its own annual elections for the positions of president, vice-president, honorary treasurer, and honorary secretary.[29] The latter position was perhaps the most crucial to the functioning of the RSC, being responsible for keeping minutes of the annual meetings, conducting official correspondence, attending to the nomination of all new fellows, maintaining the RSC library and archive, and superintending the publication of the *Proceedings and Transactions*.[30]

The process of inducting new fellows into the RSC was also established at the inaugural meeting. The Marquis of Lorne personally selected and appointed the first cohort of RSC fellows, which consisted of residents of the Dominion of Canada and Newfoundland who had "published original works or memoirs" or "rendered eminent services to literature or to science."[31] Nominations for new fellows required the endorsement of three existing fellows, two of whom needed to belong to the section to which the candidate desired to be assigned, as well as the support of the section's president and vice-president. Once this was achieved, a formal letter of nomination was sent to the honorary secretary who, in turn, forwarded the nomination to the council. The entire RSC body was then invited to vote on each nominee at the next annual meeting, with votes typically passed unanimously.[32]

The remainder of the first annual meeting was dedicated to sharing research by fellows in their respective sections. The research papers presented in these sessions were diverse and interdisciplinary, as revealed by a sample of presentations: Roman Catholic priest and historian Cyprien Tanguay on the "*Origines des familles canadiennes*" (Section I); librarian and author Alpheus Todd on "The Establishment of Free Public Libraries in Canada" (Section II); physicist James Loudon on "Hydrodynamics" (Section III); and agriculturalist William Saunders on "The Importance of Economizing and Preserving our Forests" (Section IV).[33] In addition to the reading of papers, several sections dedicated their time to discussing a particular project or initiative. The literature sections (I and II) resolved to collaborate with the offices of the Hudson's Bay Company "with the view to the formation of a Canadian Museum of Archives, Ethnology, Archaeology, and Natural History."[34] The scientific sections (III and IV) resolved to engage more closely with international learned societies, particularly the British Association for the Advancement of Science and the International Forestry Association, and to petition the Canadian government to waive duties on imported scientific apparatus and publications.[35]

The inaugural annual meeting of the RSC revealed the projects, initiatives, and agendas that would define the Society's first forty years. Most importantly, the RSC was conceived as an organization tasked with establishing networks of knowledge and power, both in Canada and abroad. The annual meeting was intended to be a venue for Canadian artists, politicians, and scholars to create and mobilize new knowledge. At the same time, the RSC's early meetings reveal a desire to physically, culturally, and intellectually conquer Indigenous peoples and their knowledge.

EXPANDING NETWORKS OF KNOWLEDGE AND POWER

The RSC's efforts to gain legitimacy during its early years were dependent on the strength of its academic and political networks, both in Canada and internationally. From the outset, the society benefited from its intimate connection to the British Crown and its representatives, particularly Governor General Lorne, husband to Queen Victoria's daughter Princess Louise. As patron, honorary president, and a frequent attendee at annual meetings, Lorne offered the RSC prestige at home and a valuable conduit to British and imperial centres of power. The RSC faithfully sent Queen Victoria (and her successors Edward VII and George V) specially-bound copies of its yearly *Proceedings and Transactions*.[36] Royal connections were actively nurtured in Canada, as well. It was common practice for RSC fellows to attend exclusive receptions, garden parties, and formal galas hosted by representatives of the Crown. Notable examples of these events included the lieutenant-governor of Ontario Sir Oliver Mowat's party in 1902, the Governor General Earl Grey's party at Rideau Hall in 1911, the Duke and Duchess of Connaught's party in 1912, and the Duke and Duchess of Devonshire's party at Government House, Ottawa, in 1919.[37]

The RSC also worked to forge a close relationship with the Dominion of Canada government during its early years. In many ways, the society was entirely dependent on the government, as its act of incorporation and annual funding grant were both established at the pleasure of Parliament. Yet, while the RSC looked admiringly to Britain and representatives of the British Crown, it often looked upon the dominion government as an inferior assembly of gentlemen in need of guidance, counselling, and education. In 1882, John William Dawson stated that it was "the practice of all civilized governments to have recourse to scientific advice," and that with the founding of the RSC "our Government can command a body of men free from the distracting influence of private and local interests and able to warn against the schemes of charlatans and pretenders."[38] This notion that the RSC alone was in possession of pure and true knowledge was pervasive throughout its first forty years, but especially so at this foundational moment. At the second annual meeting in 1883, Alpheus Todd presented an address "On the Relation of the Royal Society to the State," in which he offered a road map for building connections with the dominion government.[39] Todd asserted that the RSC had the capacity to "assist in the intellectual progress of Canada," helping citizens and their elected officials to navigate the "material development of this country ... at an accelerated pace."[40] This upward journey would be long and challenging, Todd warned, and would feature "new and heretofore unknown fields of intellectual effort ... various mental, moral and scientific questions ... [and] the colonization and organization of new territories." It was in this moment of turbulent transformation and expansion, Todd concluded, that "the counsel and co-operation of the Royal Society of Canada, both individually and collectively, may prove of inestimable advantage to the whole Dominion."

The RSC's location in Ottawa made it convenient to engage in political networking and lobbying activities. Bourinot, the society's honorary secretary, was a fixture on Parliament Hill, serving as the clerk of the House of Commons from 1880–1902. Responsible for recording minutes, certifying bills and orders, and advising the Speaker of the House on procedural matters, Bourinot was intimately familiar with the social, cultural, and political issues of the day and was a personal friend to many in the House and Senate.[41] Government officials and cabinet ministers often attended RSC meetings and corresponded with the council.[42] In 1908, Prime Minister Sir Wilfrid Laurier and Canadian High Commissioner to the United Kingdom Lord Strathcona were elected honorary vice-presidents of the society, and over the years numerous other officials were elected fellows and members of the council.[43] One particularly striking example is Duncan Campbell Scott, who was elected a fellow in 1899 while serving in the Department of the Interior.[44] Scott later moved to the Department of Indian Affairs, all the while rising through the ranks of the RSC, eventually becoming its honorary secretary in 1911 and president in 1921.[45] Despite numerous efforts to gain legitimacy by building relationships with Canadian political figures, in the eyes of the society and its fellows, it was they who were being courted. "The Royal Society is not, as it has sometimes been styled, a self-constituted body," RSC President George Grant claimed at the annual meeting in 1892. "We have been called into existence by the head of the State, and have been, substantially as well as formally, recognized by Parliament."[46]

The RSC's most far-reaching academic and political networks were established through the society's relationship with affiliated associations across the world. More than a dozen Canadian societies agreed to support the RSC when it was founded in 1882, and by the end of the nineteenth century the list had more than doubled.[47] The RSC worked to build relationships with foreign learned societies, as well. Official ties were established with the Imperial Institute in London (1889), the Smithsonian Institution in Washington (1895), the Geological Society of London (1908), the Moscow Society for the Development of Experimental Sciences (1910), the Royal Society of Literature (1913), the Royal Society of London (1916), and the Society of Chemical Industry (1921).[48] Through these partnerships, the RSC was able to exchange knowledge and ideas, and to collaborate on major projects. Perhaps most importantly to the council, relationships with affiliated societies offered it legitimacy and a sense that the RSC was rising through the ranks of the world's great learned institutions.

RSC INITIATIVES, PROJECTS, AND AGENDAS

The fellows and council leveraged their extensive academic and political connections to pursue a variety of initiatives, projects, and agendas during the RSC's first forty years. One of the most enduring legacies was the publication of the annual *Proceedings and Transactions of the Royal Society of Canada*, which created a detailed record of the life and work of the society. The first volume of the *Proceedings and Transactions* was published in 1883.[49] Typical volumes from the 1880s and 1890s included a list of fellows and their positions, a report of council, copies of letters and official correspondence, a financial report, an update from the honorary librarian, minutes of the annual general assembly, and a selection of papers presented in each of the four sections, many of which included content on Indigenous topics. Every volume featured verbatim and often lengthy reports of the RSC's affiliated societies. In 1913, a series of appendices were added to the *Proceedings and Transactions*, presenting scientific data from the Dominion Astronomical Observatory, the Meteorological Service of Canada, the Inland Revenue Laboratory Branch, the Department of the Interior Forestry Branch, and the Dominion Marine Biological Stations.[50]

In addition to the items published regularly in the front, the *Proceedings and Transactions* often featured special reports and news about major projects, such as the creation of a standardized

Figure 1.2 Copies of *Proceedings and Transactions*, Walter House, Ottawa.

Canadian history textbook for elementary school students in 1895, or the 1903 committee tasked with creating a common registry of geographical place names in Canada, and "fixing them on the map in intelligible orthography."[51] The 1895 volume contained an eighty-page bibliography of current and former RSC fellows, and the 1904 volume included an "*Inventaire chronologique des livres, brochures, journaux et revues publiés dans la province de Québec de 1764 à 1904.*"[52] Major anniversaries, celebrations, and commemorative events were also covered extensively in the volumes, such as the

Cabot Celebrations of 1897, and the 300th anniversary of Samuel de Champlain's settlement of Acadia in 1904.[53] A notable feature of the *Proceedings and Transactions* was the inclusion of numerous images, diagrams, plates, maps, sketches, and photographs, some of which contained representations of Indigenous tools, artwork, and other cultural artifacts.[54] The publication was entirely Canadian-made, from the design of illustrations and photographs to the copy editing, typesetting, and binding processes; even the paper was sourced domestically.

The RSC used the *Proceedings and Transactions* as a tool for expanding its networks of knowledge and power. Recipients of the annual volumes were numerous and diverse. All current and former fellows received hard-cover copies of the volume, as well as a host of powerful and well-connected individuals across Canada, including the lieutenant governors of the provinces and of Newfoundland, members of the Privy Council, speakers of the Senate and House of Commons, the chief justice and judges of the Supreme Court of Canada, the chief justices of the provinces, the premiers of each province, the speakers in the legislatures of each province; the minister of education in each province; the Library of Parliament, and the libraries of Canadian universities.[55] Several dozens of copies were sent abroad every year to individuals and institutions in Europe, Asia, Australasia, and South America. As RSC President Henri-Raymond Casgrain announced at the annual meeting in 1891, with the exception of Guatemala and Venezuela, "we believe we have sent the Annual Transactions over the whole civilized world ... with the confidence that it is fully worthy of Canada and illustrates the intellectual development of the country to an eminent degree."[56]

Education and public engagement with the arts and sciences was at the heart of most initiatives undertaken by the RSC during the period of this study. Prime among these was the establishment of a National Museum of Natural History and Ethnology in Ottawa. One of the first official communications sent by the council after its founding in 1882 was a circular to officers of the Hudson's Bay Company, requesting "objects of interest from all parts of British North America" that could be used to start a national collection.[57] The RSC was "extremely desirous," the circular noted, to learn about "the native tribes ... [in] those parts of the country which are as yet little known and thinly inhabited."[58] The council worried about the gradual loss of Indigenous languages, traditional histories, belief systems, and cultures across Canada, and saw a national museum as a way of preserving for future generations "implements of all kinds ... fragments of pottery ... skulls from ancient burial places ... specimens of weapons, tools, etc."[59] This campaign to preserve a record of Indigenous knowledge and culture was motivated not by a desire to regenerate Indigenous ways of life, but rather by the prestige of possessing a national collection of Indigenous artifacts and curiosities.

The RSC's campaign for "a National Museum worthy of the name" produced mixed results.[60] In 1896, the council lamented that while other recommendations of the society had been acted upon, the dominion government had "not yet seen its way to complying with this particular suggestion," and it once again urged "in the strongest possible manner the almost absolute necessity of taking some immediate step in this direction."[61] The following year, RSC fellow and Liberal Member of Parliament for Ottawa Napoléon Belcourt raised a motion in the House of Commons in support of a national museum.[62] Prime Minister Wilfrid Laurier responded positively, acknowledging that the existing collection of Canadian history and heritage "could be at any moment burned to ashes."[63] In 1898, the government announced plans for a new national museum, and former RSC President Sir Sandford Fleming held several meetings with Laurier to lobby for a design that would be "worthy of this bright era in our country's material development."[64] As the council triumphantly asserted at the annual meeting of 1899, the dominion government "have now an admirable opportunity of taking a practical step towards giving the Washington of the North some of the aspects of the Washington of the South."[65] Unfortunately for the RSC, the promise was rather more than the performance - after the election of the Conservative Borden Government in 1911, all plans for the national museum were put on hold.[66]

The RSC lobbied to establish several other national institutions in Ottawa during the late nineteenth and early twentieth centuries. Starting in the 1890s, the council made numerous overtures to the dominion government to expand the small and underfunded Archives Office, established in 1872 as an annex to the Department of Agriculture, and to create a national public archive tasked with preserving the growing collection of Canadian historical artifacts.[67] "Sufficient importance, we are afraid, has not been always heretofore paid to the preservation of historic documents relating to our past history," the council lamented in 1895, adding that "as a consequence much has been lost to posterity."[68] In his presidential address of that year, titled "The Manuscript Sources of Canadian History as Revealed by Our Archives," James MacPherson Le Moine raised the issue of a national archive more creatively: "If family papers are cherished, and claim respect in the home circle as memoirs of an unforgotten past, how much more ought to be prized, carefully garnered and preserved, the records of a whole people, that is, its public archives."[69] Unlike the national museum, the RSC found greater success in its seventeen-year campaign for a national Public Archives of Canada, which was finally established in Ottawa in 1912.

The creation of a national library was another priority item on the RSC agenda during the early twentieth century. Key to the society's goals of expanding its networks of knowledge and power and building public support for the arts and sciences, the campaign for a national library was seen by many fellows as a signature achievement for the RSC. In 1911 and 1914 the council sent deputations to the Borden government requesting a royal commission to investigate expanding the Library of Parliament into a publicly accessible institution.[70] Both overtures were denied. The pressure on the government was raised significantly in 1916 after the disastrous fire that consumed the Centre Block of Parliament. It was "most fortunate that the Library was saved," the council stated with a hint of schadenfreude, "but it cannot be doubted that it is still exposed to very great danger."[71] While the RSC was not successful in its campaign for a national library until 1953, it did gain a local victory in 1901, when the Carnegie foundation awarded the city of Ottawa funding for a new public library. The council touted the achievement at its annual meeting that year, but admitted "the satisfaction of some Canadians is somewhat marred by the fact that this praiseworthy movement in the direction of culture will owe its success to the generosity of a public-spirited millionaire of the United States."[72]

Innovations in science and technology were also actively supported by the RSC during the late nineteenth and early twentieth centuries. Beginning in the late 1880s, the society lobbied the dominion government to establish a national survey of tides and currents to assist shipping companies in navigating Canadian waters. One was eventually created in 1893.[73] In 1898, the council sent a letter to Parliament drawing its attention "to the necessity that exists for having a full and accurate map of the Dominion. . . .

At present, there is no map, large or small, available to the public, and grave inconveniences arise therefrom."[74] Five years later, in 1903, one of the first official maps of Canada was published – conspicuously absent were references to Indigenous peoples.[75] In 1900, the RSC sponsored a major expedition to the American state of Virginia to observe the total eclipse of the sun, and in 1902, it contributed to the wireless telegraphy work of Guglielmo Marconi in Newfoundland.[76] In 1907, the council struck a special committee to investigate the shift to the metric system in Canada, and another committee was tasked with raising funds for a more powerful telescope at the Dominion Observatory in Ottawa.[77] During the First World War, the RSC played a central role in the establishment of the Honorary Advisory Council for Scientific and Industrial Research, the precursor to the present-day National Research Council in Ottawa.[78] Perhaps the most notable scientific initiative undertaken by the RSC during this period was Sir Sandford Fleming's campaign to establish international standards of time. While serving as a fellow, vice-president, and president of the RSC (1882, 1888, 1889), Fleming spearheaded a worldwide movement in support of "universal time."[79] As the council asserted in its annual report of 1903, Fleming's determination had changed the world and added to the prestige of the RSC: "It was he who supplied the energy, made the calculations, rallied its friends, overcame the hostility of competitors, inspired the necessary diplomacy, initiated and directed the essential surveys, and finally compelled into accord the hesitating Governments of Great Britain and interested colonies."[80]

CHALLENGES, OBSTACLES, AND MISSED OPPORTUNITIES

The RSC faced a number of challenges, obstacles, and missed opportunities during its first forty years. A casual reading of the *Proceedings and Transactions* reveals a society that struggled with inclusion and exclusion, membership participation, organizational structure and management, and building legitimacy. In nearly every presidential address and report of council, the RSC was touted as an inclusive and open society, a clearinghouse of ideas and research. But as early as 1883, the Marquis of Lorne issued a warning to the council that the society not become an exclusive and exclusionary body. He warned that the most serious challenge to the society was "that men may be apt to take exception to your membership because it is not geographically representative." In this vein, he encouraged the RSC to expand its membership beyond Montreal, Toronto, and Ottawa. "If men be elected simply because they came from such and such a college," he argued, "you will get a heterogenous [sic] body together, quite unworthy to be compared with the foreign societies."[81] Four years later, President Daniel Wilson asserted that the RSC was "thoroughly national and representative in its object and scope," yet, in the same breath, he contradicted himself by adding that "it would be a mistake to suppose that this Society should include all our literary and scientific men, or even all those of some local standing. It must consist of selected and representative men who have themselves done original work of at least Canadian celebrity. . . . In this sense it must be exclusive in its membership, but inclusive in that it offers its benefits to all."[82]

A notable exclusion from the RSC during the period 1882–1922 was the presence or voice of women. As the historian Donald Wright has argued, gender-based exclusion was a common practice in academia and the scientific professions during the late nineteenth and early twentieth centuries.[83] The barriers for women to access a university education were particularly high in Canada, and virtually insurmountable for Indigenous women, which meant that very few held professorships or achieved the record of teaching, researching, and publishing that was often required for entry into the RSC. In the hearts and minds of many Canadians at this time, only young white men were capable of becoming scholars and intellectuals. Indeed, several founding members of the RSC were outspoken critics of women's inclusion in Canadian colleges and universities during this period, taking on leadership roles in campaigns to bar or obstruct their admission.[84]

Women were for all intents and purposes barred from membership in the RSC, and they played virtually no role in the society's administrative functioning during its first forty years. The original RSC bylaws of 1882 stated that only "persons" could be fellows, and the council frequently referred to its membership as "famous men," or "men whose achievements in science have more than equalled in fame the triumphs of statesmen."[85] The rare occasion that women were discussed at the RSC annual meetings was usually in a patronizing and chivalric context. In his presidential address of 1895, James MacPherson Le Moine commented "is not our history also lighted up with the sweet, thoughtful faces of heroic women – noble exemplars to their sex – beacons from on high, illuminating the rugged paths of struggling humanity: Madame de Champlain, the Lady Latour, Madeleine de Verchères, Laura Secord; nor is the race extinct."[86] A handful of fellows attempted to push the society to be more inclusive of women, but their efforts were often thwarted or at least dulled. In 1913, McGill University Professor John George Adami put forward an amendment to the RSC bylaws, which read: "That the Fellows shall be persons male or female, resident in the Dominion of Canada."[87] In an amendment to the amendment, which was eventually carried by the majority of fellows, University of Toronto Professor James Playfair McMurrich argued that the current wording of "persons" in the bylaws was sufficiently clear to include both men and women.[88] No women, however, were elected as fellows during the period of this study.[89] These efforts by the RSC to keep women at bay were grounded in the belief that only men could make claims to reason, objectivity, and knowledge, and that a distinct and unbreakable boundary existed between the masculine and the feminine, the serious and the frivolous, the professional and the avocational. In this respect, the RSC's eligibility requirements for admission of new fellows, both de jure and de facto, were deliberately sexist and exclusionary.

Though exceedingly rare, women did participate and actively contribute to the RSC's annual meetings.[90] The first presentation delivered by a woman took place in 1888, six years after its founding. Mrs W. Wallace Brown, a well-published expert in Passamaquoddy languages and customs, and the spouse of the local Indian Agent in Calais, Maine, spoke on the topic of "Some Indoor and Outdoor Games of the Wabanaki Indians." Although the official minutes record Wallace Brown's lecture, it was not included in the president's summary of presentations that year.[91] The next paper delivered by women took place at the annual meeting in 1896, when the historians Mary Agnes Fitzgibbon and Janet Carnochan delivered talks on "The Under-Currents of History" and "A Slave Rescue in Niagara Sixty Years Ago" respectively.[92] Women also presented reports from affiliated societies, which were published in the *Proceedings and Transactions*, including representatives of the Women's Canadian Historical Society, the Historical and Scientific Society of Manitoba, and the Niagara Historical Society.[93] The RSC's series of "Popular Lectures" often featured contributions by women and were open to the public. One in 1895 featured an evening of readings from

Canadian poets, including Archibald Lampman, Bliss Carman, and Duncan Campbell Scott.[94] Several female poets were present, but their works were recited by male colleagues. In his first presentation to the RSC, Duncan Campbell Scott read a poem written by Toronto-based poet and author Susie Frances Harrison titled "The Tree."[95] The only woman to present her own work that evening was the accomplished author and performer Pauline Johnson, who recited her signature poem "The Song My Paddle Sings" while dressed in "Indian costume."[96] Johnson might have been made an exception because of her mixed Mohawk and European heritage, or perhaps on account of her family's political connections to Lord Dufferin and the Marquis of Lorne; in any event, her performance offered a romanticized portrait of Indigenous issues that stood in stark contrast to the bleak and often violent experience of Indigenous people living in central and western Canada during that period.

Perhaps the most visible absence in the *Proceedings and Transactions*, and the RSC more generally, were Indigenous peoples and voices. Other than Johnson, no Indigenous person presented research or addressed the RSC during the forty years covered by this study, and there is no evidence that a member of this community was ever in attendance at an RSC event. Indeed, there were even concerted efforts to erase Indigenous voices. In 1890, the editor of the *Proceedings and Transactions*, John G. Bourinot, suggested that the RSC could reduce its publishing expenses by $500 if it avoided "the printing of matter in algebraic symbols or in Indian languages."[97] For some fellows, the marginalization of Indigenous peoples and their knowledge was not simply an act of convenience or frugality, but rather an essential part of the nation-building process. As journalist and founding member of the RSC John Reade explained in his 1882 lecture on the relationship between language and imperialism, "real, permanent conquest is something more than that of mere physical force. . . . It is a conquest of mind by mind, a conquest in which the victor is a teacher and the vanquished a learner. It is, in fact, a conquest of civilization."[98] In Reade's hierarchy of civilizations, language was a key determinate of success, and "the Aryan family is very definitely marked off from that of the Semites, while the differentiation is still more decided between either of these and the great horde of tongues outside their common pale."

Yet, while the RSC actively excluded Indigenous peoples, cultures, and ways of living, they were at the same time consumed, if not obsessed, with Indigenous topics. Indigenous people were one of the most commonly discussed topics at RSC meetings during the late nineteenth and early twentieth centuries, particularly in Sections I-III. Notable examples include John Reade, "The Half-Breed" (1883); Daniel Wilson, "The Artistic Faculty in Aboriginal Races" (1885); Franz Boas, "The Eskimo" (1887); Jean-André Cuoq, "*Grammaire de la langue algonquine*" (1891); Horatio Hale, "An Iroquois Condoling Council" (1895); William Douw Lighthall, "Hochelagans and Mohawks" (1899); George Bryce, "Intrusive Ethnological Types in Rupert's Land" (1903); Charles Canniff James, "The Downfall of the Huron Nation" (1906); Nathaniel Burwash, "The Gift to a Nation of a Written Language" (1911); Edward Sapir, "A Girl's Puberty Ceremony Among the Nootka Indians" (1913); Charles Marius Barbeau, "*Les Indiens du Canada depuis la découverte*" (1914); and Diamond Jenness, "The 'Blond' Eskimos" (1920).[99] A deeper reading of these articles reveals that the vast majority of RSC fellows who spoke and wrote about Indigenous issues viewed them with mixtures of curiosity and contempt. Delivered in the era of scientific racism and against the backdrop of intense international competition to collect, preserve, and display Indigenous artifacts, these presentations offer glimpses of both altruism and self-serving imperialism, two themes that defined the RSC's first forty years.[100]

Indigenous people were frequently represented in the speeches made by the governor general and president at RSC annual meetings. In 1885, the Marquis of Lorne commended fellows who were conducting research on "the ethnology of our native races ... partly owing to the diminution in the number of those races, partly owing to the change in their mode of life and their gradual adoption of European manners and customs."[101] George Lawson's presidential address of 1888 discussed the "early history of European life in Canada," and reconstructed the "wearisome toils of the forest-clearing and farm-making ... [and] the exciting warfare of human strife."[102] Despite couching his story in the language of colonization and marginalization, Lawson expressed concern about the loss of Indigenous cultures, what he called "primitive modes of life and thought," and again called for the establishment of a national museum to capture and preserve them for future generations.[103] George Dawson's 1894 presidential address echoed these anxieties about the irreversible loss of Indigenous cultures, arguing that "the investigation of the native races themselves should be systematically prosecuted till all that can be gathered in relation to them shall have been ascertained. Specimens, too, illustrating the arts, the manufactures and the anthropology of the native races should be collected and carefully preserved."[104]

Ironically, while the RSC actively excluded women, Indigenous people, and scholars of mere "local standing," it also struggled to fill seats at its annual meeting. Attendance and participation were persistent issues in the *Proceedings and Transactions*, and common grievances of the president and council in their annual reports. As early as 1887, President Thomas-Étienne Hamel noted the "meagre attendance of members," and the number of fellows who were "apparently indifferent to the work of the Society" and did not "do anything in the way of promoting the work that most of us have at heart."[105] The following year, George Lawson chastised absentee fellows in his presidential address, noting that "as our organization is of a limited membership ... it is essential that all should be active workers."[106] As honorary secretary, Bourinot often had to deal with the consequences of apathetic fellows. During the 1880s and 1890s, his annual report to the RSC typically featured a laundry list of complaints about fellows missing meetings, moving out of the country without notice, or failing to submit their nominations for elected positions.[107] In 1892, Bourinot scolded that "it would be well ... for some members to bear in mind that they owe certain responsibilities in making the Society successful, and that the position is not purely honorary."[108]

The consequences of this indifference were striking. Despite the fact that 90 per cent of RSC fellows resided between Quebec City, Kingston, and Ottawa, the average attendance for all sections at RSC annual meetings held from 1882–1892 was never higher than thirty-five of eighty.[109] Adding to these problems of attendance and participation were the frequent and sometimes numerous deaths of fellows. An average of two to three fellows passed away every year, and the number was often much higher. Four fellows died in 1895, representing a five per cent loss to the RSC membership; in 1904, three fellows from Section II died, representing 15 per cent of the section.[110] Six RSC fellows died in 1912, and twelve more passed away between 1917–1918.[111]

In response to the "exceedingly irregular" attendance at annual meetings, and the "indifference or apathy to be shown by one or two Fellows who never attend or even send excuses," the RSC Council suggested a series of reforms in the 1890s and 1900s.[112] Inactive fellows were put on the retired list, and grants were established for fellows travelling great distances to Ottawa.[113] In 1895, the number of fellows in each section was raised from twenty to twenty-five, and raised again in 1909.[114] President George Grant even went so far as to suggest the abolition of Section II (English Literature, History, and Allied Subjects), which had a particularly dismal record of attendance and publication and was in a "condition of anaemia."[115] The idea was dropped, but problems with attendance persisted into the twentieth century. Eventually, the Council resorted to calling out inactive fellows by name at annual meetings, which was met with some success. After an unusually lengthy description of Stephen Leacock's record of truancy was published in the *Proceedings and Transactions* of 1917, Leacock presented a paper in 1919.[116] Despite these efforts to both encourage and coerce, in the forty years from 1882 to 1922 the RSC never once had a full complement of fellows in attendance at its annual conference.

The council itself was responsible for some missed opportunities and errors during the first forty years of the RSC. A perennial challenge was the lack of a permanent space to host the annual meetings in Ottawa. The first nine meetings were held in the Railway Committee Room in Centre Block, a space loaned on a year-to-year basis by Sir Charles Tupper, then minister of railways and later prime minister.[117] In 1894, the RSC was granted permission to use the assembly hall of the Normal School on Elgin Street, Ottawa, an arrangement that continued for many years.[118] On special occasions, the RSC held annual meetings outside of Ottawa, including the William Molson Hall in Montreal (1891), the legislative building in Nova Scotia (1897), the University of Toronto (1902), the High School Building in St. John (1904), and the New Medical Building at McGill University (1914).[119] Throughout the period of this study, however, the council's lobbying campaign to acquire permanent space from the dominion government was unsuccessful.

The publication of the *Proceedings and Transactions* was also a recurring source of anxiety and frustration for the council. The volume covering the first meeting in 1882 was never released because a publisher was not found in time. Instead, the president and vice-president used their personal resources to publish a twenty-page booklet titled *Inaugural Meeting, 1882*.[120] Several embarrassing errors were made in the rush to publish the volume for 1883, forcing

Bourinot to print an apology on the first page: "The difficulties attendant on the printing and the illustrating for the first time of a work of this kind and magnitude are many – a consideration that may help to excuse some defects in the execution of the task ... trusting that the volumes which, it is hoped, will succeed this, may be freer from minor errors."[121]

Unfortunately for Bourinot and the council, the challenges posed by the *Proceedings and Transactions* only grew in size. The volume published in 1889 was the thinnest, yet also the most expensive to date, the result of "great and unusual delay" in the submission of papers, many of which arrived three months late.[122] The following year Bourinot warned that if the *Proceedings and Transactions* continued to shrink in size, it would not only indicate "a diminishing interest in the Society, [but], if presented to the House of Commons, might have caused remark."[123] Somewhat comically, Bourinot's most significant challenge during the following two decades was managing volumes that were too large. "Authors appear in too many cases to have elaborate second thoughts," he wrote in his report of 1893, "which cost the society sometimes a considerable sum."[124] The situation worsened in 1892, when the publisher, typesetter, and copy-editor of the *Proceedings and Transactions*, Samuel Edward Dawson of Montreal, took up a new position with the Queen's Printer in Ottawa. In his resignation letter to the council, Dawson offered a pointed critique of the final volume of his tenure: "I would remark that at no previous time in the history of the Society did the papers come in so late, or did I have so much difficulty in getting the volume out in time."[125] In 1902, for the first time in his twenty-year tenure as honorary secretary and editor, Bourinot was able to report a volume completed on time and within budget – he died later that year, a loss described by the council as "irreparable."[126]

The *Proceedings and Transactions* again fell into some disarray in subsequent years. The new honorary secretary and editor, James Fletcher, produced a half dozen volumes, encountering many of the same challenges as Bourinot with respect to the "negligence of less considerate authors."[127] The volumes for 1906 and 1907 were 1,180 and 1,228 pages long, respectively, which raised alarm within the council. "The revenue of the Society is not elastic," it stated in 1909, "and too great elasticity cannot therefore be allowed in its expenditure."[128] Fletcher died later that year, causing further disruption for the publication of the *Proceedings and Transactions*.[129] His replacement, former RSC president William Dawson LeSueur, oversaw the release of both the shortest (1911) and the longest (1915) volumes in the publication's history before passing away in 1917.[130] Perhaps the most grievous incident during this period occurred in 1905 when, after years of being untouched in a storage vault in Montreal, the RSC's collection of original copies of the *Proceedings and Transactions* was accidentally sent to a paper mill as waste. The consequences of this mistake were costly and historically significant. Original copies of certain early volumes have since become exceedingly rare, a reminder that the losses of the past are alive and well in the present.[131]

CONCLUSION

In its report of 1891, the RSC council reminded fellows that "the past has its many lessons for us who live in the present, and it would be well to have always before us something to remind us what we owe to its struggles and achievements."[132] In many ways, the *Proceedings and Transactions* offer the RSC of the twenty-first century just such a reminder. Reading these storied volumes in Walter House, it is abundantly clear how far the society has come from its humble beginnings in 1881–1882. It now has a headquarters, a permanent facility for its archives, and a membership of more than two thousand fellows; in 2018 the RSC inducted nearly 120 new fellows, one and a half times the size of the entire inaugural cohort of 1882 and vastly more inclusive with respect to gender, sexual orientation, class, race, and age. Other aspects, however, have not changed: there remains a president, honorary secretary, and council, and the RSC continues to publish cutting-edge research, though no longer through the *Proceedings and Transactions*. Annual meetings are held in Ottawa and across Canada for artists, politicians, and scholars to create and mobilize knowledge, and the society continues to navigate issues related to equity, diversity, and inclusion. Indeed, a modern-day fellow would likely feel quite familiar with an RSC annual meeting held in 1882, 1902, or 1922.

These competing impulses of continuity and change are some of the most salient themes in the *Proceedings and Transactions*. The period 1882–1922 was a transformative moment in Canadian and global history, witnessing the rise of industrialization, the expansion of the nation state, and the emergence of mass communications and transportation technologies. The volumes capture some of this

Figure 1.3 RSC Archives in Roderick A. Macdonald Room, Walter House, Ottawa.

excitement and uncertainty about the future. It is fascinating to trace how fellows grappled with topics that seemed revolutionary at the time, but that today are taken for granted: "The Longitude of Toronto" (1885), "Evolution" (1886), "A National Standard of Pitch" (1889), "Injurious Insects of Canada" (1900), "The Density of Ice" (1902), and "Relativity" (1920), to name but a few.[133] At times, the pace of change was remarkable, even by present standards. In his 1891 presidential address, Thomas Sterry Hunt stated that the "man of letters may hope to find ... encouragement and pecuniary recompense for his labour; but the student of science," he lamented, "though he may perchance gain fame, has little hope for such rewards."[134] Less than a generation later, in 1908, President Arthur Doughty painted precisely the opposite picture of the arts versus science debate: "The scientific sections express the activities of a scientific era. They deal with material things and make their appeal to the practical genius of the age. They need neither explanation nor apology; for, in popular opinion, science is held to have a basis of real utility which is lacking in literature."[135]

The *Proceedings and Transactions* also expose a vulgar side to the RSC's complicated history. One can find in these volumes some of Canada's best and brightest engaging in some of the worst and grimmest ideas in this country's history. On several occasions, I encountered pages that made me feel deeply uncomfortable, forcing me to take a walk or make a coffee to work through what I had read – the abject exclusion of women, Indigenous people, and racialized people; harmful scientific research on Indigenous minds and bodies, including the "growth of children," the "physical measurements of adults," and the challenges of locating "an Indian of pure blood"; President Robert Ramsay Wright's statements on the benefits of eugenics for dealing with "existing evils" and rooting out "feeble-mindedness"; President Frank Adams' comments that "our cold winter was one of Canada's best assets, seeing that it keeps away negroes and all those other undesirable elements of permanent population classed by the unlearned under the comprehensive title of 'dagos.'"[136] The *Proceedings and Transactions* thus expose that all of the knowledge produced and celebrated by RSC fellows took place within a context of racist and often violent imperialism, whereby powerful elites gathering in Ottawa sought to conquer and control vast swathes of the Canadian landscape. Indeed, this research reveals that the RSC played a central role in the historical marginalization of Indigenous peoples and their knowledge. As the first RSC president, John William Dawson, stated in the inaugural presidential address of 1882, "We can trace out new paths which must be followed by our successors, we have the right to plant wherever we please the trees under whose shade they will sit."[137]

Canadians today live in the shade of these "trees" planted by dozens of fellows nearly 140 years ago. For some, the legacy created by the RSC exists in its rich contribution to Canadian arts, literature, science, and innovation, or the central role its fellows played in establishing the legal, commercial, and intellectual pillars of the modern Canadian nation-state. For others, and particularly for Indigenous peoples, the early history of the RSC casts a long and dark shadow over their lives, a spectre of imperialism that continues to shape the challenges, inequities, and injustices they face every day. With a greater understanding of both the struggles and achievements of its past, the RSC has a unique opportunity to make meaningful progress toward reconciliation – and to plant the seeds of change that will guide the society's next 140 years.

NOTES

I am grateful to Constance Backhouse, Aleksandra Bennett, Jennifer Evans, Norman Hillmer, and Cynthia Milton for their invaluable contributions to this research.

1 On the history of the RSC, see Carl Berger, *Honour and the Search for Influence: A History of the Royal Society of Canada* (Toronto: University of Toronto Press, 1996); Robert Daley and Paul Dufour, "Creating a 'Northern Minerva': John William Dawson and the Royal Society of Canada," *Journal of the History of Canadian Science, Technology and Medicine* 5, no. 17 (January 1981): 3–13.
2 Royal Society of Canada, *Proceedings and Transactions of the Royal Society of Canada for the Years 1882 and 1883* 1, vol. 1 (Montreal: Dawson and Sons, 1883): lii. All *Proceedings and Transactions of the Royal Society of Canada* hereafter cited as RSC, *Proceedings and Transactions,* followed by year of publication.
3 Royal Society of Canada, *Inaugural Meeting, 1882* (Ottawa: Royal Society of Canada, 1882): 4. Hereafter cited as RSC, *Inaugural Meeting, 1882.*
4 On the negotiations that led up to and proceeded from this meeting, see Margaret A. Banks, *Sir John George Bourinot, Victorian Canadian: His Life, Times, and Legacy* (Montreal–Kingston: McGill-Queen's University Press, 2001), chap. 13.
5 John William Dawson was born in Nova Scotia in 1820. He served as the first superintendent of education for that province from 1850–1853, and as principal of McGill University from 1855–1893. Dawson was the only person to ever serve terms as president of the Royal Society of Canada (1882), of the American Association for the Advancement of Science (1882), and of the British Association for the Advancement of Science (1886). He died in 1899. Peter R. Eakins and Jean Sinnamon Eakins, "Dawson, Sir John William," in *Dictionary of Canadian Biography*, vol. 12 (University of Toronto–Université Laval, 2003), accessed 19 August 2020, http://www.biographi.ca/en/bio/dawson_john_william_12E.html.
6 Alfred Richard Cecil Selwyn was born in England in 1824. He served as director of the Geological Survey of Canada from 1869–1894, and as president of the RSC from 1896–1897. He died in 1902. Suzanne Zeller, "Sewlan, Alfred Richard Cecil," in *Dictionary of Canadian Biography*, vol. 13 (University of Toronto–Université Laval, 2003), accessed 20 August 2020, http://www.biographi.ca/en/bio/selwyn_alfred_richard_cecil_13E.html.

7   George Lawson was born in Scotland in 1827. He served as president of the RSC from 1887–1888. He died in 1895. Suzanne Zeller, "Lawson, George," in *Dictionary of Canadian Biography*, vol. 12 (University of Toronto–Université Laval, 2003), accessed 19 August 2020, http://www.biographi.ca/en/bio/lawson_george_12E.html.
8   Charles Carpmael was born in England in 1846. He served as president of Section III of the RSC in 1882 and 1886. He died in 1894. Suzanne Zeller, "Carpmael, Charles," in *Dictionary of Canadian Biography*, vol. 12 (University of Toronto–Université Laval, 2003), accessed 20 August 2020, http://www.biographi.ca/en/bio/carpmael_charles_12E.html.
9   Pierre-Joseph Olivier Chauveau was born in Charlesbourg, Lower Canada in 1820. He served as president of the RSC from 1883–1884. He died in 1890. Narcisse-Henri-Édouard Faucher de Saint-Maurice was born in Quebec City in 1844. At Lorne's request, Faucher de Saint-Maurice hand-selected the first twenty French-speaking fellows of the RSC. He died in 1897. Jean Hamelin and Pierre Poulin, "Chauveau, Pierre-Joseph-Olivier," in *Dictionary of Canadian Biography*, vol. 11 (University of Toronto–Université Laval, 2003), accessed 19 August 2020, http://www.biographi.ca/en/bio/chauveau_pierre_joseph_olivier_11E.html; Kenneth Landry, "Faucher de Saint-Maurice, Narcisse-Henri-Édouard," in *Dictionary of Canadian Biography*, vol. 12 (University of Toronto–Université Laval, 2003), accessed 20 August 2020, http://www.biographi.ca/en/bio/faucher_de_saint_maurice_narcisse_henri_edouard_12E.html.
10 Daniel Wilson was born in Edinburgh in 1816. According to one of his biographers, after moving to Canada in 1853, Wilson developed an "obsession" with analyzing human skulls. He served as the first president of the University of Toronto from 1887 until his death in 1892. Carl Berger, "Wilson, Sir Daniel," in *Dictionary of Canadian Biography*, vol. 12 (University of Toronto–Université Laval, 2003), accessed 19 August 2020, http://www.biographi.ca/en/bio/wilson_daniel_12E.html.
11 Goldwin Smith was born in England in 1823. He died in 1910. Ramsay Cook, "Smith, Goldwin," in *Dictionary of Canadian Biography*, vol. 13 (University of Toronto–Université Laval, 2003), accessed 20 August 2020, http://www.biographi.ca/en/bio/smith_goldwin_13E.html.
12 John George Bourinot was born in Sydney, Nova Scotia, in 1836. He was clerk of the House of Commons from 1880 until his death in 1902. Bourinot served as honorary secretary of the RSC from 1881–1902, and as president from 1892–1893. On Bourinot's views on race, see Bourinot, "Canadian Studies in Comparative Politics: Canada and England,"

Proceedings and Transactions, 1890, 3; Margaret A. Banks, "Bourinot, Sir John George," in *Dictionary of Canadian Biography*, vol. 13 (University of Toronto–Université Laval, 2003), accessed 20 August 2020, http://www.biographi.ca/en/bio/bourinot_john_george_13E.html.

13 The Marquis of Lorne was born in London in 1845. He served as governor general of Canada from 1878–1883, and was made Duke of Argyll in 1900. He died in 1914. P.B. Waite, "Campbell, John George Edward Henry Douglas Sutherland, Marquess of Lorne and 9th Duke of Argyll," in *Dictionary of Canadian Biography*, vol. 14 (University of Toronto–Université Laval, 2003), accessed 19 August 2020, http://www.biographi.ca/en/bio/campbell_john_george_edward_henry_douglas_sutherland_14E.html; Darin MacKinnon, "Louise and Lorne: The Vice-Regal Visit of 1879," *The Island Magazine* 48 (Fall–Winter 2000): 3–9.

14 P.B. Waite, "Campbell, John George Edward Henry Douglas Sutherland, Marquess of Lorne and Ninth Duke of Argyll (1845–1914), Governor-General of Canada," *Oxford Dictionary of National Biography*, 23 September 2004, accessed 19 August 2020. On Lorne's role in the founding of the National Gallery, see R.H. Hubbard, "The Early Years of the National Gallery of Canada," *Proceedings and Transactions*, vol. 3, series IV (June 1965): 121–129.

15 Robert M. Stamp, *Royal Rebels: Princess Louise & the Marquis of Lorne* (Toronto: Dundurn, 1988), 174. For more on Lorne's travels to western Canada, see J. MacGregor, "Lord Lorne in Alberta," *Alberta Historical Review* 12, no. 2 (April 1964): 1–14; "An Uneasy Encounter," *Canada's History* 91, no. 6 (December 2011): 14.

16 Stamp, *Royal Rebels*, 170, 180.

17 RSC, *Inaugural Meeting, 1882*, 4.

18 Ibid., 2.

19 Ibid., 6.

20 Ibid., 6–7.

21 Ibid., 7; RSC, *Proceedings and Transactions*, 1883, 6.

22 RSC, *Inaugural Meeting, 1882*, 7.

23 Ibid., 7–8. Dawson listed as sources of inspiration the Royal Society of London, the Académie française in Paris, the Smithsonian Institution in Washington, the Philadelphia Academy, and the Boston Society of Natural History.

24 Ibid., 7. Dawson explained that the reign of Queen Victoria "has been marked by the patronage of every effort for the growth of education, literature, science and art."

25 Ibid., 7.

26 Ibid., 7.
27 Ibid., i.
28 The inaugural president and vice-president for each section of the RSC were as follows: Section I – J.M. LeMoine, N.H.É. Faucher de St. Maurice; Section II – Daniel Wilson, Goldwin Smith; Section III – T. Sterry Hunt, Charles Carpmael; Section IV – A.R.C. Selwyn, George Lawson.
29 The vice-presidential and presidential terms were limited to one year each, after which a fellow remained a past-president and member of the council for three years.
30 RSC, *Inaugural Meeting, 1882*, xxxiv.
31 Ibid., 4. The inaugural fellows were later described as "learned divines, public functionaries, and scholars." RSC, *Proceedings and Transactions*, 1894, xix. For a list of members of the inaugural cohort, see RSC, *Proceedings and Transactions*, 1883, xxv.
32 RSC, *Proceedings and Transactions*, 1883, II. In 1899, the honorary secretary learned that individuals seeking membership in the RSC were offering gifts to existing fellows in exchange for nominations. The practice revealed "an absence of good taste ... dignity or self-respect," the Secretary noted. RSC, *Proceedings and Transactions*, 1899, x. In 1900, the RSC bylaws were amended in several respects: three fellows from the same section were required to nominate a new fellow; an additional round of balloted voting at the sectional level was added; a new mechanism for resolving disputes through re-voting was added; and it was clarified that each vacancy would be filled through a separate voting process, eliminating the possibility of a second-place candidate becoming a fellow. For a full listing of the Regulations of the Royal Society of Canada, see RSC, *Inaugural Meeting, 1882*, 4–6, and RSC, *Proceedings and Transactions*, 1900, 1–13.
33 RSC, *Inaugural Meeting, 1882*; Noël Bélanger, "Tanguay, Cyprien," in *Dictionary of Canadian Biography*, vol. 13 (University of Toronto–Université Laval, 2003), accessed 21 August 2020; Bruce W. Hodgins, "Todd, Alpheus," in *Dictionary of Canadian Biography*, vol. 11 (University of Toronto–Université Laval, 2003), accessed 21 August 2020; Leslie Monkman, "Reade, John," in *Dictionary of Canadian Biography*, vol. 14 (University of Toronto–Université Laval, 2003), accessed 21 August 2020; J.G. Greenlee, "Loudon, James," in *Dictionary of Canadian Biography*, vol. 14 (University of Toronto–Université Laval, 2003), accessed 21 August 2020; Ian. Stewart, "Saunders, William," in *Dictionary of Canadian Biography*, vol. 14 (University of Toronto–Université Laval, 2003), accessed 21 August 2020.
34 RSC, *Inaugural Meeting, 1882*, 5.

35 Ibid., 20.
36 RSC, *Proceedings and Transactions,* 1883, ii; Ibid., iii. Volumes of the RSC, *Proceedings and Transactions* were also sent annually to the pope and "the more important governments of Europe." RSC, *Proceedings and Transactions,* 1903, vi. The only annual meeting to be postponed during the RSC's first forty years occurred in 1910, after learning that the funeral of King Edward VII was scheduled during the same week.
37 RSC, *Proceedings and Transactions,* 1902, xlv; RSC, *Proceedings and Transactions,* 1907, xxii; RSC, *Proceedings and Transactions,* 1911, xvii; RSC, *Proceedings and Transactions,* 1912, xxvii; RSC, *Proceedings and Transactions,* 1919, xx.
38 RSC, *Inaugural Meeting,* 1882, 8.
39 RSC, *Proceedings and Transactions,* 1883, xlv; Bruce W. Hodgins, "Todd, Alpheus," *Dictionary of Canadian Biography*, vol. 11 (University of Laval–University of Toronto, 2003).
40 RSC, *Proceedings and Transactions*, 1883, xlv–xlix.
41 See Margaret A. Banks, *Sir John George Bourinot, Victorian Canadian: His Life, Times, and Legacy* (Montreal–Kingston: McGill-Queen's University Press, 2001), chap. 8.
42 RSC, *Proceedings and Transactions,* 1901, xli.
43 RSC, *Proceedings and Transactions,* 1908, xxxvi.
44 RSC, *Proceedings and Transactions,* 1899, cxxvii.
45 RSC, *Proceedings and Transactions,* 1911, 3; RSC, *Proceedings and Transactions,* 1922. The *British North America Act* of 1867 granted responsibility for "Indians and lands reserved for Indians" to the dominion government. Initially, this responsibility fell within the Department of the Secretary of State. In 1873, it was transferred to the newly created Department of the Interior, and named the Indian Branch. In 1880, the Department of Indian Affairs was created as a distinct department of the dominion government. See Brian E. Titley, *A Narrow Vision: Duncan Campbell Scott and the Administration of Indian Affairs in Canada* (Vancouver: University of British Columbia Press, 1986), 8–13.
46 RSC, *Proceedings and Transactions,* 1892, xxxi.
47 RSC, *Proceedings and Transactions,* 1883; RSC, *Proceedings and Transactions,* 1899. Notable affiliated societies included: the Natural History Society of New Brunswick, the Nova Scotia Institute of Natural Science, the Historical Society of Halifax, the Geographical Society of Halifax, the Institut Canadien, the Literary and Historical Society of Quebec, the Historical Society of Montreal, the Literary and Scientific Society of Ottawa, the Institut Canadien-Français, the Canadian Institute

in Toronto, the Entomological Society of Ontario and the Historical and Scientific Society of Manitoba.

48 RSC, *Proceedings and Transactions*, 1889, xi; RSC, *Proceedings and Transactions*, 1895, iii; RSC, *Proceedings and Transactions*, 1908, xi; RSC, *Proceedings and Transactions*, 1910, xix; RSC, *Proceedings and Transactions*, 1913, xxxii; RSC, *Proceedings and Transactions*, 1917, xiv; RSC, *Proceedings and Transactions*, 1921, iii.

49 RSC, *Proceedings and Transactions*, 1883. The first volume was eight hundred pages long, and 1,600 copies were printed at a total cost of $4,900.

50 RSC, *Proceedings and Transactions*, 1913.

51 RSC, *Proceedings and Transactions*, 1895, xv; RSC, *Proceedings and Transactions*, 1903, xxix.

52 RSC, *Proceedings and Transactions*, 1895; RSC, *Proceedings and Transactions*, 1904, l. See also, J.G. Bourinot, *Bibliography of the Members of the Royal Society of Canada* (Ottawa: Royal Society of Canada, 1894).

53 RSC, *Proceedings and Transactions*, 1897; RSC, *Proceedings and Transactions*, 1903.

54 The 1897 volume, for example, included twenty-six portraits of distinguished Canadians, forty-four illustrations, forty-four diagrams, eighty maps, and numerous facsimiles of primary source documents. The 1899 volume included 160 maps and illustrations. RSC, *Proceedings and Transactions*, 1898; RSC, *Proceedings and Transactions*, 1900.

55 RSC, *Inaugural Meeting*, 1882, 20.

56 RSC, *Proceedings and Transactions*, 1891, iii, v. A list of recipients was included in the *Proceedings and Transactions* of 1890: Argentina, Austria-Hungary, Belgium, Chile, Costa Rica, Denmark, Ecuador, England, France, Germany, Holland, India, Ireland, Italy, Japan, Malta, Mauritius, Mexico, Newfoundland, New South Wales, New Zealand, Norway, Peru, Portugal, Queensland, Romania, Russia, Scotland, Spain, South Australia, Sweden, Switzerland, Tasmania, United States, Uruguay, and Victoria.

57 RSC, *Proceedings and Transactions*, 1883, xxix. The RSC Council sent a similar circular in 1897. RSC, *Proceedings and Transactions*, 1897, xiii.

58 RSC, *Proceedings and Transactions*, 1883, xxx. The circular added that "from the more remote parts of the North-West and North-East Territories and British Columbia, scarcely any local collections could be made which would not be possessed of scientific value."

59 RSC, *Proceedings and Transactions*, 1883, xxxi.

60 RSC, *Proceedings and Transactions*, 1893, vii.

61 RSC, *Proceedings and Transactions,* 1896, xx. The Council noted that 26,000 people had visited the Geological Survey's archives in 1895.
62 Patrice A. Dutil, "Belcourt, Napolean-Antoine (baptized Louis-Antoine-Ferdinand)," in *Dictionary of Canadian Biography,* vol. 16 (University of Toronto–Université Laval, 2003), accessed 25 January 2021, http://www.biographi.ca/en/bio/belcourt_napoleon_antoine_16E.html.
63 RSC, *Proceedings and Transactions,* 1897, xi.
64 RSC, *Proceedings and Transactions,* 1898, xiv, ci; RSC, *Proceedings and Transactions,* 1899, xvii.
65 RSC, *Proceedings and Transactions,* 1899, xvii. The comparison is likely a reference to the Smithsonian Institution, founded in 1846 in Washington, DC, and originally called the United States National Museum. The first building constructed for the purpose of housing the Smithsonian collection, the Arts and Industries Building, was completed in 1881. Smithsonian Institution Archives, https://siarchives.si.edu/history/arts-and-industries-building, accessed 15 July 2020.
66 RSC, *Proceedings and Transactions,* 1912, xviii.
67 Official calls for the creation of a National Archives were made at the RSC annual meetings of 1891, 1894, 1895, 1903. RSC, *Proceedings and Transactions,* 1891, xii; RSC, *Proceedings and Transactions,* 1894, xvi; RSC, *Proceedings and Transactions,* 1903, xxvii.
68 RSC, *Proceedings and Transactions,* 1895, xxvii. The Council noted as an example the loss of the original papers connected to the Quebec Conference of 1864, which, members lamented, "cannot be found in any of the public departments."
69 RSC, *Proceedings and Transactions,* 1895, lxvii.
70 RSC, *Proceedings and Transactions,* 1911, xx; RSC, *Proceedings and Transactions,* 1914, xiii.
71 RSC, *Proceedings and Transactions,* 1916, xvii.
72 RSC, *Proceedings and Transactions,* 1901, x.
73 RSC, *Proceedings and Transactions,* 1887, v; RSC, *Proceedings and Transactions,* 1893, ix; RSC, *Proceedings and Transactions,* 1901, xxviii.
74 RSC, *Proceedings and Transactions,* 1898, xvi.
75 RSC, *Proceedings and Transactions,* 1903, xxx. The creation of an official map was politically motivated. For an account of the Alaska boundary dispute, see Norman Hillmer and J.L. Granatstein, *For Better or For Worse: Canada and the United States into the Twenty-First Century* (Toronto: Tomson Nelson, 2007), 52–56.
76 RSC, *Proceedings and Transactions,* 1898, ix; RSC, *Proceedings and Transactions,* 1902, xxix.

77 RSC, *Proceedings and Transactions*, 1907, lxxvii. In 1917, a 72-inch reflecting telescope was installed at the Dominion Observatory, at a cost of $50,000. RSC, *Proceedings and Transactions*, 1917, xxi.
78 RSC, *Proceedings and Transactions*, 1917, lxiii.
79 RSC, *Proceedings and Transactions*, 1887, 43; RSC, *Proceedings and Transactions*, 1891, lxiii, 19. Fleming presented research on "Time-Reckoning" at several annual meetings, and chaired a special committee charged with developing a scientific name for universal time: Chronocanon, Cosmochron, and Pantochron being some of the more imaginative recommendations.
80 RSC, *Proceedings and Transactions*, 1903, xix.
81 RSC, *Proceedings and Transactions*, 1883, li.
82 RSC, *Proceedings and Transactions*, 1886, iv.
83 Donald Wright, "Gender and the Professionalization of History in English Canada before 1960," *Canadian Historical Review* 81, no. 1 (March 2000): 29–66.
84 Notable examples include Goldwin Smith, who opposed the admission of women at Cornell University, and George Lawson, who fought sternly (and unsuccessfully) against the inclusion of women at Queen's University during the 1860s, even going so far as to regulate the size of mirrors installed in the women's washrooms. Ramsay Cook, "SMITH, GOLDWIN," in *Dictionary of Canadian Biography*, vol. 13 (University of Toronto–Université Laval, 2003), accessed 26 January 2021, http://www.biographi.ca/en/bio/smith_goldwin_13E.html; Suzanne Zeller, "LAWSON, GEORGE," in *Dictionary of Canadian Biography*, vol. 12 (University of Toronto–Université Laval, 2003), accessed 26 January 2021, http://www.biographi.ca/en/bio/lawson_george_12E.html.
85 RSC, *Inaugural Meeting, 1882*, 7; RSC, *Proceedings and Transactions*, 1899, xi.
86 RSC, *Proceedings and Transactions*, 1895, xc.
87 RSC, *Proceedings and Transactions*, 1913, xli.
88 RSC, *Proceedings and Transactions*, 1913, xli. McMurrich was president of the RSC from 1922–1923.
89 The first woman elected fellow of the RSC was the paleontologist Alice Wilson, in 1938. Wilson was born in Cobourg, Ontario, and is recognized as Canada's first female geologist. See M.R. Dence, "Royal Society of Canada," *The Canadian Encyclopedia* (7 February 2006).
90 Notable examples include biologist and librarian Florence Daly Lucas and teacher and nuclear physicist Harriet Brooks, both of whom were published in the RSC, *Proceedings and Transactions*. See Mary Kinnear,

"Lucas, Florence Davy (Thompson)," in *Dictionary of Canadian Biography*, vol. 14 (University of Toronto–Université Laval), 2003, accessed 25 January 2021, http://www.biographi.ca/en/bio/lucas_florence_daly_14E.html; Marelene Rayner-Canham and Geoff Rayner-Canham, "Brooks, Harriet (Pitcher)," in *Dictionary of Canadian Biography*, vol. 16 (University of Toronto–Université Laval, 2003), accessed 25 January 2021, http://www.biographi.ca/en/bio/brooks_harriet_16E.html.

91 RSC, *Proceedings and Transactions*, 1888, 41. On Wallace Brown, see W. Wallace Brown, "Chief-Making among the Passamaquoddy Indians," *Journal of American Folkore* 5, no. 16 (1892): 57–59; J. Walter Fewkes, "A Contribution to Passamaquoddy Folk-Lore," *Journal of American Folklore* 3, no. 11 (1890): 258; "Buffalo Bill: A Local Boy," St. Croix Historical Society (2017), http://stcroixhistorical.com/?p=1197, accessed 1 August 2020.

92 RSC, *Proceedings and Transactions*, 1896, xlvii. See Mary Agnes Fitzgibbon, "A Historic Banner," *Women's Canadian Historical Society of Toronto* (1896); Janet Carnochan, *St. Andrew's, Niagara, 1794–1894* (Toronto: W. Briggs, 1895).

93 RSC, *Proceedings and Transactions*, 1899, cii, xcv; RSC, *Proceedings and Transactions*, 1902, xxx. Several other women presented reports at the RSC annual meetings, including: Miss Ellerby, Women's Canadian Historical Society of Toronto; Alice Peck, Canadian Handicrafts Guild, Montreal; Margaret Ahearn, Women's Canadian Historical Society of Ottawa. RSC, *Proceedings and Transactions*, 1897, xlv; RSC, *Proceedings and Transactions*, 1905, xii.

94 RSC, *Proceedings and Transactions*, 1895, vii.

95 S. Frances Harrison, pseudonym Seranus, was a Toronto-born author, poet, and musical critic. Theodore Harding Rand, *A Treasury of Canadian Verse with Brief Biographical Notes* (New York: Dutton, 1900), 392.

96 RSC, *Proceedings and Transactions*, 1895, cxiv. On Pauline Johnson, see Carole Gerson's contribution in this volume, as well as Marilyn Rose, "Johnson, Emily Pauline," in *Dictionary of Canadian Biography*, vol. 14 (University of Toronto–Université Laval, 2003), accessed 25 August 2020, http://www.biographi.ca/en/bio/johnson_emily_pauline_14E.html.; J. Garvin, ed., "E. Pauline Johnson," in *Canadian Poets* (Toronto: McClelland, 1916), 145–156.

97 RSC, *Proceedings and Transactions*, 1890, ii.

98 RSC, *Proceedings and Transactions*, 1883, 17. On John Reade, see Cynthia Milton's contribution in this volume, as well as Leslie Monkman, "Reade, John," in *Dictionary of Canadian Biography*, vol. 14 (University of Toronto–Université Laval, 2003), accessed 25 August 2020.

99 RSC, *Proceedings and Transactions*, 1883, 1; RSC, *Proceedings and Transactions*, 1885, 67; RSC, *Proceedings and Transactions*, 1887, 35, 99; RSC, *Proceedings and Transactions*, 1891, 3, 85; RSC, *Proceedings and Transactions*, 1895, 3, 45; RSC, *Proceedings and Transactions*, 1899, 199; RSC, *Proceedings and Transactions*, 1903, 135; RSC, *Proceedings and Transactions*, 1906, 311; RSC, *Proceedings and Transactions*, 1911, 3; RSC, *Proceedings and Transactions*, 1913, 67; RSC, *Proceedings and Transactions*, 1914, 381; RSC, *Proceedings and Transactions*, 1920, xxi.

100 Nancy Stepan, *The Idea of Race in Science: Great Britain, 1800–1960* (London: Macmillan, 1982), chapters 2 and 4.

101 RSC, *Proceedings and Transactions*, 1885, iii.

102 RSC, *Proceedings and Transactions*, 1888, xxi.

103 RSC, *Proceedings and Transactions*, 1888, xxiv.

104 RSC, *Proceedings and Transactions*, 1894, lxvi.

105 RSC, *Proceedings and Transactions*, 1887, iii.

106 RSC, *Proceedings and Transactions*, 1888, xviii. Lawson added that Section IV, Geological and Biological Sciences, was the most active contributor to the RSC.

107 RSC, *Proceedings and Transactions*, 1890, vii.

108 RSC, *Proceedings and Transactions*, 1892, vii.

109 RSC, *Proceedings and Transactions*, 1894, v. Eight of the twenty fellows in Section II attended the annual meeting in 1892.

110 RSC, *Proceedings and Transactions*, 1895, xxviii.

111 RSC, *Proceedings and Transactions*, 1913, iii; RSC, *Proceedings and Transactions*, 1918, xvi; RSC, *Proceedings and Transactions*, 1919, iv. According to Statistics Canada, the average life expectancy for a Canadian male in 1920 was between fifty-seven and sixty-five years. See: www150.statcan.gc.ca/n1/pub/11-630-x/11-630-x2016002-eng.htm.

112 RSC, *Proceedings and Transactions*, 1894, x.

113 RSC, *Proceedings and Transactions*, 1892, vii; RSC, *Proceedings and Transactions*, 1894, ix–x; RSC, *Proceedings and Transactions*, 1901, viii; RSC, *Proceedings and Transactions*, 1906, v.

114 RSC, *Proceedings and Transactions*, 1895; RSC, *Proceedings and Transactions*, 1909, lxi. In the expansion of 1909, Sections I and II were raised to thirty fellows, and Sections III and IV were raised to forty fellows.

115 RSC, *Proceedings and Transactions*, 1891, xxx–xl. At the meeting in 1889, five papers were read in Section II, while seventeen were read in Section III. In the *Proceedings and Transactions* of 1905, Section II published four

papers, while Section IV published eleven. In the volume for 1921, Section II published eight papers, while Section III published fifty-two.

116 RSC, *Proceedings and Transactions*, 1917, xlvii; RSC, *Proceedings and Transactions*, 1919, xxv.
117 RSC, *Proceedings and Transactions*, 1883; RSC, *Proceedings and Transactions*, 1891.
118 RSC, *Proceedings and Transactions*, 1894; RSC, *Proceedings and Transactions*, 1895.
119 RSC, *Proceedings and Transactions*, 1891; RSC, *Proceedings and Transactions*, 1897; RSC, *Proceedings and Transactions*, 1902; RSC, *Proceedings and Transactions*, 1904; RSC, *Proceedings and Transactions*, 1914.
120 RSC, *Inaugural Meeting*, 1882; RSC, *Proceedings and Transactions*, 1883, lii.
121 RSC, *Proceedings and Transactions*, 1883, i.
122 RSC, *Proceedings and Transactions*, 1889, i.
123 RSC, *Proceedings and Transactions*, 1890, i.
124 RSC, *Proceedings and Transactions*, 1893, xiii.
125 RSC, *Proceedings and Transactions*, 1892, xv; RSC, *Proceedings and Transactions*, 1893. In 1893, the RSC hired John Durie and Son, Ottawa, as its new printer.
126 RSC, *Proceedings and Transactions*, 1904, iv; RSC, *Proceedings and Transactions*, 1903, vii.
127 RSC, *Proceedings and Transactions*, 1906, ix; RSC, *Proceedings and Transactions*, 1908, iii. "The practice of sending out several revises is fatal to a dispatch," Fletcher complained to RSC fellows in 1906.
128 RSC, *Proceedings and Transactions*, 1909, vii.
129 Ibid., ii.
130 LeSueur was RSC President from 1912–1913. RSC, *Proceedings and Transactions*, 1910; RSC, *Proceedings and Transactions*, 1911; RSC, *Proceedings and Transactions*, 1916; C.G. Holland, "LeSueur, William Dawson," in *Dictionary of Canadian Biography*, vol. 14 (University of Toronto–Université Laval, 2003), accessed 25 August 2020.
131 Rare volumes include RSC, *Proceedings and Transactions*, 1895; RSC, *Proceedings and Transactions*, 1899; and RSC, *Proceedings and Transactions*, 1905.
132 RSC, *Proceedings and Transactions*, 1891, xiii.
133 RSC, *Proceedings and Transactions*, 1885; RSC, *Proceedings and Transactions*, 1886, xv; RSC, *Proceedings and Transactions*, 1889, 11; RSC,

Proceedings and Transactions, 1900, 207; RSC, *Proceedings and Transactions*, 1902, 143; RSC, *Proceedings and Transactions*, 1920, xxiii.
134 RSC, *Proceedings and Transactions*, 1891, xxxiii.
135 RSC, *Proceedings and Transactions*, 1908, li.
136 RSC, *Proceedings and Transactions*, 1902, xvi; RSC, *Proceedings and Transactions*, 1911, xvii, xxxvii; RSC, *Proceedings and Transactions*, 1914, xli.
137 RSC, *Inaugural Meeting*, 1882, 7.

2

Duncan Campbell Scott and the Royal Society of Canada: The Legitimation of Knowledge

Constance Backhouse

In June 1983, the *National Lampoon*, a satirical and humour magazine, mocked Duncan Campbell Scott's legendary rise within the Canadian public service: "As a youth, this poet found secure employment as a copying clerk for the Department of Indian Affairs and stayed with that department for the next fifty years, occasionally winning promotions by attrition."[1] The sarcastic summary was true but somewhat misleading. Scott's ladder of ascension took him from copying clerk in 1879 to chief clerk, book-keeper, accountant, acting deputy superintendent, and then superintendent of education by 1909.[2] His final appointment was to the post of deputy superintendent general of Indian Affairs, where he served as the department's chief civil servant, equivalent to a deputy minister, from 1913 to 1932. From that vantage point, he would become Canada's "principal architect of Indian policy."[3]

In 1899, the Royal Society of Canada (RSC) honoured Scott by inducting him as a fellow.[4] He felt this recognition keenly and took it as "his national duty" to devote significant time to the society.[5] He made himself indispensable within the organization, where he served on innumerable committees over more than three decades. He was elected honorary secretary for the Society in 1911, a post he held for ten years.[6] In 1921, he was elected to its highest position as president.[7]

Was there a connection between Scott's powerful role at Indian Affairs and his elite position within the RSC? The temporal overlap suggests that there must have been some cross-fertilization between Scott's work in the two organizations. Of equal significance is the

Figure 2.1 Duncan Campbell Scott, 1915.

question of what impact Scott's RSC status may have played in cementing his political and governmental reputation as a white man with the expertise to set policy on Indigenous issues.

SCOTT'S DUAL CAREERS: PUBLIC SERVANT AND LITERARY PIONEER

Scott's career with Indian Affairs is pivotal, but it was his reputation as a literary figure that brought him into the ambit of the RSC, and it is important to examine his contributions in both realms. He was born in Ottawa in 1862, of parents who claimed English and Scottish heritage.[8] The dominant familial influence on his life seems to have been his English father.[9] Reverend William Scott was a Wesleyan Methodist preacher, whose religious calling encompassed a desire to "eradicate heathenism wherever it was to be found," and entailed efforts to Christianize the Ojibwa at the St. Clair Mission near Sarnia and the Anishnaabe on Manitoulin Island.[10] Reverend Scott's occupation kept the family moving through a series of small villages in Quebec and Ontario, and young Scott spent his high school years in Stanstead, Quebec. Financial constraints ended his formal education at the age of fifteen.[11]

Next, Reverend Scott, who was a long-time supporter of John A. Macdonald, sent a specimen of his young son's handwriting to the prime minister. In 1879, combined with the political connection, that was sufficient to garner his son a patronage appointment, a governmental entry position as copy clerk. As Brian Titley, author of the definitive work about Scott's life as a civil servant notes, it was Scott's "business acumen," "gift with figures," "devotion to organization aims," and "imperial pride" that then carried him forward to the highest post.[12]

In his years as the top power-broker at Indian Affairs, Scott oversaw encroachments upon Indigenous lands and resources, the erosion of their hunting, fishing, and other treaty rights, compulsory attendance at Indian residential schools, shockingly inadequate health care, new gender roles that diminished women's status, and the attempted annihilation of Indigenous spiritual, linguistic, and cultural practices.[13] When confronted with the appalling death rates of Indigenous children in residential schools, Scott commented in 1910: "[T]his alone does not justify a change in the policy of this Department, which is geared toward the final solution of our Indian

Problem."[14] In 1920, he wrote: "Our object is to continue until there is not a single Indian in Canada that has not been absorbed into the body politic, and there is no Indian question, and no Indian Department."[15] Observers have affixed Duncan Campbell Scott with responsibility for Canada's most destructive Aboriginal policies.[16]

Yet Scott's main interests did not lie in his governmental work. His contemporaries remarked that "the centre of his life was not in his office, where he seldom came early and never stayed late."[17] It was his contribution to the "world of *belles lettres*" and his career as a Canadian literary pioneer that took precedence for Scott. His first poem was published in 1888.[18] Two collections of poetry appeared before the century was out.[19] The decade following, he co-edited a series of "great man" biographies.[20] In 1914, he published one article in a book,[21] and three additional volumes of poetry arrived by 1921.[22]

SCOTT'S CONNECTIONS WITH THE ROYAL SOCIETY OF CANADA

Founded in 1882, the Royal Society of Canada patterned itself after the British Royal Society of London, designed to be a "senior collegium of distinguished scholars, artists, and scientists."[23] The 1883 incorporating statute proclaimed its objective to "promote learning and intellectual accomplishments of exceptional quality" in the "arts, humanities and sciences, as well as in Canadian public life."[24] Membership was restricted to individuals who had made outstanding contributions in their field of expertise. New members were elected by the existing members to receive this "highest of academic accolades."[25] It was an insular process of admission, lacking in transparency.

Nevertheless, the Society's early activities were impressive:[26] establishing a commission to produce an official register of Canadian place names;[27] lobbying the government to commission an official map of Canada;[28] measuring the 98th meridian;[29] campaigning for a national museum;[30] insisting upon the preservation of historical monuments, sites, buildings, and archives;[31] and obtaining Carnegie Foundation funds to construct the Ottawa Public Library.[32] Its annual meetings facilitated scholarly exchanges and eventually set the framework for annual "learned societies" meetings.[33]

In 1899, when Duncan Campbell Scott was first named a fellow, he was still an accountant with Indian Affairs,[34] hardly someone who was to be celebrated for "accomplishments of exceptional quality in Canadian public life." Nor was it his expertise in Indigeneity that spawned the RSC recognition, for he had little experience in "dealing directly with Indians."[35] He was a man without post-secondary education, and difficult to categorize as a scholar at this stage. The foundation for the RSC accolades must therefore have been his work as a poet and short-story writer. Although sixty years later Scott would be described as one of Canada's "Confederation poets,"[36] by the year of his induction, he had published only two collections of poems[37] and one collection of short stories,[38] along with a series of columns titled "At the Mermaid Inn" in the Toronto *Globe*[39] and some short stories in periodical magazines.[40] For a publishing career commenced in 1887, it was not "prolific," according to literary scholar Stan Dragland.[41] It would seem like slim pickings as a basis for RSC recognition.

Toronto literary critic and professor E.K. Brown speculated that Scott may have "succeeded to [Archibald] Lampman's seat in the Royal Society of Canada."[42] Lampman was a poet and intimate friend of Scott's, a graduate of Trinity College Toronto, and a postal clerk in Ottawa, who was inducted into the Royal Society in 1895, and died in 1899. His output as a poet was not dissimilar from Scott's at the time, and his position as a postal clerk indicates that government employment at the lower echelons did not entirely bar someone from Royal Society accreditation.[43] Brown's speculation may shed some light on how Scott's RSC induction was perceived, but holding "a seat" for a specific person does not accord with the selection process that the Royal Society professed to use. And the timing seems a bit tight, with Scott's induction the same year as Lampman's death leaving little time to prepare a nomination and filter it through the election process.

If one were speculating, one might just as easily ask whether Scott's wife, Belle Warner Botsford, whom he married in 1894, might have had some influence. Belle was a professional violinist from Boston who had trained at the Paris Conservatory, and she cut a swath through Ottawa society when she took up residence with her new husband. She played hostess to society women and visiting dignitaries, and was often an invited guest at Rideau Hall.[44] Although she was alleged to be a domineering woman whose relationship with her husband was somewhat strained, she would undoubtedly have wished his stature to grow, and an RSC fellowship would have helped. Although there is no surviving record of her effort to exercise influence, one should not discount the underground social networks of women, and their contributions to their husbands' careers.

Apart from such speculations, was Scott's selection as a fellow an anomaly at the time? In 1899, he was inducted with two other new fellows.[45] William Henry Drummond was an Irish-born Montreal physician with a medical degree from Bishop's College, associate editor of the *Canada Medical Record*, a professor of medical jurisprudence, and an international public lecturer. He had published two volumes of critically and popularly acclaimed poetry and two volumes of prose, was a fellow of the Royal Society of Literature of Great Britain, and was described as "one of the most popular authors in the English-speaking world."[46] William McLennan was a Montreal-born practicing notary, translator, and author, with a law degree from McGill. He had published books and articles of history, fiction, and poetry in Montreal, Toronto, and New York, and was renowned as a writer with "the accuracy of a scholar and the fine feeling of a poet."[47]

Reverend George Bryce, inducted three years later, was a Presbyterian cleric, historian, and educator with degrees from the University of Toronto and Knox College. A founder of the University of Manitoba where he became a professor of science, Bryce also helped to create the Manitoba Historical and Scientific Society. By the time of his induction, he had published seventeen papers on geology, archaeology, and the history of the province.[48] William Douw Lighthall, who was also inducted in 1902, was a Hamilton-born Montreal lawyer, politician, historian, poet, and novelist, who held a bachelor and master's of arts and a law degree from McGill. A mayor of Westmount and a founder of the Union of Canadian Municipalities and the Society of Canadian Literature, Lighthall had published books of history, philosophy, poetry, and fiction.[49] Adam Shortt, inducted in 1906, had amassed graduate degrees from Queen's and the University of Edinburgh and Glasgow. The holder of the John A. Macdonald Chair of Political and Economic Science at Queen's, he had published books on international trade and the history of Canadian banking.[50] William Lyon Mackenzie King, inducted in 1910, held a BA from University College Toronto, an LLB from Osgoode Hall, and both an MA and PhD from Harvard. He had served nine years as deputy minister and one year as minister of labour where he shaped Canada's first industrial disputes legislation, and had already been honoured as a Companion of the Order of St Michael and St George.[51] In contrast to the accountant from Indian Affairs, King had substantially greater claim to "accomplishments of exceptional quality in Canadian public life."

Scott's RSC induction should also be considered against another prominent literary figure, E. Pauline Johnson, Tekahionwake. By the year of Scott's induction, thirty-eight-year-old Pauline Johnson from the Six Nations Reserve near the Grand River, Ontario, could outdistance him in terms of her international prominence as a poet, writer, artist, and performer.[52] In 1892, Scott and Johnson had shared a stage before a Toronto audience of 400 spectators. Her performance contrasted vividly with Scott's "prose sketch," a reading that "failed to stir the crowd."[53] Contemporary journalists reported that Johnson recited from memory "A Cry from an Indian Wife," a poem based on Indigenous resistance during the Northwest Resistance and that "her recitation so startled and moved the audience that, in the finest tradition of theatrical lore, a star was born."[54] As one biographer wrote about that evening, "Pauline's stated desire was 'to set people on fire.' That she did."[55] At the height of her career by 1895, celebrated for her poetry and dramatic readings across Canada, the United States, and Britain, Johnson was not among the literary artists inducted into the RSC. Nor would she be recognized by 1913, the year of her death. It is worth adding that her gender and race, as a woman of mixed-race Mohawk and English heritage, may have disqualified her.[56] Although there was no formal rule barring women or racial minorities, for the duration of Scott's active involvement all of the fellows and officers were white and male.[57]

Still, the contrast between Scott and the other fellows who were elected around the same time is notable. It is true that there were fewer distinctions between amateur and professional researchers at the turn of the twentieth century, and there were some other fellows without university credentials.[58] But the academic backgrounds and intellectual output of Drummond, McLennan, Bryce, Lighthall, Shortt, and King would have added considerable lustre to the RSC. The reverse would have been true for Scott, for it was the lustre of the RSC that attached to the deputy superintendent. The bulk of his publications and literary acclaim came after his induction, quite possibly helped along by the RSC stamp of legitimacy.

Indeed, subsequent to his entry into the RSC, Scott published considerably more.[59] The decade following, he ventured into the field of Canadian history. In conjunction with University of Toronto professor and literary critic Pelham Edgar (honoured as an RSC fellow in 1915), he co-edited George Morang's *Makers of Canada*, a twenty-volume series of "great man" biographies,[60] compiled by two men who possessed no training as historians.[61] Scott's authorial contribution was on John Graves Simcoe, the first lieutenant-governor of Upper Canada.[62] He published another historical article in 1914, on the history of Indian Affairs, which appeared in *Canada and its Provinces*.[63] His literary output continued with additional volumes of poetry in 1905, 1906, 1916, 1921, 1926, and 1935, another volume of short stories in 1923, and several edited collections of other writers' work.[64] Despite the burgeoning publications, he has been characterized as "a minor poet"[65] and his oeuvre as "unspectacular but solid in poetry and fiction."[66] He was quoted to have said, "I have long been quite satisfied not to be taken seriously as a poet. I don't seem to be able to gain the attention of important papers or reviews, but I am not grieving. Probably I would not be able to live up to popularity."[67]

Throughout this time, his involvement with the RSC grew by leaps and bounds. The society maintained four (eventually five) different sections divided by disciplinary area.[68] Within two years of his entry as a fellow, Scott had been elected vice-president of the section on "English Literature, History and Allied Subjects," and, in 1902, he was elevated to president of the section.[69] Within the RSC committee structure, Scott accrued more power. Starting in 1903, he participated actively as a member of the printing committee, which assessed which research papers of members would appear in the annual proceedings.[70] In the absence of outlets for publication of scholarly papers in this era, the RSC *Proceedings and Transactions* became the pre-eminent national journal for dissemination. Successive RSC presidents praised Scott for his poetry in their annual presidential addresses.[71] Scott himself presented frequently at the annual meetings, often reading his poems aloud to the assembled throng.[72]

By 1909, Scott was serving on the nomination committee that selected candidates for society membership, in effect, gate-keeper for the society's roster of new fellows.[73] In 1913, he participated on a committee to design a new RSC seal.[74] From 1923 to 1932 he sat on the section's advisory committee.[75] From 1911 to 1921, his position as honorary secretary gave him an ongoing seat on the

Figure 2.2 Duncan Campbell Scott, undated.

executive of the RSC council.[76] Ian Wereley, who has reviewed all of the RSC *Proceedings and Transactions* for this period, concluded that there were years when it seemed that "Scott's name appears on every page."[77] In 1927, he was awarded the Society's Lorne Pierce Medal, and in 1930 he was appointed to the nominating committee for the Flavelle and Tyrrell Medals.[78] In 1929, he became convenor of his section's special endowment committee.[79]

Using the same skills that had ensured his unusual success in the public service – characterized by observers as "composure," "cunning," and an "air of impersonal command"[80] – Scott rode a steady trajectory to the top. Described as a "tall, bony figure" and reputed to be personally self-conscious, nervous, gloomy, aloof, dour, and even forbidding, he still managed to maintain a social circle of musicians, painters, actors, and writers.[81] It was enough to convince the RSC fellowship to install him as president of the whole society. It may have been the RSC lead that brought the University of Toronto to award him an honorary doctorate of literature in 1922.[82] It was his first degree.[83]

When the RSC elevated Scott to its most powerful position of president, it sealed his reputation as a man "rich in honours."[84] It placed its imprimatur upon a member who had by then become a known literary figure, enhancing his reputation as a "man of letters." For eight years, Scott had also been holding down the most powerful post within Indian Affairs, and the stature of the RSC presidential position must have carried considerable weight within the government department and among the federal politicians who supervised Scott's policy-setting and operational activities. At the helm of Indian Affairs, he was someone to whom his bureaucratic and political supervisors deferred because of his "reputed superior knowledge and experience of Indian matters."[85] In fact, Scott was someone who was "better acquainted with prime ministers, book publishers and newspaper editors than with Aboriginal leaders."[86]

The interconnecting threads that linked Scott's Indian Affairs post, his literary reputation, and his RSC station did not escape notice. In December 1915, the *Boston Evening Transcript* stated that Scott was "far and away the best honorary secretary who ever managed the Royal Society of Canada, wherefore writing folk can't but rejoice to celebrate his proven skill as Administrator of the intricate Indian Service."[87]

EXPLORING THE DAMAGING INTERCONNECTIONS FURTHER

First Nations, Inuit, and Métis peoples, central to Scott's civil service activities, were also evident in his literary oeuvre. Although his poetic verses were celebrated as refined and romantic, he portrayed Indigenous peoples as irrational and brutal, caricaturing them as drunken, debauched, stupid, and pagan, stereotyped "stage props" to white actors.[88] His biography of John Graves Simcoe characterized Indigenous peoples as children under beneficent protection from imperial authorities.[89] His 1914 article on the history of Indian Affairs has been described as a partisan and hostile dismissal of Indigeneity in Canadian history, amateurish musings with a "penchant for hyperbole."[90] His literary output bore clear resemblance to his Indian Affairs work, where his relations with Indigenous peoples were "invariably strained and frequently openly antagonistic," and he persistently refused to "take Indian wishes into account" in formulating or implementing policy.[91]

To what extent were his RSC activities equally bound up in this mix? Scott's status within the RSC enhanced his reputation as a white man expert in Indigenous issues, but this was not the full extent of the crossover. The RSC helped to construct a bedrock of racist ideas that bolstered the damaging policies of Indian Affairs. An organization entirely lacking Indigenous participants, the RSC gave its members little opportunity to correct their ignorance about the philosophical, political, economic, scientific, cultural, and artistic knowledge that Indigenous members might have brought to their inner circle of scholarly elites. As the other essays in this volume demonstrate, those RSC members who did claim to focus on Indigenous research, did so with a Eurocentric colonial framework that infused their publications with pernicious racist notions about "civilization" and "progress."

As president of his section in 1902–03, Scott created a committee to pressure the government for a "permanent ethnology survey" of the diverse "types" of people in Canada.[92] When the RSC chose to establish a new designated section on "Social Science and Economics" in 1909, it was in part due to growing interest in new topics of race and immigration,[93] and as a member of the RSC printing committee, Scott selected scholarly papers that focused on ethnographical distinctions between the "white races" and "aborigines or Indians."[94] In 1911, he presented a paper titled "The League of the Iroquois: Traditional History of the Confederacy of the Six Nations," which he explained had been prepared by a committee of chiefs of the Six Nation Indians of Grand River. He congratulated the group on bringing "from its shadowy basis of legend to its mechanical execution" a document that "bears witness to the degree of proficiency in the use of English to which many of them have attained." He emphasized that even the "typewritten manuscript was prepared by one of the Indians."[95] In his presentations at the annual meetings, Scott read out the papers of other fellows with descriptions of "sacrificial rites" of the Blackfoot[96] and female puberty ceremonies among the Nootka.[97]

In 1921, the year the RSC elected him president, Scott was immersed in efforts to derail emerging Indigenous political organizations. His department had mounted a concerted campaign to discredit the first leader of the League of Indians of Canada, Frederick O. Loft, a Mohawk from the Six Nations Reserve and a returning war veteran. Scott unfairly criticized Loft's wartime service and disparaged Loft's educational background, despite Loft's completion of secondary school, a feat unusual for educationally deprived Indigenous students. In fact, Loft had achieved precisely the same educational attainments as Scott, who had gone no further than high school himself.[98] Scott's actions betray a heightened sense of his own academic standing, his RSC presidential privilege apparently giving him licence to discredit those without university education.

In the 1920s, members of the Six Nations Confederacy asserted claims of autonomy, rejecting the authority of the Department of Indian Affairs on the ground that their nations had always been allies, rather than subjects, of the British Crown. They sought a declaratory judicial ruling of sovereignty and a hearing before the newly formed international League of Nations, and then lodged an appeal directly to King George V.[99] When their demands met with some public support, Scott came out swinging, characterizing their "so-called status claim"[100] as "absurd,"[101] something that he must "squelch" at the start.[102] He blamed Indigenous "vanity and general ignorance" for prompting the "unwarranted claims and foolish assumptions."[103] He began to lobby for an amendment to the *Indian Act* to make it a criminal offence to raise funds to hire legal counsel to pursue Indigenous claims. In 1927, Parliament acquiesced, making it a crime to raise money from Indigenous communities for the prosecution of Indigenous claims unless the Department of Indian affairs gave prior written consent.[104]

Other RSC fellows intervened in the sovereignty discussions. Ontario Supreme Court Justice William Renwick Riddell had adjudicated a parallel claim over Mohawk fishing rights in the famous *Eliza Sero v. Gault* case in 1921.[105] Riddell, who published more than 1,200 articles on Canadian legal, medical and social history, law, and international relations, had been inducted as a fellow in 1917.[106] Scottish by ethnicity, an "ardent imperialist" by inclination, and a jurist with copious Anglo-elite connections, Riddell made short shrift of Sero's claim.[107] Then Duncan Campbell Scott and Justice Riddell wrote back and forth about the decision, agreeing that the wider sovereignty claim was also "entirely without merit," while at the same time exchanging pleasantries about the upcoming RSC elections and its annual meeting that May.[108]

William Douw Lighthall, a Montreal lawyer who had assisted the Six Nations in making their claim in 1921, also corresponded with Scott. Lighthall, who had been inducted into the Royal Society in 1902 and served as its president from 1918–19, had included Scott's poem in his 1889 poetry anthology, giving Scott his first poetry publication in a book.[109] Relying upon the friendship that they had forged through their literary connections and linkages within the RSC, Lighthall urged Scott to rethink his quest to dismantle the Six Nations' traditional system of tribal government. According to Titley, "his friend's appeal did not move Scott."[110]

Friend or foe, the RSC served as a nexus within which powerful white men debated the merits of Indigenous autonomy. The "chief apologist for Canada's Indian policy," a man whose "role was pivotal," Scott insisted that the ultimate power and wisdom rested with the government and the men who formulated its policy.[111] The views of the RSC president took ascendance. His position that Indigenous sovereignty was a "piece of folly" turned into a "ruthless determination to crush" the sovereignty movement.[112]

Is it unfair to criticize Scott and his RSC colleagues for anti-Indigenous views and actions? Some might argue that concepts such as racism have changed over time, and people should not face opprobrium for simply reflecting the standards of their times.[113] This fails to grapple with the question of whether discriminatory beliefs are ever universally held, regardless of the era. Undoubtedly, Indigenous peoples would have viewed the world quite differently from Scott. To dismiss their perspectives is to render the standards of

Figure 2.3 Duncan Campbell Scott at piano, 1942.

the times very partial indeed. There were also some non-Indigenous people who would have disagreed with Scott.[114] Socio-cultural context is never uniform, there are always dissenting voices, and persons in Scott's position would have had some access to diverse perspectives. Scott was a "voracious and eclectic reader,"[115] and in his position as the most powerful civil servant in Indian Affairs and as a treaty negotiator, he would also have had multiple opportunities to speak with and learn from Indigenous people.[116]

What was more, Scott and the RSC fellows were some of the key people influencing the socio-cultural context. They helped to create and sanction what counted as knowledge and expertise.[117] They extolled the presumptive superiority of Western knowledge and culture, setting up racial and ethnic hierarchies, and legitimating certain kinds of knowledge while erasing others.[118] The RSC fellows served as "credentializers," men who were "guarantors of reliable knowledge" deemed central to national development.[119]

As Nell Irvin Painter notes, racism has had a historical and continuing impact but "race is an idea, not a fact."[120] The "science of race" flourished in Europe in the eighteenth century in aid of imperial colonization. Latter-day scholars established an escalating hierarchy of human taxonomy, advancing multiple racial schemes with criteria "constantly shifting according to individual taste and political need."[121] Duncan Campbell Scott, who published an essay titled "The Aboriginal Races," embraced the concept.[122] He described Indigenous people in his 1920 Indian Affairs annual report as "savages in warpaint," presenting a vision that would amuse "the superior race."[123] He was a "man who for decades, as both a major poet and a senior civil servant, helped to shape perceptions of Canada's Native peoples and peoples of mixed race and to frame and execute policies concerning their treatment and the treatment of their cultures."[124]

Academic networks created "racial ideology" through cultures of intellectual connections that were "racially exclusive, gendered, and classed."[125] As Painter explains, "These worlds were not universal. Rather they stretched in partial and particular directions, linking people who knew each other and people who knew people who knew each other."[126] The intimate bonds that emerged within the formal structures of the RSC brought together people who capitalized on their elite stature, Anglo-Saxon heritage, and useful connections to give credence to their authority.

DUNCAN CAMPBELL SCOTT'S LIFE AND DEATH

In stark contrast with the harsh lives of the First Nations, Métis and Inuit peoples his efforts did so much to restrict, Scott lived a life of affluence and plenty. In the realm of ideas with the power of persuasion, it was an asset to be rich. His three-storey, twelve-room brick home at 108 Lisgar Street was graced with a wealth of windows. A high-ceilinged music room housed a grand piano and the walls

Figure 2.4 Duncan Campbell Scott's home, 108 Lisgar Street, photographed in 1890 when it was the residence of Scott's father, Reverend William Scott.

were crowded with paintings from the likes of Emily Carr and Lawren Harris, a framed portrait of Scott by the famed photographer Karsh, and stacks of books. His first wife, Belle Botsford, kept scrapbooks of her "gilded age" dinner cards and party invitations, and Scott partook of private country club memberships and golfed with Prime Minister Robert Borden.[127] Several years after the death of his wife and one year after his remarriage to a woman young enough to be his daughter, Scott retired, took up wintering in British Columbia and Arizona, and travelled through Italy and Britain.[128]

Scott's stature owes much to the Royal Society of Canada. In Scott's *Canadian Encyclopedia* entry, three of the six honours that appear under the subtitle "Legacy" are Royal Society awards: the fellowship in 1899, the presidency in 1921, and the Lorne Pierce

Medal in 1927.[129] He retired in 1932 at the age of sixty-nine. Privately reflecting upon his years of public service, he described them as "my fifty-year imprisonment with the savages."[130] After a number of attacks of angina, Duncan Campbell Scott died of heart failure on 19 December 1947.[131] Bolstered by the RSC "seal" of recognition that had crowned him a member of Canada's intellectual elite, Scott's catastrophic Indigenous policies lived on for generations to come.

NOTES

1. E. Brian Titley, *A Narrow Vision: Duncan Campbell Scott and the Administration of Indian Affairs in Canada* (Vancouver: University of British Columbia Press, 1986) duplicates the quote at ix, and notes at 13 that most clerks "were engaged in copying letters into letter books before typewriters arrived."
2. Titley notes that Scott's temporary promotion to acting deputy superintendent occurred in 1893, following his recent promotion to chief clerk and accountant. He was replaced in the deputy superintendent post by Hayter Reed later that year, returning to his post as accountant. He continued his work as an accountant while taking on the newly created position of superintendent of education in 1909. Ibid., 14–24.
3. Ibid., 22.
4. RSC, *Proceedings and Transactions*, 1899, cxxvii.
5. Stan Dragland, *Floating Voice: Duncan Campbell Scott and the Literature of Treaty 9* (Concord ON: Anansi, 1994), 113.
6. RSC, *Proceedings and Transactions*, 1911, xx. He was replaced by Honorary Secretary Charles Camsell in 1921, although he served one additional year in 1925. RSC, *Proceedings and Transactions*, 1921, 1; RSC, *Proceedings and Transactions*, 1925, 1.
7. RSC, *Proceedings and Transactions*, 1921, xxxv.
8. Duncan Campbell Scott was born in the parsonage of the Dominion Methodist Church at Metcalfe and Queen, where his father was then the minister. Titley, *Narrow Vision*, 23. Scott's father, English-born William Scott, arrived in Canada in the 1830s. Scott's mother, Isabella (Janet) Campbell McCallum, was born in Lower Canada, and most sources identify her parents as Gaelic-speaking Scottish Highlanders. Ibid., 23; Mark Abley, *Conversations with a Dead Man: The Legacy of Duncan Campbell Scott* (Madeira Park BC: Douglas & McIntyre, 2013), 27–8. E.K. Brown ed.,

Duncan Campbell Scott: Selected Poems (Toronto: Ryerson Press, 1951) notes at xi that Scott's maternal grandparents were John MacCallum and Isabella Campbell, who "had the Gaelic" and "were emigrants from Killin in Perthshire." See also letter #162 (29 September 1946) from Duncan Campbell Scott to E.K. Brown, published in Robert L. McDougall, ed., *The Poet and the Critic: A Literary Correspondence Between D.C. Scott and E.K. Brown* (Ottawa: Carleton University Press, 1983), 176, where Scott writes: "I remember my maternal Grandmother, being held up to see her on her death-bed; then I was about five, and I can see an old face and a head with a lace nightcap; she had The Gaelic, as they say, and I've been told that her pet name for me was Gagey." The death certificate for Scott's mother gives Scott's maternal grandmother's name as Mary Campbell, birthplace Perthshire, Scotland. I am indebted to Mark Abley, Carole Gerson, and Karyn Huenemann for advising me of these references.

In contrast, one source suggests that Scott's maternal grandmother may have been an Onondaga woman from Kahnawake. David McNab, "'A Lurid Dash of Colour': Powassan's Drum and Canada's Mission, The Reverend William and Duncan Campbell Scott," in Jill Oakes et al., *Aboriginal Cultural Landscapes* (Winnipeg: Aboriginal Issues Press, 2004) notes at 265 that Scott's grandmother on his mother's side was Onondaga, "a Campbell and the country wife of Duncan Campbell Napier ... likely of the Bear clan," citing Barbara Alice Mann, *Iroquoian Women: The Gantowisas* (New York: Peter Lang, 2000). The reference to Duncan Campbell Napier indicates a possible mix-up between Duncan Campbell Scott and Duncan Campbell Napier. There appears to be no connection between Duncan Campbell Scott and Duncan Campbell Napier, although the latter's wife, Catherine Wurtele, may have had Indigenous heritage. Napier was born in Jersey, served in the army in Lower Canada, retired to Shropshire with his daughter's family, and died in Jersey. I am indebted to Carole Gerson and Karyn Huenemann for this information.

9 Rumours suggest that for much of Duncan Campbell Scott's adult life he was estranged from his mother and sisters, although some observed that this may have been attributable to his first wife's wishes. E.K. Brown, *Selected Poems*, xviii; Sandra Gwyn, *The Private Capital* (Toronto: McClelland and Stewart, 1984), 467; McNab, "A Lurid Dash of Colour," 244–69; Titley, *Narrow Vision*, 23; Abley, *Conversations*, 27–8.

10 McNab, "A Lurid Dash of Colour," 258; Robert L. McDougall, *The Poet and the Critic* (Ottawa: Carleton University Press, 1983), 1; Dragland, *Floating Voice*, 77; Titley, *Narrow Vision*, 23; Abley, *Conversations*, 55.

11 Scott's high school was the Wesleyan college, founded in Stanstead in 1872. Titley, *Narrow Vision*, 23–4.
12 Ibid., 24–5.
13 Ibid., chap. 3–10.
14 As quoted in Abley, *Conversations*, 64 without reference to the original source. Abley adds that this was said before Adolf Hitler's infamous reference to the "final solution" for Jews gave the phrase a Holocaust connection. The actual source for this statement remains unidentified. Correspondence from Abley to the author, 30 October 2019, indicates that Jonathan Lainey, Curator, First Peoples, Canadian Museum of History, had contacted both Donald Smith and Brian Tetley, neither of whom could identify a source. Abley notes: "I had quoted the phrase ... having taken it from Anthony Hall, who took it from Kevin Annett, who did not provide a proper reference." See also https://www.ictinc.ca/blog/the-final-solution-which-government-used-the-term-first.
15 Quoted in Dragland, *Floating Voice*, 87–88, citing Library and Archives Canada RG10 vol.6810, 473, Hearings testimony (1921–22).
16 Abley, *Conversations*.
17 E.K. Brown, *Selected Poems*, xxxiii; E.K. Brown, "Duncan Campbell Scott: A Memoir," in E.K. Brown, *Responses and Evaluations: Essays on Canada*, edited with introduction by David Staines (Toronto: McClelland and Stewart, 1977), 134.
18 *Scribner's Magazine* published "The Hill Path" in May 1888. Titley, *Narrow Vision*, vii and 26.
19 Barrie Davies, ed., *At the Mermaid Inn: Wilfred Campbell, Archibald Lampman, and Duncan Campbell Scott in the Globe, 1892–93* (Toronto: University of Toronto Press, 1979); Titley, *Narrow Vision*, 26.
20 Ibid., 26–7.
21 D.C. Scott, "Indian Affairs, 1763–1841," in Adam Shortt and Arthur G. Doughty, eds. *Canada and its Provinces*, vol. 4 (Toronto: Glasgow, Brook and Company, 1914), 695–725.
22 Titley, *Narrow Vision*, 27–8, 32–3.
23 Royal Society of Canada, https://rsc-src.ca/en/about/history.
24 RSC Bylaws, 3.1, 1883.
25 Library and Archives Canada, Royal Society of Canada fonds, MG28-I458, Finding Aid #1874.
26 Carl Berger, *Honour and the Search for Influence. A History of the Royal Society of Canada* (Toronto: University of Toronto Press, 1996).
27 RSC, *Proceedings and Transactions*, 1898, xiv.

28 Ibid.,1898, xvi.
29 RSC, *Proceedings and Transactions*, 1899, xxii.
30 Ibid., xvii.
31 RSC, *Proceedings and Transactions*, 1903, xxxvii.
32 RSC, *Proceedings and Transactions*, 1907, xi.
33 Library and Archives Canada, Royal Society of Canada fonds, MG28-I458, Finding Aid #1874.
34 Titley, *Narrow Vision*, notes at 14–17 that by 1893, Scott had been promoted to "chief clerk and accountant." That year, he took a few months' stint as acting deputy superintendent after Lawrence Vankoughnet was fired and before Hayter Reed replaced him that same year. Under Clifford Sifton's leadership as superintendent from 1896 to 1905, Scott remained an accountant. E.K. Brown, *Selected Poems* asserts at xx that Scott's "moderate state was heightened when he became secretary" in 1896.
35 Titley, *Narrow Vision*, 17.
36 Several others who would later be characterized as "Confederation poets" and were already RSC fellows, had considerably more formal education than Scott. Inducted in 1892, Charles George Douglas Roberts (BA, MA; University of New Brunswick) held a position as professor at King's College in Windsor, NS from 1885–95. *Canadian Encyclopedia* https://www.thecanadianencyclopedia.ca/en/article/sir-charles-george-douglas-roberts. William Wilfrid Campbell, inducted in 1894, had five years' post-secondary education. *Dictionary of Canadian Biography*, vol. XIV (1911–1920).
37 Duncan Campbell Scott, *The Magic House and Other Poems* (London: Methuen, 1893); *Labor and the Angel* (Boston: Copeland & Day, 1898). The latter included his first "Indian poems" "Watkwenies" and "The Onondaga Madonna."
38 Duncan Campbell Scott, *In the Village of Viger* (Boston: Copeland & Day, 1896).
39 Republished in Barrie Davies, ed., *At the Mermaid Inn: Wilfred Campbell, Archibald Lampman, and Duncan Campbell Scott in the Globe, 1892–93* (Toronto: University of Toronto Press, 1979).
40 K.P. Stich, ed., *The Duncan Campbell Scott Symposium* (Ottawa: University of Ottawa Press, 1980), 149–50 lists nine short stories published by 1899.
41 Dragland, *Floating Voice*, 83.
42 E.K. Brown, *The Selected Poems of Duncan Campbell Scott* (Toronto: Ryerson Press, 1951), xx.
43 Robert L. McDougall, "Lampan, Archibald," in *Dictionary of Canadian*

Biography, vol. 12, University of Toronto/Université Laval, 2003, accessed 25 January 2021, http://www.biographi.ca/en/bio/lampman_archibald_12E.html. Another Ottawa civil servant, in the Department of Militia and Defence, William Wilfrid Campbell, who had been ordained as an Anglican minister but left the church in 1891, was inducted to the RSC in 1894. Like Scott, he would later be called a "Confederation poet." Unlike Scott, he had five years of post-secondary education. *Dictionary of Canadian Biography* vol. XIV (1911–1920).

44 Gwyn, *The Private Capital*, 456; McDougall, *The Poet and the Critic*, 2; Abley, *Conversations*, 28–31, 178; Dragland, *Floating Voice*, 82, 255–9.

45 RSC *Proceedings and Transactions*, 1899, cxxvii.

46 Mary Hane Edwards, "Drummond, William Henry," *Dictionary of Canadian Biography* vol.13 (Toronto: University of Toronto Press, 1994). Drummond's works include: *The Habitant and Other French-Canadian Poems* (NY: G.P. Putnam's Sons, 1897); *Phil-o-rum's Canoe and Madeleine Verchères* (NY: G.P. Putnam's Sons, 1898); *The Ideal Life: Addresses Hitherto Unpublished* (Toronto: J. Revell, 1898); *Montreal in Halftone: a Souvenir Giving Over One Hundred Illustrations, Plain and Colored, Showing the Great Progress which the City has Made During the Past Seventy Years* (Montreal: W.J. Clarke, 1898);

47 Leslie G. Monkman, "McLennan, William," in *Dictionary of Canadian Biography*, vol. 13 (University of Toronto–Université Laval, 2003), accessed 25 January 2021, http://www.biographi.ca/en/bio/mclennan_william_13E.html. McLennan's works include: *An Outline of the History of Engraving* (Montreal, 1881); *Songs of Old Canada* (Montreal, 1886); "Anciens Montréalais, I: Bénigne Basset, Notaire Royal, 1639–1699," *Le Canada Français* (Québec), 1re sér., 3 (1890): 469–77; "A Gentleman of the Royal Guard, Daniel de Gresollon, Sieur Du L'Hut," *Harper's New Monthly Magazine*, 87 (1893): 609–26; "Montreal and Some of the Makers Thereof," Montreal Board of Trade, *A Souvenir of the Opening of the New Building, One Thousand Eight Hundred and Ninety Three* (Montreal, 1893), 7–57; *Spanish John* (New York, 1898); *In Old France and New* (Toronto, 1899).

48 Jim Blanchard and Gordon Goldsborough, *Memorable Manitobans: George Bryce (1844–1941)*, http://www.mhs.mb.ca/docs/people/bryce_g.shtml. J.M. Bumsted, "George Bryce," *Dictionary of Manitoba Biography* (Winnipeg: University of Manitoba Press, 1999).

49 *Sketch of the New Utilitarianism* (1887); *The Young Seigneur* (1888); *The False Chevalier* (1898); *Songs of the Great Dominion* (1889); *Canadian Songs and Poems* (1893); *Montreal After 250 Years* (1892).

Lighthall had also served as the president of the Canadian Authors Association. PAC, RG 10, vol. 2285, file 57-169-1A, part 2. Richard Virr, "Son of the Great Dominion: W.D. Lighthall and the Lighthall Family Papers," http://fontanus.mcgill.ca/article/download/24/22.

50 Stanley Gordon, "Adam Shortt," in *The Encyclopedia of Canada*, vol. V, ed. W. Stewart Wallace (Toronto, University Associates of Canada), 396. Article published 16 January 2008, last edited 16 April 2014. https://www.thecanadianencyclopedia.ca/en/article/adam-shortt. Shortt's work includes: *Imperial Preferential Trade from a Canadian Point of View* (Toronto, 1904), and papers on the history of Canadian banking published in the *Journal of the Canadian Bankers' Association*.

51 RSC *Proceedings and Transactions*, 1910, 1; H. Blair Neatby, "William Lyon Mackenzie King," *Canadian Encyclopedia* (15 October 2008), https://www.thecanadianencyclopedia.ca/en/article/william-lyon-mackenzie-king.

52 Veronica Strong-Boag and Carole Gerson, *Paddling Her Own Canoe: The Times and Texts of E. Pauline Johnson Tekahionwake* (Toronto: University of Toronto Press, 2000); Charlotte Gray, *Flint & Feather: The Life and Times of E. Pauline Johnson, Tekahionwake* (Toronto: Harper Collins, 2002).

53 Abley, *Conversations*, 180–2.

54 Sheila M.F. Johnston, *Buckskin & Broadcloth: A Celebration of E. Pauline Johnson – Tekahionwake 1861–1913* (Toronto: Natural Heritage Books, 1997), 98.

55 Ibid., 98.

56 Margery Fee, "Publication, Performance, and Politics: The 'Indian Poems' of E. Pauline Johnson–Tekahionwake (1861–1913) and Duncan Campbell Scott (1862–1947)," in Robert Lecker, ed., *Anthologizing Canadian Literature* (Waterloo: Wilfred Laurier University Press, 2015), 51.

57 Although the bylaws used the word "persons" to describe fellows, and did not explicitly state that membership was limited to males of European heritage, in practice only "white" males were inducted for many decades. The first (white) woman elected to the Society was Alice Wilson, a paleontologist, who joined the fellowship in 1938. Carl Berger, *Honour and the Search for Influence*, 52; Michael R. Dence, "Royal Society of Canada," in *Canadian Encyclopedia* (article published 7 February 2006), last edited 16 March 2017, https://www.thecanadianencyclopedia.ca/en/article/royal-society-of-canada. It took until 1929 before the Privy Council made a legal ruling that "persons" included women with respect to appointments to the Senate: Robert J. Sharpe and Patricia I. McMahon, *The*

Persons Case (Toronto: University of Toronto Press, 2007). Lacking RSC records on Indigeneity and race, it is difficult to know when the first Indigenous or racialized fellows were inducted. Anecdotally, it appears that Indigenous architect Douglas Cardinal may have been the first elected fellow in 2004, although he was not present for the actual induction until 2019. Annishinaabe legal scholar John Borrows appears to have been the first inducted fellow in 2007.

58 Library and Archives Canada, Royal Society of Canada fonds, MG28-I458, "Introduction to Finding Aid" #1874. William Kirby, inducted in 1884, was a tanner by trade with no academic credentials, although he had served as a magistrate (County of Lincoln), and reeve and collector of customs (Niagara). His assertion to literary claim was an 1877 historical romance situated in Quebec City, *The Golden Dog,* that became one of the nation's best-known nineteenth-century novels. *Dictionary of Canadian Biography*, vol. XIII (1901–10).

59 The RSC, *Proceedings and Transactions*, 1902, 295–6 recorded ten of Scott's magazine and newspaper publications under the "Canadian Bibliography of the Year 1901."

60 *The Makers of Canada* (Toronto: George M. Morang, 1903–1908). RSC, *Proceedings and Transactions*, 1915, 3.

61 Titley, *Narrow Vision*, 26–7.

62 Duncan Campbell Scott, *John Graves Simcoe* (Toronto: Morang, 1905).

63 Scott, "Indian Affairs, 1763–1841," 695–725.

64 The poetry included: *New World Lyrics and Ballads* (Toronto: Morang, 1905); *Via Borealis* (Toronto: Tyrrell, 1906); *Lundy's Lane and Other Poems* (New York: Doran, 1916); *Beauty and Life* (Toronto: McClelland, 1921); *The Poems of Duncan Campbell Scott* (Toronto: McClelland, 1926); *The Green Cloister: Later Poems* (Toronto: McClelland and Stewart, 1935). The volume of short stories was *The Witching of Elspie* (Toronto: McClelland and Stewart, 1923). Edited collections included *The Poems of Archibald Lampman* (Toronto: Morang, 1900, 1901, 1905); *People of the Plains* by Amelia M. Paget (Toronto: William Briggs, 1909); and *Selected Poems of Archibald Lampman* (Toronto: Ryerson, 1947).

65 S.L. Dragland, ed., *Duncan Campbell Scott: A Book of Criticism* (Ottawa: Tecumseh Press, 1974), 3.

66 McDougall, *The Poet and the Critic*, 2. McDougall noted in "D.C. Scott: A Trace of Documents and a Touch of Life," in Stich, *Duncan Campbell Scott Symposium*, 129 that his books reached "meagre critical attention" during his lifetime. G. Ross Roy, "Duncan Campbell Scott," in Dragland,

ed., *Duncan Campbell Scott* noted at 140–1 that "Scott never did have a large public; he left fame to the other poets."
67 E.K. Brown, *Selected Poems*, xxxv.
68 Section I encompassed Littérature français, Histoire et Archéologie. Section II included "English Literature, History, and Archaeology." Section III included "Mathematical, Physical, and Chemical Sciences." Section IV included "Geological and Biological Sciences." The Sections expanded as fields of knowledge increased; a fifth Section was later added for more sciences.
69 This was the name of Section II in 1901. RSC, *Proceedings and Transactions,* 1901, 3, 8, and RSC, *Proceedings and Transactions,* 1902, 1.
70 RSC, *Proceedings and Transactions,* 1903, xxxix.
71 William Douw Lighthall, "Canadian Poets of the Great War," RSC, *Proceedings and Transactions,* 1918, xli–lxv; W. Lawson Grant, "Presidential Address, Section II," RSC, *Proceedings and Transactions,* 1920, 1; Sir Robert Falconer, "The Intellectual Life of Canada as Reflected in its Royal Society," RSC, *Proceedings and Transactions,* 1932, liv.
72 See for example, RSC. *Proceedings and Transactions,* 1899, cxxv; RSC, *Proceedings and Transactions,* 1925, xxxv; RSC, *Proceedings and Transactions,* 1933, cxi.
73 This committee controlled the nominations for all Sections. All new fellows had to pass its scrutiny, and then achieve election by the existing fellows. RSC, *Proceedings and Transactions,* 1909, lxvi.
74 RSC, *Proceedings and Transactions,* 1913, xli.
75 RSC, *Proceedings and Transactions,* 1923, xxx.
76 His membership on the RSC Council continued between 1924 and 1933.
77 Ian Wereley, "Final Report: Research on the *Proceedings and Transactions of the Royal Society of Canada, 1898–1947,*" January 2019, copy on file with the RSC Truth and Reconciliation Task Force.
78 RSC, *Proceedings and Transactions,* 1924, xxx; RSC, *Proceedings and Transactions,* 1925, xvii, xxxiv; RSC, *Proceedings and Transactions,* 1927, xvii, xxxi, xxxvi; RSC, *Proceedings and Transactions,* 1928, xxi; RSC, *Proceedings and Transactions,* 1930, xxx.
79 RSC, *Proceedings and Transactions,* 1929, ix.
80 Abley, *Conversations,* 178.
81 Gwyn, *The Private Capital,* 436; Titley, *Narrow Vision,* 29; Abley, *Conversations,* 28, 79, 126.
82 Titley, *Narrow Vision,* 28.
83 Queen's University granted him a second honorary doctorate of laws in 1939. Robert L. McDougall, "Duncan Campbell Scott," in *The Canadian*

    Encyclopedia. Article published 11 August 2008; Last edited 18 January 2018. https://www.thecanadianencyclopedia.ca/en/article/duncan-campbell-scott
84 McDougall, "D.C. Scott: A Trace of Documents," 129.
85 Titley, *Narrow Vision*, 203; Abley, *Conversations.*
86 Abley, *Conversations*, 174.
87 As quoted in Abley, *Conversations*, 174.
88 John Flood, "Native People in Scott's Short Fiction," in Stitch, ed., *The Duncan Campbell Scott Symposium*, 73–83; Dragland, ed., *Duncan Campbell Scott*; E. Palmer Patterson II, "The Poet and the Indian: Indian Themes in the Poetry of Duncan Campbell Scott and John Collier," *Ontario History* vol. 59 (1967): 69–78; J.D. Logan and Donald G. French, "Duncan Campbell Scott," in Dragland, ed., *Duncan Campbell Scott* describe Scott's ballads at 61–2 as "the product of a reflective mind *thinking into* Indian mind the thoughts of a civilized man."
89 Duncan Campbell Scott, *John Graves Simcoe* (Toronto: Morang, 1909).
90 Titley, *Narrow Vision*, 32–6. Scott wrote: "It is doubtful if the Indian allegiance was of any real benefit to the British. . . . The Indians were at all times moody and fickle fighters, eager to be purchased every season with a new supply of merchandise, and quick to imagine slights and insult. There was ever present the fear of their treachery." He emphasized the contrast between "civilized governments and savage forces" adding, "altruism is absent from the Indian character," and "the apparent duty was to raise him from his debased condition." D.C. Scott, "Indian Affairs, 1763–1841," 695, 706–7, 713.
91 Titley, *Narrow Vision*, 17, 184.
92 RSC, *Proceedings and Transactions*, 1902, xiv, xli; RSC, *Proceedings and Transactions*, 1903, xxvi.
93 RSC, *Proceedings and Transactions*, 1909, lxvii.
94 Scott sat on the printing committee from 1903–04, and later on the renamed editorial committee from 1924–26 and 1931–32. The following papers were published during his tenure: Rev. Dr G. Bryce, "Several Ethnological Types of Rupert's Land," (1903); Rev. Charles Hill-Tout, "Totemism," (1903); W.D. Lighthall, "Thomas Pownell and his Services to the Anglo-Saxon Race," (1904); W.J. Wintemberg, "Examples of Graphic Art on Archaeological Artifacts from Ontario," (1924); Louis Dow Scisco, "Precolumbian Discovery by Basques," (1924); W.D. Lighthall, "Hochelaga and 'The Hill of Hochelaga,'" (1924); A.G. Doughty, "The Preservation of Historical Documents in Canada," (1924); William Renwick Riddell, "Le Code Noir," (1925); Edmund H. Oliver, "The

Beginnings of White Settlement in Northern Saskatchewan," (1925); James Y. Coyne, "The Jesuits' Mill or Mortar: The Great Dispersion of the Hurons, 1649–1651," (1926); W.J. Wintemberg, "Foreign Aboriginal Artifacts from Post-European Iroquoian Sites in Ontario," (1926); Edmund H. Oliver, "The Settlement of Saskatchewan in 1914," (1926); D. Jenness, "The Sekani Indians of British Columbia," (1931); W.D. Lighthall, "The Remoter Origins of the Iroquoian Stock," (1931); G.S. Brett, "The Intellectual Aspect of the Relations between India and the West," (1931); William Renwick Riddell, "The Last Indian Council of the French at Detroit," (1931); Douglas Leechman, "Aboriginal Paints and Dyes in Canada," (1932); W.D. Lighthall, "The False Plan of Hochelaga," (1932).

95 RSC, *Proceedings and Transactions*, 1911, 195.

96 RSC, *Proceedings and Transactions*, 1908, xli, reading a paper by Robert N. Wilson, "Indian Agent for the Blood Indians"; RSC, *Proceedings and Transactions*, 1909, 3.

97 Ibid., *Proceedings and Transactions*, 1913, xlvii and 67, reading "A Girl's Puberty Ceremony among the Nootka Indians," a paper written by Edward Sapir, PhD.

98 Public Archives of Canada RG 10, vol. 3211, file 527, 781, Scott to Sir James Lougheed, 21 February 1921, suggests without evidence that Loft's military record was not good and that he was collecting fees from Indians for his own purposes. In what Titley described as "a deliberate attempt to mislead the minister," Scott belittled Loft's schooling as merely "some education." In vol. 3229, file 571, 571, 13 June 1922, he also condemned Loft for the "emptiness of his mind." Titley, *Narrow Vision*, 102–6.

99 Titley, *Narrow Vision*, chap. 7.

100 PAC, RG 10, vol. 2285, file 57, 69–1A2, Scott to A. Meighen, 3 May 1920, as quoted in Titley, *Narrow Vision*, 115.

101 PAC, RG 10, vol. 2286 file 57,169–1, part 5, Scott to O.D. Skelton, 9 June 1925, as quoted in Titley, *Narrow Vision*, 127.

102 PAC, RG 10, vol. 2287, file 57,169–176, Scott to Gordon J. Smith, 14 April 1921, as quoted in Titley, *Narrow Vision*, 117.

103 PAC, RG 10, vol. 3229, file 571, 571, Scott to Charles Stewart, 13 September 1922, as quoted in Titley, *Narrow Vision*, 118–19.

104 On Scott's lobbying in 1924, see Paul Tennant, *Aboriginal Peoples and Politics* (Vancouver: University of British Columbia Press, 1990), 93, 111–13. *An Act to Amend the Indian Act*, S.C. 1926–7, c.32, s.6 provided: "Every person who, without the consent of the Superintendent General expressed in writing, receives, obtains, solicits or requests from any Indian

any payment or contribution or promise of any payment or contribution for the purpose of raising a fund or providing money for the prosecution of any claim which the tribe or band of Indians to which such Indian belongs, or of which he is a member, has or is represented to have for the recovery of any claim or money for the benefit of said tribe or band, shall be guilty of an offence and liable upon summary conviction or any such offence to a penalty not exceeding two hundred dollars and not less than fifty dollars or to imprisonment for any term not exceeding two months." The prohibition remained in force until 1951.

105 (1921), 64 D.L.R. 327 (Ont. S.C.).
106 RSC, *Proceedings and Transactions*, 1917, 3.
107 Riddell had a bachelor of arts and science from Victoria College, Cobourg, and received the gold medal from Osgoode Hall Law School in Toronto in 1883. He practised law in Cobourg and Toronto, was named Queen's Counsel in 1899, and appointed to the bench in 1906. Constance Backhouse, *Colour-Coded: A Legal History of Racism in Canada, 1900–1950* (Toronto: University of Toronto Press, 1999), chap. 4.
108 Ibid., chap. 4.
109 "Lighthall, W.D., 1857–1954," The William Ready Division of Archives and Research Collections, McMaster University; W.D. Lighthall, ed., *Songs of the Great Dominion*, an anthology published in London, England in 1889; Abley, *Conversations*, 107.
110 PAC, RG 10, vol. 2286, file 57,169–1, part 5, W.D. Lighthall to Scott, 3 February 1928; Titley, *Narrow View*, 128.
111 Titley, *Narrow Vision*, 134.
112 Toronto *Globe*, 2 July 1928, as quoted in Titley, *Narrow Vision*, 129, 134.
113 See Gerald Lynch, "In Defence of Duncan Campbell Scott," *Ottawa Citizen*, 30 August 2013.
114 Franz Boas, a German-born Jewish anthropologist of Scott's era, had begun to question "conventional notions of racial superiority and civilization," disputing ideas of "higher" and "lower" races. Nell Irvin Painter, *The History of White People* (New York: Norton, 2010), 228–44.
115 James Doyle, "Duncan Campbell Scott and American Literature," in Stich, *Duncan Campbell Scott Symposium*, 103.
116 Dragland, *Floating Voice*.
117 Section II of the RSC amassed many scholarly papers on this subject, all written by white men. John Reade, "The Literary Faculty of the Native Races of America," (1884); John Reade, "The Half-Breed," (1885); John Reade, "Aboriginal American Poetry: a Chapter on Comparative Literature," (1887); A.J. Hall, "A Grammar of the Kwagiutl Language,"

(1888); George M. Dawson, "Notes and Observations on the Shushwap People of British Columbia," (1891); George Patterson, "The Beothiks or Red Indians of Newfoundland," (1891); George Patterson, "Vocabulary of the Language of the Beothiks or Red Indians of Newfoundland," (1892); Douglas Brymner, "The Jamaica Maroons," (1895); Horatio Hale, "An Iroquois Condoling Council," (1895); John Campbell, "The Present Position of American Anthropology," (1895); Charles Tout-Hill, "Prehistoric Man in British Columbia," (1895); Charles Harrison, "A Grammar and Dictionary of the Languages of the Haida Indians of the Queen Charlotte Islands," (1895); E.T.D. Chambers, "The Philology of the Ouananiche," (1896); George M. Dawson, "Notes and Observations on the Kwakiool People of the Northern Part of Vancouver Island and Adjacent Coasts," (1897); Charles Tout-Hill, "Notes on the Cosmogony and History of the Squamish Indians of British Columbia," (1897); John Campbell, "The Origin of the Hiadahs of the Queen Charlotte Islands," (1897); John Campbell, "Origin of the Kootenay and Tshimsiam Indians of British Columbia affiliating both with the Malaysian Polynesians," (1898); John Campbell, "Recently Discovered Relics of the Mound Builders," (1898); Charles Tout-Hill, "Oceanic Origins of the Kwakiutl-Nootka and Salishan Stocks of British Columbia, and Fundamental Unity of Same, with Additional Notes on the Dene," (1898); W.D. Lighthall, "Hochelaga and Mohawks: A Link in Iroquois History," (1899); C.C. James, "The Downfall of the Huron Nation," (1906); Daniel Burwash, "Gift to a Nation of Written Language," (1911); W.D. Lighthall, "Signposts of Prehistoric Time," (1916); Charles Tout-Hill, "Recent Discoveries and New Trends in Anthropology," (1923); Edward Sapir, "A Bird's-Eye View of Indian Languages North of Mexico," (1923); Marius Barbeau, "The Native Races of Canada," (1927). See Lawrence J. Burpee, "List of Papers Contributed to Section II of the Royal Society of Canada, 1882–1924," in RSC, *Proceedings and Transactions*, 1925, 9–17.
118 Tamson Pietsch, *Empire of Scholars: Universities, Networks and the British Academic World 1859–1939* (Manchester: Manchester University Press, 2013), 5–6.
119 Ibid., 22, 33, 62.
120 Painter, *The History of White People,* viv–xii, 1.
121 Nineteenth-century American anthropologist Samuel George Morton classified American Indians as "a separate race somewhere midway between white and black people." For details of the contested

taxonomies, see Painter, *History of White People*, 43, 75, 168, 190–2, 200, 229–42, 383.

122 The 1923 essay appeared in the *Annals of the American Academy of Political and Social Sciences* vol. 107 (1923): 63–66; Abley, *Conversations*, 158–64.

123 Quoted by Abley, *Conversations*, 151–3.

124 D.M.R. Bentley, "Shadows in the Soul: Racial Haunting in the Poetry of Duncan Campbell Scott," *University of Toronto Quarterly* 75:2 (Spring 2006): 767.

125 Painter, *History of White People*, 119; Pietsch, *Empire of Scholars*, 79, 83.

126 Painter, *History of White People*, 201, 387.

127 Gwyn, *The Private Capital*, 456; McDougall, *The Poet and the Critic*, 2; Abley, *Conversations*, 28–31, 178; Dragland, *Floating Voice*, 82, 255–9. The tragedy in Scott's life was the death of his only child, Elizabeth Duncan Scott in 1906. Born in 1895, she died of scarlet fever at the age of eleven, in Paris where she had been sent two years earlier to attend an exclusive boarding school. Scott's Lisgar Street home has been demolished; in its place stands a twenty-two-storey-condominium called The Merit.

128 His second wife, Elise Aylen, whom he married in 1931 when he was sixty-nine years old, was born in 1893, two years before Scott's daughter. Abley, *Conversations*, 175–7.

129 The Lorne Pierce Medal, created by the Royal Society in 1926, recognizes achievement of special significance and conspicuous merit in imaginative or critical literature. McDougall, "Duncan Campbell Scott."

130 Quoted as being a "rare unguarded moment" with a "literary friend," without further details, by Abley, *Conversations*, 67.

131 Titley, *Narrow Vision*, 199; Abley, *Conversations*, 31, 177.

3

"Perhaps the white man's God has willed it so": Reconsidering the "Indian" Poems of Pauline Johnson and Duncan Campbell Scott

Carole Gerson

The title of this essay, taken from the last line of Pauline Johnson's signature poem, "A Cry from an Indian Wife" (1885; 1892),[1] emblematizes the gulf between Johnson and Duncan Campbell Scott in their literary representation of Indigenous people. In this dramatic monologue, which was Johnson's first poem to be published in a Canadian periodical, the speaker mourns the plight of her people as "starved, crushed, plundered." Yet she also embodies resistance in her scathing reference to the power of the alien "white man's God" when she proclaims – in the present tense – "By right, by birth, we Indians own these lands." In contrast, Scott's literary writings align with his professional goal to enact that power by assimilating Canada's "Indians" into "the body politic,"[2] implementing the policy that his government justified as historical necessity. In 1941, nearly a decade after his retirement, he commented, "I was never unsympathetic to aboriginal ideals, but there was the law which I did not originate and which I never tried to amend in the direction of severity. One can hardly be sympathetic with the contemporary Sun-dance or Potlatch when one knows that the original spirit has departed and that they are largely the opportunities for debauchery by low white men."[3]

While most of his literary pieces about Indigenous people acknowledged that the "doom" of a "weird and waning race"[4] involved considerable pain for those who were trapped by history, his poems that lament the inevitable destruction of Indigenous people – through miscegenation, exploitation, or cultural collapse – also reinforced the notion of the "disappearing Indian." This mindset is eloquently discussed by Thomas King in *The Inconvenient Indian* (2012), albeit he fails to mention Johnson. In 1890, when Johnson wrote to a friend that one of her goals was "to upset the Indian Extermination and noneducation theory – in fact to stand by my blood and my race,"[5] she intuitively anticipated the program of assimilation that would be associated with Scott. Because Scott didn't leave personal journals or notebooks and his biography remains unwritten, his poetic motives and processes of composition are sparsely documented, nor is there a definitive scholarly edition of his poems.[6] However, when his literary publications are examined in relation to those by Johnson, an interesting relationship emerges. While it would be an overstatement to claim that Scott's literary writings about Indigenous people intentionally countered specific works by Johnson, their chronology and other contextual evidence show they were written in full awareness of her presence and her impact.

Whereas Scott's creative writings on "Indians" were once admired as Romantic expressions of sympathy built on "the contrast of the savage powerful past of the race with its humbled present and hopeless future" in the words of the respected mid-twentieth century literary critic, E.K. Brown,[7] today these works are viewed as implicit justification of his administration of the residential school program. If Scott had not written about Indigenous people, who appear in a handful of pieces that represent a very small portion of his total oeuvre,[8] it would be easier to continue to appreciate his literary work as lyrical, aesthetic, stylish, and often very good. His 1922 Royal Society of Canada (RSC) presidential address, "Poetry and Progress," remains an eloquent argument for the value of art in a world besieged by materialism. But Scott's current public image as Canada's Hitler[9] now taints his entire body of work to the extent that in 2010 his name was removed from an Ottawa literary award[10] and in 2015 his plaque in Ottawa's Beechwood Cemetery was changed.[11] One could perhaps invoke Margaret Atwood's notion that settler Canadians are intrinsically "divided down the middle" and thereby regard the apparent disjunction between Scott's literary life and his professional life as typical of our cultural schizophrenia.[12] Poet and critic Stan Dragland wrestled with the dilemma of reconciling the administrator and the poet in his book, *Floating Voice: Duncan Campbell Scott and the Literature of Treaty 9* (1994); more recently, Mark Abley took up the challenge in *Conversations with a Dead Man:*

The Legacy of Duncan Campbell Scott (2013), without coming to any resolution. Nor do I have one to offer. Today, I find my position somewhat akin to that of Emily Nussbaum and other critics of current American culture who are asking, in light of the "#Me Too" revelations about major filmmakers and actors, "What should we do with the art of terrible men?" For Nussbaum, this question has involved re-evaluation of the work of Woody Allen, whose movies had been her hallmark of excellence in American film. In a recent NPR radio interview (15 July 2019), she said, "You don't have to solve that contradiction to engage with it,"[13] a statement that well describes Abley's book and indeed the position of anyone else who wants to give Scott some credit as a talented poet, without also crediting his untenable role in Canadian history.

This discussion engages with Scott by examining his literary representation of Indigenous people in relation to the work of Pauline Johnson, Canada's only Indigenous literary author to achieve prominence during Scott's lifetime. Given that Johnson and Scott were contemporary denizens of central Canada, both inhabiting the country's small but active literary space that expanded dramatically from the mid-1880s through the turn of the century, it is surprising that few scholars have focused directly on these two writers. In one study, Rick Monture compared the two writers' attitudes towards the position of the Iroquois within the Canadian paradigm[14] and, in another, Margery Fee's analysis of their representation in Canadian literary anthologies found that Scott's canonical dominance during the twentieth century derived from his relative longevity, his professional identity, and entrenched cronyism among the country's male literary powerbrokers.[15] However, no one has yet analyzed their personal interaction and the chronological relationship between their poems.

CULTURAL CONTEXTS

The biographical origins of the two poets did not predict there would be much contact between them. Duncan Campbell Scott (1862–1947) was born in Ottawa, the son of a Wesleyan minister, and attended Stanstead Wesleyan College. Too poor to send his son to medical school, William Scott was nonetheless sufficiently well-connected to draw on his acquaintance with Sir John A. Macdonald to secure a civil service position for his promising seventeen-year-old.[16] After beginning in 1879 as a clerk in the Department of Indian Affairs, Scott remained in Ottawa for the rest of his life as he rose through the ranks to become deputy superintendent general (the equivalent of deputy minister today) of Indian Affairs in 1913. Within this environment, he developed his artistic talents as a musician and a poet, and became a prominent local cultural leader.

In contrast, Emily Pauline Johnson (1861–1913) was born and raised in middle-class comfort in Ohsweken, Ontario, on the Six Nations Reserve. Her father, George Henry Martin Johnson, Onwanonsyshon (1816–1884), was both a hereditary and elected Mohawk chief whose fluency in the reserve's six Indigenous languages enabled his work as a translator. Johnson's English-born mother, Emily Susanna Howells (1824–1898), was a cousin of the well-known American author, William Dean Howells (a connection that proved of no assistance to Johnson). Under the guidance of her mother, Pauline was educated in the English literary classics; she was also an avid canoeist and active member of the Brantford Canoe Club. The loss of the family's income and elegant home following the death of Johnson's father in 1884 prompted her to turn to writing as a means of support; in 1892 she expanded her presence from the page to the stage, with performances of her stories and poems across Canada, in England, and occasionally in the United States. Here she enacted both sides of her identity: she performed her Indigenous poems and stories in her buckskin outfit for the opening portion of the program, then returned after intermission costumed in Victorian evening dress, in which she presented humorous skits and Romantic nature verses. Pauline Johnson's last years were spent in Vancouver, where she died of breast cancer 10 March 1913, three days before her fifty-second birthday.

D.M.R. Bentley and many other scholars have documented how the 1890s proved a critical decade in the development of English-Canadian poetry.[17] As they launched their poetic careers, Scott and Johnson crossed paths occasionally. Both participated in the landmark "Evening with Canadian Authors" of 16 January 1892, organized by Frank Yeigh for the Young Liberal Club of Toronto. This occasion marked Johnson's first serious stage appearance, where she mesmerized her audience with her recitation of "A Cry from an Indian Wife," which articulates an Indigenous view of the 1885 Northwest Rebellion. Sandwiched between the Young Liberal Glee Club singing "God Protect Our Dominion" and an untraceable "weird sketch"[18] by Duncan Campbell Scott titled "Veronica," Johnson's poem was the only political item on the program[19] and was noted as such in the press. The *Globe* printed the full text of the poem, alongside its reviewer's claim that hearing Johnson perform "was like [hearing] the voice of the nations who once possessed this country, who have wasted before our civilization, speaking through this cultured, gifted, soft-voiced descendant."[20] Scott and Johnson shared the platform again at a similar event sponsored by the Royal Society of Canada at Ottawa's Normal School on 17 May 1895, where Johnson was the hit of the evening "with a most dramatic story of an Indian girl's revenge." According to the write-up in the *Globe*, Johnson, "who wore her handsome Indian costume, made perhaps the most pronounced success of the evening, giving two numbers of her own."[21] It is intriguing to imagine the response of the staid Scott to Johnson's riveting performance of "Ojistoh," her assertive woman warrior poem, discussed later in this chapter. Delivered "with immense power and with wonderful success," it drew "enthusiastic applause from a crowded meeting composed of all classes of the community, from the Governor-General to the children of the public schools."[22]

In addition to these public appearances, there is evidence of occasional contact on a more personal level. Almost every year during the 1890s, Scott and his close friend Archibald Lampman (who died in 1899) privately printed a Christmas card with several new poems, which they sent to their friends as a seasonal greeting. Preserved at Trent University in the fonds of Pauline's older sister, Evelyn Johnson, are two such cards. The first is dated New Year's Day, 1891 and is addressed to "Miss E Pauline Johnson." It is signed "Duncan Campbell Scott" below the handwritten message: "Wishing you a very Happy New Year." The second is an unaddressed and unsigned copy of a later card, "Two Poems Written by Archibald Lampman & Duncan Campbell Scott & Privately Issued to their Friends at Christmastide 1896." As well, we know that Johnson was Scott's guest on at least one occasion: at the time of the 1895 Ottawa Normal School public reading, she gave a private recital at a dinner party that the Scotts held at their home for that evening's participants.[23] There were likely additional such events at which both poets were present. Arthur S. Bourinot, son of career civil servant John George Bourinot, an active member of the RSC and editor of its *Transactions*, later reminisced, "Literary gatherings were

Figure 3.1 Duncan Campbell Scott (*top left*) and Pauline Johnson (*top centre*). From Bourinot, "Canada in the Victorian Era: A Historical Review," *Proceedings and Transactions*, 1897, Section II, 79.

frequently held at our [Ottawa] home and I can remember peering over the bannisters at such literary figures as Wilfred Campbell, Pauline Johnson ... and ... Duncan Campbell Scott."[24] In 1897, in the *Proceedings and Transactions* of the RSC, photographs of Scott and Johnson appeared side by side in a full-page array of Canadian authors as an illustration for J.G. Bourinot's paper on "Canada in the Victorian Era: A Historical Review."[25] Interestingly, Duncan Campbell Scott's name does not appear in Bourinot's text, which cites "Frederick G. Scott, Pauline Johnson, [Charles G.D.] Roberts, Bliss Carman, Archbishop O'Brien, Speaker Edgar, Ethelwyn Wetherald, [Archibald] Lampman, and Wilfred Campbell" as the country's most notable poets writing in English.[26] For this visual display, Bourinot chose an early photograph of Johnson in everyday dress, rather than one of her publicity photographs in her buckskin costume. Centred at the top of the page and looking directly at the camera, Johnson dominates her peers (see figure 3.1). As Johnson's public was better acquainted with photographs of her in costume, exemplified in the early publicity photograph in Figure 3.2, I infer that Bourinot's choice was an overt effort to "whiten" her image, in keeping with the RSC's notions of propriety.

These occasions notwithstanding, in print Scott was remarkably reticent about Johnson, despite his frequent promotion of other writers of his generation.[27] From February 1892 to June 1893, Scott, Lampman, and fellow Ottawa poet Wilfred Campbell contributed to a weekly literary column, "At the Mermaid Inn," in the Toronto *Globe*, with commentary about a wide range of Canadian and international writers. When attention briefly turned to Johnson, it appeared in a contribution signed by Campbell, not Scott. Through the 1890s, Johnson's reputation soared: for example, she was the most prominent female poet in James Wetherell's anthology, *Later Canadian Poems* (1893), in which Scott was one of the seven featured male poets, and in such articles as Joseph Dana Miller's "The Singers of Canada," published in a prominent New York magazine in 1895.[28] Yet in 1901, when Scott wrote his own summary of "A Decade of Canadian Poetry," Johnson received less attention than many minor poets. The wording of his contrast between "Miss Johnson's virile touch and strong imagination" and "the delicacy and shyness of [Ethelwyn] Wetherald's genius"[29] implied that "genius" was something that Johnson lacked, nor did he mention her Mohawk (Haudenosaunee) identity. After this article, I can find

Figure 3.2 Publicity photograph of Pauline Johnson, circa 1892.

no further public evidence of interaction between the two writers, an absence that suggests that as he rose in the administration of the Department of Indian Affairs, Scott pulled back from overt social or literary relationships with the Johnson family. Nonetheless, in his professional capacity, he demonstrated respect for Johnson's home community of Six Nations when he encouraged a group of chiefs to publish an account of the origins of their Confederacy that appeared in the *Proceedings and Transactions of the Royal Society of Canada* in 1911.[30] And he facilitated publication by an elite Métis woman when he oversaw the production of Amelia M. Paget's *People of the Plains* (1909), described by historian Sarah Carter as a "sympathetic and positive portrait," for which he wrote an introduction in which he complimented the author's "knowledge of the Cree language and her intimacy with all the ways of the Indians."[31]

At the time of Johnson's demise in Vancouver in 1913, Scott was honorary secretary of the RSC, in which capacity he sent the society's $10 contribution for flowers for her funeral.[32] The day following her death, Scott's personal note to William Douw Lighthall (secretary of Section II of the RSC) expressed a complex response. Here is the complete text:

Dear Lighthall,
A few minutes ago your teleg arrived and after phoning the President [W. Dawson LeSueur] I sent a wire to Vancouver. I had heard nothing of Pauline's death until your message came. She was a very unusual being and worthy of much admiration [which] she always had from me. It was not the death for her to die with all her physical vigour and her spirit of curiosity about life – but we are not allowed to choose!

Best wishes and regards,
Yours faithfully,
Duncan Scott[33]

In this note, Scott's dominant emotion is surprise rather than regret, and, as in his published comment of 1901, his remarks concern Johnson as a charismatic person, rather than her writing. He refrained from saying that her death was a loss for Canadian literature. Most members of the Canadian literary community were long aware of Johnson's impending demise from cancer, having been canvassed to purchase her book of stories, *Legends of Vancouver*, which was first issued in 1911 as a fund-raiser to cover her medical bills. While Scott was presumably included in this campaign, his name does not appear among the many subscribers recorded in Johnson's fonds at McMaster University. In 1943, thirty years after Johnson's death, Walter McRaye, who had been Johnson's stage partner and manager, invited people who had known her to contribute to the book that would appear as *Pauline Johnson and Her Friends* (1947). Scott's initial response was positive: "I will try to write something about Pauline Johnson & her work. As you are aware I knew all the family & was able to do something for Evelyn. Let me know whether she is still alive."[34] Scott's ignorance that Pauline's sister, Evelyn, had died six years earlier, in 1937, seems symptomatic of his distance from the Johnsons; it is unlikely that he wrote something for McRaye, as nothing attributed to Scott appeared in the final book.

READING SCOTT AND JOHNSON TODAY

This relationship becomes more complex when we consider the chronology of Johnson's and Scott's literary writings on Indigenous people. With both writers, works with specifically Indigenous content represent a small portion of their output, yet today it is primarily these poems and stories that receive attention, despite the literary skill evidenced in much of their other work. From the beginning of her career, Johnson published poems about Indigenous issues, starting with "The Re-interment of Red Jacket" (1884), alongside many on topics that were not specifically Indigenous, such as experiences of nature and wilderness, in line with poetry by her Euro-Canadian peers like Lampman, Campbell, and Scott. Scott, on the other hand, had published nearly forty poems on various topics, starting in 1888, before the 1894 appearance of his first "Indian" poem, "An Onondaga Mother and Child" (later retitled "The Onondaga Madonna") in *The Atlantic Monthly*. During the 1880s and 1890s, much of Johnson's poetry and prose about Indigenous people appeared in mainstream Canadian periodicals, published in Toronto and Montreal, that Scott would certainly have seen: *The Week*, *The Dominion Illustrated*, the *Globe*, and *Massey's Magazine*. In addition to the poems that are the focus of this discussion, Johnson published articles about canoeing and camping, some of which referenced her Indigenous heritage.

While Scott could not have been unaware of Johnson's writings and performances, she was likely less cognizant of his literary activities. The periodical venues for Scott's "Indian" poems were American magazines that Johnson may or may not have seen: in addition to *The Atlantic Monthly* (which published "Night Hymns on Lake Nipigon" in 1900), these included *The Outlook* ("The Forsaken," 1903) and *The Smart Set* ("The Half-Breed Girl," 1906). Moreover, three of Scott's most significant "Indian" poems made their first appearance not in well-known periodicals, but in slender, author-funded volumes in small print runs with limited circulation[35] that probably didn't reach Johnson: "Watkwenies" in *Labor and the Angel* (1898), and "Indian Place Names" and "On the Way to the Mission" in *New World Lyrics and Ballads* (1904). Long after Johnson's death, Scott wrote his last "Indian" poems: "Powassen's Drum" was published in 1926 in *The Poems of Duncan Campbell Scott*, and "At Gull Lake: August 1810" and "A Scene at Lake Manitou" appeared in *The Green Cloister* in 1935. Like Johnson, Scott was an accomplished writer of short stories; "Star-blanket" (later retitled "Charcoal"), his only story to focus directly on an Indigenous character, appeared in 1904, following Johnson's ground-breaking stories of the 1890s.

When we map the chronology of Johnson's and Scott's publications, the resulting timeline suggests that not only was Scott continuously aware of Pauline Johnson, but also that his "Indian" poems and single "Indian" story were implicitly written in response to her work. And when we compare the contents of their writings, we can see that Scott frequently countered Johnson's ethos of resistance. Whereas Johnson consistently asserted Indigenous values of courage and justice, primarily through female characters who deploy whatever agency they can muster, Scott consistently depicted Indigenous people as victims of history, as articulated in 1994 by Ojibwe poet Armand Ruffo in his "Poem for Duncan Campbell Scott":

... he's always busy writing
stuff in the notebook he carries. Him,
he calls it poetry
and says it will make us who are doomed
live forever.[36]

Moreover, the prominence of Pauline Johnson may well have inflected Scott's focus on Indigenous women. Most of the "Indian" poems he published during Johnson's lifetime concern women; these also happen to be his poems that are best known today due to their recurrence in anthologies.[37] In contrast to Johnson's first-person incarnation of specific Indigenous characters, all Scott's poems present a third-person perspective, offering external observations of women who represent the turmoil experienced by people in transition: all convey defeat. When set in their chronological context (see appendix 1), each of his poems can be seen as countering previous poems by Johnson. Scott's first such poem, "The Onondaga Madonna" (1894), opposes Johnson's powerful assertion of Indigenous rights in her frequently performed and oft-reprinted "A Cry from an Indian Wife" (1885), in which her speaker curses "the fate" that brought white men "from the East / To be our chiefs."[38] Scott, on the other hand, concedes to fate when he inverts Christian mythology to describe the Onondaga mother as an anti-Madonna: she is a "tragic savage" belonging to a "weird and waning race," and her lighter-skinned child is "the latest promise of his nation's doom."[39]

In subsequent poems, Scott references the Indigenous past rather than the future, elegiacally describing a steep decline from endurance and bravery to a diminished and often corrupted present. Thus the heroic mother of "The Forsaken" (1903) is later abandoned in a cowardly fashion by her descendants[40] and the titular character of "Watkwenies" (1898; see appendix 2) is reduced from active participation in triumphant Iroquois warcraft to passive dependence on treaty money from the Indian Agent. Johnson, on the other hand, created first-person embodiments of strong Indigenous women in dramatic monologues that proved effective performance pieces, thereby offering her audiences (on both the stage and the page) an inside view of agency as well as a sense of an authentic voice. This contrast is especially telling in relation to the figure of the woman warrior, whom Johnson represented on stage in her compelling narrative "Ojistoh," which she frequently performed (including at the 1895 RSC Ottawa poetry reading which Scott attended). Whereas Scott contrasts Watkwenies's ancient memory of long-forgotten victory with her present state of disempowerment, Johnson's Ojistoh proclaims her strength with her opening declaration, "I am Ojistoh!" After she engineers her escape from her Huron abductor by seducing him in order to "[bury] in his back his scalping knife," she triumphantly concludes, "Ojistoh, still am I!"[41] – an assertion of presence that is countered by Scott's dispossessed Watkwenies.

"Watkwenies" also bears comparison with Johnson's earlier short lyric, "The Corn Husker," published in 1896 (see appendix 2). Both poems describe an old Indigenous woman reflecting on the changes she has experienced. For Watkwenies, all that is left of her "perished day" are the sounds of present-day children "playing snow-snake in the stinging cold." However, Johnson's unnamed corn husker, with "Age in her fingers, hunger in her face," thinks

[...] of the days gone by,
Ere might's injustice banished from their lands
Her people, that to-day unheeded lie,
Like the dead husks that rustle through her hands.[42]

Needless to say, Johnson's invocation of "injustice" is nowhere echoed by Scott. An accomplished sonnet that well displays its author's poetic talent, "Watkwenies" effectively contrasts the destroyed Indigenous past with the mundane present, while omitting analysis of the cause of this change. A glimmer of causality appears in his story, "Charcoal," which fictionalizes the documented history of a Blood man whose efforts to assume "the white man's ways" exploded into rebellion when he avenged his betrayal by murdering his wife's lover, injuring a white farm instructor, and shooting a Mountie.[43] The closest that Scott came to granting interiority to an Indigenous character occurs when, condemned to hang, Charcoal puzzles over the contradictions between white notions of "fair dealing" and his traditional code of vengeance. At the end, Charcoal's confusion about the "mystery" in which he is entangled earns sympathy from the reader, but the inevitable power of church and state remains unquestioned.[44]

Differences between the two writers are most striking in their contrasting representation of the figure of "The Half-Breed Girl," to cite the title of Scott's 1906 poem. Johnson seldom used the word "half-breed" and usually in derogation: spoken by the nasty cleric in her story, "As It Was in the Beginning," and rehabilitated in the gracious Lady Bennington in another story, "The Shagganappi." Not published until after Johnson's death, this story repudiated the word "half-breed," preferring "half-blood" because "breed is a term for cattle and not men," in the words of Lord Mortimer, Canada's governor general, who is the story's primary authority. Through this character, Johnson further claimed that the young hero, of Cree and French ancestry, constituted the "real Canadian" because his lineage blended "the blood of old France and the blood of a great aboriginal race."[45]

In Johnson's oeuvre, mixed-race women appeared in her fiction rather than her poetry. Several of her stories recount the decisions taken by young women who assert control after being betrayed by white lovers, whereas the mixed-race women in Scott's writings symbolize tragedy. Johnson's performance programs regularly included "A Red Girl's Reasoning," a story that is now a major focus of Johnson criticism, which was published in February 1893 in the *Dominion Illustrated Monthly*, a prominent Montreal family magazine, and the *Toronto Evening Star* (under the title "A Sweet Wild Flower"). Also of critical interest today is "As It Was in the Beginning," which first appeared in the 1899 Christmas number of the popular Toronto magazine, *Saturday Night*. Both stories were collected in Johnson's posthumous book, *The Moccasin Maker* (1913), as was "The Derelict," an ironic tale that was first published in Toronto's *Massey Magazine* in 1896, in which a mixed-race woman offers salvation to a decrepit Anglican clergyman who chooses to sacrifice his career in order to stay with her.

The main characters in Johnson's stories stand in sharp contrast to the stereotype of the compliant, self-sacrificing "Indian maiden" that she scathingly critiqued in her 1892 essay, "A Strong Race Opinion: On the Indian Girl in Modern Fiction."[46] Both "A Red Girl's Reasoning" and "As It Was in the Beginning" are set remotely on the prairies and focus on a young woman with a Cree mother. Christie Robinson of "A Red Girl's Reasoning" has a white father, while the father of Esther, in "As It Was in the Beginning," possesses the "uncertain blood" of a "half-breed."[47] Both heroines make the mistake of trusting white men. Christie marries Charlie Macdonald, a handsome surveyor with a penchant for "Indianology"[48] who weds his "little Indian wife"[49] in the same way that he collects his other trophies, only to spurn her when he learns that her parents were married by Indigenous rather than Christian ritual. Esther is taken to a residential school by a cleric named Father Paul, who deprives her of her original culture but then persuades his nephew not to marry her. Both women refuse to be victims of white treachery. Christie rejects Charlie in turn when he seeks reconciliation, while Esther poisons her weak white lover to prevent him from marrying the Hudson Bay Company factor's insipid daughter. Hence, rather than yield to their racial and sexual vulnerability, Johnson's fictional women deploy their gender to assert an agency that brings them a degree of satisfaction. While neither enjoys a conventional happy ending, they each reach what is perhaps the best conclusion that can be obtained under the circumstances.

Raised as a child of the manse and canny about the ingrained power of the church in Canada, Scott never criticized organized Christianity. He depended upon various churches to run the residential schools, and positively represented Indigenous peoples' relationships with the church in such poems as "The Mission of the Trees," "On the Way to the Mission," "Night Hymns on Lake Nipigon," and "The Forsaken." However, Christianity did not fare so well with Johnson. Although an early journalistic write-up described her as "an earnest member of the Church of England"[50] and her publications contain several positive references to Anglicans,[51] many of her creative writings repudiated institutional religion. Her strategies ranged from irony, as in "The Gopher," described as "A merry little rascal ... who dresses like a hypocrite, in soft, religious grey" and "monkeys with his conscience,"[52] to the anger that informs her depiction of Father Paul, the treacherous Blackcoat in "As It was in the Beginning." In choosing the word "Blackcoat," a term usually associated with Catholicism, to describe a cleric who belongs to an unspecified Protestant denomination, Johnson created a generic figure through whom she criticized the residential school system as a whole.

From 1906 to 1911, one of Johnson's major sources of income was her stories published in two American magazines, *The Mother's Magazine* and *The Boys' World*, both issued by the Illinois-based publisher of Sunday school materials, David C. Cook.[53] In her pieces for the specific audiences defined by the titles of these serials, Johnson's focus on good behaviour and positive moral values accorded with her publisher's social outlook, yet one of her most outspoken essays was rejected. "The Stings of Civilization" remained in manuscript,[54] presumably because its attacks on the commercialization of religion and on the capitalistic accumulation of wealth were too strong for *The Mother's Magazine*, its intended outlet. Nonetheless, perhaps unaware of their transgressive nature, *The Boys' World* published two of Johnson's stories that challenged policies of the Canadian government: "We-hro's Sacrifice" (1907), positively presents the outlawed Onondaga white dog ceremony, and "The Potlatch" (1910) celebrates this West Coast tradition, thereby ignoring the official ban first imposed in 1884 and reiterated in the revised *Indian Act* of 1895. Both stories subsequently circulated widely, as they were included in *The Shagganappi*, a posthumous collection of Johnson's stories issued in Toronto in 1913 with a dedication to "the Boy Scouts" and reprinted in 1927.

As senior administrator in the department of Indian Affairs, Scott worked to implement the assimilation of the Indigenous population through education as well as intermarriage, while writing poetry about mixed-race people that depicts them as torn between their competing identities.[55] In such poems as "The Onondaga Madonna," "At Gull Lake: August 1810," and "The Half-Breed Girl," women who are themselves part white, or bear children who are "paler"[56] than their mothers, embody discomfort and suffer accordingly. The unnamed "half-breed girl," who lives in a "stifling wigwam," is troubled by "shadows"[57] of her Scottish father's identity that haunt her psyche to the point of incapacitation. In the words of critic D.M.R. Bentley, the poem's conclusion depicts the girl "as a fearful and doomed victim of racial dualism who lives a half-life between a Scottish heritage to which she cannot gain access and a Native existence that part of her being finds odious."[58] Beautiful Keejigo, in "At Gull Lake: August 1810" (1935), one of Scott's last "Indian" poems, believes that her mixed heritage (from her Normandy father and her Saulteaux mother) qualifies her for a relationship with Nairne, the Orkney trader. She is so troubled by his rejection ("Drive this bitch to her master") that she courts death at the hands of her Saulteaux husband and his "old wives," who "[throw] her over the bank / Like a dead dog."[59]

CONCLUSION: LAST WORDS

Scott's final poetic word on Indigenous women appeared in "A Scene at Lake Manitou" (1935), in which "the widow Frederick / Whose Indian name means Stormy Sky" futilely seeks to appease the gods who have caused the deaths of her husband and her son, presumably from tuberculosis.[60] Without any stake in the future, her only recourse is to return to her trapline, where she will end her days "Alone with the silence."[61] This silence permeated Scott's poetic vision of the Indigenous future, as expressed in 1906 in "Indian Place Names." In this poem, the Canadian landscape resonates with musical names, such as Winnipeg, Meductic, and Kamouraska, left by "the dusky folk" whose "vaunted prowess all is gone, / Gone like a moose-track in the April snow."[62]

For Duncan Campbell Scott, the erasure of Indigeneity programmed by his career in the Department of Indian Affairs offered a compelling subject for poetry; for Pauline Johnson, poetry and prose provided a medium in which to assert continuity and resistance. Several generations later, Cree writer Rosanna Deerchild voiced this contrast when she stated that Duncan Campbell Scott "wrote our obituary in his poetry." She then continued: "He was killing us in words but Pauline was keeping us alive."[63]

APPENDIX I

Chronology of the first appearances of the major "Indian" Poems by Pauline Johnson and Duncan Campbell Scott, citing their final titles. Scott's works appear in italics. Significant stories appear in square brackets.

1884 "The Re-interment of Red Jacket"
1885 "A Cry from an Indian Wife"
1886 "'Brant': A Memorial Ode"
1888 "The Death-Cry"
1889 "The Happy Hunting Grounds"
1890 "As Red Men Die"
1891 "The Pilot of the Plains"
1892 "The Song My Paddle Sings"; "The Avenger"
1893 "Wolverine"; ["A Red Girl's Reasoning"]
1894 "The Cattle Thief"; "Silhouette"; *The Onondaga Madonna*
1895 "Dawendine"; "Ojistoh"
1896 "Lullaby of the Iroquois"; "The Corn Husker"; ["The Derelict"]
1897 "The Indian Corn Planter"
1898 "The Indian Legend of Qu'Appelle Valley"; *"Watkwenies"*
1899 ["As It Was in the Beginning"]
1900 *"Night Hymns on Lake Nipigon"*
1903 *"The Forsaken"*
1904 [*"Charcoal"*]
1905 *"On the Way to the Mission"*; *"Indian Place Names"*
1906 *"The Half-Breed Girl"*; *"Spring on Mattagami"*
1913 "The Ballad of Yaada"
1916 *"Lines Written in Memory of Edmund Morris"*; *"The Height of Land"*

1926 *"Powassen's Drum"*
1935 *"At Gull Lake: August 1810"*; *"A Scene at Lake Manitou"*

APPENDIX II: TWO COMPARABLE POEMS

"The Corn Husker," Pauline Johnson, 1896

Hard by the Indian lodges, where the bush
Breaks in a clearing, through ill-fashioned fields,
She comes to labour, when the first still hush
Of autumn follows large and recent yields.

Age in her fingers, hunger in her face,
Her shoulders stooped with weight of work and years,
But rich in tawny colouring of her race,
She comes a-field to strip the purple ears.

And all her thoughts are with the days gone by,
Ere might's injustice banished from their lands
Her people, that to-day unheeded lie,
Like the dead husks that rustle through her hands.

"Watkwenies,"[64] D.C. Scott, 1898

Vengeance was once her nation's lore and law:
When the tired sentry stooped above the rill,
Her long knife flashed, and hissed, and drank its fill;
Dimly below her dripping wrist she saw,
One wild hand, pale as death and weak as straw,
Clutch at the ripple in the pool; while shrill
Sprang through the dreaming hamlet on the hill,
The war-cry of the triumphant Iroquois.

Now clothed with many an ancient flap and fold,
And wrinkled like an apple kept to May,
She weighs the interest-money in her palm,
And, when the Agent calls her valiant name,
Hears, like the war-whoops of her perished day,
The lads playing snow-snake in the stinging cold.

NOTES

I am grateful to Margery Fee and Mark Abley for their helpful comments on an earlier version of this essay.

1. E. Pauline Johnson, "A Cry from an Indian Wife," in *E. Pauline Johnson, Tekahionwake: Collected Poems and Selected Prose*, eds. Carole Gerson and Veronica Strong-Boag (Toronto: University of Toronto Press, 2002), 14–15. First published in *The Week*, 16 April 1885, 315. The final line of the poem cited here belongs to the later version of 1892.
2. Duncan Campbell Scott, transcript of testimony before Special Parliamentary Committee on Proposed Changes to Indian Act, April 1920. LAC/BAC, RG10, vol. 6810, file 470-2-3, vol. 7, 55 (L-3) and 63 (N-3); from https://www.facinghistory.org/stolen-lives-indigenous-peoples-canada-and-indian-residential-schools/historical-background/until-there-not-single-indian-canada.
3. D.C. Scott to E.M. Brown, 2 July 1941. Robert L. McDougall, ed., *The Poet and the Critic: A Literary Correspondence between D.C. Scott and E.K. Brown* (Ottawa: Carleton University Press, 1983), 26.
4. From Scott's first "Indian" poem, "The Onondaga Madonna" (1894), in Glenn Clever, ed., *Selected Poetry of Duncan Campbell Scott* (Ottawa: Tecumseh, 1974), 14.
5. Johnson to Archie Kains, 20 April 1890; *Collected*, xvi.
6. Leon Slonim's dissertation, "A Critical Edition of the Poems of Duncan Campbell Scott" (University of Toronto, 1980), remains unpublished.
7. E.K. Brown, "Memoir of Duncan Campbell Scott," *Selected Poems of Duncan Campbell Scott* (Toronto: Ryerson, 1951), xix.
8. Just thirteen of Scott's poems and one story directly concern Indigenous subjects, in a total oeuvre of more than 250 poems: more than two hundred in *The Poems of Duncan Campbell Scott* (Toronto: McClelland and Stewart, 1926) plus fifty in *The Green Cloister: Later Poems* (Toronto: McClelland and Stewart, 1935) and some forty stories.
9. For Scott's use of the term "final solution" in 1910 see: https://www.ictinc.ca/blog/the-final-solution-which-government-used-the-term-first. Mark Abley's investigation shows that Scott never uttered the expression "kill the Indian in the child." See *Conversations with a Dead Man: The Legacy of Duncan Campbell Scott* (Madeira Park, BC: Douglas & McIntyre 2013), 36–37.
10. https://en.wikipedia.org/wiki/Duncan_Campbell_Scott
11. http://muskratmagazine.com/duncan-campbell-scott-was-a-dickhead/; "Duncan Campbell Scott Plaque Now Includes his Past Creating

Residential Schools," CBC *News;* CBC *Radio-Canada,* 2 November 2015; Web 23 November 2015: http://www.cbc.ca/news/canada/ottawa/duncan-campbell-scott-plaque-updated-1.3299062.
12 Margaret Atwood, *The Journals of Susanna Moodie* (Toronto: Oxford University Press 1970), "Afterword," 62.
13 Emily Nussbaum, *I Like to Watch* (New York: Random House 2019), 110; https://www.npr.org/2019/07/15/741146427/we-all-watch-in-our-own-way-a-critic-tracks-the-tv-revolution.
14 Rick Monture, "'Beneath the British Flag': Iroquois and Canadian Nationalism in the Work of Pauline Johnson and Duncan Campbell Scott," *Essays on Canadian Writing* 75 (Winter 2002): 118–41.
15 Margery Fee, "Publication, Performance, and Politics: The 'Indian' Poems of E. Pauline Johnson–Tekahionwake (1861–1913) and Duncan Campbell Scott (1862–1947)," in *Anthologizing Canadian Literature,* ed. by Robert Lecker (Waterloo ON: Wilfrid Laurier University Press, 2015), 51–78.
16 Abley, *Conversations,* 28.
17 See Bentley, *The Confederation Group of Canadian Poets, 1880–1897* (Toronto: University of Toronto Press, 2004).
18 Touchstone, "A Canadian Literature Evening," *Saturday Night,* Jan 23, 1892, 7.
19 A copy of the program survives in Frank Yeigh's scrapbook for the Young Liberal Club, Frank Yeigh papers, F 1085, Archives of Ontario.
20 "Canadian Literature: An Evening with Canadian Authors," *Globe,* 18 January 1892, 5.
21 "Social Life at the Capital," *Globe,* 25 May 1895, 9. Also see Charlotte Gray, *Flint & Feather: The Life and Times of E. Pauline Johnson, Tekahionwake* (Toronto: HarperCollins 2002), 222. During the 1890s, Pauline Johnson's name appeared on other occasions in the RSC's *Proceedings and Transactions*: in 1895 in Horatio Hale's "An Iroquois Condoling Council," (II, 47–48) and in reference to the poetry reading of 17 May (VI–VII, CXIII–CXIV); in 1896 in John Campbell's "The Ancient Literature of America," (II, 67); in 1897 in J.G. Bourinot's "Canada during the Victorian Era," (II, 23, 79); in 1910 her poem "In the Shadows" was cited in Lt-Colonial William Wood's paper, "Laurenciana," (II, 38–39); and in 1913, the RSC spent $10 on flowers for her funeral (XXXVIII).
22 "Miss Pauline Johnson's Poems," *The Week,* 23 August 1895, 927. Evidence of the popular association of this poem with Johnson includes the program for Lord and Lady Strathcona's Dominion Day reception in

London in 1899, when it was recited by Miss Minnie Hope Morgan of Toronto: "Montrealers in London," *Montreal Gazette* 17 July 1899, 7.
23 F.G. Scott (no relation) recalled this dinner in his contribution to Walter McRaye, *Pauline Johnson and Her Friends* (Toronto: Ryerson, 1947), 57.
24 Arthur S. Bourinot, ed., *More Letters of Duncan Campbell Scott* (self-pub., Ottawa: by the editor, 1960), 1.
25 J.G. Bourinot, "Canada in the Victorian Era: An Historical Review," *Proceedings and Transactions*, 1897. Section II: 3-84; writers' photographs appear on 79. https://www.biodiversitylibrary.org/item/41834#page/437/mode/1up
26 Ibid., 23.
27 Abley, *Conversations*, 181.
28 Joseph Dana Miller, "The Singers of Canada," *Munsey's Magazine* (May 1895); cited in Bentley, 273-74.
29 Duncan C. Scott, "A Decade of Canadian Poetry," *Canadian Magazine* 17.1 (June 1901); 153-58; Ibid.,154.
30 "Traditional History of the Confederacy of the Six Nations," *Transactions of the RSC*, 1911, sec. 2, 195-246. See Carl Berger, *Honour and the Search for Influence: A History of the Royal Society of Canada* (Toronto: University of Toronto Press, 1996), 40, 149. This positive attitude would later be countered by Scott's efforts to repress the Six Nations' system of local governance in the 1920s.
31 Amelia M. Paget, *People of the Plains,* 1909; rpt. with an introduction by Sarah Carter (Regina: Canadian Plains Research Centre, 2004), xxi, xxxvii. Stan Dragland suggests that Paget's book might have been Scott's source for the story of Akoose in his poem, "Lines in Memory of Edmund Morris" (1915); *Floating Voice* (Toronto: Anansi 1994), 212.
32 RSC *Proceedings and Transactions*, 1913, "Statement of Receipts and Expenditures of the Royal Society of Canada, for the years ending 30th April 1913," xxviii.
33 Scott to W.D. Lighthall, 8 March 1913, Lighthall fonds, box 8 file19, Rare Books and Special Collections, McGill University Library.
34 D.C. Scott to McRaye, 7 April 1943. Walter McRaye fonds, box 1 file 4, McMaster University Library.
35 Scott told a fellow Ottawa poet that "he had published all of his books at his own expense." Wilfred Eggleston, *Literary Friends* (Ottawa: Borealis, 1980), 112. Poetry was seldom profitable and subsidy by the author was the norm.

36 Armand Garnet Ruffo, "Poem for Duncan Campbell Scott," *Opening in the Sky* (Penctiton, BC: Theytus 1994), 25–26; 25.
37 Fee, *Anthologizing*, 52.
38 E. Pauline Johnson, Tekahionwake, *Collected Poems and Selected Prose*, ed. Carole Gerson and Veronica Strong-Boag (Toronto University of Toronto Press, 2002), 14–15.
39 Duncan Campbell Scott, *Selected Poetry of Duncan Campbell Scott*, ed. Glenn Cleaver (Ottawa: Tecumseh, 1974), 14.
40 See Lee B. Meckler, "Rabbit-Skin Robes and Mink Traps: Indian and European in 'The Forsaken,'" *Canadian Poetry* 1, (1977): 60–65. Meckler provocatively claimed that Scott's use of the word "slunk" to describe the departure of the woman's sons is "the most controversial word in the corpus of Canadian poetry," 60.
41 Johnson, *Collected*, 114–16.
42 Scott, *Selected*, 13.
43 See Leon Slonim, "The Source of Duncan Campbell Scott's 'Charcoal,'" *Studies in Canadian Literature*, 4.1 (1979): 1–4.
44 D.C. Scott, "Charcoal," [1904 as "Starblanket"] *The Circle of Affection and Other Pieces* (Toronto: McClelland and Stewart 1947), 212–22; 213, 221.
45 E. Pauline Johnson, "The Shagganappi," *The Shagganappi* (Toronto: Briggs, 1913), 11, 13. Mixed-raced Lady Bennington may have been modelled on Amelia Connolly Douglas, the wife of James Douglas, governor of the colony of Vancouver Island, or on Isabella Hardistry, the wife of Lord Strathcona. See Margery Fee, *Literary Land Claims: The "Indian Land Question" from Pontiac's War to Attawwpiskat* (Waterloo, ON: Wilfrid Laurier University Press, 2015), 127.
46 First published in the Toronto *Sunday Globe*, 22 May 1892, 1; Johnson, *Collected*, 177–83.
47 Ibid., 210.
48 Ibid., 189.
49 Ibid., 190.
50 "A Clever Canadian," *Saturday Night*, 26 April 1890, 6.
51 An early poem, "A Request" (1886), asked that Anglican missionaries go to the "North-west Indian lands" to save the souls of "Crees and Blackfeet" (Johnson, *Collected*, 21–22), and the story "We-hro's Sacrifice" includes "a great Anglican bishop" who respects the emotions of "a little pagan Indian lad" (Johnson, *Collected*, 223).
52 Johnson, *Collected*, 100.
53 Today, this press is aggressively evangelical: see https://davidccook.org/.

54 In the Johnson collection at the Museum of Vancouver; first published in *Collected Poems and Selected Prose* (2002).
55 See Lisa Salem, "'Her Blood Is Mingled with Her Ancient Foes': The Concepts of Blood, Race and 'Miscegenation' in the Poetry and Short Fiction of Duncan Campbell Scott," *Studies in Canadian Literature* 18.1 (1993): 99–117.
56 "The Onondaga Madonna," *Selected*, 14.
57 "The Half-Breed Girl," *Selected*, 43–44.
58 D.M.R. Bentley. "Shadows in the Soul: Racial Haunting in the Poetry of Duncan Campbell Scott," *University of Toronto Quarterly* 75.2 (2006): 752–70; 759–60.
59 "At Gull Lake, 1810," *Selected*, 96–99.
60 To which Scott believed that Indians had a "pre-disposition": see Duncan Campbell Scott, "Indian Affairs 1867–1912," in *Canada and its Provinces* vol. 5, section 3, "Upper Canada," eds., Adam Shortt and Arthur G. Doughty (Toronto: Glasgow, Brook, 1914). Rpt in Duncan Campbell Scott, *Addresses, Essays and Reviews,* ed. Leslie Ritchie, introduction by Stan Dragland vol. 1 (London ON: Canadian Poetry Press, 2000), 204–5.
61 "A Scene at Lake Manitou," *Selected*, 102–06.
62 "Indian Place Names," *Selected*, 36.
63 Rosanna Deerchild, "My Poem is an Indian Woman," in *Indigenous Poetics in Canada* ed. by Neal McLeod (Waterloo ON: Wilfrid Laurier University Press, 2014), 241.
64 The Woman Who Conquers [Scott's note, translating the woman's name and the title of the poem.]

4

"Sooner or later they will be given the privelage [sic] asked for": Duncan Campbell Scott and the Dispossession of Shoal Lake 40, 1913–14

Adele Perry

One could not design a better symbol of the connections between Canada's colonial project and its cultural elite than Duncan Campbell Scott if one tried. Canadian history means that we do not need to invent such a figure. Scott was the deputy superintendent general of department (DPG) of the Department of Indian Affairs (DIA) and, in that capacity, the "principal architect of Indian policy" from 1913 to 1932.[1] These were years when federal interventions into Indigenous lives, governance, and territories escalated, broadened, and intensified. Campbell Scott was also a decorated poet and writer, and a member of the Royal Society of Canada (RSC) from 1899 onward and its president in 1921–22. Campbell's career and how it was acknowledged and celebrated tells us a lot about the connections between Canada's colonial project, rooted in violent dispossession of Indigenous territories and destruction of Indigenous lives, kinship, and communities and central Canada's polite cultural elite, and how their respective legacies have been understood and evaluated.

Behind this book, and the project that inspired it, sits this fact: a man who bears central responsibility for the intensification and administration of Canadian colonialism was also a leader within the RSC. What this means for how we understand the RSC, its past, present, and possible futures, are all surely shifted by this recognition, or ought to be. In this paper, I turn the lens away from the particular history that Scott, as a colonial administrator, is most associated with: that of Indian residential schooling. My focus is instead on

Scott's connections to the loss of Indigenous land, especially reserve lands. I delve deep into the weeds of how the Canadian state dispossessed Shoal Lake 40 First Nation's resources and reserve lands in the interests of Winnipeg's drinking water. Taken as a case study, the relationship between DIA, Winnipeg's municipal government, and Shoal Lake 40 First Nation shows how we must see Scott, and via him, the RSC's story as not being tied up only with IRS, but with the ongoing loss of Indigenous lands and resources.

There are many Shoal Lakes in Canada: lakes, municipalities, First Nations, and reserves. The one that concerns me here is an Annishinaabeg or Ojibway community that borders Ontario and Manitoba. The story of how this community came to inhabit an artificial island is a story of Canadian colonialism. It is also very much a story of Scott, and his work as a colonial official, and what it means to live and work in the wake of it. My ongoing research on the relationship between the city of Winnipeg, Shoal Lake 40, and colonialism sits squarely in a moment shaped by Idle No More in the winter of 2012-3, the release of the final report of the Truth and Reconciliation Commission in 2015, the movement in support of Wet'suwet'en resistance, and the growth and expansion of a rich scholarship of Indigenous Studies. My own work is a small part of a wider effort of Winnipeggers, both Indigenous and, like myself and my family, non-Indigenous, who have called to account the relationship between this city and Shoal Lake 40, the First Nation at the source of Winnipeg's water supply.

In the 1910s, Shoal Lake 40 First Nation lost critical parts of their reserve land, and through that, their capacity to access much of what urban Canada would consider basic amenities and services. Winnipeg gained a decent, reliable, and cheap source of domestic water in 1919. In the past decade, the activism of Shoal Lake 40 and the response of Indigenous and non-Indigenous Winnipeggers have called these histories to account. What does it mean to live in a city built on Indigenous land, and where the drinking water has come, and still comes, at the direct expense of a First Nation at the other end of the pipe?

This question echoes the one that guides this volume of essays. What does it mean to be a member of an organization that was led by a man who was responsible for no small part of the worst excesses of Canada's colonial project? From the vantage point of both Ottawa and the available secondary scholarship on Scott, the dispossession of Shoal Lake 40 in the interest of Winnipeg's water is invisible, not even a footnote. Shoal Lake 40 does not appear in Brian Titley's *A Narrow Vision: Duncan Campbell Scott and the Administration of Indian Affairs in Canada*, a 1986 work that remains the best and most conclusive study of Scott as a colonial administrator. Nor does it surface in Stan Dragland's insightful call for readers to examine the uncomfortable connections between Scott's writing and his administration of Indigenous territories in Treaty Nine, directly to the east and north of Shoal Lake, or in Mark Abley's creative and scholarly "conversation" with Scott.[2]

Activists and scholars looking to bring Scott to better account have understandably tended to focus on his record with regards to Indian residential schools (IRS). At the DIA, Scott superintended the expansion and sharpening of a carceral system of residential schooling that separated First Nations, Inuit and, to a lesser extent, Métis children from their families, communities, and economies. IRS began before Scott's tenure at the DIA, and they would persist after it. But Scott's connection to the IRS system is important. Scott was appointed superintendent of Indian Education in 1909. It was during his tenure as deputy superintendent of the DIA that the IRS system reached its height, in terms of the number of institutions, the number of children who attended them, and the extent of coercive measures available for making children attend and stay at school.[3] The focus on Scott's record as a developer and administrator of IRS reflects the very real way that IRS stand as powerful symbols of the destructive totality of Canada's colonial project and how it imperiled, and continues to imperil, Indigenous life.

For all of this, IRS were not the only part of early twentieth-century Canada's colonial project, or of Scott's administration. The ongoing loss of Indigenous land and resources under Scott's tenure with the DIA also demand our attention and analysis. Dene political theorist Glen Coulthard urges us to think of "colonialism as a form of structured dispossession." He explains that Canada, like other settler colonial states, is "structurally committed to maintain – through force, fraud, and more recently, so-called "negotiations" – ongoing state access to the land and resources that contradictorily provide the material and special sustenance of Indigenous societies on the one hand, and the foundation of colonial state-formation, settlement, and capitalist development on the other."[4]

The dispossession of Indigenous lands and resources is variable, evolving, and far from over. It also occurs within particular historical and spatial contexts. In the case that concerns me here, it is in the western edge of the Lake of the Woods watershed bordering the contemporary provinces of Manitoba and Ontario in the first decades of the twentieth century. The boundary waters of Lake of the Woods had been home to Annishinaabeg and their careful economies, social relations, and practices of governance for thousands of years. The arrival of the European fur-trade in the eighteenth century shifted these histories, and, if population and food production are good indicators, in some respects enriched them.[5] The articulation of Canadian interest in the 1850s and 1860s was followed by the assertion of Canadian colonial authority from 1870 onwards. Canadian efforts to negotiate a treaty with Annishinaabeg at the North-West Angle in 1870 went sideways, in no small part because of Annishinaabeg demands. "The Saulteaux tribe seem to have been the most difficult to manage," opined the settler press in 1874.[6]

Treaty Three was concluded in 1873, with Shoal Lake 40 one of the signatory First Nations. Canada would interpret this agreement and those like it as land cession agreements. As Kate Gunn notes, a 2014 Supreme Court of Canada decision begins with the statement that the Annishinaabeg signatories to Treaty Three "yielded ownership of their territory" in exchange for reserve lands.[7] Annishinaabeg archives, both oral, material, and written, speak to a different meaning of this treaty, seeing it as "an agreement for both parties to mutually share and use the treaty lands" and "not as a surrender of jurisdictional authority to the Crown." Historian Brittany Luby shows how Annishinaabeg understandings of Treaty Three were preserved in the written record in the Paypom Treaty, created by Joseph Nolin, the Métis translator hired by the Annishinaabeg negotiators.[8]

In 1913, the City of Winnipeg needed a new water supply, as had been the case for some time. The geographically spread out and overwhelmingly Indigenous community of Red River became part of Canada through a process that was complicated, protracted, and violent. Population growth was modest in the years that followed the *Manitoba Act* of 1870 and the incorporation of Winnipeg three or four years later. It picked up in the final fifteen years of the nineteenth century and especially in the first years of the twentieth century. A mere 241 people were enumerated in the City of Winnipeg in 1871; by 1901 there were 42,340, and by 1912, 136, 035. Even accounting for civic boosters' tendency to exaggerate the city's population growth, it clearly outstripped nearly all other Canadian cities in the years between 1871 and 1921.[9] The city had tried treating water from local rivers and artesian wells, public schemes, and private ownership. An old idea about bringing water from the Lake of the Woods watershed returned when Thomas Russ Deacon was elected mayor in 1912 on what was referred to as a "Shoal Lake water ticket."[10]

The Greater Winnipeg Water District (GWWD's) plan to build an aqueduct to transport Shoal Lake water 150 kilometers west to Winnipeg depended on Shoal Lake 40 reserve lands. It was not the language or relations of Treaty, however understood and defined, that shaped the discussions around Shoal Lake 40's lands and resources in the 1910s. What did matter was the *Indian Act*. Passed first in 1876, and still in force today, the *Indian Act* represents the Canadian colonial project at its most interventionist and intractable. Historians Mary-Ellen Kelm and Keith Smith explain that the *Indian Act* distinguishes Canada's colonial project. It is a unique and totalizing piece of legislation that works "to eliminate Indigenous people through its own defining powers, to sever their connections to lands and of their families and communities, to disrupt Indigenous systems of governance, and to silence protest."[11]

In its almost century and a half of life, the *Indian Act* has been regularly revised in ways both big and small. In the final decades of the nineteenth century and the first decades of the twentieth century, the *Indian Act* was revised to further erode Indigenous control over territory and community, to increase state power, and to diminish Indigenous protest. Particularly relevant here are the changes to facilitate the access of settler governments and individuals to what the *British North America Act* calls "Lands reserved for Indians." Legal historian Douglas Harris explains how the *Indian Act* defined reserves in ways that denied the First Nations the kinds of power and sovereignty usually insured in property inherent in property law. Reserves become a peculiar form of "collective ownership" that "distributed the beneficial interest to Indian bands while retaining the legal interest and placing the responsibility in its bureaucracy to act as a trustee."[12]

When the GWWD began to plan for its aqueduct, it first sought the necessary permissions from the province of Manitoba, the province of Ontario, and the International Joint Commission. In this correspondence, an Ontario official would remind Deacon that Winnipeg's designs on Shoal Lake 40's lands involved questions of Indigenous rights, writing: "You of course understand that some of the lands in the vicinity of Shoal Lake are Indian Lands and that this Government has no control over those lands."[13] It would be months before Deacon approached the federal government and, when he did, it was with a gentlemanly request. In the spring of 1913, Deacon began to seek the approval of the International Joint Commission. In the fall of 1913, the GWWD's lawyer asked for DIA permission to "enter upon Indian Reserve No. 40" and do "preliminary survey work" there. The GWWD's respect was returned: the DIA responded prompted, politely, and positively. William Roche, the superintendent general of the DIA, consented, and asked only that the GWWD be prepared to pay for damages.[14]

This conversation between officials in Winnipeg and Ottawa shifted gears when the First Nation acted in its own interests, and made decisions about resources on its reserve. Chief Pete Redsky wanted to sell gravel and sand to the GWWD's contractor. "He has already got the Consent of Chief Redsky and the band to do so," the local Indian Agent reported.[15] A few days later, Redsky wrote to Ottawa and asked for clarity about what, exactly, were the GWWD's rights to the reserve and its resources. Could the newcomers cut green wood, could the First Nation sell wood and, if so, what would the price be? More profoundly, Redsky asked: "Has the Greater Winnipeg Water Commission made any arrangements about occupying any part of the reserve or about taking sand, gravel and timber from it?" and reminded officials of their fiduciary duties to First Nations: "We look to you to care for the interests of the Indians in this matter."[16]

Ottawa responded by stating that the First Nation could not sell gravel and sand unless it agreed to surrender its rights to them to Canada. Within ten days, Ottawa had drafted a surrender document, and Scott was instructing the Indian Agent on how to conduct a surrender process: the exact number of voting male members of the First Nation over the age of twenty-one years, residing on or near the reserve, the kind of officials present, and so on.[17] In January of 1914, twelve of a possible twenty-one eligible members voted in a surrender process, and the support of eleven of them was enough to approve the surrender of all their rights to sand and gravel on the reserve to the Department of Indian Affairs.[18] Scott explained that this was done so that the DIA could sell Shoal Lake 40's resources "for their benefit."[19]

Historians do not know a lot about how the *Indian Act* dealt and deals with resource rights on reserves, let alone the extent to which they were and are subject to surrender processes. But the particular colonial economies that have defined so much of Canada's past and present have been and still are particularly hungry for resources, whether the archetypal staples of fish, fur, and timber, or their contemporary analogs of minerals and natural gas. Economies have been and continue to be organized around the extraction of resources from Indigenous lands and moving them to markets, mainly global ones. This often involves land, in a conventional sense, but in ways that ought to condition how we see settler colonialism, and the place of land within it. What the City of Winnipeg wanted from Shoal Lake 40 was gravel, sand, timber and, most of all, water. Winnipeg acquired lawful access to these resources through the *Indian Act's* mechanism of surrender brought to bear on resource rights. But accessing Shoal Lake's water required land too: to build the intake to the aqueduct, and to build a dyke and a canal to ensure that clear water would end up in Winnipeg's mains and taps.

The land that was needed for Winnipeg to take Shoal Lake's water prompted the major land loss that would define Shoal Lake 40's geography and determine so much of its experience in the twentieth and twenty-first centuries. This is Shoal Lake 40's history alone, but it is also part of a longer and wider history whereby the small amount of land left to First Nations as "reserve" was whittled away, often as soon as it was granted. Surrender processes certainly predated Confederation and the *Indian Act*. A kind of surrender is sketched out in the Royal Proclamation of 1763, and specified in legislation that followed.[20] Between 1818 and 1838, nine First Nations in eastern Canada lost a total of eleven million acres of land to surrender.[21]

However, the pace and scale of surrender practices shifted in the period of intensive setter expansion into the territories west of the Great Lakes in the final years of the nineteenth century and particularly in the first decades of the twentieth. Sarah Carter's commanding study of how the federal government undermined Indigenous agriculture in the prairies is by necessity a study of the mass surrender of reserve lands. Officials like Frank Oliver, appointed superintendent general of Indian Affairs in the Liberal government of 1905, supported the alienation of reserve land. The *Indian Act* was amended a year later to allow the government to distribute up to 50 per cent of the purchase price of surrendered reserve lands. Carter documents how presumptions of the uselessness of reserve land, and the desirability of it being "opened up" for settlers was widespread, supported by "farmers, townspeople, merchants, railroad executives, newspapermen, and speculators." The DIA received letters from across the continent "asking whether it was true that Indian reserves were to be thrown open for settlement and just how this land might be acquired."[22]

The Annishinaabeg of St Peter's, Manitoba, hung onto their prosperous farm lands in the years that followed the signing of Treaty One and passage of the 1876 *Indian Act*. In 1907, they lost the entirety of their reserve through a surrender process that was unusually self-interested and irregular, even by the low bar of an early twentieth-century settler colonial state hungry for Indigenous land. A commission in 1911 declared the surrender of the St Peter's reserve invalid but it was not until 2008 that the federal government recognized the injustice and compensated the descendants.[23] St Peter's was unusual it the scope and totality of its loss. But this community was far from alone in losing the little land it had in these decades. Peggy McGuire-Martin's study for the Indian Claims Commission shows how a total of 21 per cent of reserve land in Manitoba, Saskatchewan and Alberta was surrendered to the Crown between 1896 and 1911 alone.[24] We have no comparative study of Ontario, or of the years following 1911 but Shoal Lake 40 was far from the only First Nation to lose land to surrender in this region and time period. In 1915, the Rainy River Annishinaabeg lost all of their reserves except one to a surrender process, losing almost 43,000 acres or 90 per cent of their land base.[25]

These surrenders required a kind of limited First Nations' consent, namely the agreement of half of the male members of the Band over the age of twenty-one at a meeting attended by an authorized government official. This was an unequivocally colonial process, and a rigid and patriarchal one. As the discussion around the surrender of the St. Peter's reserve in 1907 made clear, it was also one that was vulnerable to subterfuge and chicanery.[26]

In February of 1914, Scott asked the GWWD to clarify its plans for Shoal Lake 40, reminding it that "no rights can be granted without the consent of the Indians."[27] The GWWD escalated. The commissioner recommended that the GWWD's board "delegate someone to, at once, proceed to Ottawa to have this matter adjusted favourably for the value of this pit to the District is quite considerable."[28] When the GWWD wrote to Ottawa, it explained that Mayor Deacon would soon be there to "personally explain to you our position and furnish you with information which will indicate to you just what our desires are in this respect."[29] By early March, Deacon had visited eastern Canada to make financial arrangements to fund the costly aqueduct, and to address how the GWWD would manage the Indigenous land that undergirded the entire plan. "While in Ottawa the Mayor took up the question of securing terminals for the pipeline and the railway in Indian Reserve No. 40," the Toronto *Globe* reported, "and he reports that very satisfactory arrangements had been made."[30] In Winnipeg, the two daily newspapers published Deacon's report of the trip, sandwiching mention that a "very satisfactory arrangement was reached with the superintendent general of Indian affairs" between descriptions of his meetings with Montreal bankers and visits to the family home in Pembroke.[31] These discussions and reporting confirm Scott's effective authority within the daily administration of empire in Canada in 1913 and 1914. They also suggest something about the shape of Canada's early twentieth-century settler elite. This was a world that linked banking, the administration of Indian affairs, visits home, civic government, and an ambitious settler city in the Prairies to centres of finance and administrative control in southern Ontario and Quebec.

At Shoal Lake, the Indian Agent noted what the GWWD had already built on the reserve, anticipating that its plans would require more and more land, and that the administration would accommodate the GWWD's interests. The GWWD's "whole operations will be on the reserve," he noted, and "I suppose that sooner or later they will be given the privelage [sic] asked for." The agent anticipated that the First Nation would be asked to surrender the land, and that members would agree.[32] But Should Lake 40 would not be given the chance to agree or disagree. The mechanism that would carve a critical 3,355 acres out of Shoal Lake 40's reserve was introduced in 1911, the same year that Scott was appointed deputy superintendent of Indian Affairs. The *Indian Act* was modified to include two new ways for dispossessing reserve lands without even this limited and fragile form of consent. The amendment that attracted the most attention at the time and in historical analyses alike is section

49A, which allowed reserves adjacent to or within towns or cities with populations of more than eight thousand to be dispossessed upon the recommendation of a special court.[33] This section became a mechanics to make possible the removal of Indigenous peoples from cities, making possible the spatial separation of Indigenous and settler upon which visions of Canadian urban modernity depended.[34]

What worried the Conservative MP for Selkirk, George Bradbury, was the other amendment, section 46. This allowed railways, roads, public work, or "work designed for any public utility" to take reserve lands "without the consent of the owner" so long as the governor-in-council approved. Whatever terms there might be would be set by that office.[35] In 1911, Bradbury raised a modest kind of alarm in the House of Commons. With the memory of the disastrous surrender of the St. Peter's reserve still in mind, Bradbury argued that the wording was unclear and the principle dangerous. "The Indians are not represented in this House and have no voice in making this legislation," he explained. The new amendments removed any capacity for redress, removed requirements for consultation, and gave the superintendent general powers that were "too broad and arbitrary." Bradbury spoke of treaties, and what they meant and did not mean in a world being remade through settler majorities. "When these treaties were made, in most cases the Indians were a power in this country. The Treaties had to be lived up to; the Indians were, in many cases, able to compel the white man to keep faith with them." If the bill was to become law, the superintendent general would receive "the power to take any Indian reserve in Canada, within the scope of this Bill, without giving the Indians the opportunity to make their protest felt."[36]

Late in February 1914, Deacon wrote to Scott "for permission to purchase" the parts of Shoal Lake 40's reserve the GWWD wanted for its terminals, gravel pit, and right of way for the aqueduct. "We recognize that the Indians are entitled to reasonable compensation for this and we are prepared to pay what the Department would think just," he explained.[37] Deacon makes no note of the possibility that Shoal Lake 40 might refuse this transfer, and frames the discussion as one between settler governments. There is no possibility of Indigenous agency or refusal suggested. And indeed, there was not. The same day, Scott's assistant J.D. McLean wrote to Deacon explaining "Since the above lands may be acquired under Section 46 of the *Indian Act* a surrender from the band will not be necessary."[38]

What followed was an administrative tussle between Ottawa and Winnipeg over the terms of Shoal Lake 40's loss. The tussle was conducted by post and sometimes telegram. Deacon was not pleased to be asked to pay a separate amount for sand and gravel, and insisted that this was not part of the deal that he "went to Ottawa for." The mayor explained that the price was excessive, "much higher" than what one might pay for adjacent Ontario Crown lands.[39] Framed in these terms, reserve land was invariably up for sale and on modest terms. First Nations' resources commanded even less. Deacon insisted that Scott had agreed that the city could have the gravel and sand for nothing.[40] Scott acquiesced in the face of the mayor's advocacy for his city's interest, sending a night letter confirming that the city would pay $3.00 per acre "to cover everything."[41] The First Nation had lost its rights to a resource that Scott would go on to give away for nothing. The chief surveyor and the DIA's draftsman discussed the price for the land and lakebed, the only properties still on the table, and decided that Shoal Lake 40 would receive $1,500 for all that it had lost: the land, the lakebed, the gravel, and the sand.[42]

In the conversation that played out between Winnipeg and Ottawa about Shoal Lake in late 1913 and early 1914, Scott briefly assumed the role of protector of a limited sort of Indigenous rights. In conversation with an ambitious, western city with little to no willingness to recognize reserve lands, Scott was the one to remind Winnipeg that the First Nation's "consent" was required before work could begin.[43] But this was a brief moment, and thereafter Scott used the administrative mechanisms of the federal government's Indian policies to help Winnipeg have its way. In any real contest between Winnipeg's demands and Shoal Lake 40's interests, Scott consistently choose the former.

In March of 1914, the governor general approved the Privy Council's report recommending that the DIA be given authority to sell approximately 3,335 acres of Shoal Lake's reserve to Winnipeg.[44] In June, the administration board of the GWWD would pass a motion to accept the offer of $1,500.[45] By this point, the formal loss of land was a kind of inevitability, and also after the fact. In his careful study of the building of the aqueduct, David Ennis notes that by the time the transaction was complete, the dyke across Indian Bay had already been substantially completed.[46] The debates between Deacon and Scott during the winter of 1913 and 1914 and the use of Section 46 were both formalities that legitimated a process of dispossession that had already occurred.

Against this inevitability of Indigenous loss and settler gain, the First Nation advocated for its interests as best as it could. In July of 1914, the Indian Agent reported that he had received a hard time while distributing treaty payments on Shoal Lake 40. The "Indians was very much excited about the work of the Greater Winnipeg Water Works and requested me to tell them what right they had to operate on their Reserve, and demanded to know what they were to get for the land taken, and what quantity is taken from them." The agent sent their queries to Ottawa, which would reply with a map and a reminder that "The Corporation of the city of Winnipeg has the power to expropriate the lands required, but you may assure the Indians that their rights will be safeguarded by the Department."[47] Four years later, Pete Redsky was asking the DIA to pay up or return the land and threatened to go to Ottawa to make his point. "This is asking the Government for the pay for the Reserve," he wrote. The land the GWWD had taken "was the best part of our Reserve," good for farming, timber, and hay. "We are now very anxious for 'The district' to pay for our land, and if they are not willing to pay for our land, I think they had better hand it back. I think it is time for you to fix up with us,"[48] declared Redsky.

Ottawa would not "fix up" with Redsky and his community in 1918, or for the century that followed. There was another surrender of land to the GWWD in 1919, and one of timber rights a year later. Like other First Nations in Treaty Three, Shoal Lake 40 lived with and in the face of the enormous costs of residential schooling and damages to the environment.[49] The engineering works undertaken to ensure that clear-looking water went to Winnipeg would effectively trisect the reserve, and leave the community landlocked. This meant one thing when Shoal Lake 40 was able to rely on the rail service provided by the GWWD train, and when a commercial fishery meant that community members owned boats. But regular passenger rail service ended in 1977, and summer excursions five years later. In 1983, Ontario closed Shoal Lake's walleye fishery. Later in that decade, the City of Winnipeg blocked Shoal Lake 40's efforts to develop some of its reserve lands as cottage lots.[50] In 1998, Shoal Lake 40 was put on a drinking water advisory. The lack of a decent water supply was not the community's only concern. The only way Shoal Lake 40 members could travel off the island in the summer was on a rickety, expensive car ferry; in the winter, they walked and drove on the ice. But neither ferries nor ice roads work when the ice is breaking up in the spring or freezing in the fall. Shoal Lake 40's status as an artificially isolated and "waterless" community became, and remains, a powerful symbol of how colonialism works to resource settler communities at the expense, and sometimes painfully direct expense, of Indigenous ones.[51]

In the spring of 2019, a twenty-four-kilometre gravel road connecting Shoal Lake 40 with the Trans-Canada Highway opened.[52] Funded by Canada, Manitoba, and the City of Winnipeg, Freedom Road is an enormous political victory, a testament to the tenacity and creativity of Shoal Lake 40. With it comes the possibility of a local water treatment plant, now scheduled to open in 2021. But a road and water treatment plant cannot mitigate the myriad ways that life on reserve has been, and continues to be, rendered continually unstable, difficult, and so often inimical to life. Reserves such as Shoal Lake 40 have been dredged through what Shiri Pasternak calls "a set of exhaustive administrative regimes that undermine, erase, and choke out the exercise of Indigenous jurisdiction."[53] Reserves such as Shoal Lake 40 sustain life, community, and possibility at great costs.

The law that Scott used to disposes Shoal Lake 40 of critical parts of its reserve remains with us still. The provisions regulating surrender were revised in the major changes to the *Indian Act* made in 1951, but they were not expunged. It remains possible for the Crown to take reserve lands without consultation, and under conditions that are in important respects broader rather than narrower.[54] As Mary Eberts explains, the "Crown in its modern dress will continue to work towards completion of one element of its agenda of internal colonization, namely securing the surrender to it of Indigenous lands, and the extinguishment of Indigenous title."[55]

As I wrote this chapter, Wet'suwet'en hereditary chiefs and their supporters in northern British Columbia were working to block a Costal Gas pipeline from cutting through their territories. In January 2019, the Royal Canadian Mounted Police entered camps in Wet'suwet'en territory, arresting fourteen. A little over a year later, the RCMP again arrived with an injunction, helicopters, and military gear, arresting fourteen.[56] As Wet'suwet'en supporters across Canada occupied ministerial offices, round danced at intersections and blocked train tracks and docks, the premier leading British Columbia's New Democratic Party-Green Party coalition government speaks unconvincingly of the rule of law, and a federal government putatively committed to reconciliation has very little to say.

This is the world that settler colonialism has wrought, and one that robust Indigenous communities, intellectuals, and activists continue to challenge with their presence and their protest. Duncan Campbell Scott played a key role in honing and sharpening Canada's settler colonial project. The case of Shoal Lake 40 provides us with an example of how Scott's policies and practices contributed to the diminution of Indigenous land and resources in the twentieth century. We have no reason to think that Scott considered this an important case. Still, it reveals a great deal about him as a colonial administrator, and that, in turn, reveals a great deal about him as a writer and a scholar. As we work to build scholarly communities, organizations, and professions that challenge the hierarchies and exclusions of colonialism and racism, it behooves us to take careful account of the legacies we have inherited, and what they have cost Indigenous people.

NOTES

I would like to thank the Centre for Human Rights' Research at the University of Manitoba for a small grant that helped support this research. I would also like to thank Cuyler Cotton for his feedback on this paper and Robin Neckoway for his research assistance.

1 E. Brian Titley, *A Narrow Vision: Duncan Campbell Scott and the Administration of Indian Affairs in Canada* (Vancouver, UBC Press, 1986), 22.
2 Titley, *A Narrow Vision*; Stan Dragland, *Floating Voice: Duncan Campbell Scott and the Literature of Treaty 9* (Toronto: House of Anansi, 1994); Mark Abley, *Conversations with a Dead Man: The Legacy of Duncan Campbell Scott* (Vancouver: Douglas and McIntyre, 2013).
3 Truth and Reconciliation Commission, *Final Report, Volume I: Canada's Residential Schools: The History, Part 1, Origins to 1939* (Montreal: McGill Queen's University Press), 276–280.
4 Glen Coulthard, *Red Skins, White Masks: Rejecting the Colonial Politics of Recognition* (Vancouver: UBC Press, 2014), 7.

5 See Leo G. Waisberg and Tim E. Holzkamm, "'A Tendency to Discourse them From Cultivating': Indian Affairs Administration in Northwestern Ontario," *Ethnohistory*, 40:2 (Spring 1993): 177–180.
6 "The Qu'Appelle Treaty," [Winnipeg] *Daily Free Press*, 3 October 1874.
7 Kate Gunn, "Agreeing to Share: Treaty 3, History and the Courts," UBC *Law Review*, 51:1 (2018): 75–105. For an additional argument rejecting the reflexive framing of the numbered treaties as land cessions, see Gina Starblanket, "The Numbered Treaties and the Politics of Incoherency," *Canadian Journal of Political Science*, (2019): 1–19.
8 Brittany Luby, "'The Department is Going Back on these Promises': An Examination of Annishinaabe and Crown Understandings of Treaty," *Canadian Journal of Native Studies*, 30: 2 (2010): 203–228.
9 Alan Artibise, *Winnipeg: A Social History of Urban Growth, 1874–1914* (Montreal, McGill-Queen's University Press, 1975), 132–133. Also see Owen Toews, *Stolen City: Racial Capitalism and the Making of Winnipeg* (Winnipeg: ARP, 2018), part 1, and Mary Jane Logan McCallum and Adele Perry, *Structures of Indifference: An Indigenous Life and Death in a Canadian City* (Winnipeg: University of Manitoba Press, 2018), chap. 1.
10 On these histories, see Adele Perry, *Aqueduct: Colonialism, Resources, and the Histories We Remember* (Winnipeg: ARP, 2016); David A. Ennis, "Pressure to Act: The Shoal Lake Aqueduct and the Greater Winnipeg Water District," *Manitoba History*, 72 (Spring–Summer 2013), and "Not all Down Hill From There: The Shoal Lake Aqueduct and the Greater Winnipeg Water District," *Manitoba History*, 75 (Summer 2014); Artibise, *Winnipeg*, chap. 12.
11 Mary-Ellen Kelm and Keith D. Smith, *Talking Back to the Indian Act: Critical Readings in Settler Colonial Histories* (Toronto: University of Toronto Press, 2018), 2.
12 Douglas C. Harris, "Property and Sovereignty: An Indian Reserve and a Canadian City," UBC *Law Review*, 50:2 (June 2017): 339.
13 W.H. Hearst to Mr Mayor [T.R. Deacon], 28 May 1913, International Joint Commission Archives, 1147, box 18, Docket 7.
14 William Roche, memo, 28 October 1913, Indian Affairs, Library and Archives Canada, RG 10 [hereafter LAC, RG 10] volume 3178, file 447, 733-1A, image 5, and R.S. Stewart to R.S. McKenzie, 27 October 1913, LAC, RG 10, volume 3178, file 447, 733-1, image 4.
15 R.S. McKenzie to Secretary, Department of Indian Affairs, 29 November 1913, LAC, RG 10, volume 3178, file 447, 733-1A, image 8.

16 Chief [Pete] Red Sky to R.S. McKenzie, 7 December 1913, LAC, RG 10, volume 3178, file 447,733-1A, image 17.
17 Duncan Campbell Scott to R.S. McKenzie, 15 December 1913, LAC, RG 10, volume 3178, file 447,733-1A, image 14.
18 R.S. McKenzie, "Report of a Council Meeting held at Shoal Lake on Above Date of the Shoal Lake Band No. 40. Before Indian Agent R.S. McKenzie and Record all Voting Members, of said band over 21 Years for the purpose of surendring [sic] there [sic] rights to all the sand and gravel on said reserve, to the Department," 7 January 1914, LAC, RG 10, volume 3178, file 447,733-1, image 23.
19 Duncan C. Scott to H. Reynolds, 3 February 1914, LAC, RG 10, volume 3178, file 447,733-1, image 40.
20 This point is made in Mary Eberts, "Still Colonizing after all these years," *New Brunswick Law Journal*, 64 (January) 2013: 130
21 Kevin D. Smith, *Liberalism, Surveillance, and Resistance: Indigenous Communities in Western Canada, 1877–1927* (Edmonton: AU Press, 2009), 220–221.
22 Sarah Carter, *Lost Harvests: Prairie Indian Reserve Farmers and Government Policy* (Montreal: McGill-Queen's, 1990), 245, 244.
23 See Sarah Carter "'They Would Not Give Up One Inch of It': The Rise and Demise of St Peter's Reserve, Manitoba," in *Indigenous Communities and Settler Colonialism*, eds. Zoe Laidlaw and Alan Lester (London: Palgrave MacMillan, 2015), 173–193.
24 Richard Spaulding, "Executive Summary," Peggy McGuire-Martin, "First Nation Land Surrenders on the Prairies, 1896–1911," (Ottawa: Indian Claims Commission, 1998), xiii. Another more than 85,000 acres of reserve land was acquired for the settlement of non-Indigenous soldiers in the years following the First World War. See Sarah Carter, "'An Infamous Proposal': Prairie Indian Reserve Land and Solider Settlement after World War I," *Manitoba History*, 37 (Spring–Summer 1999): 9–21.
25 Luby, "This Department," 209. For case studies of surrender, see David Vogt and David Alexander Gamble, "'You Don't Suppose the Dominion Government Wants to Cheat the Indians': The Grand Trunk Pacific Railway and the Fort George Reserve, 1908–1912," *BC Studies*, 166 (Summer 2010): 55–72, 127–128; Steve Roe, "'If the Story Could be Hard': Colonial Discourse and the Surrender of Indian Reserve 172," *BC Studies* 138/139, (Summer/Autumn 2003): 115–136; Patricia K. Wood, "Pressured from all sides: the February 1913 surrender of the northeast corner of the Tsuu T'ina Nation," *Journal of Historical Geography*, 30 (2004): 112–129.

26 See Sarah Carter, "St Peter's and the Interpretation of the Agriculture of the Aboriginal People of Manitoba," *Manitoba History*, 18 (Autumn 1989): 46–52.
27 Duncan C. Scott to R.H. Reynolds, Chair, GWWD, 3 February 1914, LAC, RG 10, volume 3178, file 447, 733-1, image 40.
28 S.H. Reynolds to Chair and Board, 12 February 1914, City of Winnipeg Archives, Greater Winnipeg Water District fonds, [hereafter CWA, GWWD] Commissioners Reports 1913–1915, temporary box 4.
29 R.H. Reynolds to J.D. McLean, 16 February 1914, LAC, RG 10, volume 3178, file 447, 733-1, image 44.
30 "Arrangements Made to Float Winnipeg Bonds," *Globe*, 5 March 1914.
31 "Mayor Returns from Trip to Eastern Cities," *Winnipeg Tribune*, 4 March 1914; Ibid.
32 R.S. McKenzie to J.D. McLean, 23 February 1914, LAC, RG 10, volume 3178, file 447, 733-1, image 50.
33 1–2 George V., chap. 14, "An Act to Amend the Indian Act," assented 19 May 1911.
34 For a study of a Section 49A removal, see Martha Walls, "The Dispossession of the Ladies: Mi'kmaq Women and the Removal of the King's Road Reserve, Sydney, Nova Scotia," *Journal of Canadian Studies*, 50:3 (Fall 2016): 538–565.
35 1–2 George V., chap. 14, "An Act to amend the Indian Act," assented 19 May 1911.
36 George Henry Bradbury, 4 May 1911, *Official Report of the Debates of the House of Commons of the Dominion of Canada*, Third Session, Eleventh Parliament, 1910–11 (Ottawa, Parmlee, 1911), 8405–6
37 Thomas R. Deacon to Duncan Campbell Scott, 26 February 1914, LAC, RG 10, volume 3178, file 447, 733-1, image 74.
38 J. D. McLean to Thomas R. Deacon, 26 February 1914, LAC, RG 10, volume 3178, file 447, 733-1, image 76.
39 Thomas Russ Deacon to J.D McLean, 7 March 1914, LAC, LAC, RG 10, volume 3178, file 447, 733-1, image 80.
40 Ibid.
41 Duncan C. Scott to T.R. Deacon, 12 March 1914, "Night Lettergram," LAC, IA, RG 10, volume 3178, file 447, 733-1, image 80.
42 S. Bray (Chief Surveyor), 1 June 1914, "Memorandum for the Deputy Superintendent General," LAC, IA, RG 10, volume 3178, file 447, 733-1, 103.
43 Scott to Reynolds, 3 February 1914.

44 Rodolphe Boudreau, "Certified Copy of a Report of the Committee of the Privy Council, Approved by His Royal Highness the Governor General on 3rd March, 1915," LAC, RG 10 volume 3178, file 447,733-1, image 126.
45 Minutes of the Greater Winnipeg Water District Administration Board, 14 June 1914, City of Winnipeg Archive, Greater Winnipeg Water District, Minutes of Administration Board.
46 David A. Ennis, "Developing a Domestic Water Supply for Winnipeg from Shoal Lake and Lake of the Woods: The Greater Winnipeg Water District Aqueduct, 1905–1919," (MS Thesis, University of Manitoba, 2011), 21.
47 R.S. McKenzie to J.D. McLean, 20 July 1914, LAC, IA, RG 10, volume 3178, file 447, 733-1, image 112; J.D. McLean to R.S. McKenzie, 27 July 1914, LAC, IA, RG 10, volume 3178, file 447, 733-1, image 113.
48 Chief Redsky to R.S. McKenzie, 19 December 1918, LAC, RG 10 volume 3178, file 447, 733-1, image 138.
49 See Brittany Luby, *Damned: The Politics of Loss and Survival in Anishinaabe Territory* (Winnipeg: University of Manitoba Press, 2020).
50 Shoal Lake Watershed Working Group, "Shoal Lake Watershed Management Plan," 21 April 2002; http://www.mhs.mb.ca/docs/sites/gwwdstation.shtml, accessed 9 February 2020.
51 Some of this is dealt with in Perry, *Aqueduct*, and Rick Harp's preface.
52 See Jon Thompson, "What Freedom Road can Teach Ontario about Partnering with Indigenous Communities," 24 June 2019, accessed at https://www.tvo.org/article/what-freedom-road-can-teach-ontario-about-partnering-with-indigenous-communities.
53 Shiri Pasternak, *Grounded Authority: The Algonquins of Barriere Lake Against the State* (Minneapolis: University of Minnesota Press, 2017), 55.
54 Darlene Johnson, *The Taking of Indian Lands: Consent or Coercion?* (Saskatoon: Native Law Centre, 1989), 89.
55 Eberts, "Still Colonizing After All These Years," 147.
56 https://aptnnews.ca/2020/02/06/rcmp-locks-down-wetsuweten-territory-as-enforcement-of-injunction-begins/; https://aptnnews.ca/2019/01/08/14-arrested-as-rcmp-enforce-injunction-on-wetsuweten-territory/, both accessed 11 February 2020.

PART TWO

The Royal Society of Canada and Academic Writings

5

Three Fellows in Mi'kma'ki: The Power of the Avocational

John G. Reid

As Tamson Pietsch has shown, "settler universities" took a crucial role in creating narratives that normalized the experience of settler dominions.[1] Anglophone Canadian university historians of the late nineteenth and early twentieth centuries who were also fellows of the Royal Society of Canada (RSC) – such as George McKinnon Wrong, Adam Shortt, Chester Martin, and others – in their distinctive ways brought Canada inside an intellectual world that existed comfortably within a framework of imperial and settler societies.[2] Historical discourse, however, was not confined to university historians, any more than the RSC drew its members only from academic institutions. To demonstrate the widespread influence of avocational writers on matters bearing historically on Indigenous-settler relations, this essay will focus on the roles of three fellows of the RSC who lived and worked in Mi'kma'ki. None of the three were professional historians, nor were they primarily known for interventions on Indigenous matters, and yet each had a substantial constituency for broadly historical writing and a strong and characteristic perspective on Mi'kmaw-settler interactions. They exemplified the role of the RSC not just as an academic institution but also as a powerful network of writers who were invariably male and non-Indigenous.

The three fellows were of different generations, although overlapping with one another. George Patterson (1824–1897) was a Presbyterian minister and county historian of Pictou County. Patterson was also an amateur archaeologist, and he was elected to the Royal Society in 1889. Archibald MacMechan (1862–1933) was a literary scholar at Dalhousie University, elected to the Royal

Society in 1916. Well-known not only as a literary critic but also for his collection and narration of sea stories, MacMechan took a deep interest in Nova Scotia's British heritage, and it was from that perspective that his historical essays and his longer historical works such as *Red Snow on Grand Pré* (1931) took their tone. Thomas Head Raddall (1903–1994) was among Canada's best-known novelists of the twentieth century. Based in Liverpool, Nova Scotia, he was a rarity among Canadian writers in that from the age of thirty-five onwards he lived entirely by his pen. He was elected to the Royal Society in 1953. As well as being a writer primarily – though not exclusively – of novels that had historical settings and themes, Raddall wrote historical works of which the best known was *Halifax: Warden of the North* (1948). He was also, like Patterson, an amateur archaeologist, exploring Indigenous sites in Queens County. As well as being from different eras, the three fellows had distinct ways in which they engaged with their Mi'kmaw neighbours, and their areas of interest in the cultures and behaviours they attributed to Indigenous societies also differed. Yet all wrote history as an avocational pursuit, all had the ability to reach substantially wider audiences than academic historians could realistically aspire to attain, and all contributed to entrenching settler perceptions that Indigeneity presented an inherent contrast with the benefits of civilization that came with colonial settlement. Although membership in the Royal Society was not for any of them the sole validation for their influence, it did provide an important underscoring for their contentions. Each of the three offered an example of the power of avocational writing on the relationship between Mi'kmaw history and settler heritage, considered from a settler perspective.

George Patterson drew his intellectual formation from the Scottish Enlightenment, through both family association and formal schooling. Of the three fellows, he was the one who struggled the most strenuously with the nature of Indigenous resistance to colonial settlement, in that he attempted to reconcile settler traditions of armed Mi'kmaw defiance with others that recounted Mi'kmaw assistance to hard-pressed colonists. Patterson also knew Mi'kmaw individuals and drew upon their historical knowledge for both his historical and archaeological works. Yet when he described current Mi'kmaq in 1877 as "the decaying remnant of the Micmac tribe," he was following closely the understandings derived from earlier generations of Presbyterian settler ministers in Mi'kma'ki.[3] The Seceder minister

James Drummond MacGregor was Patterson's grandfather and the subject of an extended memoir published by Patterson in 1859. MacGregor served, from 1786 until his death in 1830, from a base in Pictou – though he travelled widely in Mi'kma'ki and the neighbouring territory of the Wolastoqiyik. He had been an early and outspoken opponent of African slavery, and in the memoir Patterson reproduced in full his grandfather's "A Letter to a Clergyman, Urging Him to Set Free a Black Girl He Held in Slavery" (1788), thus self-consciously placing himself in a humanitarian tradition.[4] Yet, while MacGregor, like his grandson, had personal knowledge of Mi'kmaw neighbours and was described by one of them as "a very good man," he was also convinced that the key to environmental and cultural progress was through the civilizing influence of settlement.[5] Patterson must have had only fleeting childhood memories of MacGregor, but as a young adult he had an extended association with Thomas McCulloch, Seceder minister in Pictou from 1803, founder of Pictou Academy, and later president of Dalhousie College – at both of which institutions Patterson studied with him. McCulloch too was deeply influenced by stadial theories that underpinned the notion of inevitable Indigenous societal decline in the context of settlement.[6] Patterson himself went on to study at the University of Edinburgh, after spending some three years as a newspaper editor in Pictou, and then returned to begin his ministerial career in the Pictou County village of Greenhill in 1849.[7]

In later life, Patterson became best known for his published writing, much of which was either theological or focused on laudatory biographies of ministers and missionaries. However, his interest in local history, including Indigenous-settler interactions, was most fully expressed in his history of Pictou County, first published in 1877, followed by a number of subsequent printings. The early chapter on "Pictou in the Prehistoric Period" was informed both by Patterson's own archaeological explorations – an interest that was to develop further in later years – and by drawing on the work of the Baptist missionary Silas Tertius Rand.[8] According to Patterson, this early era was recalled by later Mi'kmaq as "the golden age of their race. Then they held undisputed possession of all these regions, and were a terror to surrounding tribes."[9] As British settlement in the Pictou area came initially through a small number of New Englanders during the 1760s and then extended to Highland Scots in the following decade, tensions arose. Patterson quoted extensively from a correspondent of an earlier Pictou newspaper, who was known only by the pen name of "Philo Antiquarius":

> They [the settlers] were constrained to submit to many indignities from the aborigines, who viewed their operations with no friendly eye. These considered the settlers as usurpers of their undoubted property; and it required not a moderate portion of skill on the part of the civilized to gain the good-will of the savage, nor inconsiderable prudence to establish this amicableness when formed.[10]

Patterson himself also maintained an ambivalent view of Indigenous threat and Indigenous coexistence intermittently throughout the book. Although the Scots from the famous migrant vessel the *Hector* were met in 1773, he noted, by the "threats of the Indians," nevertheless "the Indians, as soon as the mutual terror had subsided, treated them with much kindness":

> The Indians were indeed sometimes disposed to make use of the terror which they knew their name and appearance inspired, particularly among the weaker sex, to secure their object; but it is due to that unhappy race to say, that from the time of the arrival of the Hector, they never gave the settlers any serious molestation, and generally showed them real kindness, which, when the tables were turned, so that the whites had plenty and they were needy, has not always been reciprocated.[11]

Patterson returned to this theme in a later passage dealing with the early nineteenth century, noting that "when we consider the manner in which they were deprived of their lands, and the unfeeling manner in which they have often been treated, it is wonderful that they have been so quiet and free from deeds of violence."[12] Yet the other side of his quandary was never far away, whether expressed in the unquestioning assertion that the five-year-old son of a settler family had been "stolen by the Indians," or in the pessimism that suffused his final statement in the book about the Mi'kmaw population, which in Patterson's observation was beginning to revive in terms of numbers but was nevertheless resistant to abandoning its cultural integrity:

> It is just to add that the benevolent of this country, from Dr [James] McGregor downward, have been interested in the

improvement of their social and spiritual condition. On various occasions attempts were made to educate young Indians, but these failed, partly from their own repugnance to the restraints of civilized lives, and partly from the opposition of their spiritual guides. In the year 1828, a society was formed in Pictou, called the Indian Civilization Society. But all of these efforts produced no permanent result.[13]

In later life, George Patterson continued to be a productive author, but in his writings Indigenous and settler topics became separated. He apparently had some difficulty in gaining election to the RSC, but was eventually admitted with the help of the eminent geologist Sir William Dawson, his slightly older contemporary who also came from Pictou and likewise had studied at Pictou Academy. Patterson's Indigenous work now centred on archaeology rather than history – a distinction he himself made not only through a methodology based on material culture but also through repeated use of the term "prehistoric" – and in particular he explored sites at Merigomish, on the easterly coastline of Pictou County. Publishing a paper entitled "The Stone Age in Nova Scotia," as presented to the Nova Scotia Institute of Natural Science in 1889, Patterson also donated to Dalhousie College a collection of the artifacts he had accumulated over the years.[14] While the title of his paper no doubt reinforced stadial notions of Mi'kmaw cultural development, and while Patterson advanced the possibility that the artifacts indicated the presence of "a previous race," who "occupied the ground before the Micmacs," nevertheless the rigour of his work with shell middens became the basis for subsequent research by twentieth-century archaeologists and has prompted Michael Deal to designate Patterson as "Nova Scotia's first archaeologist."[15] Patterson's contributions to the *Proceedings and Transactions of the Royal Society of Canada*, meanwhile, were primarily historical. They included a paper in 1892 on "Sir William Alexander and the Scottish Attempt to Colonize Acadia," and another in 1894 on "Sable Island: Its History and Phenomena."[16] Neither dealt, other than tangentially in the paper on Alexander, with Indigenous inhabitants. Thus, Patterson's interpretive comments on settler-Mi'kmaw interactions belonged primarily to *A History of the County of Pictou, Nova Scotia*, although his archaeological research was also important in its own right. He also sought out Mi'kmaw oral testimony, noting in the preface to the county history that in preparing the book he had "interrogated Micmacs," and in a letter of 1884 to his son he clearly continued to attach importance to "what I have been told by Old Indians."[17] Yet ultimately, Patterson was true to the conclusions already reached by MacGregor and McCulloch, that the Mi'kmaq were a people in decay, and that the path of "civilization" – despite "their own repugnance" – remained essential for this "unhappy race."

Archibald MacMechan was some thirty-eight years younger than Patterson, although it is likely that they knew one another, if only through their common membership in the Nova Scotia Historical Society, which MacMechan joined soon after arriving in Halifax in 1889 as professor of English at Dalhousie University.[18] Then aged thirty-seven, MacMechan had been a high-school teacher in Ontario following graduation from the University of Toronto, but came to Dalhousie immediately after obtaining his doctorate in philology from Johns Hopkins University.[19] Of the three fellows, MacMechan was distinctive in two important respects. He alone was a university scholar, though not trained as a historian. Secondly, he had much more limited contact with living Mi'kmaw people than did either Patterson or Raddall. Halifax-based and living within walking distance of the Dalhousie campus, MacMechan's principal impression of the Mi'kmaq of his own time seems to have come from "the sight of the stolid, brown-faced Micmacs in the market nowadays with their baskets and other wares," or the tendentious perception of "the Indian of today ... [as] a squalid, pitiable object."[20] However, as with Patterson and Raddall, MacMechan took an intense and extended interest in Nova Scotia's past. During his early years in Halifax, he presented a series of papers to the historical society, and also published two detailed scholarly editions of documents relating to the British regime at Annapolis Royal during the era following the Treaty of Utrecht.[21] Mistrustful of any historical scholarship that he regarded as dry and sterile, and an admirer of Francis Parkman's vivid portrayals of eighteenth-century North America, MacMechan favoured narratives that were characterized by imagination as much as by enquiry. As Janet Baker has pointed out, his scholarly sensibility was matched by his belief in "the animating spirit of an author."[22]

Thus, MacMechan himself declared in 1913, as quoted by Baker:

> History should not be regarded simply as so many learned, scientific tomes, made for a few scholars: it should exist as a

sentiment, a feeling. Our young Canadians may not know a single date accurately, they may not be able to pass even a high school examination in the facts of our history. I should not care a rush, if only the name Quebec awakens in their minds the thought of Champlain and Wolfe, if they cannot see the words Queenston and Chateauguay without remembering that a country's a thing men should die for at need. Therefore there can-not be too much popularization of Canadian history.[23]

For MacMechan, therefore, history was primarily an expression of heritage, and the heritage that mattered was that of Canada as a British creation. In that sense, MacMechan – as might be inferred from the shaping of his thought at the high point of imperialism among English-Canadian intellectuals – had a greater preoccupation with empire than did either Patterson or Raddall, and yet for him colonial settlement was also a critically important element of imperial expansion.[24] As indicated by his juxtaposition of the names of Champlain and Wolfe, he considered the French regime in Quebec to form an important element of Canadian history, although one brought to a salutary ending in 1759–60. Indigenous inhabitants, however, fell into an entirely different category, as violent and destructive obstacles to the attainment of the benefits of settler colonization.

This theme first came out in its full clarity in 1914 from the stark language used in MacMechan's contribution to a multi-volume history of *Canada and its Provinces* co-edited between 1913 and 1917 by Adam Shortt and Arthur G. Doughty, the dominion archivist. Volume XIII dealt with "The Atlantic Provinces," meaning at the time the Maritimes.[25] MacMechan wrote the two chapters on Nova Scotia, while W.O. Raymond contributed the two on New Brunswick and Sir Andrew MacPhail the single chapter on Prince Edward Island. MacMechan's chapters were broken at 1775, and in the second of them (going up to 1867) Indigenous history had only tangential mentions. In the first of his chapters, Mi'kmaw references began primarily with the establishment of Halifax and, soon after, Lunenburg as settler centres. In Halifax, the many problems encountered included "the hostility of the Indians. No man's life was safe outside the pickets. In spite of a guard of sixty men Dartmouth was attacked and settlers killed and scalped. Parties cutting firewood on the Basin required armed protection; and a corps of rangers recruited from New England's Indian fighters were constantly scouring the woods."[26] Stirred up by the "complete ascendancy" of a "turbulent priest," the French missionary Jean-Louis Le Loutre, MacMechan declared, "many were the massacres in the early days and deep the terror caused by them."[27] At Lunenburg, matters were just as dire, as "hapless women and children [were] cut off in the lonely clearings, killed and scalped. Without the slightest warning, a war-party would emerge from the leafy mystery of the forest, shoot, knife, tomahawk and burn, and then disappear again into the woods as silently as beasts of prey."[28] Only with what MacMechan portrayed as "the submission of the Indians" at "a grand powwow in the governor's garden in 1761" – the concluding of the treaties of 1760–61 – was "the long story of savage warfare, murders, scalpings, captures in Nova Scotia brought to a close."[29]

Thus – whether with learned allusion, as to Henry II's attributed description of Becket, or with the repeated use of imagery that cast Mi'kmaw forces as brutal and inhuman – MacMechan employed the dexterity of the skilled essayist in presenting and normalizing a crudely simplistic vision of a complex history. A much later work, *Red Snow on Grand Pré*, devoted an entire chapter to "the Indian terror." Although reporting briefly and without comment on a conversation in which "the Indians" had denounced "both French and English for encroaching on the liberties of the natives of America," adjectives and analogies again told the story, referring demeaningly to Indigenous women and, at Quebec, to "canoes filled with Indian warriors, their faces hideously streaked with vermilion, black and yellow. Cape Diamond echoed to their piercing, wild-beast yelps and screeches."[30] And in early Halifax, imperial ambitions were again impeded by "codeless savages."[31] The preface to *Red Snow on Grand Pré* made it clear that the book was not deeply researched, with some printed documents consulted as well as Beamish Murdoch's *A History of Nova-Scotia, or Acadie*.[32] "Episodes in the long series of Indian outrages are recorded in Murdoch and elsewhere," MacMechan wrote; "[m]y task has been to assemble them in order and relate them to the history of the province."[33]

MacMechan's portrayal of violent and gratuitous Mi'kmaw obstruction of colonial settlement was inseparable from his commitment to an imperial heritage. Significantly, *Red Snow on Grand Pré* was dedicated fulsomely to his friend of long standing Dugald Macgillivray, a prominent Halifax banker who was a donor to Dalhousie University and also a tireless advocate of the public celebration of the empire. In 1933, MacMechan presented Macgillivray for the honorary degree of Doctor of Laws from Dalhousie University – a degree which MacMechan himself received at the same ceremony, as did Judge George Geddie Patterson, the son of Rev. George Patterson.[34] The citation recounted Macgillivray's involvement in the raising of the Halifax Memorial Tower, celebrating the 250th anniversary of the Nova Scotia legislature, and went on to note that "to him the city owes the monuments to [Robert] Burns, [Sir Walter] Scott, to [Edward] Cornwallis, and our own founder [the Earl of] Dalhousie. These are not only adornments to the city of Halifax; they are national assets; they are additions to the aesthetic riches of Canada; and they are due to the initiative, energy and vision of Dugald Macgillivray."[35] The raising of the statue of Governor Edward Cornwallis in Halifax carried especial meaning for MacMechan, who in earlier years had conducted an extensive though unsuccessful correspondence in an effort to locate an accurate portrait painting of Nova Scotia's first Halifax-based governor.[36]

As plans for the Cornwallis statue emerged during the late 1920s – it was eventually unveiled in 1931 – MacMechan contributed an essay to the *Dalhousie Review* that praised Cornwallis as the founder of Halifax and also delivered brief though pointed remarks on Mi'kmaw resistance. The broader theme was set out at the beginning as the heritage of which Cornwallis provided a meritorious example: "men of English blood all the world over are accustomed to feel and give voice to a just pride in the achievements of their race, as a colonizing power, wherever ship could sail."[37] Macgillivray, conversely and unsurprisingly, was also an admirer of MacMechan's work, and wrote to him in December 1931 with congratulations on the Royal Society of Canada's award to MacMechan of the Lorne Pierce Medal, for literary achievement.[38] MacMechan had been a fellow of the Royal Society since 1916, although Duncan Campbell Scott as honorary secretary had taken a jaundiced view of his disinclination or inability to attend the 1916 annual meeting: "we rather make it a point that immediately after election the new Fellow should come to be introduced to the Society, which is considered an important incident and part of the regulations. However, if you find it impossible to come, we can only look forward to your presence at the next meeting."[39] Even so, just as Scott had written to MacMechan years earlier – on Department of Indian Affairs letterhead – to congratulate him on his essay collection, *The Porter of Bagdad and Other Fantasies*, so MacMechan continued to be recognized as among Canada's leading essayists, literary critics, and scholar-teachers.[40] Yet, in capacities including his membership of the Royal Society, he had also contributed powerfully to historical narratives that contrasted a supposed Indigenous savagery with the benignity of empire and colonization.

Thomas Head Raddall, some forty-one years younger, never formally met MacMechan, but in 1947 he put together a posthumous collection of MacMechan's *Tales of the Sea*, and contributed a foreword. MacMechan had been well known for being a habitual urban walker, and Raddall wrote that "my memory of him is confined to a few glimpses of an erect and dignified figure with a grey torpedo beard, walking the streets of Halifax in a curious aloof way as if he had them all to himself."[41] Raddall himself, after his family had moved from England in 1913, lived in Halifax as a youth, including experiencing the 1917 Explosion, and he remained a regular visitor to the city. However, he lived most of his adult life in Queens County, first in the rural community of Milton and subsequently in Liverpool. Employed initially as a book-keeper, he then became a full-time writer in 1938. From 1923, when he moved to Milton, Raddall travelled extensively throughout the interior areas of Queens County. Soon afterwards, he developed an interest in Mi'kmaw place names, and then (as recorded in his memoirs) began:

> [a] ... long and interesting friendship ... when I found a band of Micmac Indians living a short distance through the woods from Cowies Falls. One or two of their men laboured in the mill there, but the rest would work only as guides to hunters and fishermen. Their women made baskets for sale in Milton and Liverpool. All spoke English well but they used their own language in the home, and the older ones knew much lore of their people. At first I was interested in the meaning of Indian place-names on our timber cruiser's maps. As time went by I found their whole knowledge fascinating, and for better understanding I learned a smattering of their language.[42]

For Raddall, personal knowledge of Mi'kmaw people of his own time was a point of pride. He later recalled that loggers employed by the mill where he worked had failed to understand that the reason

Mi'kmaq, in the vicinity of the site known as Indian Gardens, upriver from Milton, had tried to dissuade them from cutting timber in the area was because it was a burial site: "I did not realize myself, until I learned more of the language, that the Indians just wanted to keep white intruders from tramping over the ashes of their forefathers."[43] Raddall continued to draw upon local Indigenous knowledge, recording for example a conversation in 1933 with "two old Micmac men at Broad River," whom he named as William Benoit Paul and Mike McCooney, as well as with McCooney's wife, who though in poor health was "highly intelligent, with a remarkable memory for Indian names and legends. When the two old men were at a loss for a name or a meaning, they often referred to her."[44]

Also beginning in the 1920s, Raddall developed a lifelong interest in Mi'kmaw archaeology. His employer in Milton, the Macleod Pulp and Paper Company, had constructed a small reservoir dam in the area of Indian Gardens in 1904, which at the time had resulted in flagrant desecration of recent burials.[45] A much larger project in 1928 was the nearby construction of a hydro-electric dam, which flooded the Indian Gardens site. Raddall and others began collections of Indigenous artifacts that had been washed down from upstream, raising for the later archaeologist John Erskine important though – given the lack of context – unanswerable questions as to the nature of the culture Erskine defined as "Late Micmac, 1400–1500."[46] Raddall's attention, however, now turned to a coastal site at Port Joli, some 25 kilometres southwest of where he was now living in Liverpool, that he heard about in 1935 from a local United Church minister. Over repeated visits with family and friends, Raddall explored a series of shell middens, recovering pottery fragments, a variety of other artifacts, and bird and animal bones. In an unpublished paper in which he described and mapped the findings, he cited the earlier work at other shell midden sites of William J. Wintemberg of the National Museum of Canada, who had been one of the professional archaeologists who had followed up on Patterson's work at Merigomish.[47] Thus, the artifact collection by Raddall had at least an indirect connection with Patterson's earlier research.

Raddall's personal interactions with Mi'kmaw neighbours and his encounters with Mi'kmaw material culture of an earlier time formed for him a starting point for his later written accounts of Indigenous topics in historical novels and non-fiction works. The novels had many Mi'kmaw characters and some Wolastoqiyik. Raddall recognized in the plotlines of key novels such as *His Majesty's Yankees* and *Roger Sudden* the military ascendancy of Indigenous forces during conflicts that accompanied British attempts to settle Mi'kma'ki prior to the treaty-making of 1760–61. He depicted ranger forces as "pitiless" scalp-hunters, and was open to portraying a verbal humiliation of the ranger leader Joseph Goreham by the Wolastoqiyik chief, Ambroise Saint-Aubin as "the most crushing rebuke ever given by a so-called savage to a white man." Nevertheless, in the novels cruelty and greed repeatedly characterized Indigenous behaviour.[48] Whether through differentiation by repeated references to brown skin colour, evocations of "blood-freezing howls," or a scene involving the main character being tortured by Mi'kmaw, readers were left in no doubt that "the savages" – even though easily manipulated by the French, and especially by Le Loutre – were inherently volatile and violent.[49]

Raddall's major work of historical writing, *Halifax: Warden of the North* (1948), had many of the same ingredients, at least during the eras leading up to the end of the American Revolutionary War, following which the Indigenous presence was absent from the narrative. Indeed, the idea for the book had arisen in part from the research Raddall had already conducted for the novels.[50] While Raddall included a substantial bibliography, he also insisted in the book's preface that "it is not a history" – which, he believed, would have required multiple volumes – but rather "a single readable book based on selective research."[51] The title came from Rudyard Kipling's 1893 poem, "The Song of the Cities," which offered a tour of the most strategically important urban centres of the British Empire and defined Halifax as "The Warden of the Honour of the North."[52] The first sentence of Raddall's text, which introduced a brief chapter on Indigenous history and related elements of French imperial history to 1713, set a pervasive tone: "The first inhabitants were a savage folk who called themselves *Meeg-a-maage*, a name which the English twisted first into Mickamuck and finally into Micmac." And "savages" the Mi'kmaq remained for the ensuing one hundred pages, or in one place "children of the forest."[53] The decision on terminology was a conscious one. A typescript draft of the book had opened with the statement that: "The first inhabitants were a wandering people," but with the last two words crossed out and replaced in handwritten form by "savage folk."[54] It was not as if an alternative language was unavailable, as more than a decade had passed since the New Brunswick Museum had published A.G. Bailey's *The*

Conflict of European and Eastern Algonkian Cultures, 1504–1700: A Study in Canadian Civilization. Owing to financial constraints, the conclusion to Bailey's study had been published subsequently as an article and, while deeply pessimistic about the eventual results for Indigenous societies, he had attributed the entire process squarely to "European invasion."[55]

Bailey and Raddall had certain similarities in biographical details. Born less than two years apart – Bailey was slightly younger – both gained election to the Royal Society of Canada in the early 1950s, Bailey in 1951 and Raddall in 1953. They must undoubtedly have met, perhaps to discuss Bailey's poetry as well as Raddall's novels, although within the Royal Society it was Hugh MacLennan with whom Raddall seems to have established a close and sympathetic relationship. Raddall's citation had been presented to the Royal Society by Queen's University historian A.R.M. Lower, who had praised *Halifax, Warden of the North* as "audacious, revealing and interesting," although in later years there would be times when Raddall shared with MacLennan a deep skepticism of academic commentaries on their books.[56] Raddall had one more substantial historical work to write, and in 1958 *The Path of Destiny: Canada from the British Conquest to Home Rule, 1763–1850* – the third volume of the Canadian History Series of his publisher, Doubleday – earned him his third Governor-General's Award.[57] In *The Path of Destiny*, Indigenous history appeared infrequently and when it did the heavily-fraught language of *Halifax: Warden of the North* was absent on most (though not all) occasions, perhaps because Indigenous forces appeared as British allies in the American Revolutionary War and especially in the War of 1812. In none of Raddall's works was there a full resolution of the paradox by which his Indigenous portrayals for the eighteenth century emphasized purportedly savage characteristics of the forebears by only a few generations of Mi'kmaq whom he counted as friends. Yet, of the many ways in which he could have closed his book of memoirs, his choice was a quotation in Mi'kmaw: "And now there is nothing more to say except the familiar phrase of my old Micmac friends when talking of things past: *Kes-pe-ah-dook-sit* – 'Here the story ends.'"[58]

Despite the differences among them, the three fellows all wrote history as an avocational pursuit. Two of the three had contacts with living Mi'kmaq that went beyond cursory encounters and influenced their view of the past. Yet none could find their way past depicting the history of colonial settlement in terms that juxtaposed notions of civilization and savagery. Savagery could, of course, be understood in more than one sense, although none of the three offered definitions governing their use of the term. Living in the woods was one portrayed characteristic that was significant to each author. "The forest sheltered them from the storm, and skins of animals afforded the warmest coverings by night and by day," wrote Patterson of "the savage life" before European contact.[59] In a similar context, both MacMechan and Raddall imagined Indigenous diplomats as child-like. According to MacMechan, for the Wolastoqiyik negotiators who met Cornwallis on board a British warship in 1749, "it was probably the first time these children of the forest had set foot in such a big canoe," while Raddall's use of the same phrase came in the context of conferences of the 1760s with Nova Scotia's lieutenant governor.[60] However, "terror" was a descriptor used by all of the authors regarding the impression made on settlers by the Indigenous presence, and both MacMechan and Raddall used imageries of violence even when there was no compelling linkage with their main subject material. When MacMechan, for example, took issue in 1906 with destructive literary reviews, the metaphor that came to mind was "the literary tomahawk and scalping-knife."[61] And when Raddall gave a television talk in 1958 on the 200th anniversary of the Nova Scotia legislature, he began by displaying "a tomahawk and a knife":

> Nasty looking things, aren't they? I found the tomahawk blade in an old Indian camp site on the Mersey River, and got one of my Micmac friends to re-haft it for me. This other thing is what we call a crooked-knife. A lot of our Indians and woodsmen in western Nova Scotia still use them in hunting. It's modelled after the ancient Micmac scalping knife.

Both Mi'kmaq, and Acadians who had evaded deportation, it seemed, "made life dangerous" in the era of the first assembly, and only with the 1761 ceremony at the governor's farm was "the reign of terror ... over at last."[62]

Of course, the idea that colonial settlement was a peaceful and benign process of civilization, and that Indigenous terror and savagery represented its antithesis was not unique to the three fellows. Nor was it propagated by them in identical or consistent ways. Patterson offered significant qualification to the formula, although still believing that civilization in the European sense must prevail. MacMechan was animated by an absorption with Canada's imperial heritage, while Raddall made a deep though implicit distinction between Mi'kmaq of the eighteenth and the twentieth centuries. For all of them, writing history was an adjunct to, respectively, religious ministry and writing, literary criticism and essay-writing, and writing fiction that was often historical in subject material but by definition a product of creative imagination. None of their historical contentions were interpretively original, and in general they reflected ideas that had wide currency in settler society. But all were highly articulate and highly literate, and membership of the Royal Society of Canada gave them access not only to a powerfully all-male and all-settler intellectual establishment but also to a platform from which their statements carried the weight of authority. Avocational as their historical writings were, they reached wide audiences and contributed notably to the entrenchment and normalization of the narrative by which colonial settlement was central and Indigenous history peripheral. Even in the twenty-first century, as efforts to restore balance to heritage commemorative patterns in Mi'kma'ki recurrently attracted accusations of erasing or falsifying a settled view of history, the influence of that normalization was felt time and time again.[63]

NOTES

For valuable comments on earlier versions of this essay, I am very grateful to the co-editors of the volume as well as to Adele Perry and Jim Walker, the assigned readers from within the project team.

1 Tamson Pietsch, *Empire of Scholars: Universities, Networks and the British Academic World, 1850–1939* (Manchester: Manchester University Press, 2013), 2–4.
2 On these and other scholars, see Carl Berger, *The Writing of Canadian History: Aspects of English-Canadian Historical Writing: 1900 to 1970* (Toronto: Oxford University Press, 1976), esp. 1–53.
3 George Patterson, *History of the County of Pictou* (Montreal: Dawson Brothers, 1877), 28.
4 George Patterson, *A Few Remains of the Rev. James MacGregor, D.D.* (Edinburgh: William Oliphant & Co., 1859); the "Letter to a Clergyman" is on 169–88. On MacGregor's opposition to slavery, see also Barry Cahill, "The

Antislavery Polemic of the Reverend James MacGregor: Canada's Proto-Abolitionist as 'Radical Evangelical,'" in *The Contribution of Presbyterianism to the Maritime Provinces of Canada*, eds. Charles H.H. Scobie and G.A. Rawlyk (Montreal and Kingston: McGill-Queen's University Press, 1997), 131–43; and for an authoritative biography covering this and other elements of MacGregor's career, Alan Wilson, *Highland Shepherd: James MacGregor, Father of the Scottish Enlightenment in Nova Scotia* (Toronto: University of Toronto Press, 2015).

5 See John G. Reid, "Scots, Settler Colonization and Indigenous Displacement: Mi'kma'ki, 1770–1820, in Comparative Context," *Journal of Scottish Historical Studies*, 38:1 (2018):190–2. The quotation is from "Biography of Peter Paul – Written February 16th, 1865, from his own Statement by an Amanuensis," unattributed newspaper clipping, "Scrapbook of Dr George Patterson on Indians," Nova Scotia Archives (hereafter NSA), MG9, vol. 5.

6 Reid, "Scots, Settler Colonization and Indigenous Displacement," 190.

7 For biographical details, see Allan C. Dunlop, "George Patterson," *Dictionary of Canadian Biography*, http://www.biographi.ca/en/bio/patterson_george_12E.html, accessed 31 May 2019.

8 See Judith Fingard, "Silas Tertius Rand," *Dictionary of Canadian Biography*, http://www.biographi.ca/en/bio/rand_silas_tertius_11E.html, accessed 31 May 2019. A number of extracts from Rand's writings were collected by Patterson in "Scrapbook of Dr George Patterson on Indians," NSA, MG9, vol. 5.

9 Patterson, *History of the County of Pictou*, 29.

10 Ibid., 62–3; for Patterson's acknowledgment to "Philo Antiquarius," see iii.

11 Ibid., 81, 92.

12 Ibid., 185.

13 Ibid., 131, 193. The reference to "spiritual guides" is presumably to Roman Catholic clergy.

14 George Patterson, "The Stone Age in Nova Scotia, as Illustrated by a Collection of Relics Presented to Dalhousie College," *Transactions of the Nova Scotia Institute of Natural Science*, 8:3 (1888–89): 231–52. The collection apparently disappeared from Dalhousie sometime during the 1920s. See Michael Deal, "George Patterson: Nova Scotia's First Archaeologist," unpublished paper, 7. I am very grateful to Michael Vance for drawing my attention to this important paper, and to Michael Deal for allowing me to consult it. For Patterson's use of the term "prehistoric," see "The Stone Age in Nova Scotia," 231, 252.

15 Patterson, "The Stone Age in Nova Scotia," 236–7; Deal, "George Patterson." See also Michelle LeLièvre, *Unsettling Mobility: Mediating Mi'kmaw Sovereignty in Post-contact Nova Scotia* (Tucson: University of Arizona Press, 2017), 88.
16 George Patterson, "Sir William Alexander and the Scottish Attempt to Colonize Acadia," *Proceedings and Transactions of the Royal Society of Canada*, 1st series, 10 (1892), section 2: 79–107; Patterson, "Sable Island: Its History and Phenomena," *Proceedings and Transactions of the Royal Society of Canada*, 1st series, 12 (1894), section 2: 3–49.
17 Patterson, *History of the County of Pictou*, iii; George Patterson to George Patterson Jnr, 17 April 1884, NSA, George Patterson fonds, MG1, vol. 745, No. 50.
18 Janet E. Baker, *Archibald MacMechan: Canadian Man of Letters* (Lockeport, NS: Roseway Publishing, 2000), 174.
19 Janet E. Baker, "Archibald McKellar MacMechan," *Dictionary of Canadian Biography*, http://www.biographi.ca/en/bio/macmechan_archibald_mckellar_16E.html, accessed 2 June 2019.
20 Archibald MacMechan, *Red Snow on Grand Pré* (Toronto: McClelland and Stewart, 1931), 160, 170.
21 Archibald M. MacMechan, ed., *Nova Scotia Archives, II: A Calendar of Two Letter-Books and One Commission-Book in the Possession of the Government of Nova Scotia, 1713–1741* (Halifax: [Herald Printing House], 1900); MacMechan, *Nova Scotia Archives, III: The Original Minutes of His Majesty's Council at Annapolis, 1720–1739* (Halifax: McAlpine Publishing Co., 1908). For the papers presented to the Nova Scotia Historical Society, see Baker, *Archibald MacMechan*, 202, note 11.
22 Ibid., 178.
23 MacMechan, "The Dean's Window," *The Standard* (Montreal), 27 September 1913, quoted in Baker, *Archibald MacMechan*, 178–9.
24 See Carl Berger, *The Sense of Power: Studies in the Ideas of Canadian Imperialism, 1867–1914* (Toronto: University of Toronto Press, 1971).
25 Adam Shortt and Arthur G. Doughty, eds., *Canada and its Provinces: A History of the Canadian People and their Institutions by One Hundred Associates*, 23 vols. (Toronto: Edinburgh University Press, 1913–17), XIII, *Atlantic Provinces*, 1914.
26 Archibald MacMechan, "Nova Scotia under English Rule, 1713–1775," in *Canada and its Provinces*, eds. Shortt and Doughty, XIII, 83.
27 Ibid., 91–2.

28 Ibid., 98. The image of "the Indian" as "a dangerous wild beast" also appeared in MacMechan, *Red Snow on Grand Pré*, 170.
29 MacMechan, "Nova Scotia under English Rule," 108–9.
30 MacMechan, *Red Snow on Grand Pré*, 106, 122.
31 Ibid., 170.
32 Beamish Murdoch, *A History of Nova-Scotia, or Acadie*, 3 vols. (Halifax: J.Barnes, 1865–7); see also M. Brook Taylor, *Promoters, Patriots, and Partisans: Historiography in Nineteenth-Century English Canada* (Toronto: University of Toronto Press, 1989), esp. 192–6.
33 MacMechan, *Red Snow on Grand Pré*, 7–8.
34 See Dalhousie University, "1892–1999 Honorary Degree Recipients," https://www.dal.ca/academics/convocation/history_traditions/honorary_degree_recipients/hon_degree_1892_1999.html, accessed 2 June 2019. For an important discussion that distinguishes the roles of the Pattersons, father and son, on Indigenous matters, see Michael E. Vance, "The Mi'kmaq, the Pattersons and Remembering the Scottish Colonisation of Nova Scotia," in *Reappraisals of British Colonisation in Atlantic Canada, 1700-1930*, eds. S. Karly Kehoe and Michael E. Vance (Edinburgh: Edinburgh University Press, 2020), 171–89.
35 Citation of Dugald Macgillivray, [1933], Archibald MacMechan fonds, Dalhousie University Archives, MS-2-82, box 29, folder 40. On the Halifax Memorial Tower, see also Paul Williams, "Erecting 'an instructive object'": The Case of the Halifax Memorial Tower, *Acadiensis*, 36:2 (Spring 2007): 91–112.
36 Beginning in 1897 and continuing intermittently to 1913, the correspondence is in Archibald MacMechan fonds, box 36, folder 1.
37 Archibald MacMechan, "Ab Urbe Condita," *Dalhousie Review*, 7:2 (Spring 1927): 199–210; quotation from 199. For a more extended consideration of the Cornwallis celebration and of subsequent controversies over Cornwallis's issuance of a scalp and prisoner proclamation aimed at Mi'kmaw people, see John G. Reid, "The Three Lives of Edward Cornwallis, *Royal Nova Scotia Historical Society Journal*, 16 (2013): 27–33.
38 Macgillivray to MacMechan, 12 December 1931, Archibald MacMechan fonds, box 10, folder 107.
39 Duncan C. Scott to MacMechan, 1 May 1916, Archibald MacMechan fonds, box 14, folder 48.
40 Duncan C. Scott to MacMechan, 20 May 1907, Archibald MacMechan fonds, box 14, folder 48. The book had been published in 1901: Archibald MacMechan, *The Porter of Bagdad and Other Fantasies* (Toronto: George

N. Morang & Co., 1901). See Carl F. Klinck and Alfred Goldsworthy Bailey, eds., *Literary History of Canada: Canadian Literature in English* (Toronto: University of Toronto Press, 1965), 341–2; Peter Waite, *The Lives of Dalhousie University, Volume One, 1818–1925: Lord Dalhousie's College* (Montreal and Kingston: McGill-Queen's University Press, 1994), 159–62.

41 Archibald MacMechan, *Tales of the Sea* (Toronto: McClelland and Stewart, 1947), foreword by Thomas Raddall, vii.

42 Thomas H. Raddall, *In My Time: A Memoir* (Toronto: McClelland and Stewart, 1976), 130–1. Raddall also recalled his early interest in place names in an article contributed in 1974 to a magazine produced at Liverpool Regional High School: Raddall, "Groundwork and Guesswork," Thomas Head Raddall fonds, Dalhousie University Archives, MS-2-202, box 7, folder 5.

43 Raddall, *In My Time*, 131–2. Raddall returned on subsequent occasions to this subject, as in "The Indian Devil," Radio Talk, 22 July 1945, Thomas Head Raddall fonds, box 50, folder 4.

44 "Information Given to T.H. Raddall in August 1933," Thomas Head Raddall fonds, box 31, folder 3.

45 [J.R. Erskine], "Micmac Notes, 1957," Thomas Head Raddall fonds, box 31, folder 3. John Erskine was "a botanist and avocational archaeologist with the Nova Scotia Museum"; Deal, "George Patterson: Nova Scotia's First Archaeologist," 9.

46 [Erskine], "Micmac Notes, 1957," Thomas Head Raddall fonds, box 31, folder 3; [Erskine], "Micmac Notes, 1958," Thomas Head Raddall fonds, box 31, folder 3. On Raddall's collection and the role of Erskine, see also Benjamin C. Pentz, "A River Runs Through It: An Archaeological Survey of the Upper Mersey River and Allains River in Southwest Nova Scotia," MA thesis, (Memorial University of Newfoundland, 2008), 15–16.

47 Raddall, "Groundwork and Guesswork," Thomas Head Raddall fonds, Dalhousie University Archives, MS-2-202, box 7, folder 5; Raddall, "Indian Kitchen-Middens in Queens County," n.d., Thomas Head Raddall fonds, box 7, folder 1; Deal, "George Patterson," 8.

48 Thomas H. Raddall, *His Majesty's Yankees* (Garden City, NY: Doubleday, Doran and Company, Inc., 1943), 161–3. On Saint-Aubin and Gorham, see Richard I. Hunt, "Ambroise Saint-Aubin," *Dictionary of Canadian Biography*, http://www.biographi.ca/en/bio/saint_aubin_ambroise_4E.html, accessed 3 June 2019; David A. Charters with Stuart R.J. Sutherland, "Joseph Goreham," *Dictionary of Canadian Biography*,

http://www.biographi.ca/en/bio/goreham_joseph_4E.html, accessed 3 June 2019.
49 Thomas H. Raddall, *Roger Sudden* (Garden City, NY: Doubleday, Doran and Company, Inc., 1945), 140–1, 143–7, 178. For a valuable further discussion, see Ian McKay and Robin Bates, *In the Province of History: The Making of the Public Past in Twentieth Century Nova Scotia* (Montreal and Kingston: McGill-Queen's University Press, 2010), 216-17.
50 Thomas H. Raddall, *Halifax: Warden of the North* (Toronto: McClelland and Stewart, 1948), ix.
51 Ibid.
52 For a text and annotations of Kipling's poem, see http://www.kiplingsociety.co.uk/poems_song_cities.htm, accessed 3 June 2019. Archibald MacMechan had already used the phrase in its full form in a tourist booklet on Halifax that he had published in 1905 for the Intercolonial Railway and other railway companies: MacMechan, *Storied Halifax: "Warden of the Honour of the North"* (n.p.: Canadian Government Railways, [1905]).
53 Raddall, *Halifax: Warden of the North*, 1, 1–101 passim, 80.
54 Typescript draft, "Halifax: Warden of the North," Thomas Head Raddall fonds, box 8, folder 9.
55 Alfred Goldsworthy Bailey, *The Conflict of European and Eastern Algonkian Cultures, 1504–1700: A Study in Canadian Civilization* (Saint John: New Brunswick Museum, 1937); Bailey, "Social Revolution in Early Eastern Canada," *Canadian Historical Review*, 19:3 (September 1938): esp. 275.
56 Raddall, *In My Time*, 302–3, 319–21; quotation on 302.
57 Thomas H. Raddall, *The Path of Destiny: Canada from the British Conquest to Home Rule, 1763–1850* (Garden City, NY: Doubleday & Company, Inc., 1957); Raddall, *In My Time*, 334. The previous two awards had been for a short story collection, *The Pied Piper of Dipper Creek* (1943), and for *Halifax: Warden of the North*.
58 Raddall, *In My Time*, 365.
59 Patterson, *History of the County of Pictou*, 29.
60 MacMechan, "Ab Urbe Condita," 205; Raddall, *Halifax: Warden of the North*, 80.
61 MacMechan, "Book and Beaver," 7 March 1906, quoted in Baker, *Archibald MacMechan*, 99–100.
62 Raddall, "'Gazette': A Talk on the 200th Anniversary of Representative Government in N.S.," 2 October 1958, Thomas Head Raddall fonds, box 50, folder 4. In notes made in earlier years (they were filed with other notes dated in 1933), Raddall had not associated this kind of knife with

scalping, commenting only that "the knife was used in various ways on the hunt and in the camp." Raddall, "The Algonquin Crooked Knife," n.d., Thomas Head Raddall fonds, box 31, folder 3.
63 See Reid, "The Three Lives of Edward Cornwallis," 34–6.

6

"Not a little disappointment": Forging Postcolonial Academies from Emulation and Exclusion

Cynthia E. Milton

When the Royal Society of Canada received its charter in 1881, the Dominion of Canada was only fourteen years old, its creation and advancement closely entwined with that of the nascent country. Looking back upon the Royal Society of Canada's (RSC) first fifty years, Sir Robert Falconer, a member of this distinguished academic association, reflected upon this symbiotic relationship in a piece titled "The Intellectual Life of Canada as Reflected in its Royal Society." Published in the RSC's *Proceedings and Transactions* retrospective issue (1882–1932), Sir Falconer began his essay by considering broadly Canadian national life, attributing to it "moderate material returns, many difficult problems, and not a little disappointment." The disappointment it seems, came by way of comparison to French-Canadian national life, which he saw as having successfully "produced a distinctive culture," one that was "compactly domiciled in the valley of the Saint Lawrence, and unified by origin, aspirations, and homeland." From his perspective, Sir Falconer felt that English Canada did not yet possess a distinctive culture as a homeland but rather was still struggling to find "an abundant intellectual harvest," or its independent expression from Britain. He, like other Fellows of the Royal Society of Canada, tended to place the blame for the failure to produce an identifiable English Canadian "intellectual life" on the difficulties posed by geography and climate. Yet, when they tried to identify what made them unique from their colonial predecessor, the Royal Society of London, or the later British Academy, they insisted upon these inhospitable lands as providing the potential for their own distinct voice as a "new country."[1]

Lost in the debates of the first fifty years of the Royal Society of Canada was the role that Indigenous peoples and their knowledge played in the creation of the new country's intellectual life. While geography received "a good share of attention" and the presence of French Canadians as equal members within one national academy was touted as a unique feature of Canadian scholarship, Indigenous peoples and knowledge were not recognized as contributing to what made Canada different from Great Britain.[2] Yet, Indigenous peoples were not entirely absent from the RSC: the RSC fellowship drew upon Indigenous knowledge in their endeavours to create a distinctive national intellectual life.[3]

This chapter addresses this double postcolonial predicament in the first fifty years of the formation of the Royal Society of Canada as its members attempted to sow and reap their intellectual harvest. The first predicament was a tension between wanting to identify a national character of a national academy as uniquely Canadian and their tendency to fall into self-assessments based on European measurements. The tendency of the day was to look to British scholars, poets, and writers, and to see their former colonial selves as lacking in comparison, while wanting at the same time to break out from this colonialist mold. This predicament was shared by other former colonies, with the globalization of European thought and its resonance and reformulations at the colonial periphery. Indeed, these former colonial outposts participated in the network of the British academic world as part of what historian Tamson Pietsch has called an "empire of scholars."[4] Yet, what made this predicament colonial was not simply the relationship of English Canadians to Great Britain (and their desire to differentiate themselves while emulating British academia), but also their relationship to Indigenous peoples and knowledge. Just as settler colonialism is a process of dispossession of lands, so too it is of knowledge; both were central to Canada's state formation.[5] This second colonial predicament – the dispossession of knowledge – points to the marginalization of Indigenous-held wisdom, experience, practice, and culture, all the while RSC scholars refashioned this knowledge through appropriation into their settler research and writings. The tragic irony is that Indigenous knowledge as held by Indigenous peoples represented an important difference from the British academy, one that seemed to have gone unrecognized by the very members who wished to claim Canadian uniqueness.

In the early decades of the Royal Society of Canada, the lines between Canada's intellectuals and government were often blurred, contributing to a perception among the RSC fellows of their importance in guiding the young nation's formation. Indeed, the RSC not only had the ear of government, but among its members sat civil servants, ministers, senators, and lieutenant governors. Since the RSC's foundation in 1882 by the Governor General Marquis of Lorne, the fellows felt that as Canada's society of savants they were obliged to inform the government on how best to shape the new nation through scientific and cultural achievements. Their ambit was broad ranging from the fine-tuning of taxation to building foundational cultural symbols. Early on, for instance, fellows established in their charter missions the creation of a national museum to house the nation's cultural and historical treasures. Four decades later, the Society still maintained this elusive ambition, when the then president of the RSC reported at the annual general meeting of 1922 that while the prime minister was sympathetic, he did not consider the moment opportune for a museum. Undeterred, the fellows continued their conversation onto the potential for public buildings to promote civic duty, commending a new municipal building in Toronto as exemplary for its inscription: "Hail to the Pioneers, their homes and deeds; Remembered and forgotten we honor here."[6] Their praise for this building and its inscription in honour of early pioneers, who had expanded European presence on Indigenous lands, illustrates the RSC's settler ambitions for the young nation.

The Royal Society of Canada's *Proceedings and Transactions* offers a contained view of the RSC's formative years and history, as Ian Wereley similarly notes in his chapter here.[7] Each volume was divided into two sections. The first section, "Proceedings," contained meeting minutes, resolutions, membership updates, and reports from RSC subcommittees and other associated societies, such as the "Women's Canadian Historical Society" and the "Historical and Scientific Society of Manitoba." The second section, "Transactions," consisted of papers presented annually before the RSC's sections.[8]

The *Proceedings and Transactions* from 1922 seems a typical volume in its organizational structure, though the editors groaned at the increasing cost of publication as each year seemed to produce a lengthier tome, 1922 being a record year of 1,226 pages.[9] After the "Proceedings and General Business," the volume launches into a presidential address, this year Duncan Campbell Scott's "Poetry and Progress." Academic papers and reports follow from the five academies at the time: Sections I and II corresponding to the humanities and social sciences in French and English respectively, and Sections III, IV, and V to mathematics and sciences. The reports and papers from the latter three sections account for more than twice the first two sections: thus, much of the volume is dedicated to describing scientific advancements by its members and invited researchers, such as "Partial Oxidation of Methane in Natural Gas," "On Photo-Electric Conductivity of Diamond and Other Fluorescent Crystals" (by a Miss M. Levi), and "The Preparation of Dust-Free Liquids." The much smaller Sections I and II include French literature and reflections on the linguistic challenges faced by French Canadians, a biography to resurrect "from oblivion" the memory of a "forgotten Loyalist" of 1808, a study on Canadian economic history, and an essay on the colonial policies of the Dominion, among other contributions to the advancement of the humanities and social sciences in Canada.

That the hard sciences, social sciences, and the humanities – both in French and English – would appear bound together in one volume since the original publication of *Proceedings and Transactions* made the Royal Society of Canada stand out among national academies as a multi-academic and bilingual society. Almost all of the anglophone contributors who took the time to reflect back on the early decades of the RSC noted these special characteristics in advancing knowledge both nationally and internationally. Indeed, when Duncan Campbell Scott gave his presidential address in 1922, he remarked that the "two languages have equal recognition and *authority* in our literature sections ... It here represents not a division of race, but a union of nationality, and joins the company of intellectuals by the dual interests of the two great sections of our people" (emphasis in the original).[10] Furthermore, for Scott, it seemed somewhat unfathomable to separate literature and science for they shared the common pursuit of perfection, what he called "ideality": "the mental process by which a poet develops the germ of his poem and perfects it is analogous to the process by which a mathematician develops his problem from vagueness to a complete demonstration."[11]

Despite their sense of uniqueness on housing literature and science in a bilingual academy in this wide-flung country, Canada's leading English-speaking intellectuals struggled with establishing their own national voice. These internal debates – tinged with not a little existential angst – would have reverberated throughout Canadian academia. These debates are evident in the first five decades of the RSC's *Proceedings and Transactions* (1882–1932). As copies of *Proceedings and Transactions* were sent to "every library, society, university, and learned institution of note in the world," readers nationally and abroad could intuit both the boldness and insecurity of its members.[12]

The RSC fellowship was ambitious and proud. It brought together the most prominent of white, male minds under one association ("Fellowship"). As Duncan Campbell Scott declared in his presidential address, "many distinguished men have joined in this Fellowship" (himself a member since 1899). Fellowship was intended to be exclusive, inviting only a select few. Women did not join the RSC until 1938, though their scholarship occasionally appeared in *Proceedings and Transactions* and their papers were read at the annual meetings and those of associated societies.[13]

Yet it was not simply these men's fellowship that mattered but rather what they produced: the foundational, national knowledge network which reflected the values and ideals of its members. As the RSC member Chester Martin wrote a decade later in an essay, "The Royal Society itself made no small contribution to the intellectual life of Canada," and the *Proceedings and Transactions* were crucial to this endeavour.[14] He quoted president Dr George Mercer Dawson as saying in 1893 that "no other country in the world can exhibit volumes more creditable on the whole in point of workmanship than those of this society," a statement which Martin deemed "without false modesty."

Yet these lofty remarks were tempered by some of the contributions published in the *Proceedings and Transactions* that suggested an underlying concern that Canada's national society was not yet good enough. Many presidents signaled what they considered Canadian academia's fragilities. John William Dawson (G.M. Dawson's father), a geologist and principal of McGill Normal School and later knighted in 1884, gave the presidential address of the Royal Society in its inaugural year.[15] In it, Dawson foresaw what would become a repeated concern over the country being too young to have a royal society: "We are sometimes told that the enterprise in which we are engaged is premature, that like some tender plant too early exposed to the frosts of our Canadian spring it will be nipped and perish. But we must remember that in a country situated as this is, nearly everything is in some sense premature."[16] Duncan Campbell Scott similarly pondered if Canadian academia had not yet come of age several decades later, stating that Canada still "struggle[d] for self-expression in a new country" and, as a consequence, "among the Canadian-born [there remained] a certain inferiority complex."[17]

This sense of inferiority was rooted in the RSC fellows' comparison of their intellectual life with that of Great Britain. Some of these writings in the first fifty years of the RSC hinted at a tension between wanting to have a distinctive Canadian voice and a constant tendency to turn their back on the actual Canada and refer to cultural registers of the "Old World," which had established the "standards" by which Canadian literature ought to have been assessed.[18]

This tension is noticeable in Scott's presidential address delivered on the evening of 17 May 1922 in the Victoria Memorial Museum "in the presence of the Honorary Patron, His Excellency Baron Byng of Vimy and a large audience."[19] While Scott praised the society, he also stated that there was little Canadian literature of note. Both a seasoned civil servant and recognized poet, Scott chose in his presentation to track the progress made in the field of Canadian literature, in particular poetry (see here chapters by Backhouse and Gerson). While Scott did not specifically deny the existence of Canadian literary arts, he did not see the presence of "a special and particular brand" either. As such, Canadian literature did not necessitate any special consideration but should "be judged by universal standards" rather than taking into consideration "the difficulties which oppress all artistic effort in new countries." Thus, despite Scott's observation that Canadian literary life "may be distinguishable to even casual perception by a peculiar blend of courage and discouragement," he did not see it as a separate literary field.[20] His speech is full of poets and authors who helped found or conformed to these "universal standards": Shakespeare, Marlowe, Webster, Coleridge, Keats, Tennyson, Wordsworth, Donne, Brooke, Owen, among others, all men of letters originating from Great Britain with an occasional mention of an American such as Walt Whitman. When Duncan Campbell Scott did focus his attention on "two such lives typical of the struggle for self-expression in a new country" – Canadian poets Archibald Lampman and Marjorie Pickthall (the former his friend and mentor) – it was in order to illustrate his point that there was nothing specifically Canadian about their writings, since "until we have faith in the power of our writers we can have no literature worth speaking about; our position in arts and letters will be secured when we find foreign critics accepting a clear lead from us."[21]

So, while Scott and other members of the RSC whose opinions graced the pages of the *Proceedings and Transactions* did think that there was something unique about Canada and hence about Canadian "intellectual life," they still felt it was "premature" to claim it as such. A much-noted impediment to the cultivation of "an abundant intellectual harvest" or even to the formation of a "'Canadian' public opinion," was the challenge posed by Canada's inhospitable climate and diverse geography, both political and environmental. As Fellow Chester Martin bemoaned at the fiftieth anniversary of the Royal Society "there are still five or six political climates across Canada .... How many English-speaking Canadians ever read a French newspaper, or any newspaper at all printed outside their own province? In that sense the greatest assets in Canadian history have not been our vast area and magnificent distances. These have been liabilities, and they will never cease to be so in our time."[22] Yet, members also acknowledge that while it was "climate and environment" that made a national voice fragile, these two factors also made Canada's intellectuals "robust."[23] Bringing bilingualism and setting into one sentence commending his predecessors, Sir Robert Falconer remarked in the same volume as Chester Martin that "the most distinguished workers in the intellectual field of Canada were stimulated by the new problems that originated in their *milieu.*"[24]

What surprises in reading through the different pieces in *Proceedings and Transactions* that reflected back on the history of the RSC is the near absence or consideration of Indigenous peoples and their knowledge to the making of a Canadian voice or to identifying the RSC's intellectual endeavours as unique. For instance, Aegidius Fauteux and Chester Martin in their paired French and English essays on "Fifty Years of Canadian History" make only passing remarks on the original inhabitants of these lands while drawing considerable attention to the landscape and climate. Sir Falconer in the same volume briefly references the study of "ethnology" that had "been enriched by the work of eminent [white, male] scholars" who "have contributed important papers to this Section, which for many years was the chief source for historical publications in Canada."[25] Even the remarkable archaeological find by the first president of the Royal Society of Canada, the geologist Sir John William Dawson, went relatively unconsidered for its role in providing a foundational national narrative: the discovery of what he thought to be the original settlement of the Hochelaga, whom Jacques Cartier encountered in 1535.[26] Similarly, the Marquis of Lorne's interest in Indigenous peoples seemed rarely mentioned in the RSC *Proceedings and Transactions*, though just prior to founding the RSC, he had journeyed through Canada meeting treaty leaders and was anxious at the loss of Indigenous artifacts to US institutions.[27]

In his presidential address before the Royal Society of Canada in 1922, Duncan Campbell Scott did not associate the Indigenous peoples of Canada with poetry (or with any of the fields of scholarship within the Royal Society of Canada), despite his keen awareness of the works of his contemporary poet Pauline Johnson of European and Indigenous ancestry (see Gerson's chapter here) and his prominent role in the federal government as Indian Affairs deputy superintendent. He did nevertheless mention in passing "natives." In the first page of his address, he wrote that French was the "first civilized language heard by the natives of this country, which is ever the pioneer language of ideals in freedom and beauty and in the realm of clear logic, criticism, and daring speculation."[28] He made a pointed plea on the need for the RSC to continue to "assist in the collection of archives and to aid in the formation of a National Museum of Ethnology, Archaeology, and National History," as had been set forth in its charter and which he considered important to "conserving and developing our intellectual resources."[29] This was a project to which Duncan Campbell Scott had been contributing for years as part of his role in Indian Affairs, requisitioning First Nations objects seized from potlatches and received from other sources for museums and for expanding his own personal collection.[30]

INDIGENOUS KNOWLEDGE IN THE RSC

The absence of Indigenous peoples in the formation of a distinctive Canadian "intellectual harvest" is surprising not because of the common practice of excluding Indigenous peoples and knowledge in most realms of settler-society institutions but because such an absence did not accurately reflect the actual work being conducted by RSC members. When one reads through the pieces published in the *Proceedings and Transactions,* it becomes evident that the RSC fellows were very much interested in Indigenous peoples and cultures, and that Indigenous knowledge influenced these intellectuals and their peers. For instance, Lucien Turner's essay "On the Indians and Eskimos of the Ungava District, Labrador" was presented by RSC Fellow Dr Robert Bell in 1887. George Dawson's contribution in the same volume, "Notes and Observations on the Kwakiool People of the Northern Part of Vancouver Island and Adjacent Coasts," appeared alongside that of German-American anthropologist Franz Boas' paper on "The Eskimo."[31] Other essays included John Schultz's 1894 "The Innuits [sic] of our Arctic," Charles Hill-Tout's 1901 "The Origins of Totemism of the Aborigines of British Columbia," Edward Sapir's 1915 "The Social Organization of West Coast Tribes," William Lighthall's 1922 "The Westmount Stone-lined Grave Race," and in the same year Claude Melançon's "Légendes de Percé." All would have been read aloud by their authors or on their behalf by members of the RSC, and discussed and debated in the annual meetings, along with scientific papers on experiments, geography, chemistry, and the like. Importantly, they would also have circulated through one of the few academic journals of the time, the RSC's *Proceedings and Transactions*.

Indeed, while the very first volume of *Proceedings and Transactions* (for the years 1882 and 1883) did not have any specific papers on Indigenous peoples, the RSC did receive reports from an affiliated organisation, the Historical and Scientific Society of Manitoba (founded in 1879). According to Rev. Prof. George Bryce's report of May 1883, the Manitoba society had six papers delivered the previous year, two of which would have included Indigenous knowledge (on the Sioux language and the Arctic regions), and one that would have aggravated the ongoing conflict over the dispossession of Métis lands by Protestant settlers.[32] By the time this volume of *Proceedings and Transactions* made its way into the fellows' homes, the president of the Manitoba society's paper, titled "The Rising in the Red River Settlement in 1869–1870," would have been read at a historical moment: the "North-West Rebellion" was reaching its pinnacle in the Battle of Batoche in May of 1885 with Riel's capture, just two years after the paper's initial presentation.

The next volume of the RSC's *Proceedings and Transactions* had four articles on Indigenous topics, two in French (out of fourteen essays) and two in English (out of five essays).[33] Two years later, half of the publications for Section II of the RSC pertained to Indigenous

(5) IMPLEMENTS AND UTENSILS.

Bow, of wood	tli-kwis'.	Pipe	wā-hat-se.
Bow string	tli-kwi-tsim.	Pipe-stem of wood	klāh'-sta-ē.
Arrow	ā-nut-lum.	Cup	kwa-as-tā'.
Notch in arrow for string	kul'-pas.	Meat-tray	tlō-a-kwē.
Arrow-head of stone	TLUU-pā-e.	Grease-bowl	tsa-pātsē.
Arrow feathers	tsul-kiuh-ste-ē.	Fire-drill	un-ā 'k.
Quiver	a-na-tlum-ātze.	Kelp oil-bottle	wā'-wa-te.
War-club (stone)	klah-stā-la.	Axe	soo-pai-oo.
Fish-club	tul'-wa-kān.	Adze	kun-tsai-oo.
War-spear	mas-to'.	Hand-adze for shaping canoe tsik'-im-in,	
Sling	yin'-ka-yō.		(Chinook jargon for iron?)
Canoe (general term)	whā'-kwunna.	Knife	'kā-wai-oo.
Canoe (large)	kwuh'-um.	Knife-handle	keowk'-pēk.
Canoe (medium)	whī-took-u'k.	Knife-point	ō-pa-ē.
Canoe (small)	whā'-who-koom.	Knife-edge	ō-whē-ē.
Fish-line	tō'-kwā-a-no-ē.	Borer	wun'-aioo.
Fish-line, of kelp	sā'-na-patl.	Stone hand-hammer	pul'-pul'-kh.
Fish-net	kē'-tlum.	Horn ladle	hā'-kē-gia.
Oolachan net	tā-katl.	Basket (for food)	lh-hā'-e.
Dipping net	how-taī-o.	Wooden water-box or bucket hā'-kat-se.	
Halibut hook	yī-kio.		

(6) FOOD.

Food	hē-ma-ōmis.	Dried halibut	kiā'-was.
Meat	ul'-tsi.	Oolachan grease	'kli'-ina.
Milk	tsā-me.	Dried berries	'ta-uk-ā'.
Juice	sa-a'k.	Dried clams	kioo'-matse.
Dried salmon	hā'-mas.	Cambium layer of hemlock	law-KH.
Dried herring-eggs	ā-unt'.	Dried sea-weed	hluk-us-tun'.
Dried meat	bumo-ul'-tsi.		

(7) COLOURS.

Black	tsoo-tla.	Red	tlā'-kwa.
Blue	tsā'-sa.	White	mel-a.
Brown	klē-āha.	Yellow	klin-kuh.
Green	klin-kuh.		

(8) NUMERALS.

One	num.	Twelve	matl-ē-gioo.
Two	matl.	Thirteen	in-tooh-icha-gioo.
Three	in-tooh.	Fourteen	mō-a-gioo.
Four	mō.	Fifteen	sik-i-a-gioo.
Five	sik'-ī-a.	Sixteen	kā-tlā-gioo.
Six	kā-tlā.	Seventeen	atle-poo'-gioo.
Seven	atle-poo'.	Eighteen	matl-kwin-ātl-gioo
Eight	matl-kwin-ātl'.	Nineteen	nā-ne-mā-gioo.
Nine	nā-ne-mā'.	Twenty	mat-sum-gioo-staw.
Ten	les-too'.	Twenty-one	nu'-num-a-kaw-la.
Eleven	num-a-gioo.	Twenty-two	a-matl-āw-la.

Figure 6.1 Excerpt from the "Vocabulary of about Seven Hundred Words from the Kwakiool Language" taken from George M. Dawson, "Notes and Observations on the Kwakiool People of the Northern Part of Vancouver Island and Adjacent Coasts, made during the Summer of 1885." RSC, *Proceedings and Transactions*, 1888, Section II, 92.

peoples: "Some Indoor and Outdoor Games of the Wabanaki Indians" by Mrs W. W. Brown; "The Indians of British Columbia" by Franz Boas; and "A Grammar of Kwagiutl Language" by Reverend Alfred J. Hall, who taught Christian texts in Indigenous languages, largely through interpreters, in what might be considered precursors to residential schools.[34]

The importance of this research about Indigenous peoples' past and present in shifting the focus away from topics related to those of European descent did not go unnoticed. As a summary report of the *Proceedings and Transactions* published in 1888 noted, "there is a charge upon us to give heed to literature and history beyond those pertaining to European settlement and civilization, we are reminded by several papers in this Section [II, English, History, Literature, and Archaeology]."[35] That is, in the late nineteenth century, the editors of *Proceedings and Transactions* identified the potential for local cultural influences on their scholarship in addition to those of Europe.

While it was not Indigenous speakers themselves who wrote these words and scholarship, the actual peoples originating from these lands nevertheless inspired settler scholars to reflect upon different themes and topics than their Old World counterparts. Though the authors of these texts remained mired in the racist and essentialist language of "totemism," "race," and "legends," and they tended to repeat paternalistic prescriptions of how to "elevate" or improve the lives of Indigenous peoples through religious and industrial education, the very publication of these essays pointed to the presence of Indigenous knowledge in Canadian academy and thus the influence of Indigenous knowledge on settler scholars. This knowledge may indeed have provided the wedge necessary for forming "small cracks in colonialist thinking" even while it could also be wielded for consolidating colonialist ends.[36]

In these aforementioned essays and other presentations before the RSC, Indigenous peoples are the objects of study for extractive research rather than seen as contributors to knowledge production or as agents in their own right. In this way the texts are largely the product of their time. But these texts would not have been written or at least not have held the information that they did without the contribution of Indigenous knowledge keepers. Knowledge (material and immaterial) was stolen, but it could also at times have been shared. Indigenous peoples gave this knowledge, choosing which stories and what knowledge to impart. Such efforts might have been part of a mutual exchange, as a means to address the challenges of physical settler colonialism of the expanding nation state, and as well to help preserve Indigenous knowledge.[37]

Settler scholars in their imaginings and understanding of the nation and landscape needed access to Indigenous knowledge. Indeed, while Canadian geography and climate were seen as the most prominent factors contributing to a Canadian "intellectual life," it was the work with and about Indigenous peoples that exposed southern Canadian scholars to the extremes of these lands. Take for instance, Sir John Christian Schultz's 1894 essay "The Innuits [sic] of our Arctic." Similar to other settler scholars, Schultz wrote in a tone that waxed nostalgic for the past of vanishing Indigenous peoples, admiring their skills and culture. Though he advocated for the Inuit's continued independence, he also argued for the expansion of Canadian colonialism, which increasingly made the Inuit "wards of the Canadian dominion," and as such under the protection of the nation state.[38] And, like some other fellows of the RSC, he gained his reputation as learned in part through transmitting what he "knew" about Indigenous peoples.

Power and knowledge go hand in hand in the social and political aspirations of John Christian Schultz, a controversial figure; his path, while exceptional in some regards, shares commonalities with other RSC fellows. Upon his death in 1896, Schultz was remembered for his divisive personality, his self-promotion, and his extensive wealth, which had been obtained through brute force and intimidation, and at the expense of local Métis communities. While florid eulogies were given at his funeral to a "devoted son" of Canada, those who knew him well remembered him as someone who incited turmoil for his own personal gain and his violent opposition to Louis Riel.[39]

Born in Upper Canada (Ontario) in 1840, John Schultz migrated west to Manitoba after his incomplete medical studies, claiming himself a physician and surgeon. In Manitoba, Schultz consolidated his economic and political wealth: he bought shares in a newspaper and set up various businesses, including a general store, which positioned him as a strong critic of the Hudson's Bay Company. In January 1868, due to debts owing, he was arrested. He broke out of prison with the help of his wife and supporters, an act of defiance that established his reputation as lawless.[40]

It was during this time that Schultz befriended a founding member of the new political party Canada First, Charles Mair. Among their shared political objectives was the promotion of Protestant migration from Ontario and the annexation of Red River into Canada, to which local resistance quickly mounted. Captured by Louis Riel during the heightened conflicts of 1869–1870, Schultz and Mair managed to escape from prison (for Schultz this was his second break out), returning to Ontario where they actively sought to stir up fiery support for the "suffering loyalists" of Manitoba. Their efforts were not just about settling this region by Protestants but also about keeping French Canadians out of the west.[41]

After an unsuccessful attempt to win in the newly founded provincial elections, Schultz managed to secure himself a federal seat in the House of Commons in March 1871. Schultz sat as a self-described Liberal but came to support Sir John A. MacDonald in his second Conservative government. In 1882, MacDonald awarded Schultz a seat in the Senate and Schultz went on to become the fifth lieutenant governor of Manitoba from 1890–1895.[42]

Just two years prior to his death, Schultz became a member of the Royal Society of Canada in 1894. Indeed, he was not the only member of Canada First to receive this honour: so too did founders George Denison (elected in 1882 and was RSC president 1903–1904), journalist, author, and poet Charles Mair (elected in 1889), and Henry James Morgan (elected in 1904). Historian Carl Berger engagingly describes these men as seeing themselves as men of letters, debating and drinking in hotel salons, sending witty correspondence, publishing and sharing their works.[43] What united them was their feeling that neither the Liberal nor the Conservative party served Canada's best interest as a young nation. Of the original five founding members (whom Schultz later joined), Berger importantly notes that they were born in Canada and all had attended college. The Canada Firsters wanted both to shed Canada's colonial yoke from Britain and to carve out a national identity and character different from the United States. As Berger writes, "like the new Dominion itself they seemed on the threshold of promising careers." They responded, Berger argues, "to the challenge that a father of Canadian Federation Thomas D'Arcy McGee had thrown down to the educated young men of the new nation: 'I invite them,' he had said, 'not to shirk from confronting the great problems presented by America to the world, whether in morals or in government. I propose to them that they should hold their own, on their own soil, sacrificing nothing of their originality; but rejecting nothing, nor yet accepting anything, merely because it comes out of an older, or richer, or greater country."[44] Indeed, they did not wish to dismantle the British Empire; what they wanted was to be a new nation, equal within the empire, and not in the shadow of the United States. By electing Canada Firsters into the fellowship, the RSC not only honoured these men's vision of a Canadian imperialism but bolstered their values within the RSC.

While the Canada Firsters who became fellows had publications of poetry or prose to their name, Schultz's membership within the RSC must have been more in recognition of his political rather than his scholarly life. He was not known for his writing, whereas Denison wrote on military history; one of Mair's most remembered literary figures was based loosely on the Shawnee leader Tecumseh, and Morgan was noted for his patriotic biographies of prominent Canadians. Schultz had, however, given talks to the Masonic Society of Manitoba and at the Historical and Scientific Society of Manitoba, both organizations for which he had been a founding member. His RSC membership undoubtedly contributed to his reputation as learned.

When Sir John Christian Schultz gave his address upon his election into Section II of the Royal Society of Canada in 1894, ("The Innuits [sic] of our Arctic"), only fourteen years had passed since "the Dominion of Canada assumed wardenship" of that region's peoples. This was a topic to which he claimed "expertise" because of his earlier seat on the Council of the Northwest Territories (1872–1876). This essay gives insight into Schultz's thinking as a new member of the nation's inner circle of savants; his earlier derision for Indigenous and Métis peoples had turned into the soft-sounding paternalism of an elder stateman. Here, Schultz attempted to present all aspects of Inuit life from food, beliefs, language, gender roles, life stages, and the transformations occasioned by Europeans.[45] The overall tone of the text seems to be one of a romanticized admiration for the Inuit, with an undercurrent of concern for how their way of life was irrevocably changing with increasing contact with outsiders. He describes the Inuit as "savage" and "strange," both derogatory terms, and early Europeans as "barbarians," "murderers," and "intruders." Contributing to the era of scientific racism, his text treats the Inuit as a homogenous people and spends considerable ink in describing their physical appearance. Most of his text, however, is dedicated to detailed descriptions of their innovations in the face of their difficult climate: the appropriateness and skill of their clothing, their housing, the design of their kayaks and their seaworthy dexterity, their hunting practices, and the importance of social networks for their survival. Schultz grounds his assertions in what he considers appropriate scholarly sources, thereby perpetuating self-referencing and the circular legitimacy of settler scholarship. While not specifically identifying his sources of information (only that they are "faithful," have "a fair opportunity of being correct," and "whose veracity, I do not doubt"), Schultz lays claim to being able to speak with certainty about a region where he does not make mention of ever having travelled, though he had sat on the Council of the Northwest Territories.

Sir John Schultz ends his essay in a common paternalistic trope of protecting the "disappearing Indian," which would also be employed by later generations of fellows of the Royal Society of Canada. And like others who argued for the need to protect Indigenous peoples from various ills brought on by interaction with Europeans and their descendants, Schultz does so by calling on Canada's obligation to them as dependents as well as by offering economic and nationalist arguments for their survival. Reflecting upon what would happen if the "white man of to-day were swept away," he concludes that the Inuit "have not, as yet, wholly lost their independence ... and would still be self-supporting and wholly independent of outside aid." Schultz sees "white man's" intervention as being the source of their loss of independence:

> [I]intoxicants, arms of precision and its ammunition he [the Inuit people] must *not* have; and this restriction our government can and should effect; the gospel must be preached to him to undo the evil already accomplished [by white men] and this end reached, it may be asked 'What then?' The answer is this, leave him to pursue his avocations till the time comes to economize him as a hunter, a boatman or pilot, the best assistants to a northern explorer. We know not yet what mineral riches are encased in these rocks within the arctic circle .... So that when the time comes, as come it will, that we [southern Canadians] may use the arctic natives in work pertaining to what may yet be a great commerce, it will be found that their powers of resisting cold and skill on the element to which they are bred from their earliest youth, will render them possibly a very important factor in the future development of arctic Canada.

Schultz reminds the audience in his closing words that the Inuit are "wards of the Canadian people," reiterating a moral argument for their protection, though only after he had expressed Inuit survival as of clear economic benefit to southern settlers.

A similar mix of admiration and paternalism can also be found in later submissions to the RSC's *Proceedings and Transactions*, such as "The Origins of the Totemism of the Aborigines of British Colombia," by Charles Hill-Tout, submitted five years after Schultz's essay on the Inuit. However, unlike Schultz, the Royal Society of Canada elected Hill-Tout in recognition of his scholarship rather than his political career. Honorary secretary of the Ethnological Survey of Canada, Hill-Tout had published *The Native Races of British North America: The Far West* (1907) and his research was foundational to the growing field of anthropology in Canada, especially in the regions of Coast Salish peoples.[46] Prior to Hill-Tout's election to the RSC in 1913, a former RSC president read "The Origins of Totemism" before the Section II English, History, Literature, and Archaeology.[47]

In this discussion on "totemism" in the west coast of Canada, Hill-Tout points to what makes naming practices, crests, and totems unique to that region and to the peoples living there, whom he refers to as "our Indians," just at Schultz had laid claim to "our Inuit." In particular, Hill-Tout takes issue with the findings of fellow ethnologists whom he criticizes for being mistaken in their analysis due to their Eurocentrism. Hill-Tout's own language is abrasive, yet he advocates incorporating the perspective of Indigenous peoples when he writes: "to take such views of the question (on naming patterns) is to look at it from the culture-state of the European, and not from that of the savage [sic]." He concludes by reminding the reader of the importance of understanding crests and totems within a non-European logic: "A superficial view of the accounts of the origin of these crests and totems will make them appear childish and absurd; but when judged by the animistic conceptions of these tribes they are really consistent and wholly rational." Hill-Tout's critique would have exasperated some of his peers who had earlier accused him of similar practices of describing "tribes" "more from a white-man's point of view."[48] Despite Hill-Tout's calls for greater incorporation of Indigenous perspectives, his own argumentation relies heavily on his own network of scholars, including Franz Boas whose work had been presented before the RSC on several occasions and the former RSC president George Dawson as "our chief sources of information on the totemic system of the northern tribes."[49]

Indigenous knowledge as translated by the RSC fellows was not just by way of external gazes upon their skills, worldviews, and subalternity but also consisted fleetingly of settler reflections upon Indigenous cultural contributions as integral to regional life. At least, this possibility of Indigenous influence on local, settler culture was raised implicitly by Claude Melançon, a scholar of French-Canadian folklore. Claude Melançon's presentation to *Proceedings and Transactions*, originally read by his colleague Marius Barbeau at the May 1922 meeting, hits a very different register than the circuitous and florid piece by Duncan Campbell Scott's "Poetry and Progress," published in the same volume, which continually praised Great Britain's bright sons but bemoaned the lack of a recognizable and sizeable Canadian voice. Melançon's essay also differs from the earlier works of Schultz and Hill-Tout in that Melançon argues, many decades later, for the necessity to save Indigenous "legends," not as a means to preserve a disappearing peoples, but to save these stories as part of a Quebec national heritage. In this way, he was similar to his mentor Barbeau who had also presented on Indigenous and Quebec "legends," much to the chagrin of some of his more traditionally-minded colleagues of the French division of the RSC. For instance, in the 1919 business meeting of Section I, francophone members had a heated debate over the inclusion of "popular traditions – a recent innovation to the Royal Society." One fellow, Ernest Choquette, "protested against the introduction of this type of work to the Royal Society, affirming that one should not rehabilitate things that educators had been trying to destroy for fifty years." Barbeau "energetically argued the opposite. Several members took part in the discussion, which did not reach a formal conclusion."[50] Ultimately, Barbeau's position prevailed as he successfully nominated like-minded fellows such as Melançon.

Claude Melançon, a journalist, a scholar of letters, and a naturalist, was elected into the Royal Society of Canada in the French division in 1943. By this point he had written novels and essays, and he had just completed his mandates as Directeur des services français du Canadien National (Director of French Services of the Canadian National, 1940–1942) and Directeur associé du service fédéral de l'information en temps de guerre (Associate Director of Federal Information Wartime Service, 1940–1942).[51] Like Duncan

Campbell Scott, Melançon spoke of imagination as leading to beauty. For Melançon, only some places were as enchanted as that of Percé on the eastern coast of Quebec, which he compared to the chateau of Sleeping Beauty: "The marvelous is universal, but popular imagination is not inspired everywhere. There are places where every fountain, each stone, seem to hide a terrible or amusing legend and others where the veil of mystery and poetry that envelops beings and things is still barely lifted."[52]

Concerned that the oral tradition and legends of the region of Percé in Gaspésie would be lost if not recorded, Melançon offers readers five rich legends that apparently had never before been in print. In the opening stories, Melançon tells how a particular fish from those waters came to have stripes; he tells another about a magic crow that repeatedly stole a frustrated fisherman's herring catch. The first story of two fishermen, one blasphemous and the other pious, is recounted mainly through dialogue, written in the jargon and tone of rural, coastal Quebec (*Pierre, le "plus grand 'sacreur'"*; *"Tiens!"*; *"gau"* – a cod's stomach). These stories read aloud brought to the halls of high academia the beliefs and language of rural, common folk. They might have been told for amusement, in part, but they were presented as saving a lost heritage: "if we do not hasten to collect them, legend, tale, and memory, they will soon vanish into oblivion."[53] Their value was as a cultural resource.

Among the five stories in Melançon's paper, two may have their origins in Mi'kmaw stories. Both are tragic love stories, and in recounting the tales, Melançon brings to the fore aspects of what he saw as Indigenous traditions and values. It is questionable how accurate his descriptions are for they were recounted in a romanticized fashion to a very particular audience. One can imagine the room in which the savants of French-Canadian society sat (or inside the homes of *Proceedings and Transactions* subscribers) when the fellows heard of the tormented Huron prisoner and the compassion of a Mi'kmaw servant who furtively conversed with him and snuck food to this warrior. The fellows heard of a secret plan to escape and perhaps the audience would have had their heart strings pulled when, on the day of the lovers' escape, all went awry on the great Rock of Percé. The Huron prisoner had been stabbed and his lover transformed into a gull by "the Great Spirit" in order "to make her forget the tragic death of her friend."[54]

Figure 6.2 Meeting of the French Section of the Royal Society of Canada, 18 November 1945. Claude Melançon is in the last row, third from the right. Marius Barbeau, who presented the essay "Légendes de Percé," is at the end of the same row on the right.

It is important that Claude Melançon had asked the RSC Fellow Marius Barbeau (secretary of the RSC the year prior and treasurer that year) to read his essay before the French Academy of the RSC, and it illustrates a tight network of scholars. Barbeau was much recognized for his work in saving lost oral history of Indigenous peoples as a founder of folklore studies in Canada.[55] Barbeau had been given the role of recording Indigenous traditions for the National Museum of Canada (founded in 1927 by an Act of Parliament, now the Canadian Museum of History), and supposedly encouraged by the work of Franz Boas, he similarly sought to save French-Canadian oral traditions. The legends of French-Canadians and Indigenous peoples became interwoven in this enterprise of saving folklore, seen as having both "scientific" and "national" value. Sir Robert Falconer in his reflections on the first fifty years of the RSC remarked on Marius Barbeau and that of earlier fellow Section I member Benjamin Sulte (elected in

1882, president 1904–05) "for the conservation of disappearing popular beliefs and social types."⁵⁶ Melançon, like other contributors to this effort to save popular folklore, focused on rural and regional oral traditions deemed subsequently as cultural patrimony in textbooks, academic publications, and tourist guidebooks.⁵⁷

Having Barbeau read his "Légendes de Percé" helped further to establish folklore as legitimate scholarly inquiry. Melançon's choice to include two Mi'kmaw stories as Quebec cultural heritage, though only one example, further suggests the possibility of Indigenous stories – though heavily romanticized – being woven into regional identity. That the stories came from French Canada might also point to a different perception of how settler expansion developed in Lower Canada – though still violent and harmful.⁵⁸ It reinforces perhaps Sir Robert Falconer's envious assessment that French Canadian national life had successfully "produced a distinctive culture," one which English Canadians had yet to build.⁵⁹

CONCLUSION: THE POSTCOLONIAL PREDICAMENT OF EMULATION AND EXCLUSION

That Melançon and Barbeau would entertain their audiences with folk stories from the rural regions of Quebec anecdotally suggests a confidence or lack of need to emulate a lofty European counterpart, a confidence that does not seem to have been shared by their anglophone colleagues in the RSC Section II. While essays included Indigenous poetry, stories, and songs such as those by John Reade in 1887 ("Some Wabanaki Songs" and "On Aboriginal American Poetry") and George Dawson's 1888 contribution, it was mainly the most prized of anglophone Canadian literature and poetry that was the focus of Section II fellows' publications in *Proceedings and Transactions*.⁶⁰ And though fellows such as Duncan Campbell Scott might mention notable Canadian authors and poets, he did so as the exception rather than the rule; he saw Canada not as lacking talent and a distinctive voice but rather as in want of a readership that recognized the authors' merits. In this way, Duncan Campbell Scott's concerns echoed in some ways those of Canada First members who wanted a unique Canadian scholarship and identity that was neither British nor American but from which they could claim their equal scholarly status. Yet, these RSC fellows did not go quite so far as to question the "royal" in the title of their national society. Nor did they consider Indigenous stories as integral or contributing to a national or regional identity as suggested by Melançon's recounting of Mi'kmaw stories. Rather, Duncan Campbell Scott, John Christian Schultz, Charles Hill-Tout, and others saw Indigenous knowledge as a resource to be extracted and saved in scholarship and museums for the good of the settler nation before vanishing.[61]

RSC fellows drew on Indigenous knowledge in their contributions to the Royal Society of Canada's annual meetings and publication, *Proceedings and Transactions*. The many essays on Indigenous topics meant that, though marginalized, Indigenous knowledge was not entirely absent from the thoughts of Canada's most prestigious academicians. Again, it must be remembered that this knowledge was filtered, a product of colonial enterprises of translating the other while transforming the other to fit into an idealized nation state. Yet, what often gets lost is an awareness that the acts of translating and transforming the other most likely led to a transformation of the self – in this case, the white men of Canadian academia who aspired to create the nation in accordance with their intellectual pursuits and findings.

The irony is that the fellows of the first fifty years of the Royal Society of Canada did not seem to understand the liberating potential that Indigenous knowledge offered for their own postcolonial predicament. While anglophone RSC members pointed to climate, geography, and the inclusion of francophone colleagues as making their voice distinctively Canadian, they still saw themselves as not living up to their British models. Mired in repeated acts of emulation of the colonial mother country and exclusion of their own colonized peoples, the RSC fellows failed to recognize that Indigenous knowledge represented an important difference from the British academy. If they had embraced their Indigenous counterparts' knowledge and welcomed Indigenous knowledge holders within their fellowship and within Canadian academia more broadly, the RSC fellows could have proudly and accurately claimed Canadian uniqueness, and thereby shed their postcolonial predicament in more ways than one.

NOTES

The author thanks John Reid, Constance Backhouse, Margaret Kovach, and the two reviewers for their comments on an earlier version of this chapter.

1 Sir Robert Falconer, "The Intellectual Life of Canada as Reflected in its Royal Society," in RSC, *Proceedings and Transactions,* vol. 20, 932, 9–25.
2 Ibid., 23.
3 The French-language publications in RSC, *Proceedings and Transactions* (*Délibérations et mémoires*) were confined mainly to the literature, poetry, and history of RSC Section I. In these essays, the authors do not seem to debate the need to find a distinctive French-Canadian voice, but rather saw their role in North America as "spreading in this continent the arts, high intellectual culture, the civilization and the splendid soul of France – the foundation of a new France in America," as Acadian Fellow Pascal Poirier (inducted to the RSC in 1889 and member of the Canadian Senate from 1885 for over forty-eight years) wrote in 1905. Such sentiments were echoed by his contemporaries in Quebec, such as Adjutor Rivard in 1908: "Let us be from the point of view of literature a province, but an intellectual province of France." The anglophone RSC members who wrote of their francophone counterparts envied them for their "distinctive culture." Falconer further remarked that the French-Canadian fellows did not need to form a separate cannon, but one that grew from France: "in the Royal Society we see the effort of its [francophone] intellectuals to recognize in Old France the primary moulds in which this culture took shape, and to claim with confidence and develop in New France affinity with the mother far way, at whose knee it learned a tongue which, in the only home that it has ever consciously known, it does not in manhood forget." Ibid., 9, 21–22.
4 Tamson Pietsch, *Empire of Scholars: Universities, Networks and the British Academic World, 1850–1939* (Manchester: Manchester University Press, 2013).
5 Allan Greer makes an important argument for the historicization of state-oriented assimilationist projects as taking different shapes and nuances. Settler colonialism as an expansion upon primarily agrarian lands describes the practices of settler expansion that "hit a high-water mark in the first half of the twentieth century." The invasion continued under a "different guise": extractivism. "Settler colonialism has not gone away, but the dynamics of colonialism have changed over time as extractivism has come to the fore in place of literal colonization by settlers.

Running parallel to this shift in the on-the-ground process of dispossession has been a change in political, legal, and ideological expressions of colonialism." It is to these latter that the RSC contributed. Allan Greer, "Settler Colonialism and Beyond," *Journal of the Canadian Historical Association* 30, 1 (2019): 73–74, 77.

6 RSC, *Proceedings and Transactions*, vol. 16, 1922, xvi–xvii. At this same meeting, the fellows present called for a committee to recommend to the minister of finance that corporations and foundations organized "exclusively for scientific, literary or educational purposes" should benefit from deducting gifts from their net income. RSC, *Proceedings and Transactions*, vol. 16, 1922: xviii.

7 In French, the volumes were first titled *Mémoires et comptes rendus de la Société royale du Canada* and later *Délibérations et mémoires*. The first volume of the RSC, *Proceedings and Transactions* was published in December 1883 and brought together the first two sessions of the Royal Society of Canada into one volume. *Proceedings and Transactions of the Royal Society of Canada for the Years 1882 and 1883*, vol. 1 (Montreal: Dawson Brothers, Publishers), 1883.

8 The Royal Society of Canada was originally proposed in 1881 with the name of "Royal Society of Canada for the promotion of Literature and Science within the Dominion" and came into being through an act of Parliament in 1882. Four academies with twenty members each made up the original RSC: Section I: "French Literature with History, Archaeology, etc."; Section II: "English Literature with History, Archaeology, etc."; Section III: "Mathematical, Chemical and Physical Sciences"; and Section IV: "Geological and Biological Sciences." RSC, *Proceedings and Transactions*, vol. 1, 1883.

9 RSC, *Proceedings and Transactions*, vol. 16, 1922. The previous year (1921) had consisted of 752 pages. By then, *Proceedings and Transactions* were being published in the same year as the RSC annual meetings (previously there had been a one-year delay). A separate section of General Business had been added, following the Proceedings, and the Transactions subsections had been expanded to five: Section I: "Littérature française, histoire, archéologie, sociologie, économie politique et sujets connexes"; Section II: "English Literature, History, Archaeology, Sociology, Political Economy, and Allied Subjects"; Section III: "Mathematical, Physical and Chemical Sciences"; Section IV: "Geological Sciences (including Minerology)"; Section V: "Biological Sciences." A series of resolutions taken at the general business meetings of 1921 expanded members of Section II and III to fifty members each and Section III to thirty. See also Wereley's chapter here.

10 Duncan Campbell Scott, "Presidential Address: Poetry and Progress," RSC, *Proceedings and Transactions,* vol. 1, 1922, xlvii–lxvii, il.
11 Ibid., il.
12 Chester Martin, "Fifty Years of Canadian History," *Proceedings and Transactions,* vol. 20, 1932: 65.
13 See Wereley's chapter here.
14 Martin, "Fifty Years of Canadian History," 65.
15 Biographical information comes from Peter R. Eakins and Jean Sinnamon Eakins, "Dawson, Sir John William," in *Dictionary of Canadian Biography*, vol. 12, University of Toronto–Université Laval, 1990, accessed 18 October 2019, www.biographi.ca/en/bio/dawson_john_william_12E.html.
16 Cited in Falconer, "The Intellectual Life of Canada," 13.
17 Scott, "Presidential Address: Poetry and Progress," lii.
18 Ibid., lii.
19 Ibid., xviii.
20 Ibid., lii–liii.
21 Ibid., liv.
22 Martin, "Fifty Years of Canadian History," 64.
23 For example, see the RSC's first secretary (and later president), John George Bourinot's 1893 essay, "Our Intellectual Strength and Weakness" wherein the author credits Canada's geography and climate as making their national intellectual life unique while largely drawing their cultural inspiration from Europe. RSC, *Proceedings and Transactions,* 1893, 3.
24 Falconer, "The Intellectual Life of Canada," 9, 14.
25 Ibid., 22–23.
26 This assertion was later challenged. See Peter R. Eakins and Jean Sinnamon Eakins, "Dawson."
27 Lorne de Marquis's engagement with Indigenous peoples and knowledge, while a mix of admiration and paternalism, was also with the interests of expansion and extraction of natural resources.
28 Scott, "Presidential Address: Poetry and Progress," li.
29 Ibid., li–lii.
30 In 1922, Scott received an inventory and subsequent shipment of First Nation objects. While efforts were made to invoice these objects, some were lost, and not all the artists remember being compensated. Ronald W. Hawker, *Tales of Ghosts: First Nations Art in British Columbia, 1922–61* (Vancouver: UBC Press, 2003), 30–31.
31 RSC, *Proceedings and Transactions,* vol. 5, 1888.
32 RSC, *Proceedings and Transactions,* vol. 2, 1884.

33 Ibid. "Les races indigènes de l'Amérique devant l'histoire" by Napoléon Legendre; "Les aborigènes et leurs rites mortuaires" by J.M. LeMoine; "The Literary Faculty of the Native Races of America" by John Reade; and "The Huron-Iroquois: A Typical Race of American Aborigines" by Daniel Wilson.
34 On Rev. Alfred J. Hall, see James C. Piling, *Bibliography of the Wakashan Languages* (Washington: Govt. Print. Off., 1894), 29–31.
35 RSC, *Proceedings and Transactions*, vol. 5, 1888.
36 Joan Sangster, "Confronting Our Colonial Past: Reassessing Political Alliances over Canada's Twentieth Century" *Journal of the Canadian Historical Association,* 28(1), 2017: 1–43.
37 See for instance, Rosalyn LaPier, *Invisible Reality: Storytellers, Storytakers, and the Supernatural World of the Blackfeet* (Nebraska Press, 2017) and Wendy Wickwire, *At the Bridge: James Teit and the Anthropology of Belonging* (UBC Press, 2019).
38 John C. Schultz, "The Innuits [sic] of our Arctic Coast," RSC, *Proceedings and Transactions,* vol. 12, 1894: 113–34.
39 Lovell Clark, "Schultz, Sir John Christian," in *Dictionary of Canadian Biography*, vol. 12, University of Toronto–Université Laval, 2003, accessed 16 October 2019, http://www.biographi.ca/en/bio/schultz_john_christian_12E.html.
40 Ibid.
41 Carl Berger, *The Sense of Power: Studies in the Ideas of Canadian Imperialism, 1867–1914* (Toronto: University of Toronto Press, 1971), 57–9.
42 Lovell Clark, "Schultz, Sir John Christian," in *Dictionary of Canadian Biography*, vol. 12, University of Toronto–Université Laval, 2003, accessed 16 October 2019, http://www.biographi.ca/en/bio/schultz_john_christian_12E.html.
43 Canada First emerged out of a meeting of five men in Ottawa in 1868 (Colonel George Taylor Denison II, Henry Morgan, Charles Mair, William Foster, and Robert Grant Haliburton). Berger, 49–51.
44 Berger, 51. Original from D'Arcy McGee, *The Mental Outfit of the New Dominion,* offprint from the Montreal *Gazette,* 5 November 1867.
45 In his text, Schultz uses the name "Innuit" [sic]. As he explains, he placed the "Eskimo" within the larger Inuit territories, thereby making a distinction between "the raw fish eaters" (the name he stated that was used by the Indigenous peoples of southeastern Labrador) and "their own proud title of 'Innuit' [sic] – the people – being seldom heard save among

themselves" (Schultz, "The Innuits [sic] of our Arctic Coast," *Proceedings and Transactions,* vol. 12, 1894, 115).
46 George Woodcock, "Charles Hill-Tout," in *The Canadian Encyclopedia.* Article published 19 May 2008, last edited 14 December 2013, https://www.thecanadianencyclopedia.ca/en/article/charles-hill-tout
47 Hill-Tout's paper was read by former RSC president Sir John Bourinot. Charles Hill-Tout, "The Origin of the Totemism of the Aborigines of British Colombia," RSC, *Proceedings and Transactions,* vol. 7, 1901, 3–15.
48 A report by Hill-Tout published in 1905 was much criticized by Franz Boas and James Teit. However, this criticism by well-known scholars did not seem to harm Hill-Tout's academic ascent as he became RSC section president. Wickwire, *At the Bridge,* 159.
49 Hill-Tout, "The Origin of the Totemism of the Aborigines of British Colombia," 7, 14. Indeed, the network of early ethnographers was fairly small and divided in their approach: Charles Hill-Tout, Marius Barbeau, and Edward Sapir were all fellows within the RSC at the same time as Duncan Campbell Scott. Franz Boas participated with his Canadian colleagues in the RSC upon invitation. James Teit, who represented a participant-observation based approach ("an anthropology of belonging") and who did much for advancing the knowledge upon which Boas, Barbeau, Hill-Tout, Sapir, and others built their careers (and museums), was not recognized by the RSC. Duncan Campbell Scott was in a position to act as RSC gatekeeper, and Teit had actively opposed and undermined many of Scott's policies as head of Indian Affairs. Wickwire, *At the Bridge,* chapter 8.
50 RSC, *Proceedings and Transactions,* vol. 13, 1919, xxii–xxiii..
51 "Melançon, Claude," *La mémoire du Québec: Le dictionnaire des noms propres du Québec,* www.memoireduquebec.com/wiki/index.php?title=Melan%C3%A7on_%28Claude%29, accessed 16 October 2019.
52 Claude Melançon, "Légendes de Percé," RSC, *Proceedings and Transactions,* vol. 16 1922, 113.
53 Ibid., 113.
54 Ibid., 118.
55 A young Marius Barbeau had similarly had his own work read before the RSC in 1914, an essay titled "Les indiens du Canada depuis la découverte," RSC, *Proceedings and Transactions* 1914, vol. 8, 1915, 381–391. Later as an RSC fellow (elected in 1916), he presented his essay, "Le folklore canadien français," which was described by a senior fellow, Sir Robert Falconer as "entertainingly discussed by our brilliant young colleague, C. Marius Barbeau." Falconer, "The Intellectual Life of Canada," 21.

Falconer may have been hinting back to a lively debate within Section I (the francophone academy) in 1919 over the inclusion of folklore in the publication of RSC, *Proceedings and Transactions*. On Barbeau, see Renée Landry, Denise Ménar, and R.J. Preston, "Marius Barbeau," in *The Canadian Encyclopedia*. Article published 19 May 2008; last edited 25 May 2015. https://www.thecanadianencyclopedia.ca/en/article/charles-marius-barbeau. Barbeau was a controversial figure, see Wickwire, *At the Bridge*, 239–42, 261–65.

56 Falconer, "The Intellectual Life of Canada," 21.
57 Jean de Berger, "Imaginaire traditionnel, imaginaire institutionnel," *La construction d'une culture: le Québec et l'Amérique française*, ed. by Gérard Bourchard (Saint-Foy : Les presses de l'Université de Laval, 1993), 104–7.
58 Allan Greer, "Settler Colonialism and Beyond," 67–70.
59 Falconer, "The Intellectual Life of Canada," 21.
60 John Reade, "Some Wabanaki Songs" and "Aboriginal American Poetry" in RSC, *Proceedings and Transactions*, 1888, 1–8; 9–34. RSC public lecture series allowed for the presentation of a more diverse range of literature, including that of women. Pauline Johnson was one of the rare women who presented her own work, her 1892 poem "The Song My Paddle Sings," RSC, *Proceedings and Transactions*, 1895.
61 For instance, consider the RSC authors MacMechan, Patterson, and Raddall discussed in John Reid's chapter here. According to John Reid, it is unlikely that MacMechan would have seen Mi'kmaw legends and stories as having cultural value. Patterson would have had difficulty with them on religious grounds. Though Raddall did collect Mi'kmaw stories in Queens and Shelburne counties, he would have used such stories "to underline difference from British colonizers rather than to inform anglophone identity." Correspondence with John Reid, 30 December 2020.

7

Nostra Culpa? Reflections on "The Indian in Canadian Historical Writing"

James W. St G. Walker

In the fall of 1966, when I was a master of arts student at the University of Waterloo, I attended a social gathering in Ottawa where a number of Indigenous youth were present. Our discussions turned to the preparations for the Canadian centennial celebrations and the history of the nation, the achievements of the "two founding nations" of French and English descent, and the efforts by "New Canadians" (neither of French nor English European immigration) to be considered a "third founding nation." The Indigenous people spoke up: "What about us? We are the *first* nations and we are left completely out of the story. What's wrong with Canadian history?"

To find an answer, when I returned to Waterloo I wrote a paper on "The Indian in Canadian Historical Writing." It earned me an "A" in a historiography course, and I gave it as a talk to a number of student and community groups during 1967. In 1968, as a PhD student at Dalhousie, I presented the paper to the history students' association. In the audience was Professor Peter B. Waite, fellow of the RSC, who encouraged me to update my evidence and offer the paper to the Canadian Historical Association (CHA). It was presented at the CHA meeting in St John's in 1971, Professor Sydney F. Wise, RSC fellow, presiding. Despite my temerity in naming and criticizing some of the historians who were there, the paper received a standing ovation. This was my first conference experience, and I assumed such a practice must be normal. In fact, it was my first and only standing ovation. The paper was also my first publication, in *Historical Papers 1971*.[1]

Discussions since 2018 with the scholars connected with the RSC's Truth and Reconciliation Task Force have prompted me to revisit that first publication. Republishing the original article in its entirety might have offered an enlightening glimpse into the norms of the historical profession in the late 1960s when I researched and wrote it. However, I was concerned by my use of outdated and cringe-worthy terminology as well as masculine presumptions of grammatical expression. I was also struck by the inflammatory nature of the racist language in the historical literature I had surveyed half a century ago. Instead of reproducing the original article here, I will briefly summarize its contents in order to offer some analysis of the early ideas of the Canadian historical profession. As Robin Winks once suggested, "one often learns more about a people from the history they write than from the history they have made."[2]

My 1971 paper involved a survey of eighty-eight titles by seventy-four authors, ranging in publication date from 1829 to 1970, including general, regional, and specialized histories in both official languages. With some notable exceptions, the survey conclusions held true despite the authors' language, date, or topic.[3] The survey findings are deeply distressing, and readers should be warned that some may find the material too painful to read. The first disturbing observation was the vocabulary that early historians used to describe Indigenous peoples. Even authors who adopted affirmative terminology, choosing words such as "brave," "dignified," "intelligent," and "hospitable," coupled the positive descriptors with condescending words such as "devoted," "happy," "faithful," even "bronzed stalwart," and "copper-hued patriot."[4] Authors who chose negative terminology used disparaging words such as "savage," "cruel," "cowardly," "lazy," "barbaric," "credulous," "fiendish," "superstitious," and "fickle," among other even more hostile terms.[5]

Historians studied in my 1971 article relied upon biased sources such as *The Jesuit Relations*, and journals from European explorers and fur-traders to characterize Indigenous peoples as "demonic" and "bloodthirsty." It was a blatant double standard when compared with Europeans in the same period who were breaking people on the wheel, burning them at the stake, sentencing them to one thousand lashes, and condemning entire populations of Africans to trans-Atlantic enslavement. Castigating Indigenous guerilla warfare techniques as "cowardly," and Indigenous treatment of prisoners as "cruel," historians rarely acknowledged the equivalent savagery of seventeenth-century European warfare and torture.[6]

Contrasted with the image of the violent Indigenous warrior was the concept of the "noble savage," whom historians praised for kindness, generosity, and hospitality. Yet even this was laden with peculiar references to a "childlike existence," and a backward "stone-age" culture that was invariably characterized as inferior to whites. Indigenous canoes, snowshoes, moccasins, toboggans, longhouses, tipis, totem poles, and decorative quill work were occasionally acknowledged, as was Indigenous expertise in forestry and hunting. However, European technology was always portrayed as indisputably superior. Historians described Indigenous living conditions as diseased and squalid, often passing over the medicinal plants and invaluable Indigenous healing knowledges that saved so many European lives. Historians criticized the status of Indigenous women, and Indigenous forms of social governance, diplomatic protocols, and alcohol consumption with little recognition of their own parallel European challenges.[7]

Equally startling was the lack of differentiation between various individuals, communities, and nations. Although some struggled to insist that "to write of Indians as if they were one people ... is historically ... absurd," most historians attributed negative traits or incidents to all Indigenous peoples, while explaining positive achievements as individual and exceptional.[8] Indigenous absence was a continuous motif. Canada's story typically began with geography, flora, and fauna, followed by the Vikings, John Cabot, Jacques Cartier, and the fur trade, with Indian trappers given less attention than the beavers they trapped. Occasionally, they came into view as allies in white peoples' wars. Few scholars suggested that the Indigenous warriors were "fighting for their own interests rather than for a Great Father overseas."[9] After 1812, Indigenous peoples almost entirely disappeared from Canadian history, emerging only fleetingly during the Red River disturbance and the subsequent North West Rebellion of 1885. Indigenous peoples were treated as peripheral except when they overlapped, or more typically conflicted, with the inevitable progress of Euro-Canadian society. They were described "as part of the setting, the environment in which the history of the European newcomers can unfold."[10]

In sum, the 1971 article characterized Canadian historical writing as reflective of "a belief in the manifest destiny of European civilization spreading across the continent from sea to sea." The good Indians were those who assisted the white movement, who occupied their reserves, and who signed away their land without resistance.[11]

THE INDIAN IN CANADIAN HISTORICAL WRITING

JAMES W. ST. G. WALKER

Dalhousie University

I began this paper with two questions: what is the place of the Indian in Canadian history, according to the writers of that history, and secondly, why is it so? My answer to those questions is what follows. To reach it I conducted a survey of the books appearing most frequently on undergraduate bibliographies for Canadian history at Canadian universities. Those books, numbering eighty eight titles by seventy four authors, range in publication date from 1829 to 1970 and they include general, regional and specialized histories in both official languages. I have divided my findings and my observations on them into four sections: the picture that is given of the Indian as a human being, and of his society; the role that is assigned to the Indian as a participant in Canadian history; some suggestions concerning the reasons for that picture and role; and finally, an attempt to discover whether the treatment of Indians varies according to the historian's language group, his time of writing, or the major emphasis of his book.

In the course of my reading I found myself asking another question, concerning the nature of Canadian history or, rather, concerning the proper and legitimate subject of study for a student of Canadian history. This supplementary question remains unanswered. I do believe, however, that I have discovered what Canadian history is not, in at least this one respect. I recognize the limitations not only of this paper but of my own experience and sophistication in our national history, but because they are honestly offered I hope that by observations will be charitably received. Robin Winks has suggested that "one often learns more about a people from the history they write than from the history they have made".* If this is so, then it may be possible to learn more from a study of the Indian in Canadian historical writing than I at first imagined on undertaking this project.

I

The picture of the Indian as a human being that is presented by writers of Canadian history is confusing, contradictory and incomplete. Clearly he is not often considered to be deserving of serious attention, or his society of scholarly analysis. Because the native Canadian appears

Figure 7.1 Reproduction of the first page of James W. St G. Walker's 1971 article "The Indian in Canadian Historical Writing."

HISTORICAL WRITING AFTER 1970

The treatment of "the Indian" in the historical writing prior to 1970 could be characterized, in the most generous of terms, as irresponsible. At that time, I expressed the hope that a growing specialized literature on Indigenous history and related disciplines would enable us to correct the damaging messages of previous interpretations, and would therefore lead to an improved position for Aboriginal peoples not only in our historical understanding but in our society. We do, after all, act according to the history we believe. When history was being written against a background of scientific racism, imperial expansion, and officially-sanctioned eugenics, the dislocation and eventual disappearance of the First Nations was considered not only foreseeable but beneficial, and their peripheral importance taken for granted. In the wake of 1960s idealism and the more sophisticated methodologies that emerged in that decade, I hoped that historians would abandon their prejudices and reconsider their approach to Indigenous history and its significance for all Canadians.

The transformation did not come quickly. Despite some truly remarkable monographs in the 1970s and early 1980s, often described as "the first wave" of a new Aboriginal history, standard accounts in Canadian history remained fixed on a national plot that neglected the Indigenous presence.[12] Indigenous writers such as Harold Cardinal, Maria Campbell, George Manuel, and Howard Adams expressed strong objections to this historical portrayal and the contemporary conditions of their communities.[13] By the 1990s and after, Canadians were witnessing the regular appearance of Indigenous issues in the daily news, from confrontations over land at Oka, Ipperwash, and Caledonia, to pollution on reserves, unequal government services to Indigenous children, revelations about residential schools and the "sixties scoop," conflicts over pipelines and resource development, and Idle No More and other resurgence movements.

More calls for change came from the Royal Commission on Aboriginal Peoples (RCAP) final report in 1996, which contained recommendations for historical revision, including the elimination of the terra nullius fiction and its legal and policy legacies, and requested that "the appropriate place of Aboriginal peoples in Canadian history be recognized." The commission called for a multi-volume history of Aboriginal peoples, and funding for the Social Sciences and Humanities Research Council (SSHRC) to facilitate the project.

This history must grant "the right of Aboriginal people to represent themselves, their cultures and their histories in ways they consider authentic." Besides curriculum reform and public education, the federal government was enjoined to "ensure that the history and present circumstances of Aboriginal peoples are communicated to immigrants and to persons becoming Canadian citizens."[14]

Even more expansive was the report of *The Truth and Reconciliation Commission* (TRC) in 2015. James R. Miller has calculated that historical material occupied about 70 per cent of volumes 1–3 with additional material in volumes 5 and 6. The discussion on *Reconciliation* in volume 6 declared that "[The] lack of historical knowledge has serious consequences for First Nations, Inuit, and Métis peoples, and for Canada as a whole," resulting in poor public policy and the reinforcement of racist attitudes. "Schools must teach history in ways that foster mutual respect, empathy, and engagement. All Canadian children and youth deserve to know Canada's honest history, including what happened in the residential schools." The Commissioners concluded that "History plays an important role in reconciliation; to build for the future, Canadians must look to, and learn from the past."[15] Among the ninety-four *Calls to Action* were the following recommendations: that age-appropriate compulsory study of Aboriginal history be included in the kindergarten to Grade 12 curriculum for all Canadian students; on special training for students in law and journalism; and for citizenship information for immigrants that would "reflect a more inclusive history of the diverse Aboriginal peoples of Canada."[16] As Chief Commissioner Murray Sinclair summarized, "Education got us into this mess, but education is the key to reconciliation."[17]

The momentum continued in the 2019 report of the National Inquiry into Missing and Murdered Indigenous Women and Girls (MMIWG) "Calls for Justice." All "elementary, secondary, and post-secondary institutions and authorities" were called upon "to educate and provide awareness to the public. . . . Such education and awareness must include historical and current truths about the genocide against Indigenous Peoples through state laws, policies, and colonial practices. It should include, but not be limited to, teaching Indigenous history, law, and practices from Indigenous perspectives."[18]

Further impetus came from waves of litigation in Canadian courts. Testimonies delivered in lawsuits regarding land claims and damages from abuse in the residential schools drew more attention to historical injustices. As early as 1973, the Supreme Court of Canada delivered a split decision on the claim of Aboriginal title put forward by the Nisga'a Nation of British Columbia (referred to as *Calder*).[19] In response, the government of Pierre Trudeau launched the Land Claims Commission to evaluate Indigenous grievances, admitting oral history evidence and the use of academic expert witnesses. The contest moved into the courts, joined in the 1990s by cases brought by residential school survivors. One of the key expert witnesses, Arthur J. Ray, concluded that the "interactive and cumulative process involving the Aboriginal, academic, and legal communities ... has been a driving force for path-breaking interdisciplinary cultural/historical research about Indigenous people. This work made the economic, legal, and political implications of Native history starkly apparent long before it became an issue in post-colonial and post-modern studies in the academy."[20]

Gradually historians and scholars in related disciplines have begun to respond. From the early stages in the 1970s and 1980s, they began to fill some gaps in the reigning narrative.[21] The 1990s saw more revisionist history of Canadian Indian policy.[22] It helped to clarify that Prime Minister Harper's insistence that Canada had never been a colonial power was an abiding, but erroneous, national myth.[23] Some scholars began to re-interpret the relationship, arguing that Indigenous peoples had ways of mitigating oppressive official policies on residential schools and potlatch illegalization that gave them some agency in the over-arching colonial situation.[24] Others disputed this approach, questioning whether "native agency" was a "colonialist alibi."[25] Although Indigenous-settler relations predominated in this literature, there were writings on what Indigenous peoples were doing in their own societies apart from resisting settler initiatives.[26]

Both trends continued into the new millennium. There have been direct rebuttals of standard accounts of the Jesuit martyrdoms, Adam Dollard des Ormeau and Madeleine de Verchères, revelation of the continuing history of the Huron–Wendat and Iroquois–Haudenosaunee peoples after "history" as previously told had abandoned them,[27] and the inclusion of specialized topics such as labour, health issues, and Indigenous law.[28] There is now a revised presentation of the numbered treaties that considers the Indigenous understanding of the relationship with settler governments and society, and explains why treaty rights are considered "sacred" by the Indigenous signatories and their successors.[29] Even the history of the fur trade is receiving new attention.[30] In addition to the inclusion of neglected content, the new literature appearing in the twenty-first century has adopted innovative methodologies, often coinciding with those suggested in the Commission reports. Indigenous sources such as oral accounts, material evidence, and origin traditions are now being studied. This has required collaboration between Indigenous writers and settler academics, along with analyses and memoirs by Indigenous authors individually who are challenging and redefining Indigenous studies today. Interdisciplinary approaches are further enriching the body of literature written by academic historians.[31] There have always been writers of history who were themselves Indigenous.[32] What is different in the last decade is the increasing visibility and influence of Indigenous historians, including Brenda Macdougall, Susan Hill, and Mary Jane Logan McCallum. The contributions of Indigenous historians are documented on the website "Shekon Neechie: an Indigenous history site."[33]

This ground-breaking scholarship has put Indigenous history on the radar of the historical profession. The Canadian Historical Association's (CHA) prestigious John A. Macdonald Prize in Canadian History (as it was called until 2018) first included a title on Indigenous history in 1978. Since then, twenty-eight such books have won or been short-listed for this honour. The CHA also inaugurated a special prize for Indigenous history in 2010. The winners have often appeared on other prize lists and their publications have become best-sellers.[34] Articles in the *Canadian Historical Review* (*CHR*) have multiplied in the past two decades,[35] as have titles on Indigenous topics listed in the journal's "Recent Publications Relating to Canada." The CHA annual meeting in 2015 hosted a panel discussion devoted to James Daschuk's *Clearing the Plains: Disease, Politics of Starvation, and the Loss of Indigenous Life*,[36] and the *CHR* published a "Forum on the Truth and Reconciliation Commission" in 2019.[37] At the 2019 annual meeting of the CHA at the University of British Columbia, there were a record thirty-eight papers and eight sessions on Indigenous topics, six TRC workshops, a sharing circle, a discussion on universities and reconciliation, and an all-day bus tour of Sto:lo Nation territory.[38]

Beyond the historical profession, the wider academy is responding to the demand for engagement with Indigenous issues. Territorial acknowledgments have become ubiquitous on Canadian campuses.

SSHRC has established several research grants and scholarships for Indigenous or settler students and scholars working on Indigenous projects,[39] many Canadian universities have responded to the TRC report with Indigenization policies including curriculum programming, research support, student assistance, community connections, and review of policies and procedures,[40] while compulsory courses on Indigenous legal systems have been added to some law school curricula.[41]

The Canadian public in general is demonstrating more and more sensitivity to Indigenous communities and their issues, historical and contemporary. For example an academic book, Daschuk's *Clearing the Plains*,[42] was at first rejected by the Aid to Scholarly Publications Program in 2009 when a reviewer dismissed it as of "zero scholarly value, do not publish." But just four years later, during the TRC hearings and Idle No More demonstrations, its publication by University of Regina Press brought enormous attention to its subject and author. In the first two years after publication, Daschuk was invited to present more than a hundred talks and interviews and his book evoked hundreds of newspaper articles, blog posts, editorials, essays, podcasts, videos, and a folk song.[43] Equally revealing of an emerging public interest, Ian Mosby, author of the 2013 article "Administering Colonial Science: Nutrition Research and Human Biomedical Experimentation in Aboriginal Communities and Residential Schools, 1942–1952,"[44] was invited to give numerous interviews and presentations to audiences wishing to hear more about residential school history.[45]

By public demand, statues of Canadian heroes such as John A. Macdonald, Champlain, and Lord Cornwallis are being removed, relocated, or re-plaqued, and, in the summer of 2019, three Indigenous titles were on the *Globe and Mail's* non-fiction best-seller list.[46] In the lead-up to the 2019 federal election, a joint statement from Canadian post-secondary student unions announced that one of their five top priorities was increased support for Aboriginal students.[47] For the leaders' debate on CBC-TV on 7 October 2019, one of the five assigned topics was Indigenous issues. In her 2019 book *From Where I Stand: Rebuilding Indigenous Nations for a Stronger Canada*, Jody Wilson-Raybould writes that "We have come a long way.... We are moving from a learning moment to an action moment."[48] Pollsters Michael Adams and Keith Neuman profiled an Environics survey of Indigenous and non-Indigenous youth aged sixteen to twenty-nine that showed that significant majorities in both groups expected meaningful reconciliation in their lifetimes.[49]

The changes since 1971 are becoming apparent. If "genocide" remains a contested term, "colonial" has been widely accepted as a valid description of the relationship between Indigenous peoples and settler society and governments. The "Indian problem" identified by Duncan Campbell Scott is being redefined as a "settler problem." Indigenous voices are starting to be heard in courts, inquiries, popular best-sellers, the Senate and House of Commons, as well as in classrooms and academic writing. However, there is no room for complacency.

At less than 1 per cent, Indigenous scholars are still significantly under-represented on Canadian university faculties.[50] Twenty-nine per cent of adult admissions into federal custody in 2017–2018 were Indigenous.[51] About one-quarter of all homicides across Canada have Indigenous victims,[52] and fewer than half of on-reserve students complete high school.[53] As inquiries and reports have indicated, there is a relationship between the way Indigenous people and their history are portrayed in educational materials and their contemporary condition.

This is the challenge faced by Canadian scholars today. It is not enough to patch select Indigenous experiences into a national story intended to explain the "success" of the Canadian nation, how it came about, and how it is to be maintained.[54] Resurgence and cultural renewal are properly the initiative of the Indigenous peoples themselves, but reconciliation is a multilateral project. Non-Indigenous scholars, including in particular members of the Royal Society of Canada, have the opportunity to grasp the practice of "reparatory history"[55] and participate in the reconciliation movement with our writing and teaching. The specialized literature offers much of the essential raw material for a radical reinterpretation of the standard time-line and underlying message of Canadian history. It is one way to compensate for *nostra culpa* in the past.

APPENDIX

Winners (*) and Short-listed Indigenous-related Titles for the CHA *Macdonald Prize (renamed in 2018 The Best Scholarly Book in Canadian History)*

2018
Susan M. Hill, *The Clay We Are Made Of: Haudenosaunee Land Tenure on the Grand River* (Winnipeg: University of Manitoba Press, 2017).

Jeffers Lennox, *Homelands and Empires: Indigenous Spaces, Imperial Fictions, and Competition for Territory in Northeastern North America, 1690–1763* (Toronto: University of Toronto Press, 2017).

J.R. Miller, *Residential Schools and Reconciliation: Canada Confronts Its History* (Toronto: University of Toronto Press, 2017).

Cecilia Morgan, *Travelers through Empire: Indigenous Voyages from Early Canada* (Montreal and Kingston: McGill-Queen's University Press, 2017).

2017
*Sarah Carter, *Imperial Plots: Women, Land, and the Spadework of British Colonialism on the Canadian Prairies* (Winnipeg: University of Manitoba Press, 2016).

Adele Perry, *Colonial Relations: The Douglas-Connolly Family and the Nineteenth-Century Imperial World* (Cambridge: Cambridge University Press, 2015).

Ronald Rudin, *Kouchibouguac: Removal, Resistance, and Remembrance at a Canadian National Park* (Toronto: University of Toronto Press, 2016).

2016
Michel Hogue, *Metis and the Medicine Line: Creating a Border and Dividing a People* (Regina: University of Regina Press, 2015)

2015
*Jean Barman, *French Canadians, Furs, and Indigenous Women in the Making of the Pacific Northwest* (Vancouver: UBC Press, 2014).

2014
*James Daschuk, *Clearing the Plains: Disease, Politics of Starvation, and the Loss of Aboriginal Life* (Regina: University of Regina Press, 2013).

Kathryn Magee Labelle, *Dispersed But Not Destroyed: A History of the Seventeenth-Century Wendat People* (Vancouver: UBC Press, 2013).

2013
*William C. Wicken, *The Colonization of Mi'kmaw Memory and History, 1794-1928: The King v. Gabriel Sylliboy* (Toronto: University of Toronto Press, 2012).

Shelley A.M. Gavigan, *Hunger, Horses, and Government Men: Criminal Law on the Aboriginal Plains, 1870–1905* (Vancouver: UBC Press. 2012).

2005
*Dominique Deslandres, *Croire et faire croire. Les missions françaises au XVIIe siécle (1600–1650)* (Paris: Fayard, 2003).

2003
*Cole Harris, *Making Native Space. Colonialism, Resistance, and Reserves in British Columbia* (Vancouver: UBC Press, 2002).

Colin Coates and Cecilia Morgan, *Heroines and History. Representations of Madeleine de Verchères and Laura Secord* (Toronto: University of Toronto Press, 2002).

2000
Patrice Groulx, *Pièges de la mémoire: Dollard des Ormeaux, les Amérindiens et nous* (Hull: Vents d›Ouest, 1998).

1999
*Mary-Ellen Kelm, *Colonizing Bodies: Aboriginal Health and Healing in British Columbia, 1900–1950* (Vancouver: UBC Press, 1998).

1997
James R. Miller, *Shingwauk's Vision: A History of Native Residential Schools* (Toronto: University of Toronto Press, 1996).

1993
*Olive Patricia Dickason, *Canada's First Nations: A History of Founding Peoples from Earliest Times* (Toronto: McClelland and Stewart–Norman: University of Oklahoma Press, 1992).

1992
*Julie A. Cruikshank, *Life Lived Like a Story: Life Stories of Three Yukon Native Elders* (Vancouver: UBC Press-Lincoln: University of Nebraska Press, 1990).

Peter S. Schmalz, *The Ojibwa of Southern Ontario* (Toronto: University of Toronto Press, 1991).

1986
Bruce Trigger, *Natives and Newcomers: Canada's Heroic Age Reconsidered* (Montreal: McGill-Queen's University Press, 1985).

1985
*Gerald Friesen, *The Canadian Prairies, A History* (Toronto: University of Toronto Press, 1984).

1980
L.S.F. Upton, *Micmacs and Colonials: Indian-White Relations in the Maritime Provinces, 1713–1867* (Vancouver: UBC Press, 1979).

1978
*Robin A. Fisher, *Contact and Conflict: Indian-European Relations in B.C. 1774–1890* (Vancouver: UBC Press, 1977).

Winners (*) and Short-listed Titles for the CHA Aboriginal History Prize

2019
*Mary Jane Logan McCallum and Adele Perry, *Structures of Indifference: An Indigenous Life and Death in a Canadian City* (Winnipeg: University of Manitoba Press, 2018).

Allan Downey, *The Creator's Game: Lacrosse, Identity, and Indigenous Nationhood* (Vancouver: UBC Press, 2018).

2018
*Susan Hill, *The Clay We Are Made Of: Haudenosaunee Land Tenure On the Grand River* (Winnipeg: University of Manitoba Press, 2017).

Marianne Ignace and Ronald E. Ignace, *Secwépemc People, Land, and Laws: Yerí7 re Stsq'ey's-kucw* (Montreal: McGill-Queen's University Press, 2017).

2017
*Maureen K. Lux, *Separate Beds: A History of Indian Hospitals in Canada, 1920s–1980s* (Toronto: University of Toronto Press, 2016).

Jean Barman, *Abenaki Daring: The Life and Writings of Noel Annance, 1792–1869* (Montreal and Kingston: McGill-Queen's University Press, 2016).

Brian D. McInnes, *Sounding Thunder: The Stories of Francis Pegahmagabow* (Winnipeg: University of Manitoba Press, 2016).

Helen Raptis with members of the Tsimshian Nation, *What We Learned: Two Generations Reflect on Tsimshian Education and the Day Schools* (Vancouver: UBC Press, 2016).

2016
*Arthur Manuel and Grand Chief Ronald M. Derrickson, *Unsettling Canada: A National Wake-Up Call* (Toronto: Between the Lines, 2015).

Emilie Cameron, *Far Off Metal River: Inuit Lands, Settler Stories, and the Making of the Contemporary Arctic* (Vancouver: UBC Press, 2015).

2015
*Elsie Paul in collaboration with Paige Raibmon and Harmony Johnson, *Written as I Remember It: Teachings (ʔǝms taʔaw) from the Life of a Sliammon Elder* (Vancouver: UBC Press, 2014)

2014
*James Daschuk, *Clearing the Plains: Disease, Politics of Starvation, and the Loss of Aboriginal Life* (Regina: University of Regina Press, 2013).

Robin and Jillian Ridington, in collaboration with Elders of Dane-Zaa First Nations, *Where Happiness Dwells: A History of the Dane-zaa First Nations* (Vancouver: UBC Press, 2013).

2013
*Leslie A. Robertson with the Kwagu'? Gixsam Clan, *Standing Up with Ga'axsta'las: Jane Constance Cook and the Politics of Memory, Church, and Custom* (Vancouver: UBC Press, 2012).

2012
* Sarah Carter and Patricia McCormack, eds., *Recollecting: Lives of Aboriginal Women of the Canadian Northwest and Borderlands* (Edmonton: Athabasca University Press, 2011).

Arthur J. Ray, *Telling it to the Judge: Taking Native History to Court* (Montreal and Kingston: McGill University Press, 2011).

2011
*Keith Thor Carlson, *The Power of Place, The Problem of Time: Aboriginal Identity and Historical Consciousness in the Cauldron of Colonialism* (Toronto: University of Toronto Press, 2010).

2010
*Shirleen Smith and Vuntut Gwitchin First Nation, *People of the Lakes: Stories of Our Van Tat Gwich'in Elders* (Edmonton: University of Alberta Press, 2009).

*Articles on Indigenous topics
in the Canadian Historical Review, by decade*

1920–29: 7	1970–79: 7
1930–39: 11	1980–89: 9
1940–49: 11	1990–99: 12
1950–59: 2	2000–09: 37
1960–69: 3	2010–19: 30

Total articles: 129

NOTES

I am grateful to my colleague Susan Roy for lending me many of her books and for her valued advice on this project.

1 James W. St G. Walker, "The Indian in Canadian Historical Writing," *Historical Papers, Communications Historiques 1971* (Canadian Historical Association: 1971), 21–47.
2 Robin W. Winks, "Canada," *The Historiography of the British Empire-Commonwealth* (Durham: Duke University Press, 1966), 70.
3 Walker "The Indian in Canadian Historical Writing," 22, 40.
4 Ibid., 22.
5 Ibid., provides detailed source references, 22.
6 Ibid., 22–3, 32–3.
7 Ibid., 23–7.
8 Ibid., 26.
9 Ibid., 30.
10 Ibid., 26–31.
11 Ibid., 37.
12 James W. St G. Walker, "The Indian in Canadian Historical Writing, 1972–1982," in *As Long as the Sun Shines and Water Flows: A Reader in Canadian Native Studies*, eds. Ian Getty and Antoine Lussier (Vancouver: UBC Press, 1983), 340–61.
13 Harold Cardinal, The *Unjust Society: The Tragedy of Canada's Indians* (Edmonton: M.G. Hurtig, 1969), and *The Rebirth of Canada's Indians* (Edmonton: M.G. Hurtig, 1977); Maria Campbell, *Halfbreed* (Toronto: McClelland & Stewart, 1973); George Manuel, *The Fourth World: An Indian Reality* (Don Mills, ON: Collier-Macmillan, 1974); Howard Adams, *Prison of Grass: Canada from the Native Point of View* (Toronto: New Press, 1975).
14 *Royal Commission on Aboriginal Peoples,* vol. V, appendix A, "Summary of Recommendations, Vols. 1–5," in particular Recommendations 1.7.1, 1.7.2, 1.10.3, 1.12.1, 1.16.2, and 5.4.12. RCAP also commissioned research that resulted, for example, in John S. Milloy, *A National Crime: The Canadian Government and the Residential School System, 1879–1986* (Winnipeg: University of Manitoba Press, 1999), and Roland Chrisjohn, *The Circle Game: Shadows and Substance in the Residential School in Canada* (Penticton BC: Theytus Books, 1997).
15 James R. Miller, "Research and Outcomes at the Truth and Reconciliation Commission," *Canadian Historical Review* (CHR) 100, no. 2 (June 2019): 163–81, and his review of the RCAP report in *BC Studies* no. 191 (Autumn 2016): 167–75.

16 Truth and Reconciliation Commission of Canada, Truth and Reconciliation Commission: *Calls to Action* (2015), www.trc.ca/assets/pdf/Calls_to_Action_English2.pdf, numbers 27, 28, 62, 63, 86, 93.
17 Quoted in *Toronto Star*, 7 September 2019.
18 *Reclaiming Power and Place*, Executive Summary of the Final Report, "Calls for Justice" number 11.1, with compulsory professional education in Indigenous history for lawyers, health providers, and social service workers, numbers 7.6, 9.3 and 10.1.
19 *Calder v. Attorney General of British Columbia*, [1973] *Supreme Court Reports* 313.
20 Arthur J. Ray, "Native History on Trial: Confessions of an Expert Witness," CHR 84, no. 2 (June 2003): 274. See also Ray's *Telling It to the Judge: Taking Native History to Court* (Montreal and Kingston: McGill-Queen's University Press, 2011), and *Aboriginal Rights Claims and the Making and Remaking of History* (Montreal and Kingston: McGill-Queen's University Press, 2016).
21 Arthur J. Ray, *Indians in the Fur Trade: Their Role as Trappers, Hunters, and Middlemen in the Lands Southwest of Hudson Bay, 1660–1870* (Toronto: University of Toronto Press, 1974); Robin Fisher, *Contact and Conflict: Indian-European Relations in British Columbia, 1774–1890* (Vancouver: UBC Press, 1977); Jennifer S.H. Brown, *Strangers in Blood: Fur Trade Company Families in Indian Country* (Vancouver: UBC Press, 1980); Sylvia Van Kirk, *"Many Tender Ties": Women in Fur-Trade Society, 1670–1870* (Winnipeg: Watson and Dwyer, 1980); John L. Tobias, "Protection, Civilization, Assimilation: An Outline History of Canada's Indian Policy," in Getty and Lussier, *As Long as the Sun Shines and Water Flows*, 39–55, and "Canada's Subjugation of the Plains Cree, 1879–1885," CHR 64, no. 4 (1983): 519–48; Bruce G. Trigger, *Natives and Newcomers: Canada's 'Heroic Age' Reconsidered* (Montreal and Kingston: McGill-Queen's University Press, 1985).
22 Sarah Carter, *Lost Harvests: Prairie Indian Reserve Farmers and Government Policy* (Montreal: McGill-Queen's University Press, 1990); Ken S. Coates, *Best Left as Indians: Native-White Relations in the Yukon Territory, 1840–1973* (Montreal: McGill-Queen's University Press, 1991); James R. Miller, *Shingwauk's Vision: A History of Native Residential Schools* (Toronto: University of Toronto Press, 1996); John S. Milloy, *A National Crime: The Canadian Government and the Residential School System* (Winnipeg: University of Manitoba Press, 1999).
23 "We also have no history of colonialism. So, we have all of the things that many people admire about the great powers but none of the things that

threaten or bother them," Prime Minister Stephen Harper, Pittsburgh, September 2009, quoted in Madelaine Drohan, "Canada As Colonial Power. Not Quite the Way We Like to Think of Ourselves," *Literary Review of Canada*, 19:1 (January–February 2011).

24 James R. Miller, "Owen Glendower, Hotspur, and Canadian Indian Policy," *Ethnohistory* 37, no. 4 (Autumn 1990): 386–415; Tina Loo, "Dan Cranmer's Potlatch: Law as Coercion, Symbol, and Rhetoric in BC, 1884–1951," *CHR* 73, no. 2 (1992): 125–65; Douglas Cole and Ira Chaikin, *An Iron Hand Upon the People: The Law Against the Potlatch on the Northwest Coast* (Vancouver: Douglas & McIntyre, 1990).

25 Robin Brownlie and Mary-Ellen Kelm, "Desperately Seeking Absolution: Native Agency as Colonialist Alibi?" *CHR* 75, no. 4 (December 1994): 543–56. D. Cole and J.R. Miller responded and M.-E. Kelm responded to their response, "Notes and Comments: Desperately Seeking Absolution: Responses and a Reply," *CHR* 76, no. 4 (December 1995): 628–42.

26 Peter S. Schmalz, *The Ojibwa of Southern Ontario* (Toronto: University of Toronto Press, 1991); Olive Dickason, *Canada's First Nations: A History of Founding Peoples from Earliest Times* (Don Mills ON: Oxford University Press, 1992); Julie Cruikshank, *Life Lived Like a Story: Life Stories of Three Yukon Native Elders* (Lincoln–Vancouver: University of Nebraska Press–UBC Press, 1990), and *The Social Life of Stories: Narrative and Knowledge in the Yukon Territory* (Lincoln–Vancouver: University of Nebraska Press–UBC Press, 1998).

27 J.T. Carson, "Brebeuf Was Never Martyred: Reimagining the Life and Death of Canada's First Saint," *CHR* 97, no. 2 (June 2016): 222–43; Emma Anderson, *The Death and Afterlife of the North American Martyrs* (Cambridge MA: Harvard University Press, 2013); Patrice Groulx, *Pièges de la mémoire : Dollard des Ormeaux, les Amérindiens et nous* (Hull: Vents d'Ouest, 1998); Colin Coates and Cecelia Morgan, *Heroines and History: Representations of Madeleine de Verchères and Laura Secord* (Toronto: University of Toronto Press, 2002); Katherine Magee Labelle, *Dispersed but Not Destroyed: A History of the Seventeenth-Century Wendat People* (Vancouver: UBC Press, 2013); T. Peace and K.M. Labelle, eds., *From Huronia to Wendakes: Adversity, Migrations, and Resilience, 1650–1900* (Norman OK: University of Oklahoma Press, 2016); Susan M. Hill, *The Clay We Are Made Of: Haudenosaunee Land Tenure on the Grand River* (Winnipeg: University of Manitoba Press, 2017).

28 Mary Jane Logan McCallum, "Indigenous Labor and Indigenous History," *American Indian Quarterly* 33, no. 4 (Fall 2009): 523–44; *Indigenous Women, Work, and History, 1940–1980* (Winnipeg: University of Manitoba

Press, 2014); "Laws, Codes, Informal Practices: Building Ethical Procedures for Historical Research with Indigenous Medical Records," in *Sources and Methods in Indigenous Studies*, eds. Chris Andersen and Jean M. O'Brien (London: Rutledge, 2017), ch. 31; and "Starvation, Experimentation, Segregation, and Trauma: Words for Reading Indigenous Health History," *CHR* 98, no. 1 (March 2017): 96–113; with Adele Perry, *Structures of Indifference: An Indigenous Life and Death in a Canadian* City (Winnipeg: University of Manitoba Press, 2018); Rolf Knight, *Indians at Work: An Informal History of Native Labour in British Columbia, 1858–1930* (Vancouver: New Star Books ,1996); M.K. Lux, *Separate Beds: A History of Indian Hospitals in Canada, 1920s–1980s* (Toronto: University of Toronto Press, 2016); Ian Mosby, "Administering colonial science: nutrition research and human biomedical experimentation in Aboriginal communities and residential schools, 1942–1952," *Histoire sociale–Social History* 46, no. 91 (May 2013): 145–72; Mary-Ellen Kelm, *Colonizing Bodies: Aboriginal Health and Healing in British Columbia, 1900–1950* (Vancouver: UBC Press, 1998); Arthur J. Ray, "Native History on Trial" (among his other works on litigation); John Borrows, *Recovering Canada: The Resurgence of Indigenous Law* (Toronto: University of Toronto Press, 2017) among his other works on Indigenous law. Perhaps the most convenient is "Challenging Historical Frameworks: Aboriginal Rights, the Trickster, and Originalism," *CHR* 98, no. 1 (March 2017): 114–35.

29 Treaty 7 Elders and Tribal Council et al., *The True Spirit and Original Intent of Treaty 7* (Montreal and Kingston: McGill-Queen's University Press, 1996); Arthur J. Ray, Jim Miller, and Frank Tough, *Bounty and Benevolence: A Documentary History of Saskatchewan Treaties* (Montreal and Kingston: McGill-Queen's University Press, 2000); James R. Miller, *Compact, Contract, Covenant: Aboriginal Treaty-Making in Canada* (Toronto: University of Toronto Press, 2009) and "Contact, Contract, Covenant: The Evolution of Indian Treaty-Making," in *New Histories for Old: Changing Perspectives on Canada's Native Pasts*, eds. Theodore Binnema and Susan Neylan (Vancouver: UBC Press, 2007), 66–91; Michael Asch, *On Being Here to Stay: Treaties and Aboriginal Rights in Canada* (Toronto: University of Toronto Press, 2014); John Borrows and Michael Coyle, eds., *The Right Relationship: Reimagining the Implementation of Historical Treaties* (Toronto: University of Toronto Press, 2017); Jean-Pierre Morin, *Solemn Words and Foundational Documents: An Annotated Discussion of Indigenous-Crown Treaties in Canada, 1752–1923* (Toronto: University of Toronto Press, 2018); D.J. Hall, *From Treaties to Reserves: The Federal Government and Native*

Peoples in Territorial Alberta, 1870–1905 (Montreal and Kingston: McGill-Queen's University Press, 2015); Marie Battiste, ed., *Living Treaties: Narrating Mi'kmaw Treaty Relations* (Sydney NS: Cape Breton University Press, 2016).

30 T. Binnema and S. Neylan, "Arthur J. Ray and the Writing of Aboriginal History," in *New Histories for Old*, 1–17; Jennifer S.H. Brown, "'All These Stories about Women': 'Many Tender Ties' and a New Fur Trade History," 25–36; Adele Perry, "Historiography that Breaks your Heart: Van Kirk and the Writing of Feminist History," 81–97 in *Finding a Way to the Heart: Feminist Writing on Aboriginal and Women's History in Canada*, eds. Robin Jarvis Brownlie and Valerie J. Korinek (Winnipeg: University of Manitoba Press, 2012); Jean Barman, *French Canadians, Furs and Indigenous Women in the Making of the Pacific Northwest* (Vancouver: UBC Press, 2014); George Colpitts, *Pemmican Empire: Food, Trade, and the Last Bison Hunts in the North American Plains 1780–1882* (New York: Cambridge University Press, 2015).

31 Blair Stonechild and W.A. Waiser, *Loyal till Death: Indians and the North-West Rebellion* (Calgary: Fifth House, 1997); Keith T. Carlson, *You Are Asked to Witness: The Sto:lo in Canada's Pacific Coast History* (Chilliwack BC: Sto:lo Heritage Trust, 2000); Bruce G. Miller, *The Problem of Justice: Tradition and Law in the Coast Salish World* (Lincoln: University of Nebraska Press, 2000); Peace and Labelle, eds., *From Huronia to Wendakes*; Helen Raptis with members of the Tsimshian Nation, *What We Learned: Two Generations Reflect on Tsimishian Education and the Day Schools* (Vancouver: UBC Press, 2016); Arthur Manuel and Grand Chief Ronald M. Derrickson, *Unsettling Canada: A National Wake-Up Call* (Toronto: Between the Lines, 2015); Elsie Paul in collaboration with Paige Raibmon and Harmony Johnson, *Written as I Remember It: Teachings (ʔəms taʔaw) from the Life of a Sliammon Elder* (Vancouver: University of British Columbia Press, 2014); Jordan Wilson, "χətə kʷθə siyáləxʷeʔəɬ ct ... Our Elders Said," preface to Susan Roy, *These Mysterious People: Shaping History and Archaeology in a Northwest Coast Community*, 2nd ed. (Montreal and Kingston: McGill-Queen's University Press, 2016), and the museum exhibit c̓əsnaʔəm, the city before the city, Musqueam Cultural Centre Gallery, Museum of Vancouver, and Museum of Anthropology, University of British Columbia, Vancouver, British Columbia, January 2015; Robin and Jillian Ridington, in collaboration with Elders of Dane-Zaa First Nations, *Where Happiness Dwells: A History of the Dane-zaa First Nations* (Vancouver: University of British Columbia Press, 2013); Leslie A. Robertson with the Kwagu'? Gixsam Clan, *Standing Up with Ga'axsta'las: Jane Constance Cook*

and the Politics of Memory, Church, and Custom (Vancouver: University of British Columbia Press, 2012); Shirleen Smith and Vuntut Cwitchin First Nation, *People of the Lakes: Stories of Our Van Tat Gwich›in Elders* (Edmonton: University of Alberta Press, 2009); Keith Thor Carlson, John Sutton Lutz, David M. Schaepe, and Naxaxalhts'i–Albert "Sonny" McHalsie, eds., *Towards a New Ethnohistory: Community-Engaged Scholarship among the People of the River* (Winnipeg: University of Manitoba Press, 2018); Julie Cruikshank, "Oral Tradition and Oral History: Reviewing Some Issues," CHR 75, no. 3 (September 1994): 403–18.

32 For a discussion of Indigenous-authored works up to 2009 see Robin Jarvis Brownlie, "First Nations Perspectives and Historical Thinking," in *First Nations, First Thoughts: The Impact of Indigenous Thought in Canada*, ed. Anna May Timpson (Vancouver: UBC Press, 2009), 21–50.

33 Brenda Macdougall, "Space and Place within Aboriginal Epistemological Traditions: Recent Trends in Historical Scholarship," CHR 98, no.1 (January 2017): 64–82; Mary Jane Logan McCallum and Susan M. Hill, "Our Historiographical Moment: A Conversation about Indigenous Women's History in Canada in the Early Twenty-First Century," in *Reading Canadian Women's and Gender History*, eds. Nancy Janovicek and Carmen Nielson (Toronto: University of Toronto Press, 2019), 23–62. The website *Shekon Neechie* (https://shekonneechie.ca/) carries a listing of Indigenous-authored titles and brief biographies of the authors from 2000. Similarly useful is the journal *Native American and Indigenous Studies*, published twice a year by the University of Minnesota Press since 2014. See also the titles on Indigenous topics in the appendix.

34 See appendix.

35 See appendix.

36 *Journal of the Canadian Historical Association* 26, no. 2 (2015): 41–81.

37 CHR 100, no. 2 (June 2019): 160–201.

38 My count based on the program.

39 https://www.canada.ca/en/social-sciences-humanities-research.html.

40 As one typical example see https://uwaterloo.ca/indigenization-strategy/updates. For an interesting description of the program at the University of Victoria see John Lutz, "Experiments in Decolonizing and Indigenizing a University History Department," Canadian Historical Association, *Intersections* 2, no. 3 (2019): 14–15. While several Canadian, American, and overseas universities have conducted reviews of their relationship to the history of slavery and the slave trade, McGill University has launched a study of its institutional connections to both transatlantic slavery and "colonialism and its impact on Indigenous communities," through their

"Call for Applications: Provostial Research Scholars on Institutions, Slavery and Colonialism," (December 2019).

41 Lakehead University Law School is one example. In December 2019, the Law Society of British Columbia announced that in 2021 all lawyers practising in the province would be required to take an online course in Indigenous history, with optional follow-up courses. Also, of interest in this respect is the authoritative *A History of Law in Canada, Volume 1. Beginnings to 1866* by Philip Girard, Jim Phillips, and Blake Brown (Toronto: University of Toronto Press, 2018) which includes close examination of Canada's three legal traditions, Indigenous, French, and English.

42 Regina: University of Regina Press, 2013.

43 Daschuk told his publisher that his book "was not as 'new' as he thought it was," CHA *Journal*, panel discussion, 2015, comment by James Daschuk, 71, comment by Ian Mosby, 54. Indeed, much of the same story had been told in Sarah Carter's *Lost Harvests: Prairie Indian Reserve Farmers and Government Policy* (Montreal: McGill-Queen's University Press, 1990).

44 *Histoire sociale–Social History* 46, no. 9 (May 2013): 615–42.

45 Crystal Fraser and Ian Mosby, "Setting Canadian History Right? A Response to Ken Coates' Second Thoughts about Residential Schools," *Active History* (April 2015). Mosby's article deserved this attention because of its merits, though its appearance in 2013 suggests the significance of "timing" in the public reception of academic research.

46 #4 *Indigenous Relations* by Bob Joseph, # 5 *Embers* by Richard Wagamese, and #8 *21 Things You May Not Know About the Indian Act*, also by Bob Joseph.

47 *Globe and Mail*, 3 September 2019.

48 Excerpted in the *Globe and Mail*, 21 September 2019.

49 *Globe and Mail*, 3 August 2019.

50 Canadian Historical Association, *Intersections* 2, no. 1 (2019): 3.

51 *Globe and Mail*, 10 September 2019. The 2016 Canadian Census showed the Indigenous population as 4.5 per cent of the Canadian total.

52 *Globe and Mail*, 23 March 2019.

53 *Toronto Star*, 14 July 2019.

54 For example, Mary Jane Logan McCallum, "Condemned to Repeat? Settler Colonialism, Racism, and Canadian History Textbooks," in *"Too Asian? Racism, Privilege, and Post-Secondary Education*, eds. R.J. Gilmour et al. (Toronto: Between the Lines 2012), 67–79, 153–54.

55 Catherine Hall, "Doing Reparatory History: Bringing 'Race' and Slavery Home," *Race and Class* 60, no. 1 (July–September 2018): 3–21.

PART THREE

Rethinking Academia and Indigeneity

8

Forensic Anthropology and Archaeology as Tools for Reconciliation in Investigations into Unmarked Graves at Indian Residential Schools

Katherine L. Nichols, Eldon Yellowhorn, Deanna Reder, Emily Holland, Dongya Yang, John Albanese, Darian Kennedy, Elton Taylor, and Hugo F.V. Cardoso

Duncan Campbell Scott was an admired Confederation poet and life-long civil servant in Canada's Department of Indian Affairs from 1880 to 1932.[1] Evidence that he was highly respected is the fact that he was made a fellow of the Royal Society of Canada as early as 1899, even serving as president from 1921 to 1922. However, since Canada's Truth and Reconciliation Commission (2008–2015), Scott is now better remembered as the architect of the shameful Indian residential school system (IRSS), particularly during his years as the deputy-superintendent of the Department of Indian Affairs from 1913 until the end of his career in 1932.[2] What is often not attributed to Scott's ignoble legacy are the residential school cemeteries and unmarked graves left behind as the result of his roles in Indian Affairs.

While Scott cannot be solely blamed, it is an indubitable fact that over the course of his career, and coinciding with his membership in the Royal Society, an alarming number of Indigenous children died in residential schools. According to Canada's Truth and Reconciliation Commission executive summary, a total of 2,434 students in their named and unnamed registries perished before 1940.[3] While Scott would have argued that he saw education and residential schools as the best path for a colonial government to "get rid of [its] Indian problem,"[4] the number of deaths give this often-quoted turn of phrase a chilling meaning. Scott's steadfast determination to implement the ideals of his day would have long term repercussions for the children who fell under his control and the communities that lost them. Halfway through his career, his enthusiasm for the policies he enforced was not dampened by the lives lost; as RSC president, he saw no reason for public officials to abandon a policy that would "continue until there is not a single Indian in Canada that has not been absorbed into the body politic."[5]

THE TRUTH AND RECONCILIATION COMMISSION OF CANADA

Recognition of the damage of the IRSS has only recently been acknowledged. In *Therapeutic Nations: Healing in an Age of Indigenous Human Rights*,[6] Athabaskan scholar Dian Million contends that Indigenous communities found it difficult to speak out against residential school abuse prior to the end of the last century.[7] It was not until 1988, Million explains, when several key texts released in mainstream Canada helped provide Indigenous authors models of truth-telling and the vocabulary to be able to "name their family atrocities using language connected to social justice movements."[8] These testimonials validated survivor experiences and have become the foundation for learning about the history and legacy of residential schools in Canada through first-hand accounts.

When the Royal Commission on Aboriginal Peoples released its final report in 1996, among its recommendations was a national investigation into the abuses suffered at residential schools.[9] Subsequently, large numbers of former students began to file lawsuits about the abuse they suffered and named the federal government and churches as defendants. Together, they successfully settled Canada's largest class action lawsuit, which brought compensation for the plaintiffs and the Indian Residential Schools Settlement Agreement (IRSSA).[10] Out of this historic five-element agreement, $60 million were set aside to create the Truth and Reconciliation Commission (TRC) of Canada and fund its five-year mandate to create a public record of the residential schooling system in Canada. In 2008, three commissioners were appointed to lead the TRC.[11] Its two main objectives were to determine the true history of Indian residential schools and to facilitate reconciliation between Indigenous and non-Indigenous peoples in Canada.[12]

About the same time as the implementation of the IRSSA, Gary Merasty, Member of Parliament for Desnethé-Missinippi-Churchill River drew attention to missing children and unmarked graves.[13] Consequently, a Working Group on Missing Children and Unmarked Burials was established, composed of archivists and representatives from national Indigenous organizations, churches, the federal government and a national organization representing survivors.[14] Representatives met throughout 2007 and 2008, and identified four fundamental questions: who and how many students died; why did they die; where are they buried; and, what happened to children who went missing?[15] The Working Group also recommended four research projects: a statistical survey of enrolment and deaths; a review of operational policies and custodial care; a study to identify unmarked burials and commemoration options; and, a means to help individual requesters through specific case research.[16] The Working Group's next steps focused on establishing protocols to access archival records and on funding options. There was no mention of developing protocols specifically for searching for cemeteries and unmarked graves or how to work with affected communities.

MISSING CHILDREN RESEARCH PROJECT

The commission adopted the Working Group's recommendations[17] and the TRC director of research anticipated a budget of $1.5 million to locate deceased children's names in archival documents.[18] The identification of deceased children would hopefully be followed up by direct scanning of cemeteries and residential school grounds using archaeological techniques designed to find subsurface anomalies such as graves. Despite these plans, the original TRC budget did not include the $1.5 million needed, and requests for funding from Indian Affairs were denied. In spite of this setback, the commission launched the Missing Children Research Project[19] in 2009 with a six-member team[20] led by Alex Maass, a previous Indian Affairs civil servant who importantly had anthropological expertise with respect to graves.[21] The goals of the Missing Children Project were to produce as complete a list as possible of children who died at school, determine their cause of death, and locate school burial sites and cemeteries using archival documentation, survivor testimony, and archaeological search methods.[22]

In the commission's executive summary, the Missing Children Project identified 3,201 student deaths in its named and unnamed registries.[23] While the majority of deaths took place before 1940, coinciding with Scott's career in Indian Affairs, the comparative data further indicates that between 1941 and 1945, the death rate for residential school children was 4.9 times higher than for Canadian school children. Even into the 1960s, the death rate for residential school children was double that of Canadian school children.[24]

It is clear then that there must be cemeteries associated with the schools in which these children died. Yet, the "Cemeteries and Unmarked Burials" chapter, only fourteen pages long, lacks vital information. The commission revealed that the Missing Children Project team was only able to visit, survey, and document burials for twenty cemetery sites across Canada.[25] The chapter does not provide a list of the school names, or a summary of the results of each cemetery visit, nor is there reference to site protection. Vaguely, the commission notes, "the locations of some of the cemeteries ... are known. The exact location of others is currently unknown."[26] In the absence of direct examination of all residential school sites, the commission utilized operational periods to estimate the schools' probability of having a cemetery.[27] Schools that opened before 1950 had higher deaths, and are therefore more likely to have cemeteries than schools that opened after 1950. While the commission does not include the exact number of cemeteries, using this model, it is likely that about ninety-five residential schools have at least one associated cemetery. This directly affects the provinces of British Columbia, Alberta, Saskatchewan, Manitoba, Ontario, Quebec, and Nova Scotia, as well as the Yukon and the Northwest Territories. This is a minimum number, as there are 139 residential schools on the TRC's list and it is possible that each one had at least one cemetery but possibly more. The mandate of the Missing Children Project was underfunded and had an impossibly large task to address in five short years. Consequently, it is unknown exactly where these cemeteries are and where the children who died at residential schools are buried.

Without a clear understanding of what remains to be done, multi-disciplinary, community-based research teams struggle to develop a suitable approach. Further complicating the issue is the lack of clear information as to what the policies were and what funding was available for schools for the purpose of reporting child deaths or burying children. While the commission asserts that the federal government's failure to provide proper funding and establish policies on acceptable care, largely contributed to unnecessarily high death rates at residential schools, they do not make similar statements regarding policies and funding relevant to recording children's deaths, notifying families, or burying children. Moreover, the commission does not connect the vulnerable and abandoned state of cemeteries to the absence of government policies during the closure of residential schools that should have ensured long-term protection. Nor does the commission comment on how these policies or lack thereof, have the potential to impact investigations into determining who died at residential schools and where they were buried.

Case Study: The Brandon Indian Residential School

The Brandon Residential School is a direct example of Scott's legacy. It was a flagship school for both the Department of Indian Affairs and the Methodist Church, yet serves as an example of the atrocities of the Canadian residential schooling system and the difficulties associated with trying to determine where children are buried. Unfortunately, with the passage of time, the collective local community memory of the school has faded, and historical facts have become illusive. Misinformation has directly impacted the community of Brandon's understanding of the legacy of the residential school and protection of the school cemeteries.[28]

In 1890, the federal government assigned $6,000 to the Methodist Church for the purpose of building an industrial school.[29] In choosing a site location, officials considered proximity to a settler community, distance from Indigenous communities, and suitable land for agricultural training.[30] The selection of the site was also influenced by city leaders in Brandon, who were willing to trade land to secure an Indian industrial school.[31] By 1891, the parties agreed that the school would be next to the Brandon Experimental Farm on the outer limits of the City of Brandon, and it subsequently opened in 1895.[32]

News of the decision to locate the school in Brandon was immediately met with resistance from Indigenous communities in the Methodists' missionary catchment area in northern Manitoba.[33] Chiefs from Berens River and Cross Lake First Nations and community members from various Nations clearly expressed their concerns about sending their children so far away with the specific fear that

Figure 8.1 Students at Brandon Residential School.

they may never see them again.[34] When the first principal took these concerns to the Department of Indian Affairs in 1894, the mandatory attendance policy implemented in 1884 was enforced.[35] It is also possible that the warrant that Scott secured in 1895 to allow the forcible removal of children from their families was utilized.[36]

The Brandon Residential School represents the problems that affected the residential schooling system. Overcrowding in 1901, 1918, and 1932 was the direct result of underfunding created by the per capita funding formula, where the amount of funding received was based on the number of children registered. In 1910, Scott created the "1910 contract" that required the government to increase per-capita grants ($100–$125 per child) so churches could make improvements to school buildings, student clothing, and food.[37] This led to further overcrowding at the Brandon Residential School as the school administrators increased the student enrollment in order to maximize funding.[38]

Overcrowding directly contributed to the spread of airborne disease. School personnel were not able to accommodate the high number of sick children, resulting in sick children staying in standard dormitories, thereby increasing the spread of pneumonia, influenza, measles, and tuberculosis.[39] In addition to airborne disease, the school did little to provide an adequate diet. Dietary investigations in 1947–1948 revealed that the school was spending

Figure 8.2 New students arrive at Brandon Residential School.

Figure 8.3 Boys with piglets.

only 44 per cent of the recommended food cost per child, causing insufficient food quantity and quality.[40] Further, food deprivation was recommended as a form of discipline as early as 1896[41] and likely continued throughout the school's operation, evidenced by the fact that in 1953 children were observed searching for food around barns on school property, for "food that should only be fed to the barn occupants."[42] Punishment ranged from sending students to jail for insubordination[43] to sending them to the mental hospital for "incorrigible behaviour."[44] A survivor recalled the cruelty of punishment experienced at the school "such as being tied to a flag pole, sent to bed with no food, literally beaten and slapped by staff."[45] Overcrowding, airborne diseases, inadequate nutrition, unsafe foods, and severe punishment would inevitably contribute to the children's deaths.[46]

By 1913, the Brandon Residential School had an expansive 960-acre agricultural farm.[47] Student manual labour was exploited, and the children were often left unsupervised[48] to work with dangerous equipment and livestock, resulting in farm accidents,[49] one of which was fatal.[50] Female students were sent as domestic servants to the homes of the school's principals,[51] which subsequently prepared some female graduates to be placed into the homes of prominent families and university professors within and outside of Manitoba.[52] Student runaways and truancy were common and were particularly high during the time of Principal Strapp (1944 to 1955)[53] to the extent that the

RCMP reported that twenty-five students fled the school in 1951.[54] The forced manual work, domestic labour, violence, abuse, and hunger are only some of the underlying reasons why children made daring escapes from the Brandon Residential School.[55]

Adults who survived their experience at the Brandon Residential School have continued to feel the impact throughout their lives. The trauma associated with the school is compounded by the complexities associated with the cemeteries. Within the community of Brandon, conflicting information surrounds the number of cemeteries associated with the Brandon Residential School, their location, whether the cemeteries are mass burial grounds, or if they even existed. Paired with this conflicting information, the difficult to access and incomplete archival record has further compounded the ability of Sioux Valley Dakota Nation and affected communities to accumulate information regarding the whereabouts of their children.

FIRST SCHOOL CEMETERY

Four children from the distant communities of God's Lake First Nation and Norway House Cree Nation died in the autumn of 1896 and so the school established its first cemetery alongside the Assiniboine River.[56] The cemetery was in use from 1896 until at least 1912 when the Brandon Public Parks Board and city council approached Principal Ferrier to purchase the school lands along the Assiniboine River to develop a suburban park.[57] The Department of Indian Affairs, Principal Ferrier, and Brandon City Council deliberated the sale for a number of years and the City of Brandon did not officially acquire the land until 1921.[58] Based on available archival records, during the period leading up to the closure of the cemetery (1895 to 1911), fifty-one names of students who died at the school from twelve different Nations have been identified.[59] The fears of the communities from which these children came were realized: their loved ones died away from home, never to be seen again.

Not only did these children die away from home, they were not even afforded a safe place to rest. At the time of the change in ownership, no provisions were made regarding protecting the cemetery. Consequently, trees were removed,[60] a public pool was constructed in 1961,[61] and all the headstones in the cemetery were removed[62] so that the site could be "bulldozed over"[63] to be used as a picnic area.[64] These changes have affected the understanding of the location and

Figure 8.4 Brandon Girl Guides at the Brandon Residential School's First Cemetery in Curran Park.

extent of the cemetery and highlight the lack of respect provided to the graves of Indigenous children who died at residential schools.

What commemoration and identification occurred was a result of community members and organizations and not the City of Brandon that owned the land. In 1963, the location of the burial ground was marked with four white stakes by Alfred Kirkness, Brandon residential school survivor and, in the early 1970s, the Brandon Rotary Club erected a hexagonal wood fence and the Brandon Girl Guides planted flowers and provided the plaque,[65] which they affixed to a large rock near the entrance.

In 2001, the City of Brandon sold the land (Curran Park) with the stipulation that the Aboriginal burial ground on the site must be left intact,[66] yet there were no rules regarding land use. In June 2002, the land was sold again to another private owner. It appears that, over time, different landowners got the impression that the

Figure 8.5 Brandon Residential School's First Cemetery, circa 2004.

memorial garden was not an official cemetery. As a result, between 2012–2017 land owner(s) denied permission for formal investigations to locate the cemetery and its boundaries or to identify unmarked graves.[67] More recently, the landowner has been willing to allow such investigations.

SECOND SCHOOL CEMETERY

Permission to construct a second cemetery on school grounds was granted in 1912,[68] but it is not until the 1950s that reference to this second cemetery reappears in archival documents.[69] The location of this cemetery is unknown as the sketch map that accompanied the original request is missing from the archival file as is the map provided by Principal Bond in 1967.[70] Even while still in use, the cemetery was not maintained. Eventually, due to obvious

Figure 8.6 Brandon Residential School's Second Cemetery, 2013.

neglect of the cemetery and continuous letters from a graduate of the school, Alfred Kirkness, Indian Affairs provided funding for a fence and cairn, and allocated $200 annually for maintenance of the cemetery. The fence and cairn were erected in 1967 and the plaque was added in 1968. The eleven names of children on the plaque are likely those who passed away between 1928 and 1957. At least five names are missing from the plaque that were on the original list provided by Principal Bond.[71] Currently, there are twelve white wooden crosses and all but one has fallen down within the cemetery fence.[72] It is possible this second cemetery operated until the school closed in 1972.

THIRD BURIAL LOCATION

It is not possible to fix precise dates to the opening and closing of these two school cemeteries. It is difficult to say with certainty that the first school cemetery closed in 1912 when Principal Ferrier requested this, or that the second cemetery north of the school is the same cemetery that he intended on opening, but with an opening date of 1928 instead of 1921. Consequently, there is a sixteen-year gap of cemetery operations, during which nine children from six different Nations are known to have died. It is possible that these children, and others who were not recorded, are buried inside and outside the second school cemetery fence.[73] Further, the Sioux Valley Dakota Nation community has concerns about unmarked graves behind the school that may indicate a third school cemetery.[74]

CALLS TO ACTION

The Truth and Reconciliation Commission released ninety-four *Calls to Action* with the aim of repairing harms caused by the legacy of residential schools. The commission advocated that improvements needed to be made to policies and programs in order to continue the process of reconciliation in Canada. To ensure work continued with residential school cemeteries, *Calls to Action* 71–76 directly address *Missing Children and Burial Information*.[75] Action 74 in particular directs the federal government to work with Indigenous Nations and churches to contact families with information of their child's grave location and to work with these families to commemorate their child's resting place. This Call to Action also states that the federal government should respond to families who would like their child reburied in their home community. Call to Action 75 calls on local stakeholders to develop strategies in order to locate, map, protect, and commemorate school cemeteries and other sites where children might be buried. Call to Action 76 recommends that the Indigenous community most affected take the lead on the project, that survivors and Elders be consulted, and Indigenous protocols be respected before any investigation of a cemetery site begins. These specific *Calls to Action* (71–76) brought attention to unmarked graves and missing children from residential schools across Canada, but do not directly address how investigations should progress or how repatriation or commemoration should unfold. The *Calls to Action* do not specifically request assistance from academics, researchers, or the academe more broadly, however, these institutions can play an important role in applying forensic and archaeological methods in the residential school context.

BRANDON'S REPRESENTATION IN THE COMMISSION'S REPORT

When discussing commemoration and protection, the commission's final report specifically referenced Brandon.[76] However, the brief discussion of Brandon's school cemeteries does not address, and the commission may have been unaware of, the complications surrounding land jurisdiction. The reality is, as we write this paper, negotiations to find and protect the first cemetery are still ongoing and are only moving forward because of the goodwill of all stakeholders.[77]

When discussing Brandon's second school cemetery, the report does not detail that within the Rural Municipality of Cornwallis, the location of the site is on federal agricultural land. The site is remote, difficult to access, and entrance requires keys to unlock two sets of gates. In the past, this restriction was due in part to protect the public from cattle, but now makes access to this important area complicated. The commission's report does not reference the number of burials or the condition of the graves. Again, as we write this paper, negotiations for land access, maintenance, and care of this cemetery are underway.

The commission's report was meant to showcase examples of attempts to address neglected residential school cemeteries. However, by overlooking the ever-present complications at Brandon, the commission reinforced community assumptions about the first school cemetery being a memorial site, omitted discussions about unkempt graves and site access to the second school cemetery, and did not address operational gaps in the cemetery records. It is difficult for those implicated in the ongoing discussions about the Brandon Residential School cemeteries to follow the commission's *Calls to Action* when its report did not present guidelines for community collaboration, procedures for search methods, or protocols for site investigations. Formal cemetery designation remains elusive, complicating efforts to identify, commemorate, and protect school cemeteries. This has left affected stakeholders to negotiate a solution on their own.

THE BRANDON RESIDENTIAL SCHOOL CEMETERIES PROJECT

Academic research regarding the Brandon Residential School burial grounds began in 2012 as part of Nichols', the first author, graduate thesis project at the University of Manitoba.[78] Sioux Valley Dakota Nation currently owns a portion of the school property. As stewards of the land, the responsibility has fallen onto them to find and protect the cemeteries and unmarked graves. The research was collaboratively designed to address cultural concerns and identify appropriate techniques to investigate survivors' accounts. The project used a variety of methods such as archival research, interviews, and archaeological and forensic search techniques.

Archaeology has developed non-invasive and invasive field practices to locate ancient and historic sites. The discipline's scientific study of the past through the excavation, recovery, and analysis of human remains and material culture have been important sources of information to understand past ways of life. More importantly, through their investigations into the past, archaeologists are able to give voice to those who were silenced and whose stories were not recorded as part of history.[79] Forensic anthropologists on the other hand, are trained in the identification and recovery of human remains from clandestine graves and outdoor crime scenes. While they generally work on cases that are of medico-legal significance in partnership with law enforcement and the medical examiner or coroner's office, the techniques and expertise of the discipline are uniquely suited to find and identify children associated with unmarked graves. Consequently, pairing techniques and technology used by both archaeologists and forensic anthropologists provides the opportunity for in-depth survey and analysis of an area to identify unmarked graves. To date, field walking to identify differences in soil density, aerial photography, controlled burns, ground penetrating radar (GPR), and electromagnetic ground conductivity (EM38) were used to systematically survey the school's property and two cemeteries. Through this investigation, 104 potential unmarked graves were identified. Paired with the fact that there are only seventy-eight recorded deaths, it is clear that more work needs to be done to understand who may be in these potential unmarked graves. No excavation can be done without engagement with affected communities and families.

The investigation into unmarked graves and cemeteries at the school has developed into a partnership spearheaded by Sioux Valley Dakota Nation and supported by faculty and students from Simon Fraser University, the University of Windsor, and Brandon University.[80] The goals of the project are to identify affected communities with children who may be buried in the cemeteries and work together collaboratively to establish a path forward, whether by registering the site as a historic cemetery, establishing formal commemoration, or applying forensic scientific methods of excavation and identification to determine who these children were and therefore restore their identity and facilitate repatriation to their home community if that is what the communities desire. In establishing this project, the team has attempted to address the commission's *Calls to Action*, but has confronted many practical problems as we translate the recommendations into applied practice.

At its heart, this project is not only community engaged but community led, where academic partners aim to support Sioux Valley Dakota Nation and associated communities attaining their goals. At least fifteen different Nations from 54 different communities had children attend or die at the Brandon Residential School and it is important to recognize these diverse Indigenous communities.[81] As a result, the vital first step in this partnership is community contact and engagement. By working to establish community relationships, we will navigate ethical, legal, and cultural complexities together, to find a resolution and honour the missing children and unmarked graves at the Brandon Residential School. With the rights of the families and Indigenous communities at the centre of our research design, we considered the implications of Call to Action number 76, which asserts that the "Aboriginal community most affected shall lead the development" of this work. We speculated about the criteria for determining the "most affected community" and who would make this decision. In this case, while the Sioux Valley Dakota Nation decided to initiate this work, as they own some of the property associated with the school, identifying additional communities affected by the legacy of the Brandon Residential School has been difficult. Therefore, oral history interviews with survivors and their relatives will help broadcast our work across Manitoba in order to ensure community engagement. Facilitating co-operation and collaboration may present some challenges as political, historical, and ontological perspectives emerge.

We also wondered about the process of informing families of the proposed work to identify graves and individuals at the Brandon Residential School. Before any further work begins, communities need to be informed and provided opportunities to determine the process and outcome. Yet, even informing communities of the work completed and potential next steps could cause harm to families and residential school survivors. As a result, we are considering what supports should be in place for families and communities to minimize harm and provide care. At the very core of this issue, we acknowledge that the children buried at the Brandon Residential School did not receive Indigenous ceremonies or gifts needed to pass into the spirit world. Additionally, since many of them came from great distances, their remains are not located within their traditional territory and the child's sacred connection to land has been lost. We anticipate that communities will have ancestral connections to these children. We acknowledge that many parents of children who attended and died at the Brandon Residential School were denied the basic human right to know what happened to their child.

With Call to Action 74, we considered how to respond to community wishes for appropriate markers when no cemetery plot maps have been found for the Brandon Residential School. Further the lack of a complete list of all children who died at the school means that it is unclear exactly where those who were recorded to have died are buried. This anonymity of children's graves has caused us to question how we and the federal government can "respond to families' wishes for reburial in home communities." Without being able to provide an exact burial location for their children and without additional details surrounding their death, it may not be possible to determine exactly where certain children are buried without excavation and invasive destructive analysis such as DNA and stable isotopes. In addition, the commission had no power to create or direct public laws in its brief call for reburial in home communities. Nor did it have a mandate to define a repatriation process. Thus, as investigators, we must navigate the awkward legal terrain to identify remains and return them to their families if that is what communities wish. We recognize that depriving families of the right to repatriation continues to inflict harms on those communities advocating for the remains to be brought home. Yet, the task is difficult, especially when Indigenous cultures are so diverse, with a range of protocols for respecting those who have passed on. For many, respect means to not disturb the grave, which may be counter to those who may want their children returned. The decision is either to excavate and attempt to identify all the children or none of them, since identities are unknown. While this seems like an impossible dilemma, we know that answers to these questions will require a considerable amount of time, discussion, planning, and respect.

With Call to Action 75, we contemplated the challenges that follow the request to, "develop and implement strategies and procedures for the ongoing identification, documentation, maintenance, commemoration, and protection of residential school cemeteries or other sites at which residential school children were buried." Determining the history and ownership of the land must happen before beginning an investigation to identify a cemetery. Site access is dependent on land jurisdiction. When residential schools were decommissioned, the chaotic process Canada created happened when no systematic plan for redistributing school properties existed. Some land fell under the control of local governments, a few Indian Bands bought the schools on their reserve, and some are in private hands. In many cases, the provinces or territories did not register these cemeteries. Private property owners had no obligation to maintain them, or in some cases, they were unaware a cemetery came with the sale. In the absence of provincial or federal protocols generating perpetual care funds, residential school burial grounds face an uncertain status. Confused accountability yielded haphazard and inconsistent preservation of these sites across the country. In a few cases, they became registered cemeteries used and managed by church organizations. More often, maintaining and repairing them fell to nearby First Nations, friendship centres, or even the goodwill of individual families and survivors. Considering these circumstances, establishing any standards to prevent neglect and destruction or to investigate them is particularly difficult. The commission reaffirms the importance of locating and identifying graves and cemeteries but remains silent on the issue of how Indigenous communities can gain jurisdictional control of these particular lands. Official silence assigns an ambiguous status for residential school cemeteries that investigators must navigate to conduct the research necessary to identify the cemeteries and those who are buried.

Without federal legislation in place to address residential school cemeteries, forward momentum is limited. Absent of a specific policy, investigators must utilize existing channels, ill-equipped to handle residential school cemeteries. Moreover, since residential school cemeteries are strewn across the country, this type of inquiry is beyond the scope of any one government Heritage Branch archaeologist. Even conducting a non-invasive survey in Manitoba entails several requirements such as applying for a heritage permit, holding a master's degree in archaeology, and securing permission to access private property. This final condition can be problematic, especially for unregistered, unmarked cemeteries. Although the provincial *Cemetery Act* administers protection, it defines a Funeral Board that administers "registered" cemeteries in the province. Consequently, residential school cemeteries receive no protection under that law, nor do they qualify as heritage sites that relevant legislation would cover. Investigators who successfully locate a residential school cemetery will find formal protection elusive.

Excavation of unmarked residential school graves is fraught with ethical and logistical dilemmas. The Brandon Residential School is no different due in part to the various stakeholders who bring forward unforeseen implications of this project. Currently, unmarked graves at residential schools occupy an interdepartmental grey area, somewhere between an archaeological and forensic context. Federal and provincial agencies have no established protocols specifically relating to their excavation. In Manitoba, protocols exist for found human remains, where once the RCMP and Medical Examiner's Office determine the remains to be of historic or pre-contact origin and a death investigation or forensic investigation is not required, the responsibility falls to the Historic Resources Branch. The Historic Resources Branch is responsible for the disposition of pre-contact and historic human remains in the province, particularly those that are found outside a recognized cemetery or burial ground. The passage of time since burial, yet at the same time, being situated in a modern context, complicates determining the jurisdictional responsibilities for possible unmarked graves. This 'in-between' status for unmarked graves is yet another legacy of residential schools. The current model of collaboration between the RCMP, Medical Examiner's Office and Historic Resources Branch is reactive. This does not anticipate cases when possible unmarked burials identified through non-invasive field survey methods must be confirmed through the process of excavation. There needs to be long-term coordination between these agencies lead by Indigenous communities and supported by allied academic researchers.

Co-ordinating our work with the Manitoba Historic Resources Branch, RCMP D-Division, and Medical Examiner's Office is necessary to start a formal investigation into the exact location of graves associated with the Brandon Residential School and possible excavation if that is the wish of partner communities. Research personnel will also partner with the Sioux Valley Dakota Nation and affected Indigenous communities to develop protocols for potential field and laboratory analyses to ensure a respectful project. This will include, but is not limited to, allocating sufficient time for ceremonies with

Elders before, during and after field work, and throughout the field work and preparation of appropriate materials. Due to the project's sensitive nature, expert researchers will have archaeological and forensic training, with a particular focus on juvenile osteology. If excavation is determined as the path communities want to follow, the remains of the children will be cared for in sacred cedar coffins, lined with red fabric, with tobacco bundles, offerings, or in any way a descendant community determines is appropriate.

If it is the wish of associated affected communities, reclaiming the identity of a child buried in unmarked graves will utilize three modes of scientific study. Once removed from a burial site, the children will be assessed to determine characteristics such as sex, age at death, and features that may help in their identification and linkage with archival records and family and survivor stories.[82] Samples will be taken of the children's teeth and bones to conduct analysis for oxygen isotopes and DNA. Oxygen isotopes from local water sources are embedded into tooth enamel through growth, that may make it possible to link children to the community they grew up in even if they died elsewhere. Isotope analysis requires the comparison of the isotopes in tooth enamel with the isotopes from the communities that children came from.[83] Determining their isotope identity will help to link them to their home community. This may then help refine the possible identification for a child to a specific community. It may then be possible to conduct DNA analysis to link that child with community or family members, thereby determining exactly to whom the remains belong. Without these methods identifying children as to age and place of birth, the number of DNA comparisons would be enormous and too expensive and difficult to implement. Therefore, the archival research, interview data, skeletal and isotopic analyses provide the complementary data that helps to narrow down the pool of potential candidates for DNA sampling.[84]

Through these scientific methods, our goal is to identify children, notify their next of kin, and facilitate the child's homecoming if that is what the affected communities' desire. We are also prepared to respect families' wishes to commemorate their child's original resting place in southern Manitoba, if they so choose. Tragically, identification might not always be possible. Therefore, the Sioux Valley Dakota Nation has offered to be the living representative for any child who cannot be identified and is unable to return home. These children will be cared for, protected, and honoured in southwestern

Manitoba. The children will be commemorated with a headstone, in order to counteract the legacy of anonymity.

REFLECTIONS AND RECOMMENDATIONS

Since residential schools emerged from federal policy, they require a national response. It is precisely because of Scott's insufficient consideration of the administration of residential school cemeteries that graves of lost children were abandoned and became unmarked. Our collaborative work at the Brandon Residential School is a case study for reconciliation, designed by academics with expertise that can make a meaningful contribution but led by the wishes of an Indigenous Nation and affected communities. Our research explores one strategy that will be a model for other researchers to reference. Although our investigation employs many scientific methods, we are cognizant that developing and maintaining respectful partnerships and building a successful multi-stakeholder consensus are just as important. While universities struggle to define institutional responses to the commission, our work with Sioux Valley Dakota Nation provides a concrete example. We deploy scientific knowledge respectfully to ensure that descendant communities have the authority to arrange culturally appropriate disposition of remains. While we are grounded in a positive scientific framework, we are not indifferent to the human conditions involved in the repatriation process. We anticipate that the guidelines, procedures, and protocols we create can be scaled up for collaborative investigations of unmarked graves and burial grounds at Indian residential schools nationwide.

Missing children and unmarked graves are forgotten human rights issues in Canada and contribute to the tragic legacy created by the Department of Indian Affairs and Scott. Regardless of the work completed by the commission, protection of residential school cemeteries remained unchanged. Jurisdiction of school cemeteries and unmarked burial grounds is tenuous, and these sacred sites, even now, are vulnerable to permanent destruction. The recent release of the National Centre for Truth and Reconciliation (NCTR) *Memorial Registry* is a good start, but simply not enough. The NCTR and other federal and provincial and territorial governmental agencies have been largely absent from discussions about identifying and protecting school cemeteries. While investigations into school cemeteries and children's burials are tangible examples of reconciliation projects, to do this work necessitates a fundamental rethinking of how cemeteries are protected in this country. Although a national strategy has not been developed, hopefully, the implementation of one will provide the jurisdiction needed for families to advocate for the protection of school cemeteries and define procedures for the repatriation of their children.

CLOSING REMARKS

Denying deceased children the dignity of an identity and burying them in unmarked graves are the symptoms of colonial violence that persist today. It sustains intergenerational trauma by preventing families from grieving for their lost children. Without a formal inquiry into deaths at residential schools, parents cannot find answers, justice, or any sense of closure. Missing children force us to confront one of the most powerful barriers to healing and reconciliation. As with so many aspects of the residential schools, justice is elusive for the survivors and their families, but through this work, we hope to see a tangible remedy for a historic wrong. This project will contribute new knowledge about Indian residential schools, a topic often avoided when discussing Canada's heritage. We will demonstrate that university-based researchers and students collaborating with First Nations can lead to progress on addressing social justice issues and human rights violation cases. Our results will have a lasting benefit for Indigenous peoples, and for all Canadians. We will add meaning to the *Calls to Action* and create an opportunity to renew a relationship now marked by mistrust. By acknowledging and acting on the issue of unmarked graves at the Brandon Residential School, we begin the work toward reconciliation. Canada cannot afford to ignore this situation and our project will heed the call.

NOTES

1 E. Brian Titley, *A Narrow Vision: Duncan Campbell Scott and the Administration of Indian Affairs in Canada* (Vancouver: UBC Press, 1986), 24, 91.
2 Titley, *Narrow Vision*, 22.
3 Truth and Reconciliation Commission of Canada (TRC), *Final Report of the Truth and Reconciliation Commission of Canada Volume 4: Canada's Residential Schools: Missing Children and Unmarked Burials*, (Winnipeg, MB: Truth and Reconciliation Commission of Canada, 2015).

4 D.C. Scott, "Deputy Superintendent General of Indian Affairs, Testimony before the Special Committee of the House of Commons Examining the *Indian Act* Amendments of 1920," Library and Archives Canada, RG10, vol. 6810, file 470-2-3, vol. 7, 55
5 Ibid.
6 Dian Million, *Therapeutic Nations: Healing in an Age of Indigenous Human Rights* (Tuscon: University of Arizona Press, 2013).
7 For examples of authors who have published about IRSS experiences see Bev Sellars and Mary Harrison, *They Called Me Number One: Secrets and Survival at an Indian Residential School* (Vancouver: Talonbooks, 2013); Joseph Auguste Merasty and David Carpenter, *The Education of Augie Merasty: A Residential School Memoir* (Regina: University of Regina Press, 2017); Edmund Metatawabin and Alexandra Shimo, *Up Ghost River: A Chief's Journey Through the Turbulent Waters of Native History* (Toronto: Vintage Canada, 2015).
8 Million, *Therapeutic Nation*, 89
9 *Royal Commission on Aboriginal Peoples*, vol. 1:36.
10 Indigenous and Northern Affairs Canada, *Indian Residential Schools Settlement Agreement* (Ottawa, ON: Indigenous and Northern Affairs Canada, 2019).
11 Truth and Reconciliation Commission of Canada, *Final Report of the Truth and Reconciliation Commission of Canada: Summary: Honouring the Truth, Reconciling for the Future* (Ottawa: Truth and Reconciliation Commission of Canada, 2015).
12 Alex Maass, "Perspectives on the Missing: Residential Schools for Aboriginal Children in Canada," in *Missing Persons: Multidisciplinary Perspectives on the Disappeared*, ed., Derek Congram (Toronto: Canadian Scholars' Press, 2016).
13 David B. MacDonald, *The Sleeping Giant Awakens: Genocide, Indian Residential Schools, and the Challenge of Conciliation.* (Toronto: University of Toronto Press, 2019).
14 Maass, *Missing Persons*; MacDonald, *The Sleeping Giant.*
15 Ibid.
16 Truth and Reconciliation Commission, *Volume 4: Canada's Residential Schools: Missing Children and Unmarked Burials.*
17 Ibid.
18 M. Milne, "The Forgotten Children: Researchers Scour Church Archives to Find Records of Students who Died at Indian Residential Schools," *United Church Observer*, 12 July 2010.

19 Truth and Reconciliation Commission, *Volume 4: Canada's Residential Schools: Missing Children and Unmarked Burials.*
20 MacDonald, *The Sleeping Giant.*
21 Alexandra Paul, "Where are the Children Buried? Truth and Reconciliation Looking into Most Horrible Chapter of Painful Residential Schools Saga," *Winnipeg Free Press*, 19 February 2011.
22 Truth and Reconciliation Commission, *Special Open House Newsletter*, (2010).
23 Truth and Reconciliation Commission, *Volume 4: Canada's Residential Schools: Missing Children and Unmarked Burials*, 15.
24 Ibid., 18.
25 Ibid., 125.
26 Ibid., 127.
27 Ibid., 127.
28 Katherine Nichols, *Investigation of Unmarked Graves and Burial Grounds at the Brandon Indian Residential School* (MA Thesis, University of Manitoba, 2015).
29 M. Gree, *Library and Archives Canada Microform Collection – School Files Series (LACMC-SFS)*, vol. 6255, file 576, part 1, c-8647, (1890), 1914.
30 H. Reed, LACMC-SFS, vol. 6255, file 576, part 1, c-8647, (1889), 1911–1913.
31 J. Miller, *Shingwauk's Vision: A History of Native Residential Schools* (Toronto, ON: University of Toronto Press, 1996), 177.
32 Department of Indian Affairs, *Indian Affairs Annual Reports*, Dominion of Canada annual report of the Department of Indian Affairs for the year ended 31st December (Ottawa; Library and Archives Canada, 1891), xiv.
33 Methodist Church, LACMC-SFS, vol. 6255, file 576, part 1, c-8647, (1888), 1906–1907.
34 Jacobs Berens, LACMC-SFS, vol. 6255, file 576, part 1, c-8647, (1891), 1995–1996.
35 H. Reed, LACMC-SFS, vol. 6255, file 576, part 1, c-8647, (1885), 2060–2061.
36 Cindy Blackstock, (8 May 2013), Child Health Policy Centre. https://childhealthpolicy.ca/mowafaghian-visiting-scholar/dr-cindy-blackstock/), retrieved from: https://childhealthpolicy.ca/wp-content/uploads/2013/04/Cindy-Blackstock-TRANSCRIPT.pdf
37 Titley, *Narrow Vision*, 86; Truth and Reconciliation Commission, *Volume 4: Canada's Residential Schools: Missing Children and Unmarked Burials*, 67.

38 J. Doyle, LACMC-SFS, vol. 6258, file 576-1, part 2, c-8648, (1932), 157; Jackson, LACMC-SFS, vol. 6255, file 576, part 2, c-8648, (1918), 30.
39 Jackson, LACMC-SFS at 30.
40 John Milloy, *A National Crime: The Canadian Government and the Residential School System, 1879 to 1986* (Winnipeg, MB: University of Manitoba Press, 1999), 266–267.
41 A. Forget, LACM-SFS, vol. 6255, file 576-1, part 1, c-8647, (1896), 2154–2155.
42 Ian Mosby, "Administering Colonial Science: Nutrition Research and Human Biomedical Experimentation in Aboriginal Communities and Residential Schools, 1942–1952," *Social History*, 46(91), (2013): 170.
43 J. Semmens, LACMC-SFS, vol. 6255, file 576, part 1, c-8647, (1896), 2152–2153.
44 J. Doyle, LACMC-SFS, vol. 6258, file 576-10, part 8, c-8650, (1938), 285–293.
45 Milloy, *A National Crime*, 284.
46 Nichols, *Investigation of Unmarked Graves*, 45.
47 "Indian Industrial school has Taken up the Raising of More Pure Bred Stock," 20 November 1913. [Clipping from an unidentified Brandon *Daily Sun* newspaper, 1, Brandon, MB].
48 Miller, *Shingwauk's Vision*.
49 Chinta Puxley, "Residential School Survivors Suffered Hearing and Breathing Problems," *Toronto Star*, 27 July 2014.
50 R. Davis, LACMC-SFS, vol. 6259, file 576-23, part 1, c-8651, (1949), 753–757.
51 J. Doyle, LACMC-SFS, vol. 6258, file 576-10, part 10, c-8650, (1940), 865–866.
52 J. Doyle, LACMC-SFS, vol. 6258, file 576-10, part 8, c-8650, (1937), 188; R. Hoey, LACMC-SFS, vol. 6258, file 576-10, part 10, c-8650, (1940), 872.
53 United Church of Canada, "Indian Residential School Records: Descriptions from the Finding Aid of the administrative records of the Conference of Manitoba & North-western Ontario," unpublished manuscript (Winnipeg, MB: United Church of Canada Conference Archivist).
54 M-E. LeBeuf, *The role of the Royal Canadian Mounted Police during the Indian residential school system* (Ottawa, ON: Royal Canadian Mounted Police, 2011).
55 Nichols, *Investigation of Unmarked Graves*, 31
56 Library and Archives Canada, *Register of Admission and Discharges – Brandon Industrial School*, Indian Affairs, RG 10, vol. 9243 (ON: Ottawa, 1895–1923).

57 T. Ferrier, LACMC-SFS, vol. 6258, file 576-9, part 1, c-8649, (1912), 1908–1909.
58 A. Johnston, "Booming City Acquire Land for Curran Park: Part Two," *Brandon Sun*, 14 February 1995, No. 27, 4.
59 Nichols, *Investigation of Unmarked Graves*.
60 A. Johnston, "Sluggish City Growth Slows Park Development: Part Three," *Brandon Sun*, 15 February 1995, No. 28, 4.
61 A. Johnston, "Recreation Board Fills Void in Administration: Part Four," *Brandon Sun*, 16 February 1995, No. 29, 4.
62 Mystery of Graves at Curran Park Solved, [Clipping from an unidentified *Brandon Sun* newspaper, 5 June] Microfilm (1963), 11.
63 Department of Indian and Inuit Affairs, *Leases & Individual Case Files – Cemetery – Brandon Residential School, Correspondence* (RG10, GRB/BAN # 2000-01600-6, box and vol. # 053, file: 577/36-7-576, part#01), Manitoba Region Federal Records Centre, Winnipeg, MB, (1963–1970).
64 Ibid.
65 Girl Guides Dedicate Plaque at Indian Children's Cemetery, [Clipping from an unidentified *Brandon Sun* newspaper, 7 June] Microfilm, (1972), 19.
66 L. Behm, "Curran Park Sold," *Brandon Sun*, Microfilm, Brandon University (MB: Brandon, 20 February 2001), A2.
67 Nichols, *Investigation of Unmarked Graves*.
68 T. Ferrier, LACMC-SFS, vol. 6258, file 576-9, part 1, c-8647, (1912), 2324.
69 Department of Indian and Inuit Affairs, *Leases & Individual Case Files*.
70 Ibid.
71 Ibid.
72 Nichols, *Investigation of Unmarked Graves*.
73 Ibid.
74 Ibid.
75 Truth and Reconciliation Commission, *Calls to Action*, 8–9.
76 Truth and Reconciliation Commission, *Volume 4: Canada's Residential Schools: Missing Children and Unmarked Burials*, 131 states: "Two cemeteries are associated with the Brandon residential school. The first is on a privately owned campground north of the Assiniboine River. The land was once the site of a public park, known as 'Curran Park.' In 1970, the Brandon Girl Guides arranged for a memorial to the cemetery to be placed in the park. A second cemetery was later established in the rural municipality of Cornwallis. There is a marker on the site that lists the names of eleven students, all but one of whom died prior to 1950."

77 When discussing the first school cemetery, the commission credits the Girl Guides for establishing a "memorial" and this implies that the site chosen in 1970 was not where the original cemetery was located.
78 Nichols, *Investigation of Unmarked Graves*.
79 K. Brownlee, *Dibaajimindww Geteyaag: Ogiiyose, Noojigiigoo'iwe gaye Dibinawaag Nibiing Onji – Stories of the Old Ones: Hunter and Fisher from Sheltered Water* (Winnipeg: MB: Manitoba Museum, 2019); Richard J. Hebda, Sheila Greer, and Alexander P. Mackie, eds., *Kwäd äy Dän Ts'ínch i: Teachings from Long Ago Person Found* (Victoria, BC: Royal BC Museum, 2017); C.H. Meloche, L. Spake, and K.L. Nichols, eds., *Working with and for Ancestors: Collaboration in the Care and Study of Ancestral Remains*, (London: Routledge, 2021).
80 SSHRC Funded Partnership Development Grant.
81 K. Figura, K.L. Nichols, L. Spake, E. Holland, J. Albanese, D. Reder, D. Yang, D. Kennedy, D. Blackbird, H. Cardoso, and E. Yellowhorn, "From home to the Brandon Indian Residential School: Addressing the colonial legacy of displaced Indigenous children through GIS and archives (1936–1952)," poster presented at the 53rd annual Canadian Archaeological Association Conference, May 2021.
82 M.E. Lewis, and G.N. Rutty, "The Endangered Child: The Personal Identification of Children in Forensic Anthropology," *Science & Justice*, 43(4), (2003): 201–209.
83 C.A. Chenery, V. Pashley, A.L. Lamb, H.J. Sloane, and J.A. Evans, "The Oxygen Isotope Relationship between the Phosphate and Structural Carbonate Fractions of Human Bioapatite," *Rapid Communications in Mass Spectrometry*, 26(3), (2012): 309–319; J.B. West, G.J. Bowen, T.E. Dawson, and K.P. Tu, eds., *Isoscapes: Understanding Movement, Pattern, and Process on Earth Through Isotope Mapping* (Springer Science & Business Media, 2009).
84 C.F. Speller, K.L. Spalding, B.A. Buchholz, D. Hildebrand, J. Moore, R. Mathewes, M.F. Skinner, and D.Y. Yang, "Personal Identification of Cold Case Remains Through Combined Contribution from Anthropological, mtDNA, and Bomb-Pulse Dating Analyses," *Journal of Forensic Sciences*, 57(5), (2012): 1354–1360.

9

Confronting "Cognitive Imperialism"[1]: What Reconstituting a Contracts Law School Course is Teaching Me about Law

Jane Bailey

Law is much richer and deeper than Western legal thought.[2]

Larry Chartrand

Numerous chapters in this book demonstrate how the Royal Society of Canada (RSC) and some of its most prominent members historically contributed to the colonization project in what is now called Canada. In chapters relating to Duncan Campbell Scott, for example, we see the critical role that Western law and policy played in colonization. Law and policy's colonizing impact, however, is not simply a thing of the past. Western law continues to be a tool of colonization. In light of this reality, it is notable that a growing number of RSC fellows and College of New Scholars, Artists and Scientists members are law professors. As such, developing a full understanding of the RSC's role in the colonization project necessitates investigation of the historic and current roles played by westernized scholarly pursuits more generally and law school education, more specifically. It also invites reflection on what decolonization efforts in this context might look like.

Such investigation and reflection require non-Indigenous College members and RSC fellows teaching and writing in law to deeply engage in the self-reflective exercise of naming and accepting responsibility for the colonizing roles we have played and continue to play inside and outside of the classroom, as well as the ways in which we benefit from colonialism. Without self-reflection, acceptance of responsibility, and deep engagement with the powerful work, guidance, and wisdom of Indigenous scholars, Elders, knowledge-keepers, students, and communities, how can non-Indigenous scholars and teachers like me revise our approaches and mindsets in ways that usefully support – rather than undermine – the projects of decolonization and reconciliation? I am a settler feminist law professor who has been teaching first-year contracts law since 2002 at the University of Ottawa, which is situated on Algonquin territory. I became a member of the RSC's College of New Scholars in 2016. This chapter reflects upon my ongoing efforts to understand both the pivotal role that the common law of contract and my teaching of its related principles have played in colonialism's attempted erasure of Indigenous laws, legal traditions, and peoples. My work on this issue arises from formal initiatives organized by others in my faculty beginning in 2015, which ultimately led to setting up "a small group of first year professors, covering all courses, who [were] committed to incorporating either a de-colonizing lens or Indigenous laws and legal orders in a clear and unambiguous way into their courses."[3] My efforts obviously pale by comparison to the unbelievably generous, kind, and exhausting work of the Indigenous and non-Indigenous scholars, colleagues, students, and community members who led and continue to lead initiatives in the University of Ottawa's law school, and all who have been and continue to be gracious enough to share their labour, knowledge, and insights with me, my students and a broader community of people who are striving to understand what it means to be an ally in responding to one of the most pressing social justice issues of our time.

This chapter is divided into three parts. Part I draws on the work of Indigenous scholars and activists to highlight the roles that education and law have played in the colonization project in what is now called Canada. Part II relies on the work of Indigenous scholars and activists to delve more specifically into how common-law legal education in Canada has contributed to colonization, as well as their insights on finding a way forward. Part III particularly focuses on how traditional common-law contracts teaching renders invisible Indigenous laws, legal traditions, and peoples, drawing on my continuing efforts to reconstitute my first-year contracts course in ways that begin to try to undo that erasure. The conclusion focuses on the moral imperative of decolonization of legal education and its benefits to all. As Marie Battiste so aptly puts it, "the decolonization of education is not just about changing a system for Indigenous peoples, but for everyone. We all will benefit by it."[4] After more than thirty years as a student, practitioner, and professor of law, I have been granted the humbling gift of beginning to imagine all that law is and can be, and to recognize law's deep connection with culture and the richness, depth and diversity of legal traditions practiced in this place now referred to as Canada.

I. COLONIZATION: THE ROLES OF EDUCATION AND LAW

The National Inquiry into Missing and Murdered Indigenous Women and Girls' (NIMMIWG) Lexicon of Terminology defines colonialism as "the ideology advocating colonization" (which is "the process by which Europeans invaded and occupied Indigenous national territories"). "Colonialism," it states is, "the attempted or actual imposition of policies, laws, mores, economies, cultures or systems and institutions put in place by settler governments to support and continue the occupation of Indigenous territories, the subjugation of Indigenous Nations, and the resulting internalized and externalized thought patterns that support this occupation and subjugation."[5] The NIMMIWG also ties colonialism to genocide, noting that "colonial structures" such as "the Sixties Scoop, residential schools, and breaches of human and Inuit, Métis and First Nations rights" empowered "a race-based genocide of Indigenous Peoples," by "leading directly to the current increased rates of violence, death, and suicide in Indigenous populations."[6] The Canadian government and its agents deployed a number of tools aimed at systematically colonizing and annihilating Indigenous peoples, their legal and cultural traditions, and their laws. In fact, many historic Canadian figures involved in the colonization project, including those from the RSC, made no effort to hide their intentions to essentially weaponize colonial systems of education and law, among others, in order to achieve their objectives. Battiste insightfully describes the systematic colonizing efforts within the Canadian education system, from Indian day schools to residential schools and to current day schools, as "cognitive imperialism," a way of capturing the market on what counts as knowledge, and what should be considered superior or inferior, often through alienating teaching methods. "Cognitive imperialism is not just symbolic cultural assimilation, but wholesale cognitive whitewashing, working through the loss of Aboriginal languages that themselves inform the perspectives and values and world views of the peoples. As a result, success has been closely associated with Aboriginal students' losing their languages and cultural connections."[7] Jeffrey Hewitt notes that once education in this cognitively imperialistic form was fully recognized as "an efficient means to expand colonization, no 'branch of learning was left untouched.'"[8] For this reason, numerous reports on the rights of Aboriginal and Indigenous peoples in Canada have called for "Aboriginal jurisdiction and control of education," with the 1996 Royal Commission on Aboriginal People describing education as the "transmission of cultural DNA from one generation to the next," shaping "language and pathways of thinking."[9] As Hewitt points out, without such control, the settler education system is both stacked against Indigenous peoples and the ability of settlers to understand "Canada's oppressive historical and ongoing actions against [them]."[10] In many ways, colonial law has played a similar role in the colonization project – beginning with claiming dominion over what can even be called law. As Larry Chartrand so incisively describes it, "Western law conceives of an obligation of law as very much an either-or proposition. You are obliged to do something – the 'law' or you are not obliged to do something – 'not law.' What if society sees obligation on a continuum of obligatory force that is circumstantial specific – a living law so to speak?"[11] Legal imperialism then is founded on first distinguishing "law" from other social and cultural orderings of relationships in society and then framing the former as superior and the latter as inferior.[12] Taking control of knowledge in this way then becomes a tool for rendering invisible laws and legal systems that live and are practised in ways that do not look like colonial legal systems.

In addition to "cognitive whitewashing"[13] through colonial legal theory and philosophy, colonial laws have been relentlessly created and imposed in order to strip Indigenous peoples of their rights and legal systems. From interpretive techniques designed to obliterate Indigenous laws relating to knowledge about treaty rights, to creation of the *Indian Act* in 1876, to legally mandated limits on Indigenous political participation, to criminalizing participation in Indigenous legal and ceremonial practices, to legal constraints on Indigenous economic pursuits, to criminalization and over-incarceration of Indigenous peoples, Canadian law has – and continues to – play a breathtakingly profound role in the attempted genocide of Indigenous peoples.[14]

II. COLONIZATION: THE ROLE OF MAINSTREAM LEGAL EDUCATION

Once the roles that education and law have and continue to play in colonization are recognized, the central part law schools play in educating about law inevitably follows. For this reason, as Hewitt highlights, the Truth and Reconciliation Commission's (TRC) recommendations point to law schools as sites of necessary reform since they "produce legal actors and, through this production line, serve as a site of colonization because in Canada law has been, and continues to be, a vehicle to oppress Indigenous peoples."[15] Notwithstanding warnings about the need for change in Canadian legal education since at least 1969,[16] the "imported legal traditions"[17] of common and civil law continue to dominate. As Chartrand compellingly argues, the unjustified dominance of these systems generally, and in law schools specifically, "diminishes the potential for a richer and deeper understanding of legal knowledge in Canada,"[18] and the silence about Indigenous laws in law schools sends an "indirect and powerful message to the public ... that Indigenous knowledge has no merit. This silence and complicity in doing nothing only reinforces colonial and racist stereotypes of Indigenous peoples being inferior and not having institutions of governance and law of their own prior to European arrival."[19] In this way, developing a richer and deeper understanding of law is not only a scholarly exercise, but an anti-racist practice of centring the legal, cultural, and spiritual depth of Indigenous peoples, communities, and nations.

Alongside the TRC's 2015 recommendations that "law schools in Canada ... require all new law students to take a course in Aboriginal people and the law"[20] and for "establishment of Indigenous law institutes for the development, use, and understanding of Indigenous laws and access to justice"[21] have come renewed calls for and initiatives toward reconciliation and decolonization in a number of law schools. However, the path in law towards not only realizing Battiste's general goal of "ethical, trans-systemic educational systems"[22] but also understanding what it means to reconcile and to decolonize in this context, and implementing necessary change is – as one would expect – a complex path that is not without risk. As Chartrand cautions, the term law may be too narrow to capture the complexity of obligations in Indigenous social orders, and inclusion of Indigenous laws within existing law schools "may result in sacrificing too much of what is uniquely Indigenous by trying to fit Indigenous peoples' normative ordering approaches that are inherently fluid and holistic in nature into a Western framework of substantive secularized legal categorization and non-fluid methodology currently employed in legal academia."[23] That said, Chartrand highlights numerous benefits that could flow from thoughtful, Indigenous-led, community-engaged inclusion of Indigenous law in law schools, including: creation of a "broader intellectual resource base" that internally empowers Indigenous peoples in community through "collective actualization of recognized value of their knowledge systems"; contributions toward richer legal theory;[24] and training for lawyers that better enables them to meet their professional obligations to both Indigenous and non-Indigenous clients on land to which common and civil law are not indigenous.[25] The University of Victoria's 2018 creation of the world's first Indigenous law degree is one impressive example of a way forward.[26] Hewitt's insights are particularly pertinent for law schools that are not yet well-placed to follow the University of Victoria's excellent example. He stresses the importance of attending to both "indigenization" and "decolonization." Under the "indigenization" priority, Hewitt includes not only incorporation of Indigenous content and courses, but also institutional change to recognize and repair failures to "make room for Indigenous legal orders, Indigenous scholars, and Indigenous legal research methodologies," including community-based researchers and knowledge keepers.[27] Within the "decolonization" priority, he includes "acknowledging historic and ongoing wrongdoings along with claiming responsibility through naming, dismantling, countering and neutralizing both the collective and individual assertions and assumptions made in relation to Indigenous peoples."[28] My limited foray into reconstituting my contracts class can neither fully achieve Hewitt's laudable priorities nor avoid the risks highlighted by Chartrand. It has, however, given me insights into some of the ways in which traditional teaching of the common law of contracts specifically serves to colonize and render invisible Indigenous law and legal traditions. Contracts is a mandatory first-year course in common-law degree programs across Canada. While the specific content of each course may vary from professor to professor, the course will typically include analysis of case law on issues such as how to determine whether a contract has been formed (Has a legally enforceable promise been made?), how to determine the exact obligations of the parties to one another, and what remedies are available when a party to a contract fails to live up to their obligations. Decisions made by judges tend to be the central focus of study, although certain bodies of legislation may also be considered. Judicial decisions from higher courts become binding on lower courts, forming bodies of precedent meant to guide the way future cases raising similar issues should be decided. A significant proportion of the precedents that continue to govern contractual relationships today were decided centuries ago, and often in the context of exchange transactions between commercial parties.

III. CONTRACT LAW TEACHING AND COLONIZATION – THE DISAPPEARING ACT

When I approached the task of reconstituting my contracts class in 2015, I encountered two aspects of myself – as both a product and a producer of colonialist methods of teaching law and understanding legal knowledge.[29] As noted above, I was prompted to do so by the decision in our faculty to work toward understanding how to, among other things, comply with the TRC's recommendations relating to law schools and legal education. My journey[30] began with an existential crisis related to reading *Canada's Indigenous Constitution* by John Borrows.[31] Midway through reading the book, I became angry and upset, and ultimately put it down for some time. I have come to recognize that my reaction was, to paraphrase Darcy Lindberg, "displaying the damage that [Borrows' discussion of Indigenous law] did to [my] conceptions of law."[32] It was only after several days of reflection that I realized my anger and upset flowed from both the shame of blithely playing an active part in Canada's violent colonialist legal enterprise and the embarrassment of recognizing that, after thirteen years of standing up in front of hundreds of students to "profess" the law, I had never really known, in fact, what law is and can be. My learning about and teaching of the common law of contract had colonized my own mind. In effect, I had become the "maze-bright rat" MacKinnon warned about in another context.[33] I had assumed, for example, that law could be relatively clearly distinguished from social norms because law was anything that ultimately the state had the power to enforce against me – something that happened mostly in or in the shadow of what happened in courtrooms. Even as I criticized common law's claims to objectivity and related denials of its fundamental role in the continued marginalization of those otherized and dehumanized by intersecting oppressions such as misogyny, sexism, homophobia, transphobia, racism, and even colonialism, I never really stopped to consider that the very definition of law by which I abided played a fundamental role in that process. Nor had I been particularly attentive to what it meant that I had been doing all of this professing at an institution that "stands on ... Algonquin sovereign territory."[34] As my awareness has grown, so too has my resolve to begin the work of reconstituting my contracts course with aspirations toward contributing to the elimination (insofar as that may be possible in a structure that is still shaped by common law concepts and categories) its colonizing and violent effects on Indigenous peoples and learners. I am also committed to ensuring that future generations of students do not walk out of my contracts class as ignorant as I have been for more than half a century, while remaining vigilant for signs of the inevitable backlash toward Indigenous members of the University of Ottawa community that arises from settler learners as they, like me, are confronted with their privilege, prejudices, and lack of awareness.

With the support of unbelievably generous colleagues and sessions led by Indigenous scholars, community members, students, and teachers too numerous to name without risking missing someone, I embarked on developing a course that seeks both to expand an ongoing feminist social-justice based questioning and critique of the authority of law and to explicitly recognize Indigenous law as law. Acknowledging Chartrand's insight that non-Indigenous scholars such as myself have no legitimate basis upon which to decide who is qualified to practice Indigenous law,[35] and thanks to insights gained from reading about Indigenous law and legal traditions, my reconstituted course aims to highlight aspects of both common law and Indigenous law that raise questions about the meaning of law, its claims to authority and obedience, and its relationship with culture.

Viewed through the lens of Sarah Morales' brilliant articulation of law as culture in her PhD dissertation focused on Hul'qumi'num law and legal traditions,[36] I began to see both the common law and Indigenous law that I read about as intimately tied to culture. Viewing law as culture, as Morales explains it, involves understanding law as coming from within and being part of everyday life.[37] The more I read through this lens, the more I recognize commonalities and differences between Indigenous and common-law legal traditions. I am also coming to better understand how difficult it is for law to command people's respect and obedience when it is or becomes disconnected from or incongruous with everyday life. In addition to providing an important opportunity for discussing this general proposition about law, Morales' law as culture framework, as well as Borrows' work, enabled me to recognize the culturally specific and exclusionary way in which I had been teaching contracts. To illustrate this, I discuss below two specific examples relating to my contract teaching that erased the cultural specificity of common-law practice or principle and, by doing so, treated related living Indigenous laws and traditions as non-existent, perfectly exemplifying the "cognitive imperialism" Battiste describes.

A) *Common Law's Requirements for Certain Agreements to be in Writing and Prioritization of Written Accounts*

Though in the Canadian common-law system only a relatively narrow category of agreements must be in writing in order to be considered legally enforceable, the common-law system has still tended to valorize writing in a number of ways. For example, the *Statute of Frauds*[38] requires that promises relating to, among other things, the sale of land, certain types of leases, and guarantees, be in writing in order to be enforced at law. Inclusion of land-related promises arguably signals a prioritization of property rights that parallels both historic and ongoing Western preoccupations with dominion over land and nature more generally.[39] It also reinforces the privileges of landowners who, in Canada, have traditionally been more likely to be white, male, and literate or have access to representatives who are.[40] The parol evidence rule, which prioritizes the written word over oral accounts of promises when interpreting contractual obligations, reinforces similar privileges.[41] As ultimately recognized by the Supreme Court of Canada in *R. v. Marshall*,[42] common-law valorization of the written word has had serious detrimental effects on Indigenous peoples' lives and laws that are based on oral traditions. A common-law preference for the written word of English and French settlers over the oral histories, stories, songs, dances, and wampum belts of Indigenous peoples in the interpretation of treaties and treaty obligations has allowed for non-Indigenous perspectives and cultural practices to prevail in ways that have been devastating to Indigenous peoples and communities.[43] Solely focusing on a Western standard that prioritizes written accounts also effectively erases Indigenous laws in the classroom, by training law students to look to writing as the only, or at least the best, way to determine whether binding obligations exist and to document the obligations parties owe to one another. It also disappears the cultural specificity of such a standard – converting it into "just how things are" or objective "truth" instead of showcasing it as a product of social, cultural, and political forces prevalent in certain Western societies.

Leading a discussion of methods for documenting law, legal obligations, and signaling solemnity with a focus on Indigenous legal traditions could become a small step toward decolonizing legal education through explicit recognition of the continuing force of Indigenous laws and legal traditions. Focusing, for example, on the encoding of Haudenosaunee independence into Gus Wen Tah–Two Row Wampum, which became the basis for agreements with the Dutch, French, and English in the seventeenth and eighteenth centuries,[44] serves not only to contextualize the historic foundations of certain nation-to-nation treaties, it also demonstrates living, ongoing obligations, and expectations for settler and Indigenous relations. Further, discussion of Tehanetorens' account of the care, attention, and ceremony associated with creating wampum strings and belts by members of the Six Nations,[45] when contrasted with scratching some words onto paper (in a language not read or spoken by other parties to the agreement) opens possibilities for recognizing this Indigenous legal tradition as an equally if not more effective mechanism for signaling solemnity or documenting parties' obligations to one another.[46] From this vantage point, putting things in writing becomes only one culturally specific, and arguably inferior, way of signaling solemnity or evidencing and recording law and legal obligations.

B) *Common Law's Presumed Unenforceability of Family Promises*

Promises must be intended by the parties to be legally binding in order to be enforced at common law.[47] In many situations, such as promises made between commercial parties or in market transactions, satisfaction of this requirement is never discussed because the intention is implicitly presumed to be present. In contrast, common law presumes that promises between family members are not intended to be legally binding, unless that presumption is rebutted with evidence.[48] Like the common-law prioritization of the written word, the presumption against the legal enforceability of family promises both reflects and reinforces a certain sort of sociocultural order in at least two ways.

First, such a presumption reinforces social inequalities. For example, as Swan, Bala, and Adamski note, common law decisions presuming that promises between heterosexual spouses are legally unenforceable "typically worked to the disadvantage of women."[49] Second, the presumption could be understood to reflect a sociocultural prioritization of market relationships over personal ones. From this perspective, the formality of intention to be legally bound will rarely impede enforcement of commercial agreements since western societies premised on capitalist orders seek to facilitate market-based transactions and dismiss promises made in the context of personal relationships as "just" reflections of "natural love and affection."[50] A common-law aversion to legal involvement in the private realm permeates in both of these situations. This aversion has been both lauded for its role in protecting the privacy and dignity of individuals from unnecessary state intrusion (a right that for Indigenous peoples has been systematically violated by colonial systems relating to child welfare, among others) and criticized for its role in, among other things, shielding domestic violence from public intervention,[51] and prioritizing property over people.

Rather than beginning a discussion around family and kin obligations and their impact on "enforceability" with a focus on the common law, leading with examples from Indigenous legal traditions offers at least two sorts of opportunities. First, it can contribute toward decolonization within the classroom by explicitly recognizing the continuing force of Indigenous laws and legal traditions. Second, it can help to reveal socioculturally-based assumptions that have served to limit Western understandings of law in ways that both lead to dismissing Indigenous law as "not law"[52] and arguably serve to disconnect common law from everyday life, thereby further undermining its claims to fidelity from anyone.

Morales' analysis of the Hul'qumi'num legal tradition, for example, offers an excellent starting point. She identifies two categories of law within that tradition: (i) *snuw'uyulh*; and (ii) family laws, both of which ground and enmesh law in relationships and social connection through seven teachings that include kinship and family.[53] As Morales puts it, "[U]niversal teachings seek to foster harmony, peacefulness, solidarity and kinship between all living beings and the natural world. In a sense, *snuw'uyulh* is a state or condition and Hul'qumi'num law functions as the device that produces or maintains the state of *snuw'uyulh*."[54] Morales explains that the bedrock of the Hul'qumi'num worldview is focused on continuing connections with "all of my relations," which include ancestors, people, and land, from which derive responsibilities and obligations.[55] Kinship also plays a fundamental role in defining and establishing the highest of legal obligations in other Indigenous legal traditions, including those of the Cree, Dene, Assiniboine, and Saulteaux Nations that negotiated treaties in what is now referred to as Saskatchewan. Within these traditions, as Cardinal and Hildebrandt note, laws of *miyo-wicehtowin* concerning good relations and *wahkotowin* governing all relations that detail the duties and responsibilities of each member of a family unit also apply to the formation of new relationships such as those between First Nations and the Crown through treaties.[56] In these traditions, law is practiced on a daily basis through interactions with the self and others and familial[57] relationships play a definitional role in determining rights and responsibilities.

Viewed in this broader context, common law's presumptions against the enforceability of family promises and favouring of armslength transactions can begin to be understood as a sociocultural product, rather than an objective reflection of what is and what is not law.[58] This in turn invites discussion around what it means for something to be legally enforceable, expanding the possibilities beyond state-sanctioned use of force to responses developed and grounded in everyday life, recognizing that even at common law, the vast majority of dispute resolution does not involve relationship-damaging litigation in a court of law. Further, it seems quite possible that conceptualizing law as something developed and practiced within day-to-day relationships could play a key role in addressing the growing public disaffection for and disconnection from law that is currently evident in many Western societies.[59]

C) Benefits and Risks

I have used the examples of the common law's preferences for the written word and presumptions against the enforceability of family promises to illustrate both the ways in which traditional common-law contracts teaching works to disappear the reality of living Indigenous laws and legal traditions as well as to illustrate how the introduction of Indigenous law might begin the work of undoing that erasure and enriching understandings of law. The potential benefits of such measures include:

- approaching and showcasing Indigenous laws as laws,[60]
- embracing critical perspectives that challenge claims to "objectivity" and "perspectivelessness" that predominate in much traditional western legal theory,[61]
- naming and recognizing the truth of how settlers and settler law have contributed to and benefited from colonization,[62]
- recognizing Canada as a poly juridical state in which Indigenous law is separate from but of equal status to common law and civil law,[63]
- recognizing Indigenous law as the living contemporary body of law that it is,[64] and
- contributing to a "broader intellectual resource base" for thinking about what law is and can be.[65]

In so doing, such an approach might contribute toward developing enriched possibilities for resolving disputes and mending relationships between communities and community members. However, the approach I have taken certainly carries with it many of the risks identified by Indigenous scholars.

First, and perhaps foremost, it might – as Chartrand suggests – sacrifice the fluid and holistic nature of Indigenous normative ordering by forcing it into common law's secularized categories and static methodologies.[66] Second, as Hewitt argues, curricular change without institutional change is unlikely to achieve objectives of decolonization and indigenization.[67] Third, as Borrows points out, a comparative framework such as the one I have suggested may co-opt Indigenous law into common-law forms and potentially reinforce common ideas that arise from comparison such as inferiority and superiority.[68] It thus runs the risk of either reinforcing existing notions of the inferiority of Indigenous laws, legal traditions, and communities or, as Alex Wilson cautions against, unrealistically oversimplifying and romanticizing them.[69] Fourth, teaching particular aspects of Indigenous laws and legal traditions abstracts them from a much larger context of Indigenous spiritual traditions, beliefs, and ceremonies in ways that may lead to inaccurate understandings.[70] Finally, it is essential to take into account the immediate impacts on Indigenous students, faculty, and staff of introducing Indigenous law into existing law schools. While community empowerment associated with recognition of Indigenous law, knowledge and legal traditions may result,[71] backlash is a seemingly inevitable result of steps toward progressive change for Indigenous peoples, as it is and has been for members of other equality-seeking communities. As a result, meaningful institutional structures and responses must be put in place. White, cis, able-bodied, settler professors may be blissfully ignorant of such backlash, because their privileges enable them to escape being targeted. For that reason, ensuring safe spaces for those targeted to describe what is happening, providing the resources they need, educating non-Indigenous members of the law school community, and sanctioning colonialist acts of violence and unkindness must be considered non-negotiable.

All of these risks, combined with an acute awareness of my own experiential limitations, my privileged social location, and the colonialist "recipe knowledge"[72] in which I am, and have for decades, been immersed raise important questions about whether the approach I am taking in my contracts course is the right one. For example, what is lost in teaching about Indigenous legal traditions based solely on reading about them rather than living them? On the other hand, if I do not incorporate the work of Indigenous scholars into my course would I effectively be shifting the burdens of reconciliation and decolonization within legal education onto the shoulders of members of Indigenous communities, in particular Indigenous colleagues and students? These are the sorts of questions with which I must continue to grapple.

CONCLUSION

It is tempting for settlers like me to think of colonization as a thing of the past. In reality, however, acts of colonization surround us every day. Just as law and education played critical roles in past practices of colonization through, among other things, "cognitive imperialism," they continue to do so today. Legal education in Canadian law schools is and continues to be a striking example of that ongoing reality. Traditional teaching about the common law of contract is certainly no exception. When contracts professors uncritically teach presumptions in favour of written accounts, and presumptions against the legal enforceability of family promises, we train future legal professionals to dismiss oral accounts as less worthy and obligations rooted in familial and kinship ties as "not law."[73] Such practices render invisible Indigenous law and legal traditions in law-school classrooms, signaling as invalid the lived and living experiences of Indigenous students within them, and unduly narrowing understandings of law in ways that impoverish us all.

The path(s) toward reconciliation and decolonization of legal education are by no means clear or unobstructed. Non-Indigenous allies must recognize our limits and take instruction from Indigenous peoples, while at the same time taking responsibility for doing the work necessary to decolonize our own minds, hearts, and practices. The movement toward a decolonized education system is not optional. It is part of a morally imperative journey toward a just society – a part that, at the end of the day, as Battiste notes, will benefit everybody[74] – including, or perhaps especially, settlers like me.

NOTES

I take full personal responsibility for all shortcomings in this chapter and in my ongoing efforts to reconstitute my contracts course. However, I must express my deepest gratitude to the Indigenous Legal Traditions Committee at the University of Ottawa's Faculty of Law, Dr Sarah Morales, Dr Tracey Lindberg, Professor Aimée Craft, Professor Larry Chartand, Dr Angela Cameron, Elder Claudette Commanda, Dr Marie Battiste, Dr Sákéj Youngblood Henderson, Tara Macdonald, Portia Larlee, Dr Val Napoleon, Dr Hadley Friedland, and Katherine Koostachin for their scholarship, activism, and insight. I wish also to recognize the powerful influence of, and to express my gratitude for the College of the Royal Society of Canada's committee that organized listening tours for College members across Canada and for the challenging and inspirational work and scholarship of Dr John Borrows and Dr Jeffrey Hewitt. Finally, I owe a never-previously acknowledged debt to Thomas Dapp (an Indigenous colleague from my first-year property class) for challenging me to think about what it means to claim to "own" a rock – a challenge that thirty years later I am only beginning to understand.

1. The quote in the title is taken from Marie Battiste, *Decolonizing Education: Nourishing the Learning Spirit* (Vancouver: Purich Publishing 2013), 162.
2. Larry Chartrand, "Indigenizing the Legal Academy from a Decolonizing Perspective," University of Ottawa Faculty of Law Working Paper Series, July 2015, https://papers.ssrn.com/sol3/papers.cfm?abstract_id=2631163 WP 2015-22, 12, accessed 12 October 2019.
3. Sarah Morales and Angela Cameron, "Small Steps on the Path Towards Reconciliation at the University of Ottawa Faculty of Law," 8 July 2016, https://reconciliationsyllabus.wordpress.com/2016/07/08/small-steps-on-the-path-towards-reconciliation-at-the-university-of-ottawa-faculty-of-law/, accessed 15 October, 2019.
4. Battiste, *Decolonizing Education*, 22.
5. National Inquiry of Missing and Murdered Indigenous Women and Girls, *Lexicon of Terminology* (Ottawa: NIMMIWG 2019), https://www.mmiwg-ffada.ca/wp-content/uploads/2019/06/MMIWG_Lexicon_FINAL_ENFR.pdf, 14, accessed 13 October 2019, https://www.mmiwg-ffada.ca/wp-content/uploads/2018/02/NIMMIWG_Lexicon_ENFR-1.pdf
6. NIMMIWG, *Lexicon*, 28.
7. Battiste, *Decolonizing Education*, 162.
8. Jeffery G. Hewitt, "Decolonizing and Indigenizing: Some Considerations for Law Schools," *Windsor Yearbook of Access to Justice* 33 (2016): 71.
9. Report of the Royal Commission on Aboriginal People Report, 1996, https://www.bac-lac.gc.ca/eng/discover/aboriginal-heritage/royal-commission-aboriginal-peoples/Pages/final-report.aspx, cited in, Hewitt, "Decolonizing," 73.
10. Report of the Royal Commission on Aboriginal People Report, 1996, https://www.bac-lac.gc.ca/eng/discover/aboriginal-heritage/royal-commission-aboriginal-peoples/Pages/final-report.aspx, cited in, Hewitt, "Decolonizing," 73.
11. Chartrand, "Indigenizing the Legal Academy," 2.
12. Battiste, *Decolonizing Education*, 32.
13. Ibid., 162.
14. I had the privilege of hearing a very powerful articulation of the appalling multi-century history of oppression through Canadian law during Dr John Borrow's keynote address, "Canada's Indigenous Constitution" during my first year orientation at the University of Ottawa Faculty of Law in fall 2016, as well as reading about it in his landmark book of

the same title; see John Borrows, *Canada's Indigenous Constitution* (Toronto: University of Toronto Press, 2010), and for viewing an exceptionally accessible and incisive description of how examples of these practices played out in what is now called Saskatchewan, see Tasha Hubbard's poignant film, *nipawistamâsowin: We Will Stand Up* (National Film Board of Canada: 2019).
15 Hewitt, "Decolonizing," 67.
16 Ibid., 75.
17 Chartrand, "Indigenizing the Legal Academy," 1.
18 Ibid., 1.
19 Ibid., 10. See also John Borrows, "Heroes, Tricksters, Monsters, and Caretakers: Indigenous Law and Legal Education," *McGill Law Journal* 61 no. 4 (2016): 807.
20 Truth and Reconciliation Commission of Canada, *Truth and Reconciliation Commission of Canada: Calls to Action* (Winnipeg: TRC 2015), recommendation 28, 3, http://trc.ca/assets/pdf/Calls_to_Action_English2.pdf, accessed 13 October 2019.
21 Truth and Reconciliation Commission, *Calls to Action*, recommendation 50, 5.
22 Battiste, *Decolonizing Education*, 167.
23 Chartrand, "Indigenizing the Legal Academy," 2.
24 Ibid., 11.
25 Ibid., 13.
26 University of Victoria, "World's First Indigenous Law Degree to be Offered at UVic," 2018, https://www.uvic.ca/news/topics/2018+jid-indigenous-law+media-release, accessed 12 October 2019.
27 Hewitt, "Decolonizing," 67–8, 70.
28 Ibid., 70.
29 Although I had previously discussed the discriminatory effect on Indigenous peoples of the common-law preference for written evidence and its aversion to extrinsic evidence in an earlier iteration of my course, I had not familiarized myself with Indigenous laws and legal traditions, nor included them in my course.
30 I now recognize that I had ignored numerous opportunities for awakening myself to the very complex realities of life and law associated with Indigenous culture, law, and legal traditions well prior to becoming a law professor.
31 Borrows, *Canada's Indigenous Constitution*.
32 Darcy Lindberg, "Miyo Nehiyawiwin–Beautiful Creeness: Ceremonial Aesthetics and Nehiyaw Legal Pedagogy," *Indigenous Law Journal* 16 (2018): 52.

33 Catharine MacKinnon, *Feminism Unmodified: Discourses on Life & Law* (Cambridge: Harvard University Press, 1987), 205.
34 Chartrand, "Indigenizing the Legal Academy," 16.
35 Ibid., 17.
36 Sarah Morales, "Snuw'uyulh: Fostering and Understanding of the Hul'qumi'num Legal Tradition," PhD diss., (University of Victoria, 2014).
37 Morales, "Snuw'uyulh," 50.
38 *Statute of Frauds*, RSO 1990, c S 19.
39 Philip Hamburger, "The Conveyancing Purposes of the Statute of Frauds," *American Journal of Legal History* 27 (1983): 354. See also E. Rabel, "The Statute of Frauds and Comparative Legal History," *Law Quarterly Review* 63 (1947): 174.
40 Robert C. Ellickson, "Property in Land," *Yale Law Journal* 102 no. 1315 (1993): 1357–8.
41 Marvin A. Chirelstein, *Concepts and Case Analysis in the Law of Contracts* (St. Paul, MN: Foundation Press, 2013): 107.
42 *R. v. Marshall*, [1993] 3 SCR 456, 177 DLR (4th) 513.
43 Harold Cardinal and Walter Hildebrandt, *Treaty Elders of Saskatchewan: Our Dream is that our Peoples will One Day be Clearly Recognized as Nations* (Calgary: University of Calgary Press, 2000).
44 Borrows, "Heroes," 75–6.
45 Tehanetorens–Ray Fadden, *Wampum Belts of the Iroquois* (Summertown: Tennessee: Book Publishing Company, 1999).
46 Fuller suggested that common law formalities served several functions, including raising the awareness of the parties to an agreement that they were undertaking obligations with legal implications, channeling certain kinds of arrangements into the legally enforceable category, and creating evidence of a legally enforceable promise. See Lon Fuller, "Consideration and Form," *Colum L Rev* 41 (1941): 799.
47 Angela Swan, Nicholas C. Bala, and Jakub Adamski, *Contracts: Cases, Notes and Materials*, 9th ed. (Markham: LexisNexis, 2015): 436.
48 *Balfour v. Balfour*, [1919] 2 KB 571 (CA).
49 Swan, Bala and Adamski, *Contracts*, 437.
50 *Balfour v. Balfour*, [1919] 2 KB 571 (CA), cited in Swan, Bala and Adamski, *Contracts*, 437.
51 Catharine MacKinnon, *Toward a Feminist Theory of the State* (Massachusetts: Harvard University Press, 1989), 191.
52 Here, I am borrowing from Chartrand, "Indigenizing the Legal Academy."
53 Morales, "Snuw'uyulh," iii.
54 Ibid., iii.

55 Ibid., 49.
56 Cardinal and Hildebrandt, *Treaty Elders,* 14, 18.
57 Here "family" extends beyond common law notions that typically confine the term to relationships created by birth, adoption, or marriage. In the Coast Salish context, Morales describes it as involving the "independent household" and the "extended household." See Morales, "Snuw'uyulh," 110.
58 Indeed, the current approach to familial promises in common law that emphasizes transaction over status or relation is, itself, a relatively recent shift associated with growing emphasis on the individual over family or community, a shift the previously presumed benefits of which have more recently come into question with the emergence of "wicked problems" such as environmental degradation, climate change, and persistent systemic discrimination against Indigenous peoples. See Henry Sumner Maine, *Ancient Law: Its Connection with the Early History of Society and its Relation to Modern Ideas* (London: John Murray, 1908).
59 With respect to Canada, for example see Adam Cotter, "Spotlight on Canadians: Result from the General Social Survey: Public Confidence in Canadian Institutions," 2015, https://www150.statcan.gc.ca/n1/pub/89-652-x/89-652-x2015007-eng.htm, accessed 13 October 2019.
60 Hewitt, "Decolonizing," 71.
61 Ibid., 76.
62 Aimée Craft, "Ki'inaakonigewin: Reclaiming Space for Indigenous Laws," Canadian Institute for Administration of Justice Annual Conference, Saskatoon, SK 2015, referenced in Hewitt, "Decolonizing," 77.
63 Chartrand, "Indigenizing the Legal Academy," 8.
64 Ibid., 816.
65 Ibid., 11.
66 Ibid., 2.
67 Hewitt, "Decolonizing," 67–8.
68 Borrows, *Indigenous Constitution*, 814.
69 Alex Wilson and Marie Laing, "Queering Indigenous Education," in *Indigenous and Decolonizing Studies in Education: Mapping the Long View*, eds. Linda Tuhiwai Smith, Eve Tuck, and K. Wayne Yang (New York: Routledge 2019), 143.
70 Cardinal and Hildebrandt, *Treaty Elders,* 1.
71 Chartrand, "Indigenizing the Legal Academy," 11.

72 Naomi Cahn, John Calmore, Mary Coombs, Dwight Greene, Geoffrey Miller, Jeremey Paul and Laura Stein, "Speluncean Explorers-Contemporary Proceedings," *George Washington Law Review* 61 (1992–93): 1779.
73 Chartrand, "Indigenizing the Legal Academy."
74 Battiste, *Decolonizing Education*, 22.

Murder They Wrote: "Unknown Knowns" and Windsor Law's Statement Regarding *R. v. Stanley*

Reem Bahdi

INTRODUCTION

Gerald Stanley shot Colten Boushie of Red Pheasant First Nation in the head on 9 August 2016. Stanley was eventually acquitted of "second degree murder and manslaughter by way of an assault or careless use of firearms"[1] by a Saskatchewan court in February 2018. Dubbed Canada's version of the Rodney King story, the *R. v. Stanley* case has revived public, policy, and scholarly debates about the injustices that mark the relationship between Canadian criminal justice and Indigenous peoples. Windsor Law responded to the *Stanley* verdict with a statement that was adopted unanimously by its faculty council. Noting that "Canada has used law to perpetuate violence against Indigenous Peoples and too often protects those who commit acts of violence against Indigenous Peoples," the faculty pledged to work towards changing the architecture of Canada's colonial legal system.[2] The faculty also expressed its solidarity with Colten Boushie's family and the Red Pheasant First Nation, deliberately using the word "murder" to describe Boushie's death, notwithstanding Stanley's acquittal.[3]

Canada has a long history of denying racism,[4] especially in its colonial engagements with and against Indigenous peoples. By specifically invoking the word "murder," Windsor Law's statement helped centre public, policy, and scholarly discussion of *R. v. Stanley* on the "unknown knowns," those things that Slavoj Zizek describes as "the disavowed beliefs, suppositions, and obscene practices we pretend not to know about"[5] but that nonetheless shape our decision-making. Windsor Law did not simply reject the verdict rendered in *R. v. Stanley*. It emphasized that the unknown knowns of law's racism against Indigenous people had to be openly acknowledged by legal institutions, including law schools. The faculty pointed out that the failure to engage with racism and colonialism, the unknown knowns in Canada's legal architecture, implicates the trustworthiness of the Canadian legal system itself.

Drawing primarily on seven volumes of transcripts from the preliminary hearing and the subsequent trial of Gerald Stanley, this chapter disentangles uncontested facts from contested ones and identifies how unknown knowns – the well documented but yet unaddressed institutional and systemic racism against Indigenous peoples – helped shaped the legal process that produced Stanley's acquittal. The analysis also draws on other primary legal sources pertaining to the period after Stanley's acquittal, including the Crown's decision not to appeal the verdict and Gerald Stanley's conviction for illegal gun ownership. Finally, the analysis presented draws on royal commissions and commissions of inquiry reports, civil society and media reports and scholarly research that details the burdens imposed on Indigenous peoples through Canadian law and policy. Brought together, these sources demonstrate multiple failures to address racism and colonialism in the *Stanley* verdict and highlight that the case represents part of a larger pattern of the legal process's inability to treat Indigenous peoples with equal dignity and worth.

It was against this context that Windsor Law issued its statement rejecting the verdict and calling for reform of law, legal institutions and legal education. Others have offered doctrinal legal analysis of the Gerald Stanley's trial and have documented the efforts of Boushie's family and community to reform Canadian law and legal institutions following the *Stanley* verdict.[6] This chapter draws on these sources but its main goal is to offer insight into the context and reasons for Windsor Law's controversial statement from the perspective of a Windsor Law faculty member.[7]

"HAPPY GROUNDHOG DAY"

Chief Justice Martel Popescul[8] of Saskatchewan's Court of Queen's Bench presided over Stanley's trial for nine days between 29 January and 9 February 2018. Chief Justice Popescul opened the fourth day of the trial with a greeting; "Happy Groundhog's Day to you."[9] The

Figure 10.1 Exhibit at the Biggar Museum, Saskatchewan.

day commemorates the measurement of a groundhog's shadow, purportedly to predict the duration of the remaining winter season. It seems out of place in a murder trial. With that greeting, Chief Justice Popescul unwittingly marked *R. v. Stanley*'s connection to a history of Indigenous injustice. In common parlance, "Groundhog Day" has come to suggest being caught in a time loop or "doing the same things repetitively."[10] From the start, the criminal justice system's interaction with Boushie and his Cree community demonstrated the troubled relationship between Indigenous and non-Indigenous peoples in rural Saskatchewan.

Biggar, the town where Stanley's trial was held, has a museum that features an exhibit about the Ku Klux Klan (KKK). Described on the museum's website as "a little more controversial," the exhibit sets out the history of the KKK in the town.[11] The pictures of the exhibit shown online include a sign that describes the KKK as a "social club" and invites visitors to learn the "secrets of the social club."[12]

Though Biggar has been home to progressive actors, the exhibit points to the influence of white supremacy in Saskatchewan's history and hints at its lingering influence in the present. The Saskatchewan KKK tried to distance itself from its American counterpart and other branches in Canada. It eschewed robes and vigilante violence but worked in the open, invoking the rule of law to achieve its goals of ensuring that Canada would be a nation of British stock.[13] Still, members of the KKK and other white supremacist groups did sometimes resort to violence. In 1991, for example, Carney Nerland, a member of a Saskatchewan branch of a white supremacist group, killed a Cree man, Leo LaChance, with an assault rifle. LaChance had entered Nerland's Prince Albert, Saskatchewan pawn shop to sell furs he had trapped.[14]

Rural Saskatchewan also has strong links with the Canadian settler colonial project. The town of Biggar was named after W.H. Biggar, lawyer to the Grand Trunk Pacific Railway (GTPR). A financially troubled enterprise, the GTPR had received significant financial support from Wilfrid Laurier's Liberal government[15] to help non-Indigenous settlement expansion into Treaty Six territory. Its tracks played a significant part in the colonization of Treaty Six territory. Not only did the railway help the western expansion of non-Indigenous settlement, it also played a significant role in taking Indigenous lands. The railway, for example, sought the annexation of land on the pretext that it was needed for rail construction when it was sought for settlement expansion more broadly. GTPR publicists and managers often openly displayed contempt of Indigenous people. GTPR's officials determined that "the cunning of the red man is inscrutable" and lamented the ways in which Indigenous leaders often brought "obscure issues" to the negotiating table.[16]

The present is built on the sediments of the past. Merleau-Ponty calls this "historical density"[17] and the Canadian criminal justice system's racism and settler colonial impulse has a high density. Communities, scholars, royal commissions, and courts have detailed the injustices imposed upon Indigenous peoples in Canada through law and legal processes. Legal doctrines such as terra nullius facilitated non-Indigenous settlement while other laws justified the domestication of Indigenous sovereignty to non-Indigenous rulers who created the Canadian state.[18] Residential schools, a system described by the Truth and Reconciliation Commission as "cultural genocide," were institutionalized primarily through the *Indian Act*.[19]

Similarly, the Missing and Murdered Indigenous Women and Girls report uses the word "genocide" without qualifying it.[20] Indigenous peoples point to the ways in which treaties between the Crown and Indigenous communities remain unfulfilled.[21] A pass system was created to keep Indigenous peoples from their lands and communities and to monitor their activities,[22] starvation was used as a weapon to further disenfranchise Indigenous peoples,[23] and residential schools took Indigenous children from their homes to further a policy of "taking the Indian out of the child."[24] Indigenous children on reserve continue to be underfunded compared to non-Indigenous children living off reserve.[25]

Within that context, Canada's criminal justice system has not served Indigenous communities well. Saskatchewan's police have a history of racism against Indigenous peoples.[26] The Saskatoon police force engaged in what they called "starlight tours," a practice where police would pick up Indigenous men at night, take them miles out of town in sub-zero Saskatchewan winters and leave them to find their way back, often without adequate clothing. An unknown number of Indigenous men were killed this way.[27] There is good argument that the practice constituted torture, which is prohibited under the Criminal Code and Canada's international obligations.[28] A provincial Commission of Inquiry that investigated the death of one young man, Neil Stonechild, commented on "self-protective and defensive attitudes exhibited by the senior levels of the police service" and noted that the "same attitudes were manifested by certain members of the Saskatoon Police Service during the Inquiry" itself.[29] Still, a systemic inquiry into racism within Saskatchewan's police forces has never been conducted.

Heidi Stark explains that criminal law was instrumental in the creation of Canadian sovereignty as the discursive depiction of Indigenous men as criminals allowed the state to deflect from its own criminality, while courts were deployed to quell Indigenous resistance to colonial expansion and violence in the lands that are now known as Saskatchewan.[30] In 1885, Indigenous leaders were hastily tried and found guilty of various offenses following The Frog Lake Resistance. "In addition to the eight Indigenous leaders hanged in 1885, an additional forty, including Chiefs Big Bear and Poundmaker, were sentenced to the Stony Mountain Penitentiary for treason. Another 100 Indigenous people were tried for criminal offenses with 60 convicted."[31]

Currently, less than 5 per cent of the population in Canada is Indigenous, yet Indigenous men make up 28 per cent of those behind bars, Indigenous women 43 per cent, and Indigenous youth 46 per cent. Some argue that the Canadian carceral system highlights the commodification of Indigenous bodies.[32] Jillian Rogin has demonstrated that the Gladue process, the very thing that was supposed to reduce Indigenous over-incarceration, is applied by courts in ways that make bail all the more difficult for Indigenous accused to secure.[33] In addition, the way in which the legal, health, and social systems failed Tina Fontaine has raised further questions about the capacity of Canadian institutions to value Indigenous lives.[34]

R. V. STANLEY: THE BASIC FACTS

There is no question that Gerald Stanley killed Colten Boushie. The only question about Boushie's death is whether Stanley intentionally killed him, whether he killed him out of carelessness, or whether Stanley's gun went off as a result of a freak accident in circumstances that did not implicate intention or carelessness. Stanley could have been found guilty of second-degree murder, which required intentional, but not planned, killing.[35] Alternatively, Gerald Stanley could have been found guilty of manslaughter or carelessly using his gun in close proximity to Boushie.[36]

Stanley had the right to be presumed innocent until proven guilty; he did not have to prove his innocence. The onus fell on the Crown to prove all the elements of the charges against Stanley beyond a reasonable doubt. The adversarial process would determine the results. Colten Boushie's family was not a party to the proceedings and the two sides, Indigenous and non-Indigenous, would be kept apart throughout. Indigenous community members would be allowed to bring an eagle feather to the proceedings[37] but were discouraged by the presiding judge from showing any emotion.[38] The trial was between the Queen, represented by the attorney general, and Gerald Stanley who was represented by a criminal defence team. The witnesses included members of the RCMP, forensic investigators, two gun experts, two lay witnesses, Gerald's son Sheldon Stanley, and three of Colten Boushie's friends who were with him on the Stanley farm. Gerald Stanley, the accused, also testified.

Ultimately, Gerald Stanley was found not guilty on all counts. He was exonerated by a jury that acts as the finder of facts. Unlike the

United States, juries in Canada deliberate in private and are bound to confidentiality. The court thus does not present any factual findings in a published decision. The transcripts, however, help reconstruct the overall picture of what happened that day and offer a glimpse into how various actors within the legal system, from the RCMP to the lawyers and the judge, viewed the charges against Stanley.

The day of the 9 August 2016 shooting began with twenty-two-year-old Colten Boushie and his friends, Eric Meechance, twenty-three, Cassidy Cross-Whitestone, eighteen, Belinda Jackson, twenty-four, and Kiora Wuttunee, seventeen, spending time on the Red Pheasant Reserve where they lived. The friends decided to go swimming and piled into Kiora's grey SUV, headed for the river near Maymont, about forty minutes away.[39] They were on their way home when they realized that the grey SUV's muffler was dragging and one of the tires had blown so driving home would be impossible. As such, the group pulled into the Stanley farm intending to ask for help. Cassidy Cross-Whitestone, the driver of the grey SUV, testified that a nearby farmer had driven him home on a previous occasion when he had needed help. He had that experience in mind when he drove into the Stanley's driveway at around 5 p.m.[40]

Gerald Stanley, fifty-six, his spouse Leesa, and their son, Sheldon, were home. Unbeknownst to Boushie and his friends, Gerald Stanley served as a mechanic to the local community, often helping people coming in off the road with their vehicles.[41] He was also a rancher. Gerald and Sheldon were fixing a fence on their farm when they heard a vehicle noisily navigating their long driveway. At first, they assumed that one of the local farmers had arrived but soon realized that the vehicle on their property belonged to a stranger.

What happened next is contested. At trial, Cassidy Cross-Whitestone testified that Eric Meechance had jumped out of the grey SUV, approached an ATV (all-terrain vehicle or quad) and tried to start it. Eric Meechance denied that he wanted to steal the ATV. Both Gerald and Sheldon Stanley testified that one of the young men had tried to steal the ATV. Gerald Stanley testified that he saw three young men, not two, get out of the vehicle and enter his shed as well as the vehicles parked on his driveway. He assumed that they were up to no good.

All of the witnesses agreed that Sheldon and Gerald Stanley began yelling and that the young men then jumped back into the SUV with Cassidy Cross-Whitestone again in the driver's seat. He put the vehicle in reverse, stopping it as he got close to Gerald Stanley, who reached out and kicked the rear tail light. Cross-Whitestone then changed gears to head out the driveway when Sheldon, who had been standing off to the side, [ran towards the vehicle] and hit the windshield with a hammer. Gerald Stanley testified that he was worried about Sheldon's safety; he had seen vehicles drive into people to kill them on TV.[42]

Sheldon Stanley's testimony was clear. He had approached the vehicle, not the other way around. Sheldon Stanley stated that he ran towards the car and struck the windshield because he was mad. As Sheldon attacked the car, Gerald Stanley went to a nearby shed to get a gun. Hindered by a dragging muffler and a blown tire, the grey SUV tried to leave the farm with Cross-Whitestone at the wheel, himself hindered by fear, alcohol, and now a broken windshield. Cross-Whitestone hit a parked vehicle belonging to Leesa Stanley. He testified that the grey vehicle stalled with the impact. By then, Gerald Stanley had come out with a Soviet manufactured semi-automatic Tokarev TT33, a handgun he used to scare away animals. Frightened, Cross-Whitestone and Meechance jumped out of the vehicle and tried to escape on foot.

Stanley testified that he fired two shots in the air, wanting to scare the group. Cross-Whitestone and Meechance said that the shots rang past their heads as they were running. After he fired the shots, Stanley testified that he was certain that the gun was empty.[43] He had removed the magazine and held it in his left hand with the gun in his right. With Cross-Whitestone and Meechance gone, Gerald Stanley approached the grey SUV with Colten, Belinda, and Kiora inside. Colten Boushie had moved into the driver's seat in an apparent attempt to drive himself and his friends to safety.

As he approached the SUV, Gerald Stanley said that he felt pure terror. He spotted the riding mower that his wife had been using earlier in the day to mow the lawn but he could not see his wife. He said that he thought that the grey SUV had run her over. Gerald Stanley ducked to check under the vehicle but did not see her. In his closing arguments, Bill Burge, the Crown Prosecutor, suggested that Gerald Stanley was not telling the truth about fearing that his wife was under the mower[44] but this point was never pressed with Stanley or any of the other witnesses.

Gerald Stanley testified that he approached the driver's side of the grey SUV with his gun in his hand with the intention of removing the keys from the ignition. He put his left hand into the driver's seat window, across the steering wheel, and turned off the ignition. He testified that he had to move a metal rod out of the way in order to get to the keys. It was later discovered that the metal rod was a gun. Stanley testified that as he put his body into the car window, he did not know where his right hand was positioned though he was carrying his gun in that hand. He insisted, however, that none of his fingers were on the gun's trigger. In other words, he was conscious of the position of his fingers on his right hand. But he was not conscious of where his hand was positioned. As his left hand reached across the steering wheel, Gerald Stanley recalled that Colten Boushie resisted somewhat against the pressure of Stanley's body in the window. Then, Stanley's gun fire precisely at the moment that it was aimed at the back of Colten Boushie's head. The bullet entered the back of Colten's head, killing him.

Gerald Stanley said that he killed Boushie by accident. Stanley testified that his gun had experienced a "hang fire" or a delayed and unexpected firing of a bullet. "Boom, it just went off," Stanley told the court.[45] Other than Gerald Stanley, Belinda Jackson was the only person to observe the shooting. Her account was very different. She said that Gerald Stanley aimed the gun at Colten Boushie's head and deliberately killed him.[46] She did not see Stanley try to remove the keys. She saw him take deliberate aim and kill Colten.

Sheldon Stanley did not see the shooting. He testified that after he smashed the grey SUV's windshield and watched the severely hampered vehicle hit his mother's parked SUV, he ran inside to get his car keys to chase the fleeing group with his car. The RCMP later found several improperly stored guns in the Stanley home.[47] By the time Sheldon Stanley came back outside, his father had already shot Colten Boushie.

Leesa Stanley also emerged from the house after the shots were fired. She instructed her son to call 911. A trained nurse, she did not approach Boushie or his friends. Meanwhile, Belinda Jackson, and Kiora Wuttunee tried to help their friend. But it was too late. Belinda Jackson testified that she heard Leesa Stanley say "[t]hat's what you get for trespassing." At that point, Belinda Jackson hit Leesa Stanley but didn't continue because "Kiora was screaming that, just stop, he's going to – he's going to shoot you, too." The Stanleys then went back into the house, called the police, with a 911 call placed at 5:37 p.m., brewed coffee, and sat in silence.

When the police arrived, they detained Gerald, Leesa, and Sheldon Stanley but Leesa and Sheldon were then released on the spot while Gerald was arrested. Gerald Stanley was charged with second-degree murder. Ten days later, on 19 August, he was released on $10,000 bail with other conditions, including that he stay away from the Boushie family. In addition to arresting Gerald Stanley, the RCMP also arrested all four of Colten Boushie's friends after they had left the property and charged them with mischief.[48]

Stanley's defence team's main argument was that Colten Boushie was killed by accident. Stanley's gun had malfunctioned. There had been a hang fire which is the result of a delay between pulling the trigger on a gun and the firing of the bullet.[49] A hang fire could theoretically explain why the gun went off even though Stanley testified that his finger was not on the trigger. The jury heard from four witnesses about hang fires, two experts and two lay witnesses. The experts testified that hang fires are exceedingly rare but possible and that they generally take place within a second.[50] More than a second would have lapsed between the time that Stanley fired the warning shots, and the time he walked towards the grey SUV and shot Boushie.

Overall, the expert evidence was confusing. The experts described in great detail how different guns work. But the jury was not able to ask questions directly to the witness to ensure that they clearly understood the conclusions being drawn and jurors were discouraged from asking questions through the presiding judge.[51] Although the experts testified that hang fires are exceedingly rare and that they generally occur within approximately one second of the last pull of the trigger, evidence was also presented from manuals that suggested that the possibility of a hang fire should be assumed for one minute.[52] In addition to an expert witness, the defence introduced two lay witnesses who testified about personal experiences with a hang fire. One recounted a story of shooting gophers forty years earlier when he was fifteen and experienced a hang fire. Although his gun was different and forty years had passed, his testimony was allowed to stand. Law professor Kent Roach points out that this testimony was not sufficiently cross-examined or distinguished from the testimony of the expert witnesses.[53]

The Crown presented the clearest indication of the problem with the hang fire defence during its closing remarks to the jury: if Stanley had indeed checked his gun to ensure that it was empty as he testified he had, then a hang fire would be impossible.[54] But this conclusion was not put to either Stanley or the expert witnesses. Ultimately, the hang fire theory overshadowed another issue – why did Stanley approach the vehicle with three passengers inside with a gun, even if he did think that it was empty, when safety protocols, which Stanley testified he knew about, dictated that one must always assume that a gun is loaded? At trial, Gerald Stanley was asked to demonstrate how he had held his gun when he approached Boushie. The RCMP had carefully confirmed that the gun Stanley used to demonstrate was empty. Even so, defence lawyer Scott Spence asked Stanley to ensure that the gun was not pointed at anyone because, as Spence put it, "I'm a scaredy cat."[55] Gun safety manuals were presented. All confirmed that one should always assume that a gun is loaded, even if it is not. Stanley testified that he was aware of this safety protocol. In light of this evidence, Stanley's handling of the gun would appear to be careless even if he did not intend to shoot Boushie. Yet Stanley was completely exonerated.

RACISM AND COLONIALISM AS "UNKNOWN KNOWNS"

"Unknown knowns," the "unconscious beliefs and prejudices that determine how we perceive reality and intervene in it,"[56] that surfaced throughout the legal process combined to compromise the Crown's case. None of the "unknown knowns" are new. They represent instances of the systemic injustice faced by Indigenous peoples in Canada for over a century. First, all potential Indigenous jurors were deliberately excluded from the jury to ensure that only non-Indigenous jurors participated in the verdict. Second, there was no consideration of the impact of trauma and distrust of police on the testimony and recall of Colten Boushie's friends. Instead, their testimony was largely discredited, lending further force and credibility to Gerald Stanley's own testimony and the theory that he killed Colten Boushie by accident because of an extremely rare hang fire. Third, the defence spent a significant amount of time, unhindered by the Crown, in priming the jury to understand Colten Boushie and his friends as dangerous and incorrigible. The Crown did not address implicit bias at any point in the legal process, even though the defence narrative relied on specific Indigenous stereotypes.[57] Finally, the judge's instructions to the jury were incomplete because they did not address the ways in which bias and stereotyping might taint decision-making.

CRAFTING AN ALL-WHITE JURY

A few days before the Stanley trial began, Scott R. Spencer, Stanley's lead defence lawyer, issued a statement to advise the media that neither Stanley nor his family would give interviews. Spencer took the opportunity to express his dismay at some of the media coverage. "Gerry's trial is not a referendum on racism," he wrote, and "race has nothing to do with the proper outcome of Gerry's trial."[58] When jury selection was held a few days later, Spencer proceeded to reject every Indigenous-looking person who had been called to present themselves as potential jurors.

Using peremptory challenges, a now repealed provision of the Criminal Code, Spencer ensured that the jury that would determine the facts of the case and render a verdict on Colten Boushie's death would be an all-white jury. During the jury selection process, both the Crown and the defence were entitled to peremptory challenges, the right to dismiss a juror without giving reasons.[59] The jury would not be representative of Colten Boushie's community or the general population in the Biggar area but would instead represent Gerald Stanley's community.

The Supreme Court has repeatedly linked a representative jury to adjudicative impartiality:

> The perceived importance of the jury and the *Charter* right to jury trial is meaningless without some guarantee that it will perform its duties impartially and represent, as far as is possible and appropriate in the circumstances, the larger community. Indeed, without the two characteristics of impartiality and representativeness, a jury would be unable to perform properly many of the functions that make its existence desirable in the first place.[60]

The Court elaborated in the *Kokopenace* case: "The role of representativeness ... not only promotes impartiality, it also legitimizes the jury's role as the 'conscience of the community' and promotes public trust in the criminal justice system."[61]

Indigenous exclusion from juries in Canada is well documented.[62] The impact of this exclusion can have substantive and symbolic consequences. The inclusion of Indigenous jurors has the potential to enhance perspective taking. That Indigenous perspectives might encourage jurors to consider a fuller perspective of views and help jurors reach unbiased understanding of the facts has also been well documented.[63] Recently retired Chief Justice Beverley McLachlin called this perspective-taking "conscious objectivity."[64] At the end of the day, the people on the jury decide who they will believe and why. They will also decide what weight to give to the evidence and will make the inferences necessary to determine the accused's guilt or innocence. If jurors empathize or understand one perspective more than another, or if implicit biases threaten their impartiality, they are deprived of the opportunity to reflect fairly on the evidence and arguments presented to them. Moreover, a representative jury has symbolic value: it sends the message that all communities can participate as equals within the justice system. The value of jury representativeness takes on added significance in communities divided by racism and colonialism that have a history of one group sitting in judgment of another. Saskatchewan is such a community.

The defence was entitled to use its peremptory challenges, but the Crown could object so that the racially driven selection process might have been put on the record and, if warranted, made the subject of an appeal. The Crown did not raise the issue.[65] Were it not for press reports and advocacy by lawyers and Indigenous communities, this issue would never have become public. After the trial, Assistant Deputy Attorney General Anthony Gerein issued a public statement indicating that there would be no appeal and noted that criticism of the jury implied that all twelve jurors had acted improperly.[66] Gerein made no distinction between intentional wrongful acts and unconscious or implicit bias, even though the Supreme Court has explained that bias or discrimination need not be intentional.[67] One can be critical of the jury's verdict in light of the composition without suggesting that the jury intentionally failed to do justice in the case.

TRAUMATIZED WITNESSES

Colten Boushie's friends were traumatized by their experiences on the farm, with the police, and in the courtroom. Belinda Jackson had witnessed her friend shot in the head at point-blank range. The RCMP engaged in a high-speed chase with one of the young women in the back seat of the cruiser. The officers reportedly explained that "they were in a rush when they got in the vehicle and weren't aware there was a person in the back seat."[68] As a result of an internal RCMP investigation into the two officers' conduct, they "received guidance on safe handling of prisoners."[69] Cassidy Cross-Whitestone and Eric Meechance ran for their lives as Gerald Stanley fired his gun. Cross-Whitestone would later receive trauma counselling after giving his testimony. No one considered the impact that the trauma of seeing a friend shot and killed and fearing for one's own life might have had on Colten Boushie's friends, three of whom testified at his trial.

Eric Meechance, who had been picked up by the RCMP and arrested after he fled Stanley's farm, learned that Colten had been killed when Belinda and Kiora were brought into the North Battleford prison. "Belinda came in first and said, 'He's gone.' Kiora came in later and was crying."[70] Belinda Jackson, the only person to witness Colten Boushie's death, testified that she was held in jail for nineteen hours without food, questioned, and released. Her detailing of events changed significantly between the original questioning by police and her testimony at trial. She explained the discrepancies by saying that she was traumatized by the events, had been drinking, and could not immediately remember everything that she had witnessed. She added that she was distrustful of the police and that distrust influenced her decision to lie to them. As an Indigenous woman, she had reasons to distrust the police who have been directly implicated in violence against missing and murdered Indigenous women and girls.[71] She remained firm in her testimony under cross-examination that Stanley had aimed at Boushie.

In his closing statement, the Crown attorney indicated that he would not be relying on Belinda Jackson's testimony, suggesting that she was not credible.[72] At no point were the Crown's witnesses given the benefit of knowledge and expertise that the legal system has developed about trauma and memory. Writing with reference to sexual assault cases, the Department of Justice instructs its employees, including Crown prosecutors, that "[t]he science of memory and psychological trauma must be applied to interview approaches and techniques," and cautions that trauma can lead to inconsistent statements. The use of "lie detection techniques" in such circumstances can inhibit memory[73] and ultimately undermine the search for truth.

Belinda Jackson had witnessed her friend's death. She also had the specific and general trauma of interaction with police.[74] But, considerations about psychological trauma and memory were not extended to Belinda Jackson or the other Indigenous witnesses in *R. v. Stanley*. Belinda's testimony was dismissed, and memory gaps and inconsistencies in her evidence were taken as indication of her unreliability and lack of credibility. With forensic evidence washed away because the RCMP had not protected the crime scene from the significant rain that fell in the three days that they waited for a warrant to re-enter the scene,[75] Sheldon and Gerald Stanley's version of events took on additional weight.

PRIMING: THE DEFENCE'S CASE

Gerald Stanley's defence team spent a significant amount of the trial detailing the events that transpired before Cassidy Cross-Whitestone drove onto the Stanley farm. The details went into developing the narrative of Indigenous youth whose dangerousness knew no bounds. In his opening, lawyer Scott Spencer used words like "terror,"[76] "terrorists,"[77] and "home invasion"[78] to describe the actions of Colten Boushie and his friends even though they had never entered the Stanley home and Colten Boushie was the victim of Gerald Stanley, not the other way around. But, as Spencer reminded the jury, "for farm people, your yard is your castle."[79]

A defence witness described the noise and commotion that the grey SUV created as it sped past a school.[80] Cross-Whitestone's criminal record was put into evidence even though he was a juvenile offender.[81] Another witness described how Colten Boushie and friends came on their farm prior to pulling into the Stanley farm, tried to steal a vehicle, and caused significant damage to property.[82] The group had been drinking for a long period before arriving at the Stanley farm. In his testimony, Cassidy Cross-Whitestone indicated that he consumed more than thirty shots and had begun drinking the morning that Colten was killed.[83] Belinda Jackson's drinking was covered in great detail as well.[84] Toxicology reports were presented to demonstrate that Colten Boushie had high levels of alcohol in his system.[85]

While all of these facts were uncontested by the Crown, their relevance to Gerald Stanley's conduct was never clearly established. Stanley did not know about the reckless driving, the attempted thefts, the destruction of property, or the drinking. How could Cross-Whitestone's speeding past a Bible school, a fact unknown to Gerald Stanley, explain why Stanley pointed a gun at Colten Boushie's head? Even if Stanley had known about the speeding, the link is hard to understand. All of these facts were presented to help the jury draw the conclusion that Gerald Stanley should have been afraid of Boushie and his friends regardless of his knowledge of them.

Gerald Stanley's lawyer stoked the jury's fears and biases by placing emphasis on events that predated the arrival of the group on Stanley's farm. Gerald Stanley argued that his gun went off by accident. But he needed a good story to explain why he needed a gun in the first place and why it was reasonable rather than careless that he should take his gun to the window of a vehicle filled with people when gun safety protocols insist that gun users always assume that a gun is loaded.

Gerald Stanley may have subjectively feared Colten Boushie and his friends but there was never any consideration at the trial of whether that fear was rooted primarily in Stanley's own prejudices and circumstances. The National Farmers Union has pointed to fear's problematic role in shaping everyday judgment in rural Saskatchewan:

> The National Farmers Union (NFU) is deeply concerned by the news that 93 per cent of Saskatchewan Association of Rural Municipalities (SARM) annual convention delegates voted in favour of a resolution calling on the federal government to "expand the rights and justification for an individual to defend or protect himself, herself, and persons under their care and their property. This resolution, put forward under the shadow of last summer's tragic shooting of Colten Boushie by a Biggar-area farmer, reveals the dangerous undercurrent of fear and aggression in rural Saskatchewan. This is not the way to address problems faced in rural areas.[86]

The NFU understood Stanley's fear as part of a larger narrative that has defined and destroyed lives. Rachelle Ternier, NFU's Saskatchewan coordinator, continued, "[w]e, the NFU, affirm the value of people over property. We do not support the ongoing colonial violence that continues to damage the social fabric of Saskatchewan."[87]

In addition to fear, the defence created the narrative that the case was about the right to defend one's property, even though Stanley did not explicitly argue defence of property.[88] Scott Spencer's declaration that "for farmers, your yard is your castle," rang true for many in Gerald Stanley's community, some of whom expressed the view that Stanley was justified in killing Boushie.[89] In the narrative presented by the defence, fear and castle are intertwined in a logic that renders Indigenous people out of place. What is it about a group of people in a vehicle with a flat tire that makes them appear out of place to a part-time mechanic who is used to people showing up unannounced on his property? One of the group members sat on an ATV and may have even started it up but some yelling seemed enough to scare him off the ATV. Did the group's Indigenous identity have something to do with Stanley's professed fear and his immediate sense of needing to scare the group off the Treaty Six land that he claimed for his own? Stanley's defence stoked of fear to reinforce the longstanding settler colonial project and consolidate the displacement of Indigenous peoples with the narrative that they are on our land and are here to steal or harm, not the other way around.

THE CHARGE TO THE JURY: MISSING ELEMENTS

Chief Justice Popescul advised the jury that if the Crown had failed to demonstrate its case beyond a reasonable doubt, Stanley had to be found not guilty. Citing phraseology provided by the Supreme Court and often repeated by criminal court judges, he explained:

> A reasonable doubt is not an imaginary or frivolous doubt. It is not based on sympathy for or prejudice against anyone involved in the proceedings. Rather, it is based on reason and common sense. It is a doubt that arises logically from the evidence or from the absence of evidence.[90]

What do "reason" and "common sense" require, and from whose perspective these should be assessed? The jury was never instructed on these points.

Reason and common sense are not neutral or abstract terms in law. On the contrary, they are given content by the embodied experiences of those who wield these terms. Writing in another context, Supreme Court Justices Claire L'Heureux-Dubé and Charles Gonthier observed:

> The sticking point is, of course, recognition that the application of "logic" and "common sense" may, in any given case, show "rank prejudice." As Dawson, *supra*, rightfully points out, at p. 316, "[legal standards] are not simply neutral mechanisms to facilitate

substantive debates, but take their place in a normative structure." As such they may be used to perpetuate "rank prejudice." Though the determination of what is relevant is often represented as involving a neutral standard applied objectively, both history and the magnitude of the harm done suggest otherwise.

From my perspective sitting in Windsor, reason would dictate that Stanley, a part-time mechanic, might have easily surmised that the group had come to the farm in need of help from the fact that the vehicle in which Colten Boushie and his friends were driving had a dragging muffler and a flat tire. One member of the group went to an ATV but seems to have run away when yelled at. Even if the Stanleys were uncertain about the group's motives, the anger that both Sheldon and Gerald Stanley displayed towards the group puzzles me. After he attacked the group's vehicle with a hammer and set off a chain of events that led to Boushie's death, Sheldon Stanley admitted at trial, "I was mad." Gerald and Sheldon's conduct when the SUV appeared on their property appears to me to be an overreaction driven by irrational fear, inordinate rage, or both. Similarly, from my perspective, common sense would not have dictated that Gerald Stanley run to get his gun or that he would fire warning shots in the air, or that he would have approached the car in which Colten Boushie was seated with a gun in his hand, whether he thought that it was loaded or not. Again, these actions, to me, betray fear, rage, or both. They do not suggest common sense.

Stanley's reaction to Boushie and his friends perhaps made sense to the jury because they had been primed to see Boushie and his friends as incorrigible, reckless, and dangerous criminals while the judge's instructions to the jury did not attempt to distill or disentangle the relationship between common sense, fear, and biases. To put it simply, bias can be passed off as "reason" and "common sense", especially in the most biased of contexts. In *R. v. Williams,* a unanimous Supreme Court found that the trial judge improperly failed to "warn the jury, either in his opening or closing addresses, to be aware of or to disregard any bias or prejudice that they might feel towards Williams [the accused] as a native person" and the Court noted that where widespread bias exists, the judge can take judicial notice of it without requiring arguments or evidence on that point.[91]

Exploring "settler common sense," Mark Rifkin explains that "settlement – the exertion of control by non-Natives over Native peoples and land – gives rise to modes of feeling, generating kinds of affect through which the terms of law and policy become imbued with a sensation of everyday certainty."[92] Common sense foregrounded and validated Gerald Stanley's emotions, placing his fear above scrutiny and rendering the claim that a man's farm is his castle a natural, necessary, and neutral contention that needed – and ultimately received – reaffirmation in the law. In charging the jury, Chief Justice Martel Popescul made no mention of any of the accumulated knowledge about Indigenous experiences with the justice system. Consistent with the defence claim that the trial was not a referendum about race, the judge did not explain what might constitute bias or how bias might influence assessments of fact. The appeal to reason and common sense masked the appeal to fear and stereotypes. Reason and common sense facilitated the defence attempt to conjure up feelings of fear that form the structures of settler solidarity in rural Saskatchewan while simultaneously hiding those structures from view.

"SHUT UP AND TEACH"[93]

Against this context, Windsor Law's faculty council unanimously adopted its statement on 27 February 2018. The statement reads in part:

> Canada has used law to perpetuate violence against Indigenous Peoples and too often protects those who commit acts of violence against Indigenous Peoples. Just like racism, law is learned. This means legal education is part of the problem too. What happened to Colten Boushie and law's response to his murder are tragic, unnecessary and unacceptable. We stand with Colten Boushie's family. We stand with Red Pheasant First Nation. We stand with Indigenous Peoples. We stand with Indigenous scholars, students, activists and families who remind all of us of our moral responsibilities as guests in the Territories of the Three Fires Confederacy to generate change.

Not surprisingly, Windsor Law's statement was met with some criticism. Queen's University law professor Bruce Pardy was particularly vociferous. He criticized Windsor Law's statement because faculty members were not at the trial. He argued that the statement revealed the extent to which legal education had "lost its way" and suggested that Windsor Law was un-Canadian.[94]

Windsor Law described Boushie's killing as a "murder" and, by implication, inferred that Stanley is a "murderer." Labelling someone who has been exonerated by the legal system a "murderer" is hardly an insignificant act, especially when that label is given by an entire faculty of law, most of whom are members of the legal profession, and who teach students aspiring to become members of that profession. On its face, the label appears to deny Stanley the benefit of due process, one of the most fundamental principles of the Canadian legal system. However, it is this writer's opinion, expressed as a faculty member, that Windsor Law's actions were made to emphasize that both the accused and victim are entitled to fair proceedings. Windsor Law's use of the word "murder" to describe Gerald Stanley was a provocative strategy to show that the legal process is flawed in that it is often practised, understood, read, and remembered from the perspective of non-Indigenous peoples. Opting for more neutral language, such as "the killing of Colten Boushie," would have risked ignoring the legal system's colonial and racists roots and thereby minimized the ways that systemic racism underpinned Gerald Stanley's trial.

CONCLUSION

Windsor Law's statement points to the fact that legal scholars and practitioners need to ask questions that extend beyond the verdict itself. The role of the academic is to help "raise the proper question."[95] The larger questions that must come out of Colten Boushie's untimely death include: is the Canadian criminal justice system trustworthy enough to sit in judgment of Indigenous peoples; is the Canadian criminal justice system capable of distinguishing between guilt and innocence when Indigenous peoples come before it, or are its truth finding functions weighed down by bias and prejudice; and, does the legal system's treatment of Indigenous peoples reinforce their status as human beings worthy of being treated with equality dignity and respect by Canada's legal system?

NOTES

1 Royal Reporting Services Ltd, transcripts, R. v. Stanley, in the *Court of Queen's Bench for Saskatchewan, Judicial Centre for Battleford*, volumes 1 to 7 (29, 30, 31 January and 1, 2, 5, 6, 8 and 9 February 2018); R. v. Stanley, 2018 SKQB 27 (CanLII), http://canlii.ca/t/hrow8, retrieved on 18 September 2019 (cameras in court room); R. v. Stanley, 2018 SKQB 27 (CanLII), http://canlii.ca/t/hrow8, accessed 18 September 2019 (preservation of evidence).
2 "Windsor Law's Statement on Stanley Trial Verdict," University of Windsor – Faculty of Law, 27 February 2018, http://www.uwindsor.ca/law/2018-02-16/windsor-laws-statement-stanley-trial-verdict.
3 Ibid.
4 See Constance Backhouse, *Colour-Coded: A Legal History of Racism in Canada, 1900–1950* (Toronto: University of Toronto Press, 1999).
5 Slavoj Zizek, "What Rumsfeld Doesn't Know That He Knows About Abu Ghraib," in *These Times*, 21 May 2004, https://www.lacan.com/zizekrumsfeld.htm.
6 See Kent Roach, *Canadian Justice, Indigenous Injustice* (Montreal: McGill-Queen's, 2019) for an analysis of the case by a criminal legal scholar, and Tasha Hubbard, nîpawistamâsowin: We Will Stand Up (2019), a documentary focused on the hearing, its shortcomings and Boushie's community.
7 I offer my own analysis in this chapter and do not aim to represent the views of Windsor Law colleagues or the institution more generally.
8 Connie Samson, "RCMP Can't Stop Nerland Inquiry," *Windspeaker.com*, 1992, https://windspeaker.com/news/windspeaker-news/rcmp-cant-stop-nerland-inquiry.
9 Transcripts at T487.
10 "Groundhog day," *Urban Dictionary*, https://www.urbandictionary.com/define.php?term=Groundhog+day.
11 Karen Morrison, "Sask. Gallery Sheds Light on Town's Dark Days," *The Western Producer*, 26 March 2009, https://www.producer.com/2009/03/sask-gallery-sheds-light-on-towns-dark-days/.
12 Biggar Museum and Gallery, Royden Donahue Exhibit Gallery, https://www.biggarmuseum.com/collectionsexhibits.htm.
13 James M. Pitsula, *Keeping Canada British: The Ku Klux Klan in 1920s Saskatchewan* (Vancouver: UBC Press, 2013), 44.
14 Martha Shaffer, "Criminal Responses to Hate-Motivated Violence: Is Bill C-41 Tough Enough?" *McGill Law Journal* 41, no. 1 (1996): 199.

CanLIIDocs 61, http://www.canlii.org/t/2bhr, accessed 11 November 2019.
15 Frank Leonard, *Thousand Blunders: The Grand Trunk Pacific Railway and Northern British Columbia* (Vancouver: UBC Press, 1996), 5.
16 Ibid., 173.
17 Mark Rifkin, *Settler Common Sense: Queerness and Everyday Colonialism in the American Renaissance* (Minneapolis: University of Minnesota Press, 2014).
18 Amar Bhatia, "Statehood, Canadian Sovereignty and the Domestication of Indian Legal Relations," *Decolonizing Law*, forthcoming.
19 Truth and Reconciliation Commission of Canada, *Honouring The Truth, Reconciling for the Future: Summary of the final report of the Truth and Reconciliation Commission of Canada* (Ottawa: Truth and Reconciliation Commission of Canada, 2015), http://nctr.ca/assets/reports/Final percent20Reports/Executive_Summary_English_Web.pdf.
20 *A Legal Analysis of Genocide, Supplementary Report of the National Inquiry into Missing and Murdered Indigenous Women and Girls* (Ottawa: National Inquiry into Missing and Murdered Indigenous Women and Girls, 2019).
21 Sylvia McAdam–Saysewahum, *Nationhood Interrupted* (British Columbia: University of British Columbia Press, 2015).
22 F. Laurie Barron, "The Indian Pass System in the Canadian West, 1882–1935," *Prairie Forum* 13, no. 1 (1988).
23 James Daschuk, *Clearing the Plains: Disease, Politics of Starvation, and the Loss of Indigenous Life* (Regina: University of Regina Press, 2013).
24 Andrew Woolford, *This Benevolent Experiment: Indigenous Boarding Schools, Genocide and Redress in Canada and the United States* (Winnipeg: University of Manitoba Press, 2015).
25 *First Nations Child & Family Caring Society of Canada et al. v. Attorney General of Canada (representing the Minister of Indigenous and Northern Affairs Canada)*, 2019 CHRT 39 (CanLII), http://canlii.ca/t/j3n9j, accessed 24 August 2019.
26 Human Rights Watch, *Submission to the Government of Canada on Police Abuse of Indigenous Women in Saskatchewan and Failures to Protect Indigenous Women from Violence* (2017), https://www.hrw.org/news/2017/06/19/submission-government-canada-police-abuse-indigenous-women-saskatchewan-and-failures.
27 Farida Deif, *Submission to the Government of Canada on Police Abuse of Indigenous Women in Saskatchewan and Failures to Protect Indigenous*

Women from Violence (Human Rights Watch, 2017), https://www.hrw.org/sites/default/files/supporting_resources/canada_saskatchewan_submission_june_2017.pdf.

28 Criminal Code of Canada, s. 269.1.
29 Honourable Mr Justice David H. Wright, "Report of the Commission of Inquiry Re: Neil Stonechild," October 2004, https://publications.saskatchewan.ca/#/products/9462.
30 Heidi Kiiwetinepinesiik Stark, "Criminal Empire: The Making of the Savage in a Lawless Land," *Theory & Event*, 19 no. 4, 2016.
31 Ibid., 3.
32 InFocus, "Justice System an 'Industry' Profiting off Indigenous Offenders and Victims," *APTN News*, 28 March 2019, <https://aptnnews.ca/2019/03/28/justice-system-an-industry-profiting-off-indigenous-offenders-and-victims>.
33 Jillian Rogin, "Gladue and Bail: The Pre-Trial Sentencing of Aboriginal People in Canada," *The Canadian Bar Review* 95, no. 2 (2017).
34 *A Place Where It Feels Like Home: The Story of Tina Fontaine*, prepared by Manitoba Advocate for Children and Youth (Winnipeg, 2019), https://manitobaadvocate.ca/wp-content/uploads/MACY-Special-Report-March-2019-Tina-Fontaine-FINAL1.pdf.
35 Criminal Code, s. 231(2).
36 Criminal Code, s. 232(1) and s. 86 (1): "Every person commits an offence who, without lawful excuse, uses, carries, handles, ships, transports or stores a firearm, a prohibited weapon, a restricted weapon, a prohibited device or any ammunition or prohibited ammunition in a careless manner or without reasonable precautions for the safety of other persons."
37 Transcript, T704.
38 Ibid.
39 John Cairns, "Witness Breaks Down under Cross Examination," *Battleford News-Optimist*, 31 January 2018, https://www.newsoptimist.ca/news/local-news/witness-breaks-down-under-cross-examination-1.23160950.
40 Debbie Baptiste v. Gerald Stanley 1246118 (SKQB 2018.)
41 Guy Quenneville, "What Happened on Gerald Stanley's Farm the Day Colten Boushie was Shot, as Told by Witnesses," *CBC News*, 6 February 2018.
42 Transcript, T687.
43 Transcript, T697.
44 Transcript, T864.

45 Manisha Krishnan, "Why Gerald Stanley's Defence Doesn't Make Sense to Gun Experts," *Vice*, 14 February 2018. See also Kent Roach, *Canadian Justice, Indigenous Injustice*, 4.
46 Transcript, T414.
47 Stanley was subsequently fined $3,900 and received a ten-year ban on gun ownership. "Mr Stanley frankly wishes he never owned a gun ... Mr Stanley has no desire to ever hold a gun again," said Scott Spencer (Stanley's lawyer): "Gerald Stanley to Pay $3,900 and Receive 10-Year Ban on Gun Ownership for Improper Firearm Storage," CBC *News*, 16 April 2018.
48 Transcript, T223.
49 Ibid., T608.
50 Ibid., T455–T602.
51 Ibid., T524–T525.
52 Ibid., T590.
53 Kent Roach, *Canadian Justice, Indigenous Injustice*, 139.
54 Transcript, T863.
55 Ibid., T697.
56 Slavoj Zizek, "Rumsfeld and the Bees," *The Guardian*, 28 June 2008, https://www.theguardian.com/commentisfree/2008/jun/28/wildlife.conservation.
57 *Radek v. Henderson Development (Canada) and Securiguard Services (No. 3)*, 2005 BCHRT 302 (CanLII), http://canlii.ca/t/ho8j7, accessed 18 August 2019.
58 "Stanley Trial 'Not a Referendum on Racism': Defence Lawyer," *Saskatoon StarPhoenix*, 26 January 2018, <https://thestarphoenix.com/news/local-news/stanley-trial-not-a-referendum-on-racism-defence-lawyer>.
59 Brian Manarin, *Canadian Indigenous Peoples and Criminal Jury Trials: Remediating Inequality* (Toronto: Lexis-Nexis, 2019).
60 *R. v. Williams*, 25375, (SCC. 1998).
61 *R. v. Kokopenace*, 35475, (SCC 2015).
62 See for example the 1991 report of Manitoba's Aboriginal Justice Inquiry (following the murder of Helen Betty Osborne and the death of J.J. Harper that implicated a Winnipeg police officer) and the 2001 report of the implementation commission for the recommendations of the 1991 Manitoba report. See also *First Nations Representation on Ontario Juries*: Report of the Independent Review Conducted by The Honourable Frank Iacobucci, February 2013.
63 Ibid.

64 Right Honourable Beverley McLachlin, "The Civilization of Difference," LaFontaine-Baldwin Symposium, Halifax, 7 March 2003, https://www.scc-csc.ca/judges-juges/spe-dis/bm-2003-03-07-eng.aspx, and Beverly McLachlin, "Judging in A Democratic State," Sixth Templeton Lecture on Democracy University of Manitoba, 3 June 2004, https://www.scc-csc.ca/judges-juges/spe-dis/bm-2004-06-03-eng.aspx?pedisable=true.

65 See Kent Roach, *Canadian Justice, Indigenous Injustice* at chap. 5 for on overview of the law related to jury selection and the Crown's failure to challenge for cause.

66 Dave Deibert, "Gerald Stanley Trial: Complete Transcript of Public Prosecution's Decision to not Appeal Case," *Saskatoon StarPhoenix*, 8 March 2018, https://thestarphoenix.com/news/local-news/gerald-stanley-trial-complete-transcript-of-public-prosecutions-decision-to-not-appeal-case.

67 See, for example, *Quebec (Commission des droits de la personne et des droits de la jeunesse) v. Bombardier Inc. (Bombardier Aerospace Training Center)*, 2015 SCC 39 (CanLII), [2015] 2 SCR 789, http://canlii.ca/t/gk9vn, accessed 24 September 2020.

68 Charles Hamilton, "RCMP Clears Itself of Misconduct in Colten Boushie Investigation, CBC News, 2 November 2017, https://www.cbc.ca/news/canada/saskatchewan/colten-boushie-investigation-rcmp-1.4383816.

69 Ibid.

70 Cairns, "Witness Breaks under Cross Examination," *Battleford News-Optimist*. Kent Roach reviews how Stanley's lawyer challenged the credibility of the Indigenous witnesses in *Canadian Justice, Indigenous Injustice* at chap. 7.

71 Pamela Palmater, "Shining Light on the Dark Places: Addressing Police Racism and Sexualized Violence against Indigenous Women and Girls in the National Inquiry," *Canadian Journal of Women and the Law*, 28 no. 2, (August 2016): 253–284.

72 Testimony, T856.

73 Department of Justice, "The Impact of Trauma on Sexual Assault Victims: How Trauma Affects Memory and Recall," https://www.justice.gc.ca/eng/rp-pr/jr/trauma/p4.html.

74 On Indigenous peoples and police interaction trauma, see *Campbell v. Vancouver Police Board (No. 2)*, 2019 BCHRT 128 (CanLII), http://canlii.ca/t/j178m, accessed 18 September 2019; *Campbell v. Vancouver Police Board (No. 3)*, 2019 BCHRT 145 (CanLII).

75 Transcript, T120.

76 Ibid., T607.

77 Ibid.
78 Ibid., T606.
79 Ibid.
80 Ibid., T613.
81 Ibid., T385.
82 Ibid., T642.
83 Ibid., T350.
84 Ibid., T448.
85 Ibid., T842.
86 National Farmers Union, "NFU Finds SARM Resolution Deeply Concerning, Will Not Solve Rural Problems," 17 March 2017, https://www.nfu.ca/nfu-finds-sarm-resolution-deeply-concerning-will-not-solve-rural-problems/.
87 Ibid.
88 Transcript, T852: Stanley's lawyer's summation to the jury emphasized, "This is a terrible accident. It's not a marked departure. Things happen. When you create this type of home invasion, fear-filled, high-energy roller coaster ride, when you create that, you create an opportunity for there to be an accident and a tragedy. And that's what happened here." It should be noted that Boushie and his friends never entered the Stanley's home and that Boushie himself remained in or near his friend's car at all times.
89 Gina Starblanket, "Gerald Stanley and the castle narrative," as settler colonialism and privileging of one story over another, podcast audio, 20 February 2018, https://policyoptions.irpp.org/magazines/february-2018/gerald-stanley-castle-narrative/.
90 Transcript, T880–T881.
91 *R. v. Williams*, 1998 CanLII 782 (SCC), [1998] 1 SCR 1128, pars 6–13, http://canlii.ca/t/1fqsg, retrieved on 24 August 2020.
92 Mark Rifkin, *Settler Common Sense: Queerness and Everyday Colonialism in the American Renaissance* (Minneapolis: University of Minnesota Press, 2014), 1.
93 Ken Montgomery, "Shut Up and Teach: Confronting the Power of Racialized Hero Discourses of Soldier and Nation," *Power and Education* 6, no. 2 (2014) 169–81.
94 Bruce Pardy, "The Social Justice Revolution has Taken the Law Schools. This Won't End Well," *The National Post*, 27 February 2018, https://nationalpost.com/opinion/the-social-justice-revolution-has-taken-the-law-schools-this-wont-end-well.
95 Slavoj Zizek, "Philosophy, the 'Unknown Knowns,' and the Public Use of Reason," *Topoi* 25, no. 1–2 (2006).

11

History in the Public Interest: Teaching Decolonization Through the RSC Archive

Jennifer Evans, Meagan Breault, Ellis Buschek, Brittany Long, Sabrina Schoch and David Siebert

In a very real sense, we were destined to fail. The goal of our MA course was to research the history of the Royal Society of Canada (RSC) for the ways in which it was implicated in the history of violence against Indigenous people, whether directly, through the building of residential schools or more surreptitiously through the caricature and exclusion of Indigenous knowledge, world making, and history from the greater Canadian story. We were inspired by the decolonial impetus behind Ann Stoler and Gayatri Spivak's work, which sheds light on the way imperial imaginaries were constructed and reproduced by colonial functionaries, who wrote their own histories in opposition to the subaltern who could not speak. Convinced we were on the side of right, we began our research buoyed by the belief that we would be overwhelmed by evidence of wrongdoing.[1] Perhaps we cannot be faulted: the archive's charms are many, especially the holdings of Library and Archives Canada (LAC), which form, quite literally, the stuff of national memory.[2] What makes its way into the histories we write is inevitably fraught, a product of a complex matrix of settler-colonial relationships that continue into the present day. No matter what was to be found inside the carefully ordered files of the RSC fonds, some of it governed by arcane privacy restrictions, there was no getting away from the fact that the evidence in the archive, housed in a building situated, not insignificantly, on unceded and contested land, remains a vestige of colonial relations not entirely relegated to history.[3] And we were, and remain, a part of that legacy too and the way it still grips us all, in different ways, today.

This chapter was conceptualized, researched, and written collectively over the course of four months in early 2019 by students and the instructor of "History in the Public Interest," a master's level public history course at Carleton University. In it, we explore the challenges of doing this kind of work intellectually, as settlers of a certain age and generation operating within the very academic institutions buttressed by learned societies and their professors, and practically, given what sources have found their way into the archive. Guided by Indigenous critique of white settler knowledge formations, we provide a snapshot of what we discovered to serve as a kind of a primer for future research, while also thinking through the absences and gaps in the historical record and what they mean for reconciliation today.

First, we will discuss our way into the sources alongside the method we chose to implement when surveying the RSC fonds at LAC. Then, we drill down into the lives, work, influence and impact of several of the core personalities of the society's early years, including William Ganong, Edward Sapir, and George Stanley. We end with a brief discussion of the intersection of personal, business, and scholarly networks, national as well as transnational, for how they contributed to the maintenance of colonial power. We opted to analyze fellows less notorious than the RSC president and deputy superintendent of Indian Affairs, Duncan Campbell Scott, though the men we chose (and of course they were always men) were well-established in government and scholarly life by the time they became connected to the society.

Our argument is that the RSC played a core role in establishing what counted as legitimate inquiry within the scholarly networks and social and intellectual bonds of this educated elite. These explorations in language, folklore, and history – so central to mid-twentieth century Canadian identity – were forged on the backs of romanticized, stereotypical, and outright racist ideas around Indigenous ways of life. The body of knowledge these early RSC fellows created placed Indigenous people and their traditions outside the bounds of culture and heritage and thus – in the hands of administrators like Scott and those who followed in his place – justified Indigenous dispossession from ancestral lands and the removal of Indigenous children from their homes and parents. While it is true these men did not believe themselves to be orchestrating cultural genocide, they played an integral part in building the intellectual infrastructure that made it possible in the first place.[4] Their legacy lives on to this day.

Before beginning our project, we realized that we needed to cultivate a method that respected the traditions that were so royally wronged by academic inquiry. Fellows of the RSC – academics but also civil servants, clergymen, anthropologists, politicians, poets, translators, librarians, and scientists – saw Indigenous communities and their languages as opportunities for personal and career gain through extractive academic study, with little consultation or reciprocity. Their goal was to support Canadian intellectual innovation, which included the growth of the nation's learned professions, universities, and cultural institutions. These were nation builders in the classic sense, intent on forging a Canadian equivalent to the great European academies of art, literature, and science. This was not soft power; as Carl Berger puts it in his history of the society: "it was a logical extension of the political consolidation of the colonies."[5]

METHODOLOGY AND PRIVILEGE

Given that all aspects of Canadian intellectual life owe their moorings to these men and their scholarship, our approach would have to be different. Fortunately, this was no regular graduate course. We met with and reported back to stakeholders in the RSC offices in Ottawa, located in a stately redbrick home in socially-stratified Centretown. We conducted class each week in Walter House, in rooms sponsored by the country's major universities, a few short blocks from the Supreme Court and Centre Block, a constant reminder that this history was very much, still, all around us. We were given access to the extant onsite archive, locating medals and ephemera not yet transferred to LAC. We blogged our early archival discoveries, and enjoyed the support of the RSC Task Force on Truth and Reconciliation to hire a researcher, Ian Wereley, who spoke with us about his experiences analyzing the *Transactions*, the results of which are in this volume. And we presented our work to Cindy Blackstock, who rushed to Walter House one snowy April between hearings on Parliament Hill, reminding us of the urgency of our work in the context of the Government of Canada's ongoing human rights violations against Indigenous children and youth. We benefitted from our affiliation with the society and with our home university, Carleton, when seeking research support at LAC, and we benefited too from the fact that these institutions were keen to gather an audience for the work. We were motivated, somewhat romantically, that we were doing right after so much wrong. We only began to realize the stakes when we started exploring a series of readings by Indigenous scholars to prepare us for our undertaking. Here, we came face to face with the inescapable fact that structural racism was not a thing of the past; it enveloped us on our journey as well.

Leanne Betasamosake Simpson put it most bluntly: decolonization is an admirable goal, but is it truly achievable when we continue to live at a time of land dispossession, violence against Indigenous women and girls, and extractive resource policy management that continues to privilege settler health, institutions, knowledge, and power?[6] From the comfort of our lofty intentions, suddenly we were forced to stare down the hard questions: was the search for justice in the historical record another way of assuaging our own guilt? Would we not just be re-centering white settler history, told anew? How might we rectify this, or is it even doable? A step in the right direction, we thought, would be to document how networks of knowledge production and power undergird the exploitative role of settler-colonial cultural imaginaries in what has passed as research excellence. When left unexamined and unchecked, as has been the case all these years, these networks perpetuate notions of self and other, settler and colonized, and animate policy decisions then as now, perpetuating white colonial state sovereignty.[7] Unless subjected to scrutiny, and made explicit, as Dallas Hunt has observed elsewhere, it continues to permeate through the archive, ensuring that "Indigenous peoples [remain] either absent, depicted as ciphers of the real individuals they are meant to represent, or presented as always already disappearing from the landscape."[8]

As we trekked down to meet with portfolio archivists at LAC, we came face to face with the enormity of the problem of using the tools of hegemonic history to do the work of decolonization. Built after an act of parliament in 1953, the national archive is itself a testament to the spirit of settler Canadian cultural identity. Fellows of the society were involved in the very call to create it. One of this country's longest-standing learned institutions, connected in an intricate intellectual web to the other dominions of the British Empire, the RSC was keenly interested in the work of the nation's best and brightest, those whose research shaped government policy, university curricula, museum collections, and scientific discovery.[9] The archive was not the only institution supported by the RSC; the society spearheaded the construction of the National Library as well, while at the same time the president of the French-language section, Charles Marius Barbeau, helped fill the collections of the Victoria Memorial Museum, which now houses the Museum of Nature, with artifacts procured from Indigenous people in dubious ways.[10] Society fellows were central to these undertakings, from rank and file members to the presidents themselves. While Duncan Campbell Scott has been exposed for his racism as the architect of residential schools, fellows like Barbeau and those under examination here are celebrated, even today, as icons in their respective fields, suggesting the scale and urgency of decolonization if we are to take reconciliation seriously as a mandate for our academic and cultural institutions.

As Crystal Fraser and Zoe Todd have argued elsewhere, colonial institutions like LAC and the RSC buttressed distinct cultural representations of what it meant to be Canadian on the backs of "Indigenous voices, bodies, economies, histories, and socio-political structures" who were the foils of these very formulations.[11] Worse still, and it remains to be pieced together sufficiently, their scholarship served government policy aimed at limiting self-government and the maintenance of Indigenous traditions.[12] If the texture of Indigenous life was hard to come by in the RSC fonds, would we be able to read sources of hegemonic power and knowledge against the grain in ways that might honour Indigenous resilience? The short answer is no. We were to fail, most egregiously in fact, at re-centering Indigenous experience. The story we were about to uncover remained a product of the colonial imagination, bound to the "colonial logic of difference" which David Garneau has characterized by its "drive to see, to traverse, to know, to translate (to make equivalent), to own, and to exploit."[13] Even if we engaged in a self-critical practice of retributive research, our own privileged position as a member of the RSC's College of New Scholars and as white settler students in a Canadian university is not easily transcended. Instead, our goal became how to write up this early period of RSC history without perpetuating the perils and pitfalls of extractive history.

EXTRACTIVE HISTORY

One of the most egregious acts of RSC fellows in their interactions with Indigenous lives and traditions was their unbridled extraction of stories, material culture, and traditions. Sociologist Lisa Tilley explains that extractive, piratic research perpetuates Western models of epistemology at the expense of other ways of seeing and knowing the world.[14] Such a methodology is predicated on a "political economy of knowledge" where "how it is refined as intellectual property ... comes to alienate participating knowers."[15] It was common for fellows of the Royal Society to employ extractive methods in their work on or with Indigenous, Inuit, and Métis peoples.[16] William F. Ganong was but one of many examples. A professor of botany and member of an illustrious Maritime family, Ganong turned his attention to the Indigenous nomenclature of New Brunswick out of a love for the province rather than goals of career advancement and networking.[17] In fact, he paid little attention to historical trends of the day, preferring topics more suited to his training in science. What he did write on the history of his province's place names was largely ignored during the first half of the twentieth century. It wasn't until the latter part of the century that it began to gain prominence.[18]

Ganong had a working knowledge of both Maliseet and Mi'kmaq place names, and for decades was the leading English scholar of the Acadian period.[19] However, his focus on the disenfranchised populations of New Brunswick was not without its issues. Like many scholars of the time period, his work relied heavily on Indigenous informants. Upon hearing about his research, whether out of pride or altruism, many people from these same communities approached him independently to provide information for his work. Despite their importance to his undertaking, Ganong was wary that their information might be "unreliable."[20] He described one of his chief informants, Jim Paul, as "an awful liar."[21] Ganong's biographer claimed he might be able to look past the lying as long as he remained "adept at disentangling interlayered fact and fiction."[22]

Inspired to complete this research and "record the evidence before it vanished," Ganong set out to "save" Indigenous knowledge before it was "lost forever." However, his inability to fully trust Indigenous communities reinforced historical assumptions around white settlers as infinitely more qualified to preserve Indigenous culture, disenfranchising Indigenous people and their traditions in the process as inferior to Western ways of knowing. Ganong's Indigenous informants were conduits of knowledge; they were not knowers in their own right. White Canadianness, in the form of Ganong's scholarship and perceived superior conservation methods, normalized a relationship of power around who was better positioned to safeguard these traditions.

Recently, scholars in various fields have begun to evaluate how academia can confront and overcome these "piratic" research methods. Collaboration between researchers and research participants is one method.[23] Acknowledgment of the various "intersecting levels of privilege and power" that come with advanced training as researchers is also crucial for decolonizing our process. A.B. Wesner, J. Pyatt, and C.N.E. Corbin argue that collaboration across difference is another way to give back in critical, meaningful ways. Research methods and fieldwork "must be constructed such that knowledge is produced across divides, collaboratively, and with attention to inscription of privileged interests, as well as being explicitly tied to the material politics of social change."[24] We deliberately crafted our project with this vision of collaboration in mind, even if some of the pitfalls of our research were difficult to overcome.

REGIONAL, NATIONAL, AND INTERNATIONAL TIES

Although the RSC was a national academy of excellence, it constituted a diverse membership that included sons of prominent political and entrepreneurial families alongside foreign nationals and temporary residents. Despite the intensely regional aspect of the society, with more than 90 per cent of fellows living between Toronto, Kingston, and Ottawa, it nevertheless managed to connect diverse constituents to a common cause: the intellectual founding of the nation.[25] In their meetings in the Centre Block of Parliament, where the men would gather three or four days every third week of May – "close to the Queen's birthday" – to conduct the business of nominating candidates for membership and medals and hearing the presidential address, they would listen to a selection of position papers that would later be published in the *Transactions*, and sent to research libraries as far away as the Soviet Union and the South Pacific.[26] In research papers in the *Transactions*, and in the field work they undertook in Canada's far-flung communities, they developed a common scholarly language, allowing new categories of analysis to evolve for the interpretation of language, culture, and social groups.

In its early history, surprisingly few of the elected fellows were even born in Canada. While several of the French-Canadian fellows looked to intellectual and religious traditions on the European continent, these nascent RSC networks operated through a kind of buzz-and-pipeline effect. From their disparate parts of the country, their work for the RSC allowed them to develop a shared sense of purpose, alongside scholarly norms and practices that connected the periphery of these settler colonial institutions and scholars to the centre of Britain.[27] The trans-local links worked in several unique ways. They connected the diverse spaces and places within Canada back to Ottawa, the society's hub and home of the federal government, the nation's cultural institutions, and its "Ottawa Men" civil servant elite. However, they also are connected through the *Transactions* and other scholarly networks forged by members themselves back to the United Kingdom.[28] Increasingly in the twentieth century, especially in the years after the First World War, academic and industrial stakeholders and institutions in the United States came to exert an influence in the society. This was especially true of universities and philanthropic organizations like the Carnegie Foundation, which suggests a subtle shift away from traditional British imperial connections towards American cultural, capital, intellectual, and economic hegemony.[29] Turning to the travails of three other RSC fellows with ties to other parts of Canada and the world beyond Ontario who wrote prodigiously on Indigenous issues, we are able to appreciate how their regional endeavours connected to several distinct networks. This suggests the importance of these Indigenous topics to their personal and professional development, alongside the project of nation-building, which undergirded virtually every part of their undertakings.

EDWARD SAPIR

An unlikely candidate for RSC membership was the itinerant Jewish American anthropologist and linguist Edward Sapir. Emigrating to New York City as an infant from poverty and pogroms in Pomerania and raised on the Lower East Side with the help of an enterprising mother and his own quick wits, Sapir benefitted in unimaginable ways from being at the right place at the right time. A student of Franz Boas at Columbia University, funded by a full scholarship he won in high school, he studied philology and the linguistic structures of his mother tongue, German, before branching out to other languages and sitting in courses in anthropology.[30] A true interdisciplinarian, he migrated around departments, his talent obvious to those around him. It was not long before Sapir was offered a place in a graduate program, where he studied Germanics with a minor in Sanskrit. Anthropology and ethnographic research occupied a sizeable part of his doctoral studies and, by the end of his degree, he had been scouted personally by Boas, who channeled funding from the National History Museum to send Sapir to the US and Canadian west coast. There he was to conduct field work so that he might further his mission to sensitize students to "what was valuable in foreign cultures ... and those elements in our own civilization which are common to all mankind."[31]

When a position opened up in Ottawa with the anthropological division of the Canadian Geological Survey to investigate "the native races of Canada, their distribution, languages, cultures, etc., etc., etc., and to collect and preserve records of the same," Sapir was ecstatic to bring what he believed to be the most modern, scientific methods to projects that had heretofore been the domain of amateurs supported by learned societies.[32] He too felt he was on the side of right. His work with Indigenous groups on the West Coast also afforded him the opportunity to continue and extend Boasian methods to debunk evolutionary, scientific racism in favour of more site- and cultural-specific ethnography.[33] His fieldwork in Canada would be instrumental in positioning him as the intellectual heir to his mentor. Indeed, he would one day lead the American Anthropological Association committee that would recommend the standardization of writing on Indigenous languages, while systematizing the classification system the discipline would employ well into the 1960s. And he would establish a place for ethnological approaches that emphasized phonetic and linguistic paradigms as a supplemental field of anthropology. By the time he left Ottawa and the anthropological division, first for the University of Chicago and then Yale, he had re-categorized museum collections at the Victoria Memorial Museum, analyzed several Indigenous language groups from the Nootka in Alberni to the Abenaki, Malecite, Micmac, Montagnais, and Rupert's House Cree, and regaled countless audiences with tales of Canada's Other.[34]

For Sapir, Ottawa represented professional and financial security and a chance to start a family. He and his first wife Florence made a home (even if they moved several times), took family vacations to the Gatineau Hills like other civil servants of his standing, and socialized with society husbands and wives including Marius Barbeau, an established folklorist in his own right and a fellow member of the museum's anthropology wing.[35] The Ottawa appointment also provided an opportunity to cement anthropology on Canadian soil, if only as part of the Geological Survey and not yet in a Canadian university. Sapir was eager to teach and had tried to lobby for a position at McGill and the University of Toronto, even appealing to cultural nationalism to substantiate the need for locally trained experts. But anthropology would have to wait several years to be fully ensconced as a discipline and Sapir had to content himself with a government position, one that nevertheless afforded him the opportunity to speak for Indigenous people on a range of issues, as was the way for Boasian anthropologists, who felt they served as conduits between local culture and public knowledge.[36]

In Sapir's efforts to serve as a liaison between the Canadian government and Indigenous culture and traditions, one sees the contradictory logic of settler colonialism at work. On the one hand, he clearly wanted to use his connection to the Geological Survey as leverage with which to help those in his Indigenous support network. In several instances, he took direct action in letters and petitions to Duncan Campbell Scott, then deputy superintendent for Indian Affairs, asking the department to take a stance on the inferior health provisions on reserve, the continued illegality of the potlatch, and even the pilfering of wampum belts from the Iroquois League at Six Nations, which would finally be returned in 1988.[37] In this sense, his method was not purely extractive; he sincerely hoped to use his knowledge and connections for the reduction of Indigenous suffering. He even wrote at great length about the complexity and immense distinctiveness of Indigenous cultures in his 1916 text for the Geological Survey, *Time Perspective in Aboriginal American Culture*.[38] His study of the Nootka similarly reflects great complexity.[39] On the other hand, the overarching thrust of his work with Indigenous partners and communities was motivated out of the same sense of salvage that guided most anthropologists of the time. Language and linguistic structures served as scripts that made ancient traditions intelligible. But these same cultures, like the artifacts he ordered and collected with near messianic zeal, needed to be properly recorded and maintained.[40] Even his informants, although essential to research collecting stories and transcribing them phonetically, were rarely viewed on par with the anthropological team back in Ottawa. For him, there was a strict separation between Indigenous knowledge and anthropological science.

Future scholars will have to piece together what it means that both Sapir and Barbeau conducted their research into Indigenous languages and culture at precisely the same time that members of the Canadian government, including RSC President Duncan Campbell Scott, were setting up the infrastructure of residential schools, designed to "de-Indianize" children by distancing them first and foremost from their own linguistic tradition.[41] Our preliminary research revealed one thing clearly: conducting ethnography and linguistic anthropology as a salvage expedition relegates Indigenous knowledge to the past, which makes it that much easier to refuse Indigenous people their rightful place in Canada's present.

GEORGE STANLEY

Whereas Edward Sapir and Marius Barbeau represent the particulars of the Ottawa story, another RSC scholar, George F.G. Stanley, exemplifies the regional outgrowth of the society in the ensuing decades of the twentieth century. As Stanley himself stated in his autobiography, "I did not become a historian because it was in my blood, or more correctly, in my genes. I became a historian because I was brought up in surroundings that stimulated an interest in history during my formative years."[42] In particular, Stanley's road to becoming a historian as well as his role in the discipline can be demonstrated through him as a person as well as through his written work, which both represent the Canadian West and the Prairies. In 1907, Stanley was born in Calgary, Alberta, to parents who had moved west following the "opening" of the Canadian frontier.[43] Growing up in the Prairies, Stanley was exposed to different experiences than the "Ottawa Men."[44] In particular, the West had higher proportions of Indigenous communities than other regions, so it was not uncommon for Stanley to come into contact with Indigenous people as part of his day-to-day. Stanley also grew up listening to stories from relatives and family friends who had participated in the settlement period, some of whom had even met famous figures such as Louis Riel.[45] These factors led to Stanley's curiosity about the Prairies and their history.

However, it was not until later in life, while attending the University of Alberta, that Stanley's curiosity transformed into an academic interest in Canadian history. His professor, A.L. Burt, fostered a thirst for knowledge regarding explorers, politicians, *coureurs des bois*, and soldiers, and while this was not entirely Western focused, it was the beginning of the path to Stanley becoming a historian.[46]

Interestingly, his real interest in Western Canada as a historical topic was kindled during his studies at Oxford. After his proposal to work on François Bigot was rejected due to lack of sources, a professor suggested Louis Riel as a topic. It was this suggestion that brought Stanley's interest full circle from the childhood stories he had heard to writing on Riel himself. He admitted to having wanted to write the story of Riel since childhood but that he had never considered that he could be the one to do so.[47] However, as someone in the academic world, Stanley now had the knowledge and ability to be that scholar who introduced Canada to the story of Louis Riel and the West. His graduate work was only the beginning.

Stanley's written collection also represents the West and its role in the national history of Canada. Despite the fact that the majority of Stanley's published works related to military topics, his personal interest in Louis Riel and the West continually rose during his career. Stanley was not the first to write on Western Canada during the settlement period but he had certainly gained a reputation in the field by the 1960s.[48] His major works in this area of history included *The Birth of Western Canada,* written in 1936 and based on the research discovered during his doctorate at Oxford, a related article entitled "Western Canada and the Frontier Thesis" in 1940, a biography of Louis Riel in 1963, and *The Collected Writings of Louis Riel,* a five-volume set published in 1985. Stanley's topic focus did not really change much over time. His writing mainly discussed the process and troubles of frontier settlement, where he argued that many of the issues and conflicts arose from the "invasion and exploitation of new areas by European peoples."[49] Yet, the basis of his arguments also revolves around the problematic notion of a clash between "primitive and civilized peoples."[50] Like Sapir, Stanley sympathized with Indigenous populations. Yet, his own writing perpetuated Western notions of what society should look like. Stanley's aim was always to prove the importance of the West and its people in Canada's nation building story. But in executing that goal, certain elements of the region's history became lost.

As Mary Jane McCallum has pointed out, Stanley is guilty of marginalizing Indigenous history within that story.[51] Furthermore, the Métis and First Nations groups he does chronicle appear as preludes to the national myth and their resistance as a failure due to their backward nature when confronted with civilization. Dallas Hunt argues that it is not uncommon for Indigenous histories to become lost after contact. He adds that if Indigenous stories are included they are usually done so in a manner that incorporates "well-known Indigenous people into the 'great men of history.'"[52] Stanley's writing on Louis Riel is the perfect example of this characterization. Riel is written about in a way that compartmentalizes his story into a generic history of the West. Not only does this approach lose the fulsomeness and authenticity of Riel's life and impact but, as Dallas Hunt argues too, the Indigenous great man approach often overshadows the multiple Indigenous histories and stories that do exist. Ganong, Sapir, and Stanley made attempts to preserve Indigenous perspectives and identities, either through language or history, but the knowledge formations they utilized actually served to flatten out if not silence real Indigenous voices. Despite this, Stanley and his work is significant in Canadian academic history and the history of the RSC because he represents the dominant trends in how scholars wrote about and conceptualized Canadian, and particularly Western or Indigenous, history during the twentieth century.

In addition to issues with the written representation of Indigenous people, Stanley also provides an example of how a scholar can reinforce and also later push back against extractive methods. Stanley's initial works on Indigenous history, including *The Birth of Western Canada,* "Western Canada and the Frontier Thesis," and *Louis Riel,* were all written from a Eurocentric Canadian perspective despite the fact that Stanley was sympathetic to Métis experience during the settlement of the West. His intention in writing these works was a response to the fact that no scholar had effectively written a history of western Canada in the 1930s or a biography of Louis Riel by the 1960s.[53] His aim was to write these histories because they were lacking in the scholarly field not because it would entirely benefit the Indigenous people of Canada.

However, later in his career, Stanley was part of a project that seemed to push back against these extractive methods, at least a little. *The Collected Writings of Louis Riel* a five-volume set, in which Stanley was invited to be the general editor, was published with a different intention than previous works on Louis Riel. The aim of *The Collected Writings of Louis Riel* was to provide students, educators, and the general public with all of the written works of Louis Riel exactly as they had been written in their original language.[54] Therefore, each volume included only a foreword, an introduction, and then Riel's work. Stanley wrote in volume five that "by providing a complete coverage of Riel's writings, we hoped to eliminate bias and lead to a greater understanding of what the Riel risings of 1870 and 1885 were all about."[55] The objective of presenting history in this way was that those interested in Louis Riel's writing, whatever their background, could decide how to interpret the sources themselves.[56] In Stanley's case, *The Collected Writings of Louis Riel* is a late-in-life effort to become a better historian of the West and Indigenous people, and the works were less about furthering scholarship and more about what others could take away from reading Riel's work. However, doing this kind of work as a privileged, white settler means that mistakes are almost certainly going to be made. RSC scholars William Ganong, Edward Sapir, and George F.G. Stanley professed a legitimate and often personal interest in documenting the cultures and lives of Indigenous people. Sapir accomplished this by documenting the languages of individual Indigenous groups through Ottawa's Geological Survey, while Ganong and Stanley took a more regional approach to discover how the history of the Maritimes and Prairies affected Canada as a whole. In the process, Ganong, Sapir, and Stanley overshadowed the actual voices and histories of the Indigenous people they were studying within the mythos of Canadian state formation. Even though Stanley eventually pushed back against this extractive and western framework of knowledge by the end of the twentieth century, his earlier works still contributed to the loss of Indigenous voices in Canadian history. While they may not have intentionally sought to harm Indigenous populations, their work nevertheless had a damaging effect on what was considered legitimate scholarship in their various arenas.

BEYOND THE DISCIPLINES

In the middle decades of the twentieth century, the reach of the RSC was extensive. The society had fellows with connections to universities abroad, to other academic societies, and even in political office. George F.G. Stanley's involvement in the RSC network began as a graduate student in the 1930s when he was awarded an RSC travel grant to cover part of his studies at Oxford's Keble College. This demonstrates two components in the intersectionality of the Royal Society. First, while it was and remains an institution for established and well-recognized scholars, it also played a role in encouraging the next generation of academics to pursue scholarship. The second is that the Royal Society had an international presence not only through the published

Proceedings and Transactions, but also through the students that they supported. As Tamson Pietsch notes in *Empire of Scholars*, the British academic system was built upon a similar series of networks that British and settler universities, scholars, students, and societies used to further their academic aims. The RSC and the students it supported clearly took advantage of these networks to construct an international presence and reputation. By sending the brightest minds abroad, those students could learn from some of the best universities in the British Empire, while also representing what Canadian scholars or scholarship had to offer to the world of academia.

Established scholars also represented the intersectional nature of the academy itself as they participated in a variety of offices or in leadership positions in learned societies. In the case of Stanley, he became a fellow of the Royal Historical Society in 1939 and the Royal Society of Canada in 1953. Additionally, he was a member of the Canadian Historical Association, of which he served as president from 1955 to 1956. Stanley took great pride in his involvement with both the Royal Society of Canada and the Canadian Historical Association. He believed that even within the societies, scholars should aim to take their work in various directions, to different scholarly communities. In particular, Stanley felt that only the best academics should gain membership to the RSC and that due to the interdisciplinary nature of the society, they must also have an interest in and ability to think critically about other fields. When the CHA transitioned from a Canadian history organization to a new association of Canadian historians studying any historical topic, Stanley helped institute a series of sub-divisions modelled after the American Historical Association and the Royal Society of Canada, which he believed would allow for a degree of autonomy. In both cases, Stanley felt that academic societies by necessity must be interdisciplinary. While it was important for a society to have subdivisions to allow some self-sufficiency, it was also crucial that the scholars within each division would be able to engage critically with members of another. It was his belief that an individual could only be called "scholar" if they met this criterion.

THE COLONIAL PROJECT

The interdisciplinary nature of the RSC is also reflected in the fluidity with which these networks of influence pervade one another. It is critical in researching the impact of the Royal Society of Canada as a networking hub to make explicit the relation between academic qualifications and social connections that served as foundations for influential friendships between powerful men in various fields, while excluding those who lacked the necessary cultural capital to gain traction. One of the consequences of these exclusive network systems is that they serve to alienate the researcher just as much as they do the rest of the uninitiated. For those who approach the coterie of such a boys' club from without, it can be difficult to find a foothold when so much is inaccessible. Our research team went into this project hoping for a smoking gun only to be met with frustration when so many of the threads comprising the web of influence are deliberately meant to be invisible to onlookers. In the end, it was necessary for us to make use of our own interdisciplinary approach to hold our own.

The embodied and linguistic cultural capital valued by the RSC historically emphasized the importance of assets such as French and English language ability, hegemonic masculinity, and comfort in reinforcing the status quo to perpetuate colonial power relationships. It was, by design, an environment in which the academically-minded and well-connected man of means could feel perfectly at ease. Bestowing titles, medals, and honours upon members and friends (and here too much research remains to be done), the RSC serves the function of institutional cultural capital, becoming a prism through which all the beams of separate assets can be filtered into a single, economically tradeable measure of worth. Finally, the academic nature of the branches of the RSC (science, social science, the arts) ensured that RSC members almost certainly have access to some amount of objectified cultural capital – privileged knowledge of understanding the taste-makers of their various fields. Certainly, this is true of Duncan Campbell Scott and his poet peer group. But as we have seen here too, it was also the story of other members, from Edward Sapir to Marius Barbeau, William Ganong to George Stanley.

The hard truth ends up being that the longer the colonial project of Canada has existed, the more entwined the threads of contact and colonization have become; it is nearly impossible to follow one thread from its origin in a file box in LAC all the way to a direct, clearly defined result of an action taken by an RSC member. It is a tangled web of relationships across time and space – personal, professional, academic – which have led to actions and events far beyond the imaginations of the original perpetrators. The forms that colonization takes can be more or less apparent, but the results of knowledge generation in the academy in Canada have an impact on the ground. The academic pursuit of knowledge is not outside or immune to politicization. The RSC's role in Canada – uniting scientists and connecting their research, plays into the imperial ambitions of the state of Canada as a whole. The foundation of Canada's markets and industry rests on Indigenous land and resources, especially the extraction of natural resources, and the corpus of knowledge acquired by the science community is directly linked, and not yet fully unexplored. The discovery, mapping, and research development done by RSC members contributed to the removal of Indigenous title from their land, the removal of Indigenous people's physical presence from their place, as well as the removal of resources from that land for the benefit of the colonial state. Future researchers will need to tell this story.

NOTES

Many thanks to Cindy Blackstock for placing this subject on the agenda of the RSC, and her unrelenting belief and advocacy of a better way forward. And to colleagues Jennifer Adese and Zoe Todd whose brilliance, activism, and drive is a model for change in and outside of the classroom.

1 Gayatri Chakraborty Spivak, "History," in *A Postcolonial Critique. Towards a History of the Present* (Cambridge, UK: Harvard University Press, 1999), 242. See also Ann Laura Stoler, *Along the Archival Grain: Epistemic Anxieties and Colonial Common Sense* (Princeton, NY: Princeton University Press, 2010).
2 According to Jacques Derrida, "[T]here is no political power without control of the archive, if not memory. Effective democratization can always be measured by this essential criterion: the participation in and access to the archive, its constitution, and its interpretation," in Jacques Derrida, *Archive Fever: A Freudian Impression*, trans. Eric Prenowitz (Chicago: University of Chicago Press, 1995), 4, note 1.
3 Stefan Berger, "The Role of National Archives in Constructing National Master Narratives in Europe," *Archival Science* 13, no. 1 (March 2013): 1–22.
4 Adam Muller, "Troubling History, Troubling Law: The Question of Indigenous Genocide in Canada," in *Understanding Atrocities:*

Remembering, Representing and Teaching Genocide, ed. by Scott W. Murray (Calgary: University of Calgary Press, 2017), 83. See also Andrew Woolford and Jeff Benvenuoto, "Canada and Colonial Genocide," *Journal of Genocide Research*, 17:4 (2015): 373–390.

5 Carl Berger, *Honour and the Search for Influence. A History of the Royal Society of Canada* (Toronto: University of Toronto Press, 1996), 5.
6 Leanne Betasamosake Simpson, "Indigenous Resurgence and Co-Resistance," *Journal of the Critical Ethnic Studies Association*. 2:2 (Fall 2016): 21.
7 Here Audra Simpson is particularly helpful for the way she parses the ontological and emotional stakes that continue to position, disfavourably, Indigenous claimants of state violence as wounded without considering the policies, structures, institutions, and actors that continue to circumscribe Indigenous life. See "Reconciliation and its Discontents: Settler Governance in the Age of Sorrow," University of Saskatchewan, 16 March 2018 https://www.youtube.com/watch?v=vGl9HkzQsGg&feature=youtu.be.
8 Dallas Hunt, "Nikikiwan: Contesting Settler Colonial Archives through Indigenous Oral History," *Canadian Literature*, no. 230–231 (2016): 25, accessed 25 March 2019, http://link.galegroup.com.proxy.library.carleton.ca/apps/doc/A510652404/CPI?u=ocul_carleton&sid=CPI&xid=1285846d.
9 Tamson Pietsch, *Empire of Scholars: Universities, Networks and the British Academic World 1850–1939* (Manchester: Manchester University Press, 2013).
10 Although the current CEO of the Museum of Nature lauded Barbeau as guided by reconciliation before it was even on the agenda, scholarly approaches to the Canadian father of anthropology argue that his research was more in keeping with the prevailing colonial mindset, which included undermining Nisga'a efforts at self-government. See Julia Roe, "The Mystic Dragon Beyond the Sea: Ethnographic Fantasy in Barbeau's Depiction of West Coast Indigeneity," *The Corvette* no. 2 (2015–2016): 54–70. Mark O'Neill's interview and comment on Barbeau may be found here:https://artsfile.ca/museums-mission-of-truthful-history-more-important-that-ever-ceo-oneill-says/.
11 Crystal Fraser and Zoe Todd, "Decolonial Sensibilities: Indigenous Research and Engagement with Archives in Contemporary Colonial Canada," in *Decolonizing Archives*, https://www.internationaleonline.org/media/files/03-decolonisingarchives.pdf, 33.
12 Andrew Nurse, "Marius Barbeau and the Methodology of Salvage Ethnography in Canada, 1911–1951," in *Historicizing Canadian*

Anthropology, eds. Julia Harrison and Regna Darnell (UBC Press, 2006), 52–64.
13 David Garneau. "Imaginary Spaces of Conciliation and Reconciliation," *West Coast Line* 74 (2012): 29.
14 Lisa Tilley, "Resisting Piratic Method by doing Research Otherwise," *Sociology*, 51 vol. 1 (February 2011): 28, https://doi.org/10.1177/0038038516656992.
15 Tilley, "Resisting Piratic Method."
16 More research needs to be done on ways in which fellows of the RSC might have been influenced by Indigenous "informants" and knowledge keepers. Blackfeet historian Rosalyn LaPier argues that Blackfeet people worked willingly with ethnographers to be sure their knowledge was recorded for future generations and shared only those stories they wanted to be made public. See Rosayn LaPier, *Invisible Reality: Storytellers, Storytakers, and the Supermatural World of the Blackfeet* (Omaha: University of Nebraska Press, 2017). Before his death, the late Kainai scholar Narcisse Blood was working on how the Canadian Blackfoot world view influenced the work of psychologist Abraham Maslow. See N. Blood and R. Heavyhead, "Blackfoot Influence on Abraham Maslow," lecture delivered at University of Montana, 2007, stored at Blackfoot Digital Library, retrieved from http://blackfoot-digitallibrary.com/en/asset/blackfoot-influence-abraham-maslow-presented-narcisse-blood-and-ryan-heavy-head-university-mo. Thanks to reader 1 for the suggestions.
17 Ronald Rees, *New Brunswick was His Country: The Life of William Francis Ganong* (Halifax: Nimbus Publishing Limited, 2016), ix.
18 "William Francis Ganong," *New Brunswick Literary Encyclopedia*, accessed 25 March 2019, http://stu-sites.ca/nble/g/ganong_william_francis.html.
19 Rees, *New Brunswick was His Country*, 151.
20 Ibid., 162–3.
21 Ibid., 165.
22 Ibid., 165.
23 Wesner, "The Practical Realities of Giving Back," 3.
24 Ibid., 4.
25 See Ian Wereley's contribution in this volume.
26 Carl Berger, *Honour and the Search for Influence*, 12.
27 Tamson Pietsch, *Empire of Scholars*, 120.
28 J.L. Granatstein, *Ottawa Men: The Civil Service Mandarins, 1935–67* (Toronto: University of Toronto Press, 1992).
29 On this, see Berger, *Honour and the Search for Influence*.

30 Regna Darnell, *Edward Sapir: Linguist, Anthropologist, Humanist* (Berkeley: University of California Press, 1990).
31 Darnell, *Edward Sapir*, 14.
32 A letter from Reginald Walter Brock, Queen's professor and president of the Survey Sapir in June of 1910 in Darnell, *Edward Sapir*, 42.
33 Boas is a contentious figure in modern anthropology, seen variously as spawning interest in Indigenous subjectivities and cultures or justifying settler colonialism by propagating the notion that they were on the decline, decaying, or being usurped. For two distinct approaches to the motivation, impact, and outcomes of Boas's research, see Isaiah Lorado Wilner, "Transformation Masks: Recollecting the Indigenous Origins of Global Consciousness," in *Indigenous Visions: Re-Discovering the World of Franz Boas*, eds. Isaiah Lorado Wilner and Ned Blackhawk (New Haven: Yale University Press, 2018).
34 Darnell, *Edward Sapir*, 76.
35 Andrew Nurse, "My How Things Have Changed: Marius Barbeau and the Politics of Amerindian Identity," *Ethnohistory* 48.3 (2001): 433–472. "Barbeau was arguably the most prominent anthropologist in Canadian history. After the First World War his work on Tsimshian and traditional French-Canadian cultures earned him two honorary doctorates, three Prix-Davids, honorary fellowships to his alma mater Oriel College and the American Philosophical Society, and a host of other awards, as well as public recognition. Although he spent most of his career with the Anthropology Division and (after a bureaucratic reorganization of Canadian government anthropology) the National Museum, Barbeau also served as an examiner for new appointments to the Department of Indian Affairs, as a federal delegate to UNESCO, and on a variety of other government committees and commissions. He also taught at the Universities of Ottawa, Montreal, and Laval, where he was named Ancien professeur d'Anthropologie et de Folklore after his retirement." Nurse, 436.
36 Darnell, *Edward Sapir*, 55.
37 Letter from Sapir to Scott dated 19 March 1914, Museum of History; Letter from Sapir to Boas 19 February 1915, Museum of History; and Sapir to Scott 16 May 1914, Museum of History, all three cited in Darnell, *Edward Sapir*, 55–57.
38 Edward Sapir, *Time Perspective in Aboriginal American Culture, A Study in Method*, Geological Survey Memoir 90: No. 13, Anthropological Series (Ottawa: Government Printing Bureau, 1916).
39 Edward Sapir, "Some Aspects of Nootka Language and Culture," *American Anthropologist* 13:1 (January 1911): 15–28.

40 Richard Handler, "The Dainty and Hungry Man: Literature and Anthropology in the Work of Edward Sapir," in *Observers Observed: Essays on Ethnographic Fieldwork*, ed. by George W. Stocking Jr (Madison, WI: 1983), 208–31.

41 John Milloy, *A National Crime: The Canadian Government and the Residential School System, 1879–1986* (Winnipeg: University of Manitoba Press, 1999).

42 George F.G. Stanley, "The Making of an Historian: An Autobiographical Essay," in *Swords and Ploughshares: War and Agriculture in Western Canada*, ed. by R.C. Macleod (Edmonton: University of Alberta Press, 1993), 3.

43 Stanley, "The Making of an Historian," 3–4.

44 This is Jack Granatstein's term for the early generation of civil servants.

45 Stanley, "The Making of an Historian," 7.

46 Ibid., 9.

47 Ibid., 11.

48 George F. G. Stanley, *The Birth of Western Canada: A History of the Riel Rebellions* (Toronto: University of Toronto Press, 1961), x.

49 From Preliminary Research done at Oxford: Library and Archives Canada, Royal Society of Canada fonds, MG 28 I 458, Container 117/118, RSC Overseas Bursary Students – Reports, "Riel Rebellion by George F.G. Stanley – Oxford Excerpt," 1934, 9.

50 Stanley, *The Birth of Western Canada*, 49; Library and Archives Canada, MG 28 I 458, Container 117/118, 9; John Perry Pritchett, "Review of *The Birth of Western Canada: A History of the Riel Rebellions*," *The American Historical Review* 42 No. 3 (1937): 569; Stanley, "Western Canada and the Frontier Thesis," 110.

51 Mary Jane McCallum, "Conclusion: The Wages of Whiteness and the Indigenous Historian," in *Indigenous Women, Work, And History, 1940–1980* (Winnipeg: University of Manitoba Press, 2013), 233, 236.

52 Dallas Hunt, "Nikîkîwân I: Contesting Settler Colonial Archives through Indigenous Oral History," *Canadian Literature–Littérature Canadienne: A Quarterly of Criticism and Review (Univ. of British Columbia, Vancouver)* no. 230/231 (2016): 1.

53 Regarding the 1930s: John Perry Pritchett, Review of *The Birth of Western Canada*, *The American Historical Review* 42, no. 3 (1937): 568; regarding the 1960s: C. P. Stacey, review of *Louis Riel*, *The Canadian Journal of Economics and Political Science* 30, no. 4 (1964): 609.

54 George F. G. Stanley, *The Collected Writings of Louis Riel: Les Écrits Complet De Louis Riel* (Edmonton: University of Alberta Press, 1985), vol. 1, xxxii; George F. G. Stanley, *The Collected Writings of Louis Riel: Les Écrits Complet De Louis Riel* (Edmonton: University of Alberta Press, 1985), vol. 5, 2, 6.
55 Stanley, *Collected Writings of Louis Riel*, vol. 5, 2.
56 Stanley, *Collected Writings of Louis Riel*, vol. 1, xxxii.

12

Cause and Effect: The Invisible Barriers of the Royal Society of Canada

Joanna R. Quinn

The Royal Society of Canada was created in 1882 to promote national scientific research and development in the nascent country. Like other institutions created in those early days, the Royal Society of Canada (RSC) recognized scholarly excellence as it has traditionally been understood throughout the Western world: as performance and achievement in the academy. It valued specific traditions of thought while it disadvantaged others; it gave little or no thought to other ways of knowing that failed to fit within the strictures that had been produced and reproduced by the men who founded the society. The structures of the society were set up in such a way as to produce invisible impediments that kept out anyone who did not "fit." In particular, Indigenous people and Indigenous knowledge were completely excluded. This essay explores the concept of structural violence, and uses it as a lens to explore the institutional barriers that were erected, and the ultimate result of such barriers.

The RSC was established by the Parliament of Canada in 1883 for the purpose of fostering Canadian intellectual thought through scientific research:

> First, to encourage studies and investigations in literature and science; secondly, to publish transactions annually or semi-annually, containing the minutes of proceedings at meetings, records of the work performed, original papers and memoirs of merit, and such other documents as may be deemed worthy of publication; thirdly, to offer prizes or other inducements for valuable papers on subjects relating to Canada, and to aid researches

already begun and carried so far as to render their ultimate value probable; fourthly, to assist in collection of specimens with a view to the formation of a Canadian Museum.[1]

The progenitor of the Royal Society of Canada was the fourth Governor General of Canada, the Marquess of Lorne, John George Edward Henry Douglas Sutherland Campbell, the 9th Earl of Argyll. Lorne was excited at the possibility of what he thought of as an intellectual "Canadian renaissance."[2] Canadian historian Carl Berger notes that "there was a mood of optimism about Canada's prospects generally in the early 1880s and a measured hopefulness about its intellectual possibilities."[3] Governor General Lorne therefore set about putting in place a series of institutions that would ensure that "adornment and elevation of thought is coincident with sterner effort."[4] Almost in tandem, during his five-year term in office, Lorne created the Royal Canadian Academy of Arts, and the National Gallery of Canada in 1880. These were seen as a "quickening movement in the new country's intellectual life; ... a striving for cohesion, a bringing together of dispersed individuals and institutions. It was a logical extension of the political consolidation of the colonies."[5] The creation of the Royal Society of Canada in 1882, therefore, came about as a part of that grand view. "Membership [in the Royal Society] was to be a counterpart to the titles of honour bestowed by the crown on deserving soldiers and statesmen in recognition of exceptional service to the state."[6]

During the same period, across the country, new and non-denominational universities were being created.[7] For these new institutions, "professors would not be selected on account of their denominational tendencies, but for their literary and scientific requirements."[8] The University of Toronto was founded in 1850 out of the Church of England-controlled King's College. The University of Ottawa emerged in 1866 out of its Catholic beginnings. Queen's University became a non-denominational university in 1881, breaking with its Church of Scotland foundations. McMaster University was incorporated from the Toronto Baptist College and Woodstock College in 1887.[9] My own university, the University of Western Ontario, was created in 1878 from Huron College, affiliated then as now with the Church of England.[10]

The universities were part of that same intellectual movement that Governor General Lorne wished to cement. The heads of prestigious universities of the time were at the leading edge of this movement, including those from McGill; Queen's; University College, Toronto; and Dalhousie University – along with colleagues from the Geological Survey of Canada and the House of Commons, and it was these men who came together to found the society.[11] A total of eighty men were recognized as fellows of the society in that initial cohort.[12] The society they established still stands as a testament to those early ideas about excellence of intellectual thought.

STRUCTURAL VIOLENCE

The excellence they sought to recognize, though, was of a very specific type, and the recognition of the society was intended only for a select few. The knowledge that was recognized for its excellence was firmly Eurocentric. And while they faced accusations of "exclusivity" and "self-perpetuation,"[13] the men who established the society had no intention of creating anything like a "popular assemblage ... in which fools could not be kept in their places."[14] Instead, they sought to replicate their own experiences, and their own ideas about what constituted "excellence" – never considering "scholarship or practice that [was] unconventional [or] outside the mainstream of the discipline."[15]

In this way, the Royal Society of Canada, like so many institutions of its time, inaugurated policies that excluded the work of many people from the society altogether. Only work done by men of a certain type were included. Others were never included because the work they did was not seen as being important, because their ways of knowing and being were not considered to be "science." The society effectively said that there was one "true" kind of knowledge that should be respected, and that *that* knowledge would be honoured by the society. It gave little or no thought to other ways of knowing that failed to fit within the parameters that had been produced and reproduced in the men who founded the society, or else it viewed that "other" knowledge as deficient, backward, primitive, and inconvenient. Those ideas have prevailed until today.

This form of injustice – referred to as "structural violence" in the peacebuilding literature – "works slowly ... and is typically built in to the very structure of society and cultural institutions" like the Royal Society.[16] Structural violence takes place when social structures prevent people from reaching their full potential. By denying a space for any scholarship that fell outside the purview of what Governor General Lorne and others felt to be appropriate, the society entrenched a set of expectations about who and what was important.

This constitutes a form of violence and injustice for three reasons: First, it denies any importance of the contribution of any person who is left out of the conversation being had within the society. Second, it continues to privilege those who are already on the inside and disenfranchise those who remain on the outside – effectively demonstrating that anything other than that *particular* kind of contribution is unworthy and unwanted, thereby also relegating its author to that same "unfit" category. Third, it further produces fear and suspicion of any work that sits outside the normal sources of "art and empirical science ... creat[ing] barriers to discriminate against people who do not share them."[17]

As such, the founders of the society formed what Berger calls "a closed coterie,"[18] even as the society's first secretary, John George Bourinot, argued "that the society, by encouraging the coming together of people widely differing in politics, religion, and opinion, was helping to break down asperities and prejudices."[19] And while such "sheer diversity" might have seemed radical at that time, by today's standards it was certainly not.[20] The eighty charter members were still, after all, white men; thirty-three of the first cohort of eighty fellows had been born in Britain.[21] Berger notes that "the closest the society ever came to questioning the very principle of limited membership was in the inter-war discussion over 'associate' fellows."[22]

Those invisible impediments effectively contributed to the establishment of an intellectual hierarchy in Canada. It is notable, in the laudatory histories of universities like Western, for example, that the universities strove to cultivate this same form of excellence. Two of the founding faculty members of Western's medical faculty were part of the inaugural cohort of the Royal Society of Canada: Richard M. Bucke and William Saunders, who became president of the Royal Society in 1906. As with the fellows of the Royal Society, all of the first faculty members and those who served on Western University's first council were white men. And all of them were affiliated with the Church of England – even the first president, Isaac Hellmuth, who had been born Jewish in Poland, had converted to Christianity and ordained in the Church of England such that only then was his "churchmanship" deemed to be acceptable.[23] This demonstrates the importance that was attached to one's British-ness (or French-ness, for those at universities in Quebec) and the distinct characteristics required for acceptance in these universities.

In their actions and interactions both at their home universities and in the company of the fellows of the Royal Society, those men began a tradition of recognizing particular forms of scholarship and standardizing the artistic and scientific disciplines, publishing what they called "a repertory of all the intellectual work in this country."[24] What was not acknowledged was the work that was left out, and work that was pejoratively deemed to be unacceptable. Really, they effected a kind of "cross-contamination" in thinking from the Royal Society to the leading intellectual institutions of the time, and vice-versa. The ideas that emerged from the Royal Society were transmitted to its fellows, who then took them back to their own universities and other institutions.

IMPACTS OF STRUCTURAL VIOLENCE

This way of thinking, about who and what should be "counted" when research excellence was tallied in Canada, had inestimable impacts. These effects were then perpetuated within the Royal Society, within universities across Canada, and across the larger Canadian society. Four of these are explored below: the impact on Canadian legal structures; the impact on student and faculty populations at Canadian universities; the "objectification" of Indigenous people; and the current state of the Royal Society of Canada.

Political and Legal Structure

Scholars have noted that "the university is basically reflecting what's happening in the rest of society."[25] Moreover, the early Canadian universities, and the Royal Society itself, explicitly sought to shape that society. The society's roots were in some ways indistinguishable from those of the senior government officials of the day and the government supported it fully; the first meeting of the Royal Society, for example, was held in the chambers of the Canadian Senate,[26] and many fellows were strongly affiliated with the political apparatus of the state. "A substantial number – about one-quarter in 1890 – were employed by governments as clerks in legislative assemblies or the House of Commons ... or in such government agencies as the Public

Archives or the Geological Survey."[27] At one point, "the office of the clerk of the Commons ... became, in effect, the clearing-house and administrative centre of the organization."[28]

The 39th President of the Royal Society was civil servant Duncan Campbell Scott. From 1913–1932, Scott worked in the Department of Indian Affairs, eventually taking up the post of deputy superintendent,[29] and there is no question that his work both for Indian Affairs and for the Royal Society overlapped considerably. The policy of the day was assimilation, and Scott worked hard to effect it. He wrote:

> I want to get rid of the Indian problem. I do not think as a matter of fact, that the country ought to continuously protect a class of people who are able to stand alone ... Our objective is to continue until there is not a single Indian in Canada that has not been absorbed into the body politic and there is no Indian question, and no Indian Department, that is the whole object of this Bill.[30]

Thus, the legislation of Indigenous people and communities, and the sanction of their agency, was of paramount importance to people like Scott, and "hostility to Aboriginal cultural and spiritual practice continued well into the twentieth century."[31] The *Indian Act* was first introduced in 1876, only a few short years before the Royal Society was established – and again, there is no accident in the deliberateness of the coincident nation-building project of both the society and the legislation. Robert Joseph notes that the *Indian Act* "is a piece of legislation created under the British rule for the purpose of subjugating one race – Aboriginal people ... The *Act* gave Canada a coordinated approach to Indian policy rather than the pre-Confederation piece-meal approach."[32] The *Indian Act* remains in place at the time of writing.

The policies enacted under the *Indian Act*, which determined "status" and the subsequent duties owed to Indigenous people by the Crown, were discriminatory and often violent. While some RSC Fellows including George Monro Grant, the principal of Queen's College (now Queen's University), advocated for the rights of the Indigenous people living in British Columbia,[33] in fact, many of the early RSC presidents were geographers, engineers, explorers and botanists working in the interest of finding the route for the Canadian Pacific Railway for settlement to proceed, and therefore directly responsible for some of the physical violence committed against Indigenous people at that time. At the very least, they were paternalistic. Worse, they provided the pattern for human rights violations, both direct and structural violence, in other parts of the world, including apartheid in South Africa.[34]

As a direct consequence of that thinking, Indigenous people were kept apart from the mainstream Canadian society. Through policies like that which established the Indian Residential Schools system, for over a century, Indigenous children were kept out of classrooms and thereby prevented from taking up what were considered acceptable intellectual activities in mainstream Canadian institutions. Worse still, their communities' own intellectual traditions were seen as illegitimate and regressive, and their use was denied by successive governments; ceremonial traditions like the sun-dance and the potlatch were prohibited under national legislation.[35] The effect of this was to consign Indigenous knowledge-keepers to the periphery, and to prohibit their practice of Indigenous intellectual traditions. The patterns laid out by such legislation were taken up by the Royal Society of Canada and replicated in universities across the country in the pursuit of "excellence." Berger notes "the unappreciated role of inertia and vanity in the persistence of institutions,"[36] and this is of significant importance in understanding how and why universities and the Royal Society were able to so soundly exclude Indigenous knowledge and methodologies from their recognition.

Student and Faculty Populations

The colonial system very clearly privileged a certain type of knowledge, necessarily carried out by a certain type of scholar: until 1938, for example, when Alice Wilson was elected, women were excluded from the Royal Society; at that time, the RSC "Council agreed to interpret the word 'persons' in its bylaws as meaning individuals of either sex."[37] But despite decisions like this, taken some fifty years after the society was established, Indigenous scholars, for example, are not represented in either the fellowship of the Royal Society or in the College in any large number.

This exclusion mirrored the institutional barriers that were in place in universities across the country, which specified who was either to be trained in Canadian universities or who was to be hired by them. With some notable exceptions, Indigenous students were excluded from universities across the country – and those who did graduate were liable to lose their Aboriginal status as a result.[38] There is evidence, for example, of only a very few Indigenous students who were afforded such an opportunity in the era in which universities were beginning to flourish. Two such students lived not far from London, Ontario, where Western University is located, yet went elsewhere for their education, even though Western's precursor, Huron College, existed at the time: Kahkewaquonaby Peter Edmund Jones, an Ojibwe of the Mississaugas, was raised at Muncey, near London, Ontario, and graduated with an M.D. from the University of Toronto in 1866. Oronhyatekha Peter Martin, a Mohawk from Six Nations Reserve, graduated from Oxford University in 1862 and went on to earn both an M.B. and an M.D. from the University of Toronto in 1866 and 1867, respectively.[39] Another Mohawk student from Six Nations, Rev. Isaac Bearfoot, *did* graduate from his studies in theology at Huron College in 1876 – where he continued to serve on the very governing council that created Western University for several years.[40] Decades later, there are scant records of people like Annie Maude (Nan) McKay, a Métis from the Northwest Territories, who graduated from the University of Saskatchewan in 1915 and continued to work there for the rest of her career. But these stories are few and far between.

Indigenous faculty members with positions in Canadian universities, however, were even fewer – and remain so even today. Following the *Calls to Action* of the Truth and Reconciliation Commission, universities have deliberately begun to hire Indigenous faculty members, but their numbers remain limited in the Canadian academy. Much of that obtains directly from Indigenous students' lack of access to university education – a direct consequence of the structural violence that has perpetuated their exclusion from the system. Harvey Mccue noted that "in 1967, there were only 200 Indigenous students enrolled in Canadian universities out of a total Indigenous student population of about 60,000."[41] The Council of Ontario Universities reports that even today, only 6,500 of the total 515,000 students enrolled in Ontario universities are Indigenous.[42] In 2012, the Chiefs Assembly on Education framed it in a bigger-picture way: "Only 4 per cent of First Nations people on reserve, and 8 per cent in total, have a university degree, compared to 23 per cent of the population."[43] Those who do go to university face significant funding problems and other barriers to access.[44]

The relative absence of Indigenous faculty and students, however, is what might be seen as the thin edge of the wedge, since Indigenous ways of knowing and being have been almost completely excluded from institutions of higher learning in Canada. In Ontario, for example: "Founded by and for European settlers, Ontario's universities have excluded Indigenous voices and played an active role encouraging the colonization of Indigenous lands, nations, and peoples."[45] Those Indigenous scholars who have managed to gain purchase in the Canadian academy have had to do so by somehow "proving" their value within the Eurocentric norms and systems of recognition that were created by and perpetuated by the Royal Society and its member institutions – the very systems that have sought to exclude them and to minimize their value. That is, the Indigenous scholars who have prevailed have had to demonstrate their relevance within the system of what is deemed "acceptable" within the university structures. At the same time, they must hold their Indigenous knowledge and responsibilities, and their important work in communities and on intellectual questions that not only fail to count, but are openly derided in academic circles. They have had to prove their excellence in the mainstream Canadian system by using methodologies not seen as legitimate by that same system.

Objectification

Even when they have prevailed, Indigenous scholars have had to fight another battle: Quite unlike the sentiment "Nothing about us without us," Indigenous people and their ways of knowing and being have traditionally been seen by the fellows of the Royal Society as objects to be examined, rather than as intellectual agents with much to contribute to the research dialogue. The impetus, in part, for the formation of the Royal Society began when Governor General Lorne "learned that the Smithsonian Institution had been [in the Canadian prairies] gathering Indian artifacts and had carted them off to Washington, D.C."[46] The Royal Society was to "assist in the collection of specimens for "a Canadian Museum of archives, ethnology, archaeology and natural history.'"[47] This mission was also the basis for the National Museum created by Lorne in 1880.

"The character of the Aboriginal peoples and their tribal divisions, languages, and customs figured prominently" in the publications of the Royal Society in its first two decades.[48] The ethnological work was carried out by early fellows including Franz Boas on "Baffin Island Inuit mythology and customs"; Jean-André Cuoq focused on "the complexity and beauty of Algonquin grammar"; George M. Dawson, who "acquired a good deal of information about the Aboriginal groups of British Columbia, including comparative vocabularies"; and Daniel Wilson, who documented the "funeral rites of Aboriginal people, the nature of the 'half-breed'... and the dialect of the habitant."[49] In some cases, Indigenous "informants" were willing collaborators.[50]

This scholarly activity denied virtually any agency on the part of Indigenous people, and consigned them solely to the status of something like museum exhibits. They were not included as fellows in the Royal Society of Canada. In fact, rather than even seeking to include them in any meaningful exchange, for the most part the Royal Society applied itself to gathering a "collection of Indian lore and relics before those people disappeared altogether."[51] One somewhat notable example that specifically includes the voices of Indigenous people is detailed by Berger, who reports that "one of the last reports, curiously, was compiled by a group of chiefs of the Six Nations, who, encouraged by Duncan Campbell Scott, published an account of the origins of their confederacy."[52] The work itself lists Scott as "presenting" the work,[53] and all modern references to this report in the subsequent literature often list Scott as the author of the work[54] – despite the work of the chiefs. So not only were they largely excluded; when they *were* included, others took credit for their work.

Effects on the Modern-Day Royal Society of Canada

The effect of the creation and perpetuation of the institutional barriers that blocked the inclusion of Indigenous people from universities and from the Royal Society is borne out in a stark way in its modern context. Still, today, there exist markers of excellence and success that are deeply Eurocentric and patriarchal. Fellows and College Members of the Royal Society of Canada are beneficiaries of the policies that sought to disenfranchise and exclude communities of scholars, and it is important for the RSC to recognize its discriminatory past. There are two related consequences, in particular, that bear some mention here.

The first of these consequences has been the exclusion of Indigenous scholars themselves from the Royal Society. The society does not keep data on the "ethno-racial" make-up of its membership.[55] Therefore, any attempt to uncover information about when the first Indigenous scholar was inducted, or the names of earlier Indigenous scholars working with the Royal Society, is not available. Colloquially, it seems that the first Indigenous scholar to have been nominated was likely the architect Douglas Cardinal in 2005, though for various reasons, he was only inducted at a ceremony in 2019. The first Indigenous scholar to have been inducted was likely the legal scholar John Borrows in 2007.

The creation of the College of New Scholars, Artists and Scientists in 2014 intentionally sought to break with the tradition of exclusion. In its first cohort, there were several leading Indigenous scholars, Chris Andersen, Carrie Bourassa, and Kiera Ladner, whose work focuses on Indigenous belonging, inclusion, recognition, and treatment. Subsequent members have included other top Indigenous scholars, and the College has elected more Indigenous scholars each year. Yet even in its nomination and selection process, the College has not thoroughly decolonized its recognition of research excellence.[56] For example; committees continue to look for markers of "success" defined in deeply Eurocentric terms, and struggle to understand that success as anything other than what they, themselves, have achieved, in a way that is familiar to them. The perpetuation of that kind of recognition remains deeply problematic.

Second, this has meant that Indigenous ways of knowing and being have been excluded by the Royal Society. As a consequence, the Royal Society is fundamentally disconnected from any kind of "systematic study of the structure and behaviour of the physical and natural world through observation and experiment"[57] – what is generally called science – that is informed by Indigenous knowledge and methodologies. The Truth and Reconciliation Commission of Canada noted that "too many Canadians still do not know the history of Aboriginal peoples' contributions to Canada."[58] That is almost wholly true of the Royal Society of Canada.

PERSISTENT INVISIBLE BARRIERS

There is a danger, of course, in pretending that including only a small handful of Indigenous scholars within the Royal Society – and then only those who are seen to have suitably conformed to Eurocentric expectations about excellence in both form and substance – should be celebrated as anything more than a hollow gesture. This kind of surface-level change is deeply problematic. The danger is that the people embedded firmly within the structures of excellence of the Royal Society that has privileged Eurocentric knowledge and related metrics of excellence could become complacent in thinking that the Royal Society has gone far enough in its reforms. If this is not coupled with real institutional reform, the induction of a few Indigenous scholars could be a form of tokenism. The worry is that this kind of self-congratulation could instead lead to the reproduction of the same kinds of barriers to inclusion that have continued to exist, and that nothing will change. Much work remains to fundamentally change the foundations of the Royal Society of Canada and to remove these obstacles.

Bona fide goodwill does indeed exist within the Fellowship and within the College to make needed structural changes, at least in some quarters. But two concerns are immediately apparent. First, it is not clear that the members have recognized a basic principle of reconciliation, which is that the dominant group – in this case, scholars from within the settler colonial population – must be prepared to give up some of the power and authority over the question of excellence that it appropriated at the creation of the Royal Society, in order that the marginalized group can (re)claim the space it should legitimately occupy. In this case, that means being willing to relinquish their monopoly on "excellence" and on "scholarship," and willing also to cede some of their own recognition to methodologies and ways of knowing that will make many profoundly uncomfortable. LaCapra writes of the need for people to become "unsettled" as a first step in the possibility of real change.[59] Whether that will emerge stands in question.

Second, if structural violence is addressed only in a tokenistic way, no real transformation can take place. Without interrogating the deep-seated inequalities and forms of exclusion that exist, but, rather, paying a kind of lip-service to a reform that barely scratches the proverbial surface of these problems, the invisible barriers to the recognition of Indigenous ways of knowing as a form of excellence, and to the recognition of those Indigenous scholars who build on those traditions in their work, will persist.

It is impossible to sufficiently underscore the importance of Cindy Blackstock's disquieting address to the Royal Society in 2016. Coupled with the then-recent report of the Truth and Reconciliation

Commission and its *Calls to Action*, Blackstock's remarks stood as a clarion call. Her remarks should have served as a launching point for real introspection and true reform. Yet in the four years that have since elapsed, relatively little has been accomplished. Universities across the country have likewise done very little in breaking down the invisible barriers of structural violence. And although it is true that important change is rarely effected quickly, the work of the Royal Society on this issue has been slow. The society must now heed that call in a real way.

THE WAY FORWARD

Decolonizing the Royal Society and its member institutions, universities and research centres across Canada is needed. A conversation about this has begun. Ben Lewis writes:

> Decolonizing all levels of our education system is crucial. An urgent and fundamental commitment from our educational institutions is required to increase awareness of the horrors of colonization and to create a society that embraces, supports, and makes space for the vibrant First Nations, Inuit, and Métis cultures that have survived. Many universities have taken up the TRC's *Calls to Action* and made public commitments to Indigenization and reconciliation. Strategies have been developed, new supports have been created for Indigenous students, Indigenous studies program offerings have been bolstered, and some Ontario universities now offer courses in languages, including Algonquian, Nishnaabemowin, and Ojibwe. However, there is real concern these initiatives do not reach the foundations of the academy. The past year has seen several resignations of Indigenous academic leaders who argue that university governing bodies are not committed to the work required for reconciliation and decolonization. This prompts the core question we explore in this issue: Are universities doing enough to respond meaningfully to the TRC's final report and the continuing colonization in higher education?[60]

The Royal Society of Canada helped to construct the scaffolding of both the universities that are now its institutional members, and of Canadian society at large. Its Fellows and College members are, to a large extent, the beneficiaries of the kinds of policies that sought to disenfranchise and exclude communities of scholars, including Indigenous scholars and their knowledge and methodologies, from the Canadian academy. Decolonization has to go further than what Lori Campbell *et al.* describe as "Indigenization aimed at supporting the adaptation of Indigenous students and employees into a settler-colonial university that remains largely unchanged by their presence. Even when well intentioned, Indigenization as inclusion puts the onus on Indigenous people. And, if the TRC taught us anything, it is that settler-colonial institutions, not Indigenous people, are the ones that should be doing things differently."[61]

Jeong notes that "equality means overcoming obstacles related to institutional, cultural, attitudinal and behavioural discrimination."[62] In this case, as a first step, that necessarily means that Indigenous scholars and their scholarship must be included as valued members of the Royal Society of Canada, and that the excellence of those scholars and of their research be recognized as being of "conspicuous merit."[63] The Truth and Reconciliation Commission of Canada asked that "the paternalistic and racist foundations of the residential school system be rejected as the basis for an ongoing relationship. Reconciliation requires that a new vision, based on a commitment to mutual respect, be developed."[64] In doing so, as a second step, the Royal Society must acknowledge its discriminatory past and the ways in which it constructed the inequalities and discrimination that have continued to face Indigenous people in Canada. Those very foundations will require the important third step: fundamentally changing the foundations of the Royal Society to remove the obstacles and seeking to remove the barriers to the full and equal appreciation of Indigenous knowledge and ways of knowing, and of those who stand as the guardians and repositories of that knowledge.

All of this requires, though, that fellows and College members, as well as the secretariat of the Royal Society, "get uncomfortable [and] do the work" that is needed to address the discrimination that is inherent, both in the Royal Society of Canada and its member institutions.[65] The Royal Society has played a role as a "federation that [has been] of considerable importance in Canadian intellectual life."[66] It might be argued that the society and its fellows did not know the harm they were doing in imposing a Eurocentric model of what should constitute excellence to which public universities in Canada sought to rise. However, if it is to continue with any credibility in the post-Truth and Reconciliation Commission era, the Royal Society must now face such challenges head-on by admitting its role and by seeking to change. By carrying out this kind of decolonization work, the Royal Society and its member institutions, universities across the country, will become stronger. The direct result will be the transmission of both enlightened values and important scholarly work to the broader Canadian public – a role that the Royal Society of Canada has played since its creation.

NOTES

1 An Act to Incorporate the Royal Society of Canada, Statutes of Canada, 1883, c. 46; Preamble.
2 P.B. Waite, "Campbell, John George Edward Henry Douglas Sutherland, Marquess of Lorne and 9th Duke of Argyll, Governor General and Author," *Dictionary of Canadian Biography* (Toronto and Quebec: University of Toronto–Université Laval, 1998–2019), available from http://www.biographi.ca/en/bio/campbell_john_george_edward_henry_douglas_sutherland_14E.html; accessed 19 October 2019.
3 Carl Berger, *Honour and the Search for Influence: A History of the Royal Society of Canada* (Toronto: University of Toronto Press, 1996), 4.
4 Waite, "Campbell."
5 Berger, *Honour and the Search for Influence*, 5.
6 Berger, *Honour and the Search for Influence*, 6.
7 The universities that emerged in this period were not yet entirely "secular," since they still had very close ties with Christian churches.
8 James J. Talman and Ruth Davis Talman, *"Western" – 1878–1853: Being the History of the Origins and Development of the University of Western Ontario During its First Seventy-Five Years* (St. Thomas, ON: The Sutherland Press, 1953).
9 See John R.W. Gwynne-Timothy, *Western's First Century* (London: University of Western Ontario, 1978), 32–37.
10 Talman and Talman, *"Western,"* 4.
11 Berger, *Honour and the Search for Influence*, 4.
12 Ibid.
13 Ibid., 7.
14 Ibid., 6.
15 Western University, *The Employment Equity Guide* (June 2014), 11,

available from https://www.uwo.ca/equity/diversity/employment/resources_tools.html; accessed 20 October 2019.
16 Ho-Won Jeong, "Challenges for Peace," in *Peace and Conflict Studies* (Aldershot: Ashgate, 2000), 20–21.
17 Jeong, "Challenges for Peace," 23.
18 Berger, *Honour and the Search for Influence*, 21.
19 Ibid., 24.
20 Ibid., 9.
21 Ibid., 11.
22 Ibid., 135.
23 Gwynne-Timothy, *Western's First Century*, 54, 53–63.
24 RSC, *Proceedings of the Royal Society of Canada / Délibérations de la Société royale du Canada* (1898), xv.
25 Frances Henry in Jackie Wong, "Equitable Campuses, but for Whom?" *University Affairs* 8 Nov. 2017.
26 Waite, "Campbell."
27 Berger, *Honour and the Search for Influence*, 9
28 Berger, *Honour and the Search for Influence*, 14.
29 Berger, *Honour and the Search for Influence*, 14; see also "Duncan Campbell Scott (1862–1947)," Canadian Poetry Archives (The National Library of Canada), http://www.collectionscanada.gc.ca/wapp/canvers/bios/escott.htm; accessed 21 October 2019.
30 *The Indian Problem, Residential Schools, National Archives of Canada, record group 10.6810, file 470-2-3, vol. 7, 55 (L-3) and 63 (N-3)*.
31 Truth and Reconciliation Commission of Canada, *Honouring the Truth, Reconciling for the Future: Summary of the Final Report of the Truth and Reconciliation Commission of Canada* (Winnipeg: Truth and Reconciliation Commission of Canada, 2015), 5.
32 Robert Joseph, "21 Things You May Not Have Known About the Indian Act," Indigenous Corporate Training Inc., [blog] 2 June 2015, available from https://www.ictinc.ca/blog/21-things-you-may-not-have-known-about-the-indian-act-; accessed 21 October 2019.
33 "George Monro Grant," *Dictionary of Canadian Biography*, vol. XIII (1901–1910), available from http://www.biographi.ca/en/bio.php?id_nbr=6748.
34 Hon. Jody Wilson-Raybould, Minister of Justice and Attorney General of Canada, "Separate Journeys, Similar Path: Truth and Reconciliation in Canada and South Africa," a speech delivered at the University of Cape Town Law School, Cape Town, South Africa, 30 March 2017.

35 See, for example, Christopher Bracken, *The Potlatch Papers: A Colonial Case History* (Chicago: University of Chicago Press, 1997).
36 Berger, *Honour and the Search for Influence*, x.
37 Berger, *Honour and the Search for Influence*, 52.
38 Truth and Reconciliation Commission of Canada, *Honouring the Truth, Reconciling for the Future*, 54.
39 Gayle M. Comeau-Vasilopoulos, "Oronhyatekha," *Dictionary of Canadian Biography* (Toronto and Quebec: University of Toronto–Université Laval, 1998–2019), available from http://www.biographi.ca/en/bio/oronhyatekha_13E.html, accessed 21 October 2019. See also "Oronhyatekha," *Wikipedia*, available from https://en.wikipedia.org/wiki/Oronhyatekha, accessed 21 October 2019.
40 Bearfoot is spelled both "Bearfoot" and "Barefoot" in the literature. See Talman and Talman, *"Western,"* 16, and Gwynne-Timothy, *Western's First Century*, 78.
41 Harvey A. Mccue, "Education of Indigenous Peoples in Canada," *The Canadian Encyclopedia*, 6 June 2011 (updated by Michelle Filice, 18 July 2018), available from https://www.thecanadianencyclopedia.ca/en/article/aboriginal-people-education, accessed 19 October 2019.
42 Council of Ontario Universities, "By the Numbers," [website] available from https://ontariosuniversities.ca/resources/data/numbers, accessed 19 October 2019.
43 Chiefs Assembly on Education, "A Portrait of First Nations and Education," Palais des Congrès de Gatineau, Gatineau, Quebec, 1–3 October 2012, 3.
44 Truth and Reconciliation Commission of Canada, *Honouring the Truth, Reconciling for the Future*, 151.
45 Ben Lewis, "A Time for Action," *Academic Matters: OCUFA's Journal of Higher Education* (Spring 2019): 2.
46 Waite, "Campbell."
47 RSC Statute, Preamble.
48 Berger, *Honour and the Search for Influence*, 37.
49 Ibid. 37–38.
50 Rosalyn LaPier, *Invisible Reality: Storytellers, Storytakers, and the Supernatural World of the Blackfeet* (Lincoln, NE: University of Nebraska Press, 2017).
51 Berger, *Honour and the Search for Influence*, 41.
52 Ibid., 40, citing Committee of the Chiefs, presented by Duncan Campbell Scott, "Traditional History of the Confederacy of the Six Nations," *Transactions of the Royal Society of Canada* 5 (1911), s.11, 195–246.

53 Committee of the Chiefs, presented by Duncan Campbell Scott, "Traditional History of the Confederacy of the Six Nations," *Transactions of the Royal Society of Canada* 5 (1911), s.11, 195–246; available from https://archive.org/details/cbarchive_51740_traditionalhistoryofthecon-fede1911/page/n2; accessed 21 October 2019.
54 See, for example, Christopher Vecsey, "The Story and Structure of the Iroquois Confederacy," *Journal of the American Academy of Religion* 54.1 (Spring, 1986): 79–106.
55 Executive Director of The Royal Society of Canada email to author 17 October 2019.
56 After the first year of the college, the nomination procedure changed. In addition to nominations by fellows and institutional members, college members may also nominate candidates.
57 Dictionary.com, "Science," available from https://www.dictionary.com/browse/science?s=t, accessed 27 October 2019.
58 Truth and Reconciliation Commission of Canada, *Honouring the Truth, Reconciling for the Future*, 8.
59 Dominick LaCapra, *History in Transit: Experience, Identity, Critical Theory* (Ithaca: Cornell University Press, 2004).
60 Lewis, "A Time for Action," 2.
61 Lori Campbell, Shannon Dea, and Laura McDonald, "Get Uncomfortable, Do the Work: The Role of Faculty Associations Following the Truth and Reconciliation Commission," *Academic Matters: OCUFA's Journal of Higher Education* (Spring 2019): 8.
62 Jeong, "Challenges for Peace," 25.
63 Berger, *Honour and the Search for Influence*, ix.
64 Truth and Reconciliation Commission of Canada, *Honouring the Truth, Reconciling for the Future*, vi.
65 Campbell et al., "Get Uncomfortable, Do the Work," 12.
66 Berger, *Honour and the Search for Influence*, ix.

PART FOUR

Future Directions

Memorandum to the Royal Society of Canada

Editors' Note: In July 2019 in Saskatchewan, at a "RSC Listening Tour," the incoming president of the RSC and the then president of the College of the RSC (Jeremy McNeil and Joanna Quinn) asked how to better orient practices within the RSC and become more inclusive of Indigenous knowledge systems, knowledge keepers, and scholars. The authors of this Memorandum offered the following assessment and recommendations. The editors of this book reproduce this Memorandum here as an example of dialogue within the RSC on how the RSC, as an old and venerated institution, grapples with becoming more inclusive and recognizes the role it played in excluding, marginalizing, and expropriating Indigenous knowledge. Emerging from Dr Blackstock's gracious efforts to bring the RSC to account (in her letter to the president reproduced in the introduction to this book), the RSC Council unanimously approved on 11 September 2017 the creation of a Truth and Reconciliation Task Force to consider the RSC's historic and ongoing responsibilities with respect to Truth and Reconciliation with First Nations, Inuit, and Metis communities. All of the RSC authors of this Memorandum are part of this RSC Task Force.

MEMORANDUM TO THE ROYAL SOCIETY OF CANADA
14 OCTOBER 2019

To: Dr Jeremy McNeil, incoming President, R.S.C. and Dr Joanna Quinn, President of the New College of Scholars, R.S.C.
From: Drs. Marie Battiste, O.C., F.R.S.C., J. Y. Henderson, F.R.S.C.; Endorsed by Dr John Borrows, F.R.S.C.; Dr Margaret Kovach, New College of Scholars of the R.S.C.; Dr Kiera Ladner, New College of Scholars of the R.S.C.; Dr Vianne Timmons, O.C., President, University of Regina; Dr Jacqueline Ottmann, Vice-Provost Indigenous Engagement, University of Saskatchewan
Re: Request for the Royal Society of Canada to consider decolonizing the RSC to include Indigenous holders of Indigenous knowledge systems and languages.

As a beacon of celebration for diverse Eurocentric knowledges, the Royal Society of Canada (RSC) has contributed to the widespread diffusion and celebration of excellence of scholars, evident in over 2000 Canadian scholars, artists, and scientists, peer-elected as the best in their field. RSC now has the opportunity to expand its reach to other knowledge systems in Canada. This brief paper offers why RSC now should undertake the next step to be a leader in celebrating and encouraging excellence among Indigenous scholars in multiple Indigenous knowledge systems and begin a process of decolonization of its foundations and aim for reconciliation with diverse Indigenous knowledge systems.

The RSC was established in the colonial era in 1883. It has reflected the values of the colonial system and ignored Indigenous or traditional knowledge system and its processes, sources and its exemplary role models and leaders. It has, however, used the peoples, cultures and lands as sources of theory and investigation, and built disciplinary knowledges and methods to theorize their observations and problematizing. By their perceptions and research methods, British colonial academic attitudes held that Indigenous people and their knowledge systems were not just different, but deficient, backward, primitive and inconvenient, thus needing to be replaced with European languages, knowledges, values, beliefs, and institutions. British values and policies of forced assimilation through schools and government policies were imposed on Indigenous peoples disrupting their lifestyles, economic and cultural well-being, meaning-making, supportive cultural foundations, spiritual beliefs, family and community survival as Indigenous peoples while also appropriating their land, removing them and erasing evidence of their existence. The colonial attitudes of superiority have not left this nation and its institutions. The Final Report of the Royal Commission on Aboriginal Peoples (1996) and the Truth and Reconciliation Commission (2015) have urged Canadians, government and institutions to shed their colonial attitudes and relearn their responsibilities framed in the original treaties and agreements to honour their promises to share their prosperity, to honour Indigenous peoples' rights to their land, to their self-determination, and their cultures, languages and knowledges. This reconciliation is not a separation of peoples, but a renewed collaboration of knowledge systems and new learning, especially of the value of diversity, inclusion, and responsibility.

Over the last forty plus years since the federal policy on Indian Control of Indian Education, Indigenous peoples have been advancing Indigenous knowledge systems and languages in schools and generating new scholarship, methodologies, protocols and relationship with Eurocentric knowledge in the curriculum, as well as requiring researchers to come to them with new attitudes, ethics and frameworks. This required administrators and educators to ethically explore, accommodate and understand the interrelationship of the diverse knowledge systems of Canada systematically. This transformative work has generated a cognitive symbiosis of these knowledge systems with their dignity, ethical and honourable approaches and principles.

In 1982, Canada ended its lingering colonial relations with Great Britain as a decolonizing agenda. In attempting to generate a post-colonial nation, Canada patriated the foundational inherent Aboriginal powers and rights and the treaty reconciliation of Aboriginal nations. It reaffirmed a new constitutional order based on constitutional supremacy and the rule of law that guarantees the effective enjoyment of the constitutional rights of Aboriginal peoples, both collectively and individually. With this constitutional affirmation and several Supreme Court challenges and clarifications, Indigenous knowledge is now a holistic knowledge system that is constitutionally protected in Canada by Aboriginal and treaty rights. This is unique and exceptional protection.

These judicial affirmations of unique constitutionally-protected knowledge systems have generated reforms in educational systems of Canada. That reform has mobilized one of the intellectual transformations in both the humanities and the sciences, beginning with policy and ethics.

The Canadian Institutes of Health Research, Natural Sciences and Engineering Research Council of Canada, and the Social Sciences and Humanities Research Council of Council have issued the *Tri-Council Policy Statement on Ethical Conduct for Research involving Humans* (2018). The Tri-Council policy statement includes a chapter on research involving Aboriginal Peoples that acknowledges the unique constitutional rights of Aboriginal peoples (p.106) and Indigenous or traditional knowledge and law (pp.108–09). This acknowledgment is based on respect for human dignity, which is the core of ethical values and human rights. This respect for the inherent human dignity of Indigenous knowledge enhances Indigenous peoples' capacity to maintain their cultures, languages, identities and well-being. It supports the full participation in, and contributions of, Indigenous people and their knowledge system to Canadian society and beyond.

The Tri-Council policy statement, developed with the participation and consent of Indigenous scholars and Elders in Canada, has adopted a negotiated, minimal, operational definition of Indigenous or traditional knowledges. It has four key attributes. First, it is an expression of an intellectual, social and cultural heritage that holistically links a people to the land and seas, that generates a cosmology and cognitive orientation. Second, Indigenous knowledge belongs to specific peoples rather than the public domain and creates specific law about who can use, teach, know and continue to use certain parts of that knowledge. Third, Indigenous knowledge is continuously being nurtured, developed and refined similar to other knowledge systems. Fourth, Indigenous knowledge is an inherent right to lifelong learning.

Indigenous knowledge systems embedded in the constitutional rights of Canada recognize eleven different Indigenous language families and over sixty distinctive languages in Canada. Though negatively affected by Eurocentric colonial historical and political relationships, Indigenous knowledge systems and their languages continue to have a deep history and foundations connected to their land and place, to relations both human and nonhuman, to wisdom developed from personal gifts, exploration, experimentation, and revelation, as well as a shared culture and communally-activated learning in place over much time and through many generations. These knowledges have been the source of Indigenous peoples' continued survival and resilience, a source for their on-going renewal of those relations. Additionally, it is the source of their joy and community aspirations for their future. Without these exceptionalities and excellence, these Indigenous peoples and nations would not have survived and persisted in their places, through impoverished conditions and exceptional traumas and violence upon them. Those exceptionalities and contributions have been largely ignored by the educational institutions of Canada, except for stories told of heroes and heroic events.

The global movement for the recognition of the rights of Indigenous Peoples in the last quarter of a century has generated a legal rights framework in the United Nations *Declaration of the Rights of Indigenous Peoples*, and mobilized a global awareness of and respect for Indigenous peoples' knowledges, their ethics, their protocols, principles, and methodologies, as well as new protections. With the Truth and Reconciliation Commission pressing for social justice and cognitive reconciliation, Canadian institutions are advancing reconciliation on multiple fronts. Yet, to achieve these objectives, they require the leading intellectual organization of Canada to expand its recognitions and reconciliations with Indigenous scholars working in Indigenous knowledge systems, with diverse methodologies and research that go beyond conventional Anglo-Eurocentric disciplinary knowledge, and to link to and with these knowledge systems and their languages to reveal an honourable and equitable Canadian thought.

Among those organizations beginning to mobilize around some parts of this agenda are Universities Canada and the Council of Ministers of Education in Canada, who have advanced the inclusion of Indigenous education in universities and schools and have promoted this agenda nationally even more so since the recent Truth and Reconciliation Commission *Calls to Action* rely on the UN *Declaration of the Rights of Indigenous People* (2007) as a guide to reconciliation. The Association of Deans of Education (2010) advanced an Accord on Indigenous Education that speaks to respect, inclusion, and recognition of Indigenous knowledges. Universities across Canada have unilaterally advanced the research ethics of Indigenous peoples, with new behavioral ethics and many more scholars have conducted research with Indigenous peoples to arrive at new understandings and inspirations from them. The educational reforms with and by Indigenous peoples/scholars also have contributed to the growth of Indigenous peoples' research in Indigenous communities and created a cognitive nexus for a trans-generational alliance between knowledge systems. This nexus is unfolding and generating many innovative dialogues, quandaries, and growing opportunities for both Indigenous and non-Indigenous scholars. It has caused a proliferation of literature on Indigenous knowledge.

Only recently, a few Indigenous scholars in the universities have notably been nominated to become Fellows of the RSC or Members of the New College for their work in explaining constitutional rights, Indigenous knowledge and laws, and educating Canadian scholars and politicians. To succeed in this nomination process, they are expected to perform and be judged based on their excellence and scholarly outputs within and contributions to Anglo-Eurocentric post-secondary institutions. Their profound scholarly contributions have been addressed primarily to Anglo-Eurocentric disciplinary knowledge systems and its gazes, forms, productions and expressions. Their achievements have been based on Eurocentric disciplinary and interdisciplinary methodologies, theories, narratives, and languages that demonstrate specific exceptionalities. Their excellence has not been recognized for contributions to their Indigenous knowledge systems, laws or their communities.

The global consensus is now evident in the UN *Declaration* that has affirmed Indigenous knowledges and rights worldwide. It clarifies the scope and rights that are already protected by the Canadian constitution. Article 31 provides that Indigenous peoples have the right to maintain, control, protect and develop their cultural heritage, traditional knowledge and traditional cultural and artistic expressions. It provides that, in conjunction with Indigenous peoples, states shall take effective measures to recognize and protect the exercise of these rights. These include both tangible and intangible knowledge and heritage.

The RSC has yet to consider honouring the diverse Indigenous knowledge systems and languages where excellence also resides. The RSC has yet to consider what is considered exceptional from the Indigenous peoples' themselves. The RSC's Task Force on Reconciliation was and is continuing to illustrate the complicity of the fellows and the RSC to cognitive imperialism of Aboriginal peoples. As recognized leaders in the Royal Society of Canada, we request the RSC leadership to advance the decolonization of the Royal Society of Canada. At its minimum, we seek recognition and reconciliation to the constitutional affirmation of Indigenous knowledge, cultural expressions and languages enfolded in aboriginal and treaty rights in Canada. Moreover, such a transformative step needs to honour Indigenous contributions to the cognitive advancement, self-determination and well-being of their peoples not just to Canadian thought. It needs to affirm and honour excellence in experimentation, exploration and diffusion in Indigenous knowledge, languages, ceremonies and traditions that contribute to the uniqueness of the institutions and knowledges of Canada.

14

Golden Eagle Rising: A Conversation on Indigenous Knowledge

Shain Jackson and Cynthia E. Milton

Through the medium of Zoom videoconferencing, Coast Salish artist and lawyer Shain Jackson and settler academic Cynthia Milton discuss his artwork on the cover of this book, *Double-Headed Golden Eagle (Ch' ask-in) Rising*. In this conversation, they reflect upon different knowledge systems, law, art as truth-telling, colonialism, residential schools, and justice that comes with knowing the truth.

CYNTHIA: Let's start with your piece, *Double-Headed Golden Eagle (Ch'as-kin) Rising*. You tell stories of *Ch'as-kin*, the Golden Eagle, as a supernatural, larger-than-life creature embodying and exemplifying power, courage, and prestige. Why do you think these stories resonate today? Of course, there are many stories, so why these stories in particular?

SHAIN: By and far, I think it speaks largely to our worldview as shíshalh people prior to contact, and it still obviously permeates and continues to this day to a large extent despite attempts to derail it. Our status was based on what we gave of ourselves to society. For instance, look at our potlatch or feasting system: our leaders were our leaders because we revered them. Their authority wasn't based on punishment. Respect didn't come because someone could bring down the weight of the state upon others. Do you respect judges, lawyers, and police officers because you revere them? No, but because they can bring the weight of the state down upon you, and this is frightening.

Figure 14.1 Shain Jackson, *Double-Headed Golden Eagle (Ch' ask-in) Rising*.

In our culture then, the Golden Eagle is among the most powerful of supernatural beings. Are we afraid of it? No. This creature could swoop down and take everyone out in one fell swoop, but we're not fearful. It represents power and courage. We revere this creature because it helps everyone out: "Do you need some beams in your longhouse lifted? Well, I will help you lift them, but you also have to help out. If folks are starving, I am going to work with the Killer Whale and we are going to go around with other supernatural creatures and work together to bring the salmon back."

This is what I mean by prestige. There are still a lot of us who live by these teachings of public service. Those teachings coincide with a humility. So, when we seek positions of leadership, most of the time, it's because we've been pushed into that role because we have those skills. We don't seek power for the sake of it.

Looking at the Golden Eagle's double heads: this was a human rights figure. At contact, 70 per cent of the European population – indeed more because 50 per cent would have been women – were oppressed. Women in our communities always had the vote! [Laugh]

Two-spirit people were not only embraced in our society, but they were lifted up to have the strengths, acumen, intuition, the feelings of both male and female, woman and man; two sexes in one person was something to us quite unique and something that needed to be exalted, not oppressed. And certainly, at the time, not killed!

CYNTHIA: I understand that you had a particular experience with a shishálh Elder when you were a new, young lawyer that etched the story of the Golden Eagle into your mind. What was that experience?

SHAIN: Again, the laws. Moving back, when I was a young lawyer, I followed more Western notions of status and law. I wasn't necessarily as humble as I should've been. I used to go back to my community and connect with Elders that I looked up to. But I was a big shot: a lawyer! So, on a Friday night, I went to bingo because this was where everybody got together. A renowned Elder asked me to come over and sit down and chat with him about "my law." He asked, "Why don't you tell me about your law? You seem to have a bit of a chip on your shoulder. You think your law is better than our law?"

I am still very embarrassed to this day, but at that time, I did not consider our laws as laws. I had grown up with these things: practices, customs, traditions, but I didn't consider them laws. I couldn't understand how they were implemented, used, formulated. But he told me stories (he was a storyteller), so he asked me about common law. I explained that essentially it was about two people or parties in a dispute (whether a criminal or civil matter) and they would go and tell a judge their story. The judge in his or her infinite wisdom would come up with a solution and that would be written down as precedent, and carried on as precedent. Or they would look back and find something else that was similar and use that as precedent. Well, he [the Elder] took this and said, "Well, ok, I tell stories all the time. What's the difference?" At the time, I perceived it as different because colonial law was written down in black and white; it could be passed down from generation to generation; it could be worked with; it could be implemented; people could read it.

The Elder stated that I should look around our band hall at the art on the walls. This Elder said, "What do you mean about written language? It's everywhere. What do you think all this is?" He looked around him. Every bit of artwork in our band hall, not just on the walls, in the rafters, and on the tables, but around people's necks, dangling from their ears, pinned to their shirts.

CYNTHIA: So, this art is telling these stories that are representative of Indigenous law?

SHAIN: Well, there are two ways of looking at it. First of all, yes, figures tell stories and when we see these stories, we are reminded; these images remind us of the stories. But even more so, there is some very intense symbolism in these pieces. And because we have an oral tradition that is tied so tightly to the art, this is what we read. It's not "like" a written language. It "is" a written language.

Again, look at the double heads of on the Golden Eagle, representing not just equality between men and women but our two-spirit people. Look also at the horns. On the Eagle or other figures, the horns are the equivalent of an SCC [Supreme Court of Canada] on the first page of a judgement. That is the highest law; it means "pay attention, this is what you have to listen to." Other images, for instance, the Salish Eyes [which can be found in the frame around *Double-Headed Golden Eagle (Ch'as-kin) Rising*]. The eyes often come in multiples of four; these are lessons that are constantly inculcated into our entire being. The number four represents holistic things, like the four seasons, and the four stages of life and the responsibilities you have in these stages. This is something that really differentiates us from European society. It represents unity within diversity. It represents a very sophisticated version of society in that it is the law. When someone comes from some other place, we welcome them. One of the biggest figures is the Welcoming Figure from Coast Salish culture. It is not some big angry statue with a spear or something like that but rather has its hands out in a welcoming gesture. Four corners' teachings: welcome the people who are from outside; take your gifts whether your teachings or resources, things you created and offer them; take them in reciprocity. There are tons of teachings about humble reciprocity. Take what they have to offer. Make yourselves stronger together, and then you are able to raise yourselves up. So, when we hold up our hands [in the welcoming gesture], which is a very Coast Salish thing, it can mean "thank you"; it means respect. I've been taught that a very important meaning is that we hold up each other.

CYNTHIA: You said that the oral is tied to art, and that oral evidence and stories can be used as evidence in a court of law. You imply that this should be the case as well for art. Could you speak more about art as truth-telling?

SHAIN: Some things are undeniable when we look at the land, and the way we codify our history and law. We can go back many, many generations with our Double-Headed Eagle as well as with our Double-Headed Sea Serpent. The lessons are the same around equality but the stories go back forever. You see them in pictographs; they've been around for hundreds, if not thousands, of years. There are petroglyphs and stone sculptures that again go back. If you know how to read them, they have a very intense, sophisticated meaning very much like the Golden Eagle. Everything around it, guides the way we live as societies, law. I wonder why we [Indigenous peoples] were seen as a threat. Again, you come into this society where there's substantive equality. Speaking of gender equality: we just unearthed a woman warrior in our territory; a woman shrouded in arrowheads and spearheads. This woman was a bad ass.... If someone could take on the role, they took on the role. Their [settlers'] concern over our laws and way of life was really directed at our egalitarianism, both social and economic. What a threat to a stratified, monarchical (and later supposedly democratic) system! This threat still exists today.

CYNTHIA: In your piece, the *Double-Headed Golden Eagle (Ch'as-kin) Rising*, there is writing engraved in the background. What is this writing and what is the juxtaposition between the two?

SHAIN: The messaging here is that I was trying to find some analogies. I wanted to liken Golden Eagle law to something found in colonial law. And we do have a lot of laws related to Golden Eagle law. They didn't come into effect until relatively late in our [Canadian] history. I would dig into the civil code, constitutional law, statutory law, looking to find different provisions. The most I could find were some equivalents in human rights law. One of my messages when myself and our current shíshalh chief met with [Prime Minister Justin] Trudeau in 2018 was that this is our Golden Eagle law. In any event, there were sections that I couldn't find equivalents to. Canada's legal system is quite punitive. Golden Eagle law compels through emotions and desires to be worthy, the giving of ourselves. It may sound pollyannish, but we are living in a diseased society now. Some of the provisions I was looking for I could only find in extreme cases: if someone is in need, you have to help them. It's so disturbing to walk around in the Downtown Eastside [Vancouver]. That would have never happened in our societies. There were no slums in our society. How could you?

CYNTHIA: The text comes from the Canadian Charter of Rights and Freedoms?

SHAIN: It's a mix and match of [Canadian] laws that seemed befitting of Golden Eagle law. Interestingly, I couldn't find many laws that compelled someone to act to help other citizens. I found a maritime law that said a captain has to help a stranded boat and something in the Quebec civil code. I found these two provisions in Canadian law.

CYNTHIA: What do you think when you hear of the Royal Society of Canada?

SHAIN: To be quite honest, I didn't know much about it before I was contacted by you. Since then, I have looked it up and had a little gander. I like where you are going with this book which is why I don't mind being involved. To me it's disturbing that something that could be, or something that purports to be, this amazing intellectual grouping of people putting out these amazing papers, books, and information, would tie its hands behinds its back when dealing with Indigenous knowledge. One of the biggest messages I would give is that it's not too late to try and tap into some of this. Putting out these notions: this is how you control a society by fallacies about groups, races, religions, creating hate.

CYNTHIA: A hundred years ago, Duncan Campbell Scott was the president of the RSC [Royal Society of Canada].

SHAIN: There's a direct connection between these racist views that were propagated [and the RSC].
I don't think he was stupid. Look, I believe 99 per cent of humanity is amazing, caring human beings, maybe misinformed and willfully blind. But when furnished with the truth, they'll do the right thing. Truth necessitates justice. We are in this amazing era of truth-telling right now, which is fantastic. I am going to be very direct: Duncan Campbell Scott, I think he was among the 1 percent. I think he was methodical in what he was trying to do. There was an agenda and a willingness to build the propaganda around that agenda. He [and the RSC] completely turned a blind eye to some amazing Indigenous knowledge. Obviously, that knowledge didn't feed into his agenda.

CYNTHIA: As you know, in the past two weeks, the remains of 215 children were confirmed to be buried in the Tk'emlups Kamloops Indian Residential School. That's the legacy of that era of Duncan Campbell Scott and others. How does art help us get to the truth of those 215 souls?
Is this too broad a question?

SHAIN: No, but let me process it though. [Pause] Give me a second. You know, a lot of processing that we've been doing over the last week or two has been about grieving and dealing with it. There is no shock in finding them. There are many of us who have been talking about this for years. There are other mass graves across Canada. Look at what this has unearthed. It has unearthed a world of trauma. I don't even want to think about how much [more suffering has occurred among Indigenous people] as a result over this last week. It's difficult.

Let's circle back to the more academic thoughts about it. Yes, this man [Duncan Campbell Scott] made this possible by trying to propagate some version of reality to these folks that somehow we were unworthy of basic human rights because we were "uncivilized," that we were less than. At the same time, since he was so intelligent, he was withholding much of the knowledge that we had. Many Indian Agents and vicars and others, they knew what we had, they knew our human rights views were extremely sophisticated but were a challenge to their position. I was recently interviewed by Dana Lepofsky, an archaeologist, who, with others, just put out a paper titled, "Scientists' Warning to Humanity."[1] It was about the risks of neglecting Indigenous knowledge. And here we are again. It has taken us this long to try and catch up with regards to human rights. But here we are sitting on the precipice of destroying all of human civilization as we know it because we can't get a hold on climate change because we can't stop consuming.... We've been warning about this. This is the thing about our teachings: they just get pushed aside for elite agendas.

CYNTHIA: I am going to quote you to yourself. In one of your pieces, you wrote "let the truth rain down."

SHAIN: Yes, "and let justice follow." In this day and age of fake news and obfuscation on our social media and regular news, if we are going to focus on anything, it is going to be "to tell the truth." Truth is what gets people engaged to act. People actually don't believe that climate change is as bad as it is. People didn't believe that our people were being abused in residential schools that much. [They thought] "maybe a bit here and there in the odd, isolated circumstance." In the last week, I've been running into people [since the confirmation of the mass grave of children in Kamloops residential school], who've said, "Oh my God, I never knew." We've been trying to tell you guys this for years! We did a commission on it! It's been in the news! They chose not to listen. But truth necessitates justice. If people are able to get the truth en masse, then there is justice. There are two ways society changes: through education (which is truth telling) or intense suffering.

CYNTHIA: Shain, thank you very much. I appreciate your sharing.

SHAIN: I appreciate this too. I hope to spend the next year sailing on a boat and finishing my novel.

CYNTHIA: Well, if you get in trouble, some sea captain will be obligated to help you.

SHAIN: [Laugh] Or the Golden Eagle.

NOTE

Álvaro Fernández-Llamazares et al. "Scientists' Warning to Humanity on Threats to Indigenous and Local Knowledge Systems," *Journal of Ethnobiology*, 41(2), 2021: 144–69.

AFTERWORD

Closing Circle Words

Margaret Kovach

A full cup of coffee nearby, I eye my keyboard unable to write. I am to craft an *Afterword* for this book and I know what is expected. An *Afterword* is a literary device holding space at the conclusion of a book for a closing commentary. It might comment on the genesis of the book or inspire a continuing conversation on the book's topic. I do not contest these aspirations for closing off this edited volume. Yet, it is the term *Afterword* that blocks me, signifying, as it does, a reflection on a project done. Words will not come. I reach for my coffee and my eyes land upon a small soapstone carving on my desk. A gift to me from Indigenous graduate students for giving a talk on Indigenous methodologies. The carving is Coyote. Lost in an imaginary moment, Coyote awakens and eyes me with an irksome glance then dryly says, "You're an academic, a shapeshifter of language, a conjurer of prose. Re-imagine this *Afterword* and transform it into something else."

I think *Postscript*. This might work, as a *Post-Script* is similar to an *Afterword* but with less convention. Still, both words imply something that is done, over, the final act, the curtain call. I know that it is the connotation of colonialism being in the past that troubles me, given the topic of this book. The topic of this book is colonialism. Specifically, it points to the birth and persistence of Canadian scholarship as a colonial construct. There is a desire by the Canadian body politic to view colonialism as finished business but in this edited volume we, the contributors, argue that the colonial mind is adaptive and that this country's colonial affliction is not over. Still, I am stuck. Words such as afterword, post, colonialism are too often tied together and evoke the frequent Canadian coffee shop and classroom banter of "it's in the past, Indigenous people should move on" and this vexes my Indigenous mind. It is as Tommy Orange writes in *There, There*: "People want to say things like "sore losers" and "move on already," "quit playing the blame game.""[1] I look back at Coyote and search for another word to hold the spirit of this book. Instinctively, I type *tapwê* and it appears on my screen. *Tâpwê* is Nêhiyaw for truth and in its practice trust endures. Space breaks open and, with a swill of coffee, I recognize that this is not an *Afterword* but rather thoughts to close the circle for today.

Why this edited volume? What did we, the editors and the contributors, wish to achieve? At its most primary, this anthology concerns itself with the colonial production and reproduction of scholarship in Canada. The topic of colonialism in Canadian scholarly literature is not new. In 2020, there exists a collection of publications by scholars of diverse identities analyzing the ideology, policy, culture, and architecture of settler colonialism in knowledge production. In demarcating the colonialist substructure of Canadian scholarship, this book contributes to the growing canon of decolonial literature. However, several pivotal events within Canada over the past several years have compelled this particular book and a response by members of the Royal Society of Canada.

In 2015, the Truth and Reconciliation Commission of Canada released its final report.[2] The Truth and Reconciliation Commission arose from the 2007 *Indian Residential Schools Settlement Agreement*. The latter is a settlement from the largest class-action suit in Canadian history. Initiated by survivors of the Indian residential schools, the *Indian Residential Schools Settlement Agreement*[3] is an agreement between residential school survivors, the Assembly of First Nations, Inuit representatives, a consortium of churches, and Canada. The *Agreement* signifies the Canadian state and the churches' responsibility for the abuse and neglect suffered by students while at Indian residential schools. The *Agreement* details several compensatory provisions for damages suffered by survivors, including a common experience blanket payment of monies to each survivor, an independent assessment process to assess the amount of monetary reparation for each individual case of abuse, a commemoration fund for community-based projects, provision for health and healing services including the Aboriginal Healing Foundation (1998–2014), and monies for a Truth and Reconciliation Commission. Schedule "N" of the *Indigenous Residential Schools Settlement Agreement* outlines the mandate of the Commission:

> There is an emerging and compelling desire to put the events of the past behind us so that we can work towards a stronger and healthier future. The truth telling and reconciliation process as part of an overall holistic and comprehensive response to the Indian Residential School legacy is a sincere indication and acknowledgment of the injustices and harms experienced by Aboriginal people and the need for continued healing. This is a profound commitment to establishing new relationships embedded in mutual recognition and respect that will forge a brighter future. The truth of our common experiences will help set our spirits free and pave the way to reconciliation.[4]

Beginning in 2007, the Truth and Reconciliation commissioners and Canadians were called to bear witness to the testimonies of the abuse Indigenous people experienced in Canadian state-sanctioned residential schools. In public gatherings across Canada, through the indelible force of Indigenous oracy, Indigenous peoples spoke the truth and Canadians listened. It hurt. Indigenous residential school survivors told Canadians what some of us knew and many did not: the Indian residential school system is an open bloodied gash that continues to wound and has yet to fully heal. Healing this wound will require a collective effort. Reconciliation is not the perfect remedy. The wound inflames and chafes. However, it offers the possibility of healing so long as Canadians choose to counter racism and inequities. *The Final Report of the Truth and Reconciliation Commission of Canada* identifies the way forward by outlining more than ninety *Calls to Action*, including, but not limited to, education, child welfare, justice, and research.

In 2007, the same year the Truth and Reconciliation Commission began its work, the First Nations Caring Society of Canada and the Assembly of First Nations lodged a human rights complaint against Canada through the Canadian Human Rights Tribunal on First Nations child welfare. The complaint asserted that First Nations children and youth were being actively discriminated against by the Canadian state through the mechanism of inequitable federal funding policy for on-reserve child welfare services. In 2016, shortly after the release of the Truth and Reconciliation Commission's final report, the Canadian Human Rights Tribunal ruled in favour of First Nations and Canada was ordered to compensate First Nations. During the nine years of the tribunal hearing, the federal government tried to shut down the case down eight times on technical grounds.[5] As I write these words in 2020, the Canadian state has yet to fully compensate First Nations as obliged by the tribunal.

In 2015, the Liberal government announced a National Inquiry into Missing and Murdered Indigenous Women and Girls. The final report of the inquiry released in 2019 entitled *Reclaiming Power and Place: The Final Report of the National Inquiry into Missing and Murdered Indigenous Women and Girls* exposed the systemic basis of the tragic violence perpetrated against Indigenous women and girls in Canada. The report documents the human and Indigenous rights violations that Indigenous women and girls have endured.

The findings of the Truth and Reconciliation Commission, the Human Rights Tribunal on First Nations Child Welfare, and the National Inquiry into Missing and Murdered Indigenous Women and Girls cast a sharp light on racism against Indigenous peoples. In 2016, converging with these benchmark events, Cindy Blackstock, a forceful advocate for First Nations, including the aforementioned child welfare complaint, was appointed honorary fellow of the Royal Society of Canada. She was invited to give the keynote address at that year's Royal Society annual meeting. Blackstock, in turn, invited the Royal Society of Canada to have a good think about the Royal Society's history. She reminded Royal Society members that reconciliation stalls when colonial skeletons are sheltered in closed-off corners. It was time, she said, for the Royal Society of Canada to reckon with Duncan Campbell Scott, given his association with the society and the violence he perpetrated against Indigenous Peoples. The Truth and Reconciliation Task Force of the Royal Society of Canada agreed. This edited anthology is one response.

From the far and near history of colonialism within the shifting Canadian landscape, several motivations animate this anthology. One purpose is to explore the historical role of the Royal Society of Canada in the complicit and explicit colonization of First Nations, Métis, and Inuit peoples. In doing so, there is a desire to hold accountable the words, language, policy, and actions arising from its members. We point specifically to Duncan Campbell Scott, a fellow from 1899–1947. In 1921–22, he was president of the RSC. During this period, he found favour among the Canadian elite while using his influence to batter Indigenous societies through the mechanisms of public policy and scholarly authority. Thus, this edited volume seeks to reckon with this history and in this sense it has a focus on the past.

Afterword: Closing Circle Words

This anthology moves, equally, with a forward purpose of calling-out colonialism in contemporary Canadian scholarship to resist ongoing colonial reproduction in knowledge production. In reading the contributions by each author in this edited volume, I sense a collective longing to tell a fuller story. One after another, each chapter asserts that Canadian scholarship has been formed and embedded in a White settler politic, a colonial affliction marked by a Canadian settler consciousness conflicted about Indigenous people. Certainly, this conflicted consciousness does not apply across the board. Influential settlers, as Duncan Campbell Scott, were not conflicted on Indigenous erasure and so weaponized Canadian policy in an attempt to rid Canada of the "Indian problem."[6] Nor was a 2018 Saskatchewan all-white jury conflicted in acquitting Gerald Stanley for the murder of Colten Boushie of Red Pheasant First Nation. From an Indigenous perspective, Indigenous peoples are not conflicted about erasure either. This is our homeland. In the face of harm done to Indigenous people, we continue to strive for peaceful co-existence, but we will not be erased.

The inerasable presence of Indigenous peoples exists within a persisting marginalization in Canadian society. Within the intellectual life of Canadian scholarship, this dynamic has manifested in the seeming paradox of erasure and salvage scholarship aimed at Indigenous culture. Even though salvage and erasure may seem at odds, both signal a deficit gaze upon Indigenous peoples. From the earliest days of the Royal Society of Canada, an ethos of Indigenous erasure marks its history.

In each of their chapters (in Part I and II respectively), Ian Wereley and Cynthia Milton reference the *Proceedings and Transactions* of the Royal Society of Canada and comment upon how these records expose a pattern and practice of racial and ethnic exclusion within this establishment. Though the Royal Society of Canada, as Milton states, sought a distinctive Canadian scholarship forged in the unique geographic conditions of the land, the early Royal Society fellows simultaneously craved both a distinct Canadian identity and a homogenous scholarship mirroring the Anglo-Saxon old world.

Through archival records, Constance Backhouse points to Duncan Campbell Scott and his desire to rid Canada of Indigenous peoples. Backhouse writes that from the period of 1913 to 1932, Scott sought eradication of Indigenous peoples through a policy cluster aimed at encroaching land rights, inadequate healthcare, and forced attendance at residential schools. In Canadian history, Scott as civil servant of the Canadian state becomes the principal architect of Indigenous erasure in Canada. Carole Gerson, in her chapter, brings Pauline Johnson (1861–1913), the poet of Mohawk lineage, into our consciousness. In focusing on the literary and intellectual life in the early days of this country, Gerson writes of Johnson's prominence as a poet and a contemporary of Duncan Campbell Scott. Gerson's chapter includes a photograph of Johnson from the 1897 *Proceedings and Transactions* of the Royal Society of Canada alongside several Canadian authors, including Scott. Johnson was invited to read poetry at an evening of readings for the Royal Society of Canada in 1895[7] but a formal relationship with the RSC does not advance beyond this point.

Adele Perry writes of how Scott used his influence in the dispossession of Indigenous land rights. In colluding with Winnipeg Mayor Thomas Russ Deacon in 1913–1914, Scott directed his intellectual energies toward stripping reserve land from the Annishinaabeg. This resulted in the creation of Section 46 of the *Indian Act,* an Indian land removal clause to allow for the dispossession of Indian lands if in the interests of "public works." The appointment of Scott as a fellow in 1899 and his elevation to RSC president in 1921–1922 points to the colonial disposition of the Royal Society of Canada in matters of Indigenous relations during this time.

In his chapter, John Reid notes the role of three lesser-known Royal Society fellows in shaping settler-Indigenous hierarchical relations. Through their literary work, Archibald MacMechan, George Patterson, and Thomas Head Raddall all assisted in the racial diminishment of Mi'kmaw peoples. As fellows, all three spoke with the weight and authority of the Royal Society of Canada. James Walker's chapter charts a more contemporary history, where he shares extracts from a 1971 historical paper he wrote entitled, "The Indian in Canadian Historical Writing." In critically reflecting upon 1970s Indigenous representation in history chronicles, he spotlights how the "good" Indigenous person was represented as compliant and subservient to the settler state.

As this text goes to press in 2021, words fail as Canadian society learns of the 215 unmarked burial sites of children who attended the Kamloops Residential School. We reach out to the Tk'emlúps te Secwépemc in sorrow and support. Katherine Nichols, Eldon Yellowhorn, Deanna Reder, Dongya Yang, John Albanese, Darian

Kennedy, Emily Holland, Elton Taylor, and Hugo Cardoso's chapter on the investigations into unmarked graves alerts us to Canada's Truth and Reconciliation Missing Children Project and the children who never came home. Moral righteousness requires that settler society rethink its relationship with Indigenous peoples.

In their chapters respectively, Jane Bailey then Reem Bahdi focus on a persistent colonialism in contemporary Canada. In linking the past and present, Jane Bailey points to the practice of erasure thriving in post-secondary classrooms. Specifically, she calls out the conscious and unconscious practice of everyday Indigenous erasure in contemporary Canadian legal education as law professors uncritically valorize Western legal jurisprudence and rituals while ignoring Indigenous laws. In Reem Bahdi's account of the trial of Gerard Stanley for the murder of Colten Boushie, we see the Canadian legal system deployed in service of racial abhorrence toward Indigenous peoples. In the conclusion of her chapter, Bahdi astutely questions, "Is the Canadian criminal justice system trustworthy enough to sit in judgment of Indigenous peoples?" As these authors demonstrate, we see a country actively seeking to expunge Indigenous presence from this land. It seems Indigenous erasure is pro forma, only to be reminded of the "salvage scholarship" existing in Canadian knowledge production. Several authors in this edited volume write of this problematic accompanying a debauched inclusion of Indigenous peoples.

Jennifer Evans, Meagan Breault, Ellis Buschek, Brittany Long, Sabrina Schoch, and David Siebert bring us into scholarship of today's academy through their chapter. During a 2019 graduate course in public history at Carleton University, these authors revisited the complicated, contradictory nature of the Canadian colonial project. They reference the work of Edward Sapir, Marius Barbeau, William Ganong and George Stanley, who were members of the Royal Society of Canada in its early operation. Sapir, Barbeau, Ganong, and Stanley were also researchers of Indigenous culture. As with Scott, these four Royal Society fellows were influential in the colonial foundations of Canadian scholarship. Yet, unlike Scott, they sought to save Indigenous culture and were "salvage scholars" when it came to Indigenous peoples. In bridging the history of the Royal Society to the present day, Joanna Quinn articulates how the development and promotion of a national scientific research body became a white, male, monolithic project. These early actions paved the way for the structural violence situated within institutional systems that produce and reproduce invisible walls to keep the "unwanted" out unless on colonial terms. The challenge, Quinn argues, is to dismantle tangible and intangible walls of exclusion.

Erasure or salvage? Either way, it is objectifying. Where Canadians fall on the erasure-salvage continuum is beyond the scope of this commentary; however, it is not off the mark to say that Indigenous Peoples live in the head of the Canadian settler psyche and have for a long while now. Resolution will not come easily because colonial relations are deep in the bones of Canadian society, the Canadian state, and Canadian scholarly establishments. Yet Canadian scholarship that subsists in the absence of a full and equitable Indigenous presence is detrimental to us all.

At this point in our history, Indigenous peoples have not been afforded full inclusion, accompanied by voice and respect. And so, in the form of a letter, the collective voice of Indigenous scholars Marie Battiste, John Borrows, J. Y. Henderson, Margaret Kovach, Kiera Ladner, Vianne Timmons, and Jacqueline Ottmann. This letter requests that the Royal Society of Canada acknowledge its continued complicity in its imperialist approach to Indigenous people, culture, and scholarship. In an era of truth-telling and reconciliatory aspirations, the signatories of this letter seek an end to Indigenous erasure and salvage scholarship and in its place a move toward full recognition of Indigenous contributions to the scholarship of this land. This edited volume concludes with a conversation between Shain Jackson, artist of the cover art, *Double-Headed Golden Eagle (Ch' ask-in) Rising*, for this book and Cynthia Milton. Shain Jackson's words from the closing chapter resonate: "In the last week, I've been running into people [since the confirmation of the mass grave of children in Kamloops residential school], who've said 'Oh my God, I never knew.' We've been trying to tell you guys this for years! We did a commission on it! It's been in the news! They chose not to listen. But truth necessitates justice."

If there is to be respect for Indigenous scholars, the anti-colonial way forward requires that Indigenous scholarship be recognized within scholarly institutions at a deep level. Specifically, this will require several efforts: a) that Indigenous scholarship, as governed by Indigenous knowledge systems and practices articulated in the *United Nations Declaration of the Rights of Indigenous Peoples*, be explicitly acknowledged within tenure and promotion policies within Canadian universities; b) that both senior university leadership and the collegium work together to ensure that Indigenous scholars have the option to be adjudicated for tenure and promotion based upon Indigenous scholarship standards; and c) that the racism and shame that diminishes Indigenous scholars within academic environments desist. Anti-colonialism and anti-racism must not take a backseat in times of fiscal restraint. These efforts will require operationally-funded educational resourcing and accountability measures to move away from the erasure-salvage continuum to a relationship of respect and equity. The Royal Society of Canada is well-situated to be a powerful influencer in these *Calls to Action*.

To not see Indigenous erasure or salvage scholarship in the history of powerful Canadian institutions such as the Royal Society of Canada is to choose not to see. To read this edited volume and not be awakened to Indigenous exclusion, past and present, is a choice. Still this Canada, struggling with a truth and reconciliation that chafes, has not yet written its final word of who we are. Day by day, year upon year, decade after decade, Indigenous peoples persist. Each day we find an ally. In the pages of this book, the contributors bring Indigenous intellectual contributions into view. Through our words, we seek to open doors, cast light on dark corners, bring into the consciousness that which has been hidden in plain view. Through our bookish, erudite words we say to Indigenous peoples of this land: I see you. You matter. *Ekosi*

NOTES

1 Tommy Orange, *There There* (Toronto: McClelland and Stewart, 2018).
2 Truth and Reconciliation Commission of Canada, *The Final Report of the Truth and Reconciliation Commission of Canada Volume 1, Canada's Residential Schools: The History, Part 1, Origins to 1939* (Winnipeg: Truth and Reconciliation Commission of Canada, 2015).
3 Legal Services Society of British Columbia, *Indian Residential Schools Settlement: The Common Experience Payment and the Independent Assessment Process* (Vancouver, B.C.: Legal Services Society, 2013), http://www.llbc.leg.bc.ca/public/pubdocs/bcdocs2014/541693/indian-residential-schools-settlement-eng.pdf.
4 "Schedule 'N' – Mandate for The Truth and Reconciliation Commission," The Indian Residential School Settlement Agreement, 2007, retrieved from http://www.residentialschoolsettlement.ca/settlement.html.

5 Cindy Blackstock, "The Complainant: the Canadian Human Rights Case on First Nations Child Welfare," *McGill Law Journal* 62, no. 2 (2016): 285.
6 National Archives of Canada, Record Group 10, vol. 6810, file 470-2-3, vol. 7, 55 (L-3) and 63 (N-3).
7 Proceedings of the Royal Society of Canada, retrieved from https://www.biodiversitylibrary.org/item/40773#page/129/mode/1up.

Contributors

JOHN ALBANESE is an associate professor of anthropology and forensic science at the University of Windsor. He has been pursuing a biocultural approach for investigating human variation using identified skeletal collections with a focus on developing and testing skeletal identification methods for bioarchaeological and forensic contexts. He occasionally assists the local police force in forensic investigations and is involved in the investigation of human rights violations in Canada and internationally.

CONSTANCE BACKHOUSE is a University of Ottawa law professor. She has published a number of prize-winning books including *Petticoats and Prejudice: Women and Law in Nineteenth-Century Canada* and *Colour-Coded: A Legal History of Racism in Canada, 1900–1950*. An RSC Fellow since 2004, she served as president of the Academy of Social Sciences from 2015–17. She was named to the Order of Canada in 2008. For more details, see www.constancebackhouse.ca.

REEM BAHDI is an associate professor in the Faculty of Law, University of Windsor where she teaches access to justice, human dignity and Arabs, Muslims and the law. Her research explores how stereotyping has shaped legal outcomes and examines how legal methods have perpetuated inequality within the law. She is interested in law and justice in both the Canadian and Palestinian contexts.

JANE BAILEY is a full professor at the University of Ottawa Faculty of Law (Common Law) where she teaches contracts, cyberfeminism and technoprudence. Jane co-leads The eQuality Project, a SSHRC-funded partnership initiative focused on young people's privacy and equality in digitally networked spaces, including the impacts of technology-facilitated violence and abuse (in both individual and corporate forms). She became a member of the RSC's New College in 2016.

DR MARIE BATTISTE is emerita professor from the University of Saskatchewan, a fellow of the Royal Society of Canada since 2013, a Pierre Elliott Trudeau Fellow (2019–2022), and 2019 honorary officer of the Order of Canada. Her scholarly interests are in the production and dissemination of research and knowledge that transforms education through decolonization of knowledges and education.

CINDY BLACKSTOCK, a member of the Gitxsan First Nation, serves as executive director of the First Nations Child and Family Caring Society and a professor at McGill University. Working with First Nations communities and children of all diversities, Cindy's areas of work include Indigenous children's rights, culturally based equity, and human rights law.

MEAGAN BREAULT has a background specializing in modern European history as well as experience in Indigenous history and digital Geographic Information Systems (GIS). Her bachelor's degree comes from the University of Saskatchewan and she obtained her master of arts degree from Carleton University. She currently works as a research associate at Know History in Calgary.

ELLIS BUSCHEK is a graduate student with a masters in history, with a focus on modern Canadian history, food history, and the factors which helped facilitate the crafting of a dominant national identity circa Canada's centennial. Specifically, his research is concerned with the production and consumption of food-related cultural content, and the relationship between this content, colonialism as a Canadian reality, and multiculturalism as a burgeoning ideal, in Canada during the 1960s. Ellis is also interested in the relationship between identity and the arts, as well as Canada's treatment of the LGBT community and the mentally ill, and aspires to bring this into conversation with his research into the Canadian culinary scene.

HUGO F.V. CARDOSO earned his PhD in anthropology from McMaster University in 2005. He has many years of research, teaching, and professional experience in museums, archaeology, and forensics. In 2013 he joined the Department of Archaeology at Simon Fraser University where he is chair and associate professor. He is also co-director of SFU's Centre for Forensic Research. He is a member of the Royal Society of Canada's College of New Scholars, Artists and Scientists since 2018.

JENNIFER EVANS is a member of the RSC College of New Scholars, Artists and Scientists and a professor of history at Carleton University, where in the winter of 2019 she taught the History in the Public Interest seminar. Meagan Breault, Ellis Buschek, Brittany Long, Sabrina Schoch, David Siebert came to the course with diverse interests, some in the history of racism and eugenics in Germany, others in the cultural politics and legacy of white supremacy in contemporary Canada. This collaboratively written chapter was the culmination of course work.

DR CAROLE GERSON (FRSC) is professor emerita in the English Department at Simon Fraser University and has published extensively on Canada's literary and cultural history, with a focus on early Canadian women writers. In 2011, her book, *Canadian Women in Print, 1750–1918*, won the Gabrielle Roy Prize for Canadian criticism and in 2013 she received the Marie Tremaine medal from the Bibliographical Society of Canada. Her most recent book, co-authored with Peggy Lynn Kelly, is *Hearing More Voices: English-Canadian Women in Print and on the Air, 1914–1960* (Ottawa: Tecumseh Press, 2020).

SAKEJ HENDERSON, JD, IPC, FRSC is research fellow at the College of Law, University of Saskatchewan, and member of the Chickasaw Nation.

EMILY HOLLAND completed her PhD at the University of Toronto in 2013 and was hired as a biological anthropologist at Brandon University in 2014. She is a practicing forensic anthropologist and regular consultant to the Manitoba Office of the Chief Medical Examiner, the RCMP, and municipal police forces. Her research investigates infant and child health in the past, techniques of skeletal analysis, and taphonomy in Manitoba.

SHAIN JACKSON is Coast Salish from the shishálh First Nation in Sechelt, British Columbia. Mr Jackson is a lawyer and an artist, and has represented the interests of Indigenous communities and organizations throughout British Columbia in relation to a broad array of issues. He is the president of Spirit Works, a First Nations owned and operated company and an executive director of Golden Eagle Rising Society, an organization whose aim is the protection of Indigenous lives. www.spiritworks.ca

DARIAN KENNEDY is the Sioux Valley Dakota Nation Community Liaison for the Brandon Indian Residential School Cemetery Project. He has strong ties to Garden Hill, Sioux Valley, Swan Lake, and Roseau River. He is working towards a bachelor of arts at Brandon University focusing on Native studies and anthropology.

MARGARET KOVACH (Sākohtēw pīsimw iskwēw) is of Nêhiyaw and Saulteaux ancestry from Treaty Four territory in Southern Saskatchewan. She is a professor in the Department of Educational Studies, Faculty of Education, University of British Columbia (Vancouver campus) and a member of the College of the Royal Society of Canada. Her award-winning book, *Indigenous Methodologies: Characteristics, Conversations, and Contexts* (University of Toronto), now in its second edition (2021), explores the role of Indigenous knowledge, theory, and Indigenous community partnership in research.

BRITTANY LONG has a bachelor of arts in history from the University of New Brunswick. She is currently working on her master's thesis at Carleton University which exams post war memory and historical interpretation of female Nazi perpetrators.

CYNTHIA E. MILTON is the associate vice president of research at the University of Victoria and professor in the Department of History. Dr Milton is past president of the College of New Scholars of the Royal Society of Canada (2016–2018), former Canada Research Chair in the Department of History at the Université de Montréal (2007–2017), and fellow of the Pierre Elliott Trudeau Foundation (2019–2020). Her interdisciplinary research studies inclusive modes of truth-telling, transitional justice, memory, and cultural interventions in the construction of historical narratives after state violence. Her publications include *The Art of Truth-telling about Authoritarian Rule* (2004), *The Many Meanings of Poverty* (2007),

Curating Difficult Knowledge (2011), *Art from a Fractured Past* (2014), and *Conflicted Memory* (2018).

KATHERINE L. NICHOLS is a PhD candidate in an interdisciplinary program that allows her to work with faculty in the Department of Indigenous Studies and the Department of Archaeology at Simon Fraser University (SFU). She is a graduate fellow of SFU's Community-Engaged Research Initiative (CERi) and is affiliated with the Centre for Forensic Research. Her current work stems from research started during her MA at the University of Manitoba done in partnership with Sioux Valley Dakota Nation, which focuses on locating cemeteries at the Brandon Indian Residential School in Manitoba.

ADELE PERRY is distinguished professor of history and women's and gender studies at the University of Manitoba. She is a settler historian of nineteenth- and twentieth-century colonialism and the author of *On the Edge of Empire: Gender, Race, and the Making of British Columbia* (2001), *Colonial Relations: The Douglas-Connolly Family and the Nineteenth-Century British Columbia* (2015), and *Aqueduct: Colonialism, Resources, and the Histories We Remember* (2016). Perry is a past president of the Canadian Historical Association, and current director of the University of Manitoba's Centre for Human Rights Research.

JOANNA R. QUINN is a past president of the College of the RSC. She is associate professor of political science and director of the Centre for Transitional Justice and Post-Conflict Reconstruction at the University of Western Ontario. Dr Quinn has written widely on the role of acknowledgment in Uganda, Canada, Fiji, Haiti, and Solomon Islands. Most recently, she is the author of *Thin Sympathy: A Strategy to Thicken Transitional Justice* (Penn Press, 2021).

DEANNA REDER (Cree Métis) is chair of the Department of Indigenous Studies and associate professor in the Department of English at Simon Fraser University. She was inducted into the College of New Scholars in the Royal Society of Canada in 2018. She is co-editor of *Learn, Teach, Challenge* (2016), *Read, Listen, Tell* (2017), *Honouring the Strength of Indian Women* (2019), the July 2020 edition of the journal, *Ariel,* and the co-author of *Cold Case North* (2020).

JOHN REID is professor emeritus of history at Saint Mary's University and senior research fellow of the Gorsebrook Research Institute. His research and publications have focused largely on northeastern North America in the seventeenth and eighteenth centuries, including settler colonialism and imperial-Indigenous relations, while more recently he has turned his attention to the history of sport. He is a fellow of the Royal Society of Canada, a former co-editor of *Acadiensis: Journal of the History of the Atlantic Region*, and has also served as president of the Shastri Indo-Canadian Institute.

DAVID SIEBERT is a dual citizen of Canada and New Zealand, and was born in Ottawa, Canada. He recently graduated with a master of arts from the School of Indigenous and Canadian Studies with a focus on heritage conservation.

SABRINA SCHOCH has a master of arts in public history from Carleton University. Her thesis is entitled "Queer Commemorative Silences: Public Memory and Lesbian Persecution Politics." She currently works for Immigration, Refugees and Citizenship Canada as an archivist for the Syrian Resettlement Memory Project.

ELTON TAYLOR, (Dakota) is a member and Councilman for Sioux Valley Dakota Nation (SVDN) and the son of residential school and day school survivors. As a SVDN Council member, he has overseen the Brandon Residential School project for several years and understands the importance of completing this work and bringing history to light.

JAMES W. ST G. WALKER is professor in the Department of History at the University of Waterloo, where he specializes in the history of human rights and race relations and African-Canadian history. Walker is a member of the Order of Canada and a fellow of the Royal Society of Canada.

IAN WERELEY, is a social and cultural historian interested in the past, present, and future of Canada. He received his PhD in history from Carleton University in 2018. He volunteers as adjunct curator of the history of energy at the Canada Science and Technology Museum, Ottawa, and serves as executive director of the Canadian Association for Graduate Studies.

DONGYA YANG is a full professor in the Department of Archaeology, and associate dean of research and graduate studies in the Faculty of Environment at Simon Fraser University. He received his PhD in anthropology from McMaster University in 1998. His research is focused on ancient DNA analysis of human, animal and plant remains to retrieve genetic information to help enhance archaeological investigations. Since 2000, he has been running a dedicated ancient DNA laboratory at Simon Fraser University.

ELDON YELLOWHORN is from the Piikani Nation. He received a bachelor of science in geography in 1983 and a bachelor of arts in archaeology in 1986 at the University of Calgary. He studied archaeology at Simon Fraser University, completing is master of arts in 1993, and at McGill University, completing his PhD in 2002. He is a full professor at Simon Fraser University where he established the Department of First Nations Studies in 2012. He is a long-time member of the Canadian Archaeological Association where he served as president (2010–12).

Index

Abley, Mark, 77n14, 89–90, 106n9, 113
Aboriginal Healing Foundation, 336
Aboriginal Justice Inquiry (Manitoba), 273n62
academia (*see also* universities): effect of its ties to government on Indigenous peoples, 302–4; and extractive history, 281–2; fascination with Indigenous knowledge, 159–63; feelings of inferiority of, 155–8; interdisciplinarity of, 290; interest in Indigenous folklore, 168–71; international ties of, 289–90; need of Indigenous knowledge to understand Canadian landscape, 163, 333; recent engagement with Indigenous issues, 186–8, 199n40, 200n41; role of in harms to Indigenous peoples, 5; split between French and English on Indigenous knowledge, 171–2
Adami, George, 14, 38
Adams, Frank, 46
Adams, Howard, 183
Adams, Michael, 187
Adamski, Jakub, 240
Allen, Woody, 90
Almeda-Cote, Iris, 12
Andersen, Chris, 308
Annishinaabeg, 112, 114, 118
Art as truth-telling, 326, 330–1
Assembly of First Nations (AFN), 336, 337

Bailey, A. G., 142–3
Baker, Janet, 136
Bala, Nicholas C., 240
Barbeau, Marius: as colleague of E. Sapir, 284; as D. C. Scott contemporary at RSC, 177n49; photo, 170; posts and awards of, 295n35; and procuring of artifacts, 280, 293n10; readings at RSC meetings, 168, 170, 177n55
Battiste, Marie, 231–2, 234, 244
Bearfoot, Isaac, 305, 314n40
Belcourt, Napoléon, 34
Bell, Graham, 3

Bentley, D. M. R., 91, 103
Berger, Carl, 164, 278, 299, 301, 304
Biggar, Saskatchewan, 252–3
Biggar, W. H., 253
Bigot, François, 287
Blackfoot, 24, 70, 294n16
Blackstock, Cindy: address to RSC, 4–5, 309–10, 338; and RSC Task Force, 5, 278; urges RSC to educate members on D. C. Scott, 5, 16; writes two letters to RSC on TRC recommendations, 3, 4–5, 12–16, 17n2
Blood, Narcisse, 294n16
Boas, Franz: as contentious figure in modern anthropology, 295n33; and Hill-Tout, 177n48, 177n49; papers of, 160, 162; and race, 85n114; work presented at RSC, 167, 170, 284
Bond, Principal (Brandon Indian Residential School), 213, 214
Borden, Robert, 74
Borrows, John, 81n57, 236, 245n14, 308
Botsford, Belle W., 63–4, 74
Bourassa, Carrie, 308
Bourinot, Arthur S., 92, 94
Bourinot, J. George: background, 48n12; as clerk of the House of Commons, 30; reads Hill-Tout paper, 177n47; research on Teutonic superiority, 24; RSC papers by, 94, 175n23; on RSCs' aims, 301; work for RSC, 26, 39, 41, 43
Boushie, Colten (see also *R. v. Stanley*), 250, 256–9, 263, 268, 275n88

Bradbury, George, 120
Brandon Indian Residential School: history, 207–11; history of first cemetary, 211–13, 214, 228n76, 229n77; and land jurisdiction questions over its cemetaries, 216; second cemetery, 213–15, 228n76; third cemetery, 215
Brandon Residential School Cemeteries Project, 216–22, 223–4
Brooks, Harriet, 54n90
Brown, E. K., 63, 89
Brown, Mrs. W. Wallace, 38
Bryce, George, 64, 160
Bryce, Peter H., 13–14
Bucke, Richard M., 301
Burge, Bill, 257
Burt, A. L., 286
Byng, Julian, 157

Campbell, Lori, 311
Campbell, Maria, 183
Campbell, Wilfred, 79n43, 94
Canada, Government of (*see also* Department of Indian Affairs): attempts to negotiate treaty with Annishinaabeg, 114; and Brandon Indian Residential School, 207; failure to compensate on Indigenous child welfare, 337–8; and *Indian Residential Schools Settlement Agreement*, 336; lobbied by RSC for national institutions, 34, 35–6, 69; lobbied by RSC for permanent home, 42; role in Shoal Lake aqueduct, 116–17; RSCs early ties to, 29–30, 154; and surrender of Indigenous land, 116–18,

126n24; and TRC calls to action on missing children, 215; TRC's comments on residential school funding of, 207
Canada First movement, 163–5, 171, 176n43
Canadian culture: and Indigenous folklore, 168–71; lack of distinction in, 152; made unique by Indigenous knowledge, 153; RSCs' feeling of inferiority about, 155–8; split between French and English on Indigenous knowledge, 171–2
Canadian Historical Association (CHA), 186, 189–93, 290
Canadian Historical Review (CHR), 186
Canadian Human Rights Tribunal, 337
Canadian Pacific Railway (CPR), 17n6
Cardinal, Douglas, 81n57, 308
Cardinal, Harold, 183, 241
Carman, Bliss, 39
Carnegie Foundation, 35, 283
Carnochan, Janet, 38
Carpmael, Charles, 23, 48n8
Carter, Sarah, 96, 117, 118
Casgrain, Henri-Raymond, 33
Chartrand, Larry, 233, 234, 235, 237
Chauveau, Pierre-Joseph-Olivier, 23, 26, 48n9
Choquette, Ernest, 168
Christianity, 102
Clearing the Plains; Disease, Politics of Starvation, and the Loss of Indigenous Life (Daschuk), 186, 187

cognitive imperialism, 232–3, 238
cognitive whitewashing, 233
collaboration, 282
colonialism (*see also* imperialism): acceptance of by historians, 188; of Canadian education system, 232–3; of Canadian law, 233–4, 238–41, 243–4; change of its focus over time, 173n5; context of for *R. v. Stanley* trial, 252–4; D. C. Scott's role in, 111, 124; defined, 232; and dispossession of Indigenous knowledge, 153; and dispossession of Indigenous lands, 17n6; and dispossession of Shoal Lake 40's land and resources, 112; and erasure of Indigenous peoples, 339; as form of structured dispossession, 113–14; and Grand Trunk Pacific Railway, 253; and *Indian Act,* 115; and J. C. Schultz, 163; perpetuated by networks of knowledge production, 279; role of Western law in, 230; RSC history of, 3, 4, 232, 320–1; RSC tie to, 276–8, 280, 291–2; self-reflection on by non-Indigenous lawyer, 230–1, 236–7; settlers seeing as finished business, 335–6; of surrender process, 118; tie to genocide, 232; in universities, 306; and unmarked graves of residential schools, 224; of violence in Saskatchewan, 265
Cook, David C., 102
Corbin, C. N. E., 282
Cornwallis, Edward, 139, 144
Coulthard, Glen, 113

criminal justice system, 254–5, 260, 269
Cross-Whitestone, Cassidy, 256–7, 263, 264
Crowfoot, Chief, 24

Daschuk, James, 186, 187, 200n43
Dawson, George, 17n6, 40–1, 156, 160, 168, 171
Dawson, John W.: background, 47n5; discovery of settlement of Hochelaga, 158–9; helps G. Patterson, 135; and inaugural meeting of RSC, 22–3, 26–7, 46, 156–7; on RSC's duty to advise government, 29
Dawson, Samuel E., 43
Deacon, Thomas R., 115, 116, 119, 120, 121
Deal, Michael, 135
decolonization: and amending law, 239, 240–1; and developing a law of contracts course, 237–8; importance of, 231–2; and law schools, 234–5, 244; L. B. Simpson on, 279; of research process, 282; of RSC, 310–12, 324–5, 342, 343; suggestions for, 342–3
Deerchild, Rosanna, 104
Denison, George, 164, 165
Department of Indian Affairs (DIA): and Brandon Indian Residential School, 205, 208, 214; role in Shoal Lake aqueduct, 116–17, 118–22; and surrender process for reserve land, 116–18
Derrida, Jacques, 292n2
Des Ormeau, Dollard, 185

De Verchères, Madeleine, 185
Double-Headed Golden Eagle (Ch'as-kin) Rising (Jackson), 326–8
Doughty, Arthur, 45, 137
Douglas, Amelia C., 109n45
Dragland, Stan, 63, 89, 113
Drummond, William H., 64

Edgar, Pelham, 66
education and colonialism, 232–3, 244
Eliza Sero v. Gault, 71
Ennis, David, 121
Erskine, John, 141, 149n45
extractive history, 280–1, 285–6, 287–8

Falconer, Robert, 152, 158, 170–1, 178n55
Faucher de Saint-Maurice, Narcisse-Henri-Edouard, 23, 48n9
Fauteux, Aegidius, 158
Federation for the Humanities and Social Sciences, 16
Fee, Margery, 90
Ferrier, Principal (Brandon Indian Residential School), 211, 214
First Nations Caring Society of Canada, 337
Fitzgibbon, Mary A., 38
Fleming, Sanford, 17n6, 34, 36, 54n79
Fletcher, James, 43
Fontaine, Tina, 255
Fraser, Crystal, 280
Freedom Road, 123
Frog Lake Resistance, 254
Fuller, Lon, 247n46

Ganong, William F., 281
Garneau, David, 280
genocide: Canadian law and, 234; colonialism's tie to, 232; as contested term, 188; need for education on, 184; RSC's role in, 277; unqualified use of term, 253, 254
George V, King, 70
Gerein, Anthony, 262
Gladue process, 255
Gonthier, Charles, 266–7
Goreham, Joseph, 142
Grand Trunk Pacific Railway (GTPR), 253
Grant, George, 17n6, 30, 42, 303
Great Britain, 29, 157–8, 283, 290
Greater Winnipeg Water District (GWWD), 115–16, 118–22
Greer, Allan, 173n5
Gunn, Kate, 114

Hamel, Thomas-Étienne, 41
hang fire theory, 258, 259–60
Hardisty, Isabella, 109n45
Harper, Stephen, 185, 195n23
Harris, Douglas, 115
Harrison, Susie F., 39, 55n95
Hellmuth, Isaac, 301
Hewitt, Jeffrey, 233, 234, 235, 242
Hildebrandt, Walter, 241
Hill, Susan, 186
Hill-Tout, Charles, 167, 177n47, 177n48, 177n49
Historical and Scientific Society of Manitoba, 160
Howells, Emily S., 91
Howells, William D., 91
Hudson's Bay Company, 163
Hul'qumi'num legal tradition, 240–1

Hunt, Dallas, 279, 287–8
Hunt, Thomas S., 45

imperialism (*see also* colonialism): cognitive, 232–3, 238; of collection of Indigenous culture, 40; of knowledge produced by RSC, 46; of Lorne of Marquis' advice to Macdonald, 24; of Lorne of Marquis' view, 27; racism used to support, 73; and RSC's ties to British Crown, 29; tie to language of, 39; and writing of A. MacMechan, 137, 138–9, 145
The Inconvenient Indian (King), 89
Indian Act, 115, 117, 119–20, 123, 303
Indian Residential Schools Settlement Agreement (IRSSA), 204, 336
indigenization, 235, 311
Indigenous knowledge/knowledge keepers: academia's need of, 163, 333; academia's trade of help for, 285–6; advances in protection of by Canadian state, 321–3; benefits and risks of including in law school, 241–3; and C. Blackstock's prodding of RSC on, 3; and C. Hill-Tout, 167–8; deemed illegitimate, 286, 304, 306; dispossession of, 153; examples of its use in Western laws, 239, 240–1; G. F. G. Stanley's marginalization of Indigenous history, 287–8, 289; harm done to by extractive history, 280–2; how its marginalization aided imperialism, 39; how law is represented by, 328–30,

331; how loss of languages harms, 233; including within law schools, 234–5; incorporating into law of contracts course, 237–8; its role in making Canadian culture unique, 153; recent popularity of Indigenous history, 186–7; RSC fascination with, 7, 33, 39–41, 159–63, 306–7; RSC founders' views on, 278; RSC procurement of its artifacts, 280; RSC's French-language historians see as part of Canadian culture, 168–71; RSC's interest in salvaging, 34; RSC's lack of interest in, 153, 158–9, 308; using art as way of codifying history and law, 330

Indigenous peoples (*see also* specific nations): as absent or disappearing, 279; backlash against due to progressive change, 243; changes for in Canadian society in recent years, 185–8; and criminal justice system, 254–5, 260, 269; D. C. Scott's efforts to deny rights of, 61–2, 70–1, 73, 88; D. C. Scott's portrayal of, 69, 83n90; dispossession of lands, 17n6; effect of link between academia and government on, 303–4; and erasure-salvage continuum, 339, 342; E. Sapir's work with, 284, 285; exclusion from juries, 261–2; and first official map of Canada, 36; G. F. G. Stanley's contact with, 286; global movement in legal rights for, 323; history at universities, 304–6; how P. Johnson's themes of Indigenous courage elicited negative Scott work, 98–104, 105; J. C. Shultz's feelings on, 163, 165–7; and litigation in courts, 184–5; Marquis of Lorne's relationship with, 24; outcry from on residential schools, 207–8; paternalistic attitude towards, 165–7; portrayal in history writing post-1970, 183, 185–6; portrayal in history writing pre-1970, 180–1, 183; racial context of *R. v. Stanley* trial, 252–4; regular appearance in news from 1990s, 183–5; as RSC members and performers, 39, 81n57, 304, 307–8; RSC's obsessive fascination with, 39–41; RSC's tokenistic move toward reconciliation with, 308–10; RSC views on, 24, 277, 278, 307; stoking fear of in *R. v. Stanley* trial, 264–6; suggestions for decolonization of its scholarship, 342–3

International Joint Commission, 116

Jackson, Belinda, 256, 258, 262–4
Jackson, Shain, 326–34
Jeong, Ho-Won, 311
Johnson, E. Pauline: and "A Cry from an Indian Wife," 88, 91–2, 99; anticipates assimilation of Indigenous people, 89; biography, 91; chronology of her writings on Indigenous people, 97, 104–5; death, 96–7; history of her contact with D. C. Scott, 91–7, 159; how her themes of

Indigenous courage elicited negative Scott work, 98–104, 105; lack of critical analysis of her poetry compared to D. C. Scott's, 90; photos, 93, 95; and RSC, 39, 65, 107n21, 178n60
Johnson, Evelyn, 92, 97
Johnson, George H. M., 91
Jones, Kahkewaquonaby Peter E., 305
Joseph, Robert, 303

Kelm, Mary-Ellen, 115
King, W. L. Mackenzie, 64–5
kinship, 241
Kipling, Rudyard, 142
Kirby, William, 81n58
Kirkness, Alfred, 212, 214
Ku Klux Klan (KKK), 252–3

LaCapra, Dominick, 309
LaChance, Leo, 253
Ladner, Kiera, 308
Lampman, Archibald, 39, 63, 92, 94, 157
land surrender, 116–18, 123, 126n24
LaPier, Rosalyn, 294n16
Lepofsky, Dana, 333
Laurier, Wilfrid, 30, 34
law and colonialism, 233–4, 243–4
law of contracts: benefits and risks of including Indigenous law in teaching of, 241–3; description of course in, 235–6; developing a decolonized course in, 237–8, 246n29, 246n30; examples of colonialism in, 238–41, 248n57, 248n58
law schools, 234–5, 241–3

Lawson, George, 23, 40, 41, 48n7, 54n84
Leacock, Stephen, 42
Le Loutre, Jean-Louis, 138, 142
Le Moine, James M., 35, 37–8
LeSueur, William D., 44, 57n130, 96
Lewis, Ben, 310
L'Heureux-Dubé, Claire, 266–7
Lighthall, William D., 64, 71, 96, 160
Lindberg, Darcy, 236
Loft, Frederick O., 70, 84n98
Lorne, Marquis of: background, 49n13; and foundation of RSC, 22, 24, 26, 27, 299; interest in Indigenous artifacts and people, 159, 175n27; relationship with Indigenous peoples, 24; on research into Indigenous people, 40; on RSC being exclusionary, 36–7; ties to British Crown, 29
Lower, A. R. M., 143
Luby, Brittany, 114
Lucas, Florence D., 54n90

Maass, Alex, 205
Macdonald, John A., 24, 61, 90, 164
Macdougall, Brenda, 186
Macgillivray, Dugald, 138–9
MacGregor, James D., 133, 134
MacKinnon, Catherine, 236
MacLennan, Hugh, 143
MacMechan, Archibald: probable view of Indigenous folklore, 178n61; RSC connection of, 131–2, 139; work which comments on Mi'kmaq, 136–40, 144, 145, 148n28

Mair, Charles, 163–4, 165
Manuel, George, 183
Martin, Chester, 131, 156, 158
Martin, Oronhyatekha Peter, 305
McCallum, Mary Jane Logan, 186, 287
McCooney, Mike, 141
Mccue, Harvey, 305
McCulloch, Thomas, 133
McGee, Thomas D., 164–5
McGuire-Martin, Peggy, 118
McKay, Annie M. (Nan), 305
McKenzie, R. S., 126n18
McLachlin, Beverley, 262
McLean, J. D., 120
McLennan, William, 64
McMurrich, James P., 38
McNeil, Jeremy, 319
McRaye, Walter, 97
Meckler, Lee B., 109n40
Meechance, Eric, 256, 257, 263
Melançon, Claude, 168–9, 170, 171
Merasty, Gary, 205
Methodist Church, 207–11
#Me Too generation, 90
Mi'kmaw: A. MacMechan work that comments on, 136–40; avocational writers' impact on, 131, 132, 143–5; derogatory descriptions of, 144; G. Patterson work that comments on, 132–6; RSC interest in folklore, 169, 171; T. H. Raddall's experience of and writing on, 140–3
Miller, James R., 184
Million, Dian, 204
Milloy, John, 14–15
Milton, Cynthia, 326–34

Missing Children Research Project, 205, 206–7
Monture, Rick, 90
Morales, Sarah, 237, 238, 240–1
Morgan, Henry J., 164, 165
Mosby, Ian, 187, 200n45
Murdoch, Beamish, 138

Napier, Duncan Campbell, 75–6n8
National Archives, 279–80
National Centre for Truth and Reconciliation (NCTR) *Memorial Registry*, 223
A National Crime (Milloy), 14–15
National Farmers Union (NFU), 265
National Gallery of Canada, 24, 299
National Inquiry into Missing and Murdered Indigenous Women and Girls (NIMMIWG), 184, 232, 254, 338
National Research Council, 36
Nerland, Carney, 253
Neuman, Keith, 187
Nisga'a, 185, 293n10
Nolin, Joseph, 114
Nussbaum, Emily, 90

Oliver, Frank, 14, 117–18

Paget, Amelia M., 96
Paget, F. H., 14
Painter, Nell I., 73
Pardy, Bruce, 268–9
Parliament of Canada: and Bryce report on residential schools, 14; G. Bradbury speaks for Indigenous in, 120; passes bill to stop Indigenous raising money

for sovereignty, 70–1, 84n104; RSC dependence on, 29, 30
Pasternak, Shiri, 123
Patterson, George: probable view of Indigenous folklore, 178n61; RSC connection of, 131, 135; work which comments on Mi'kmaq, 132–6, 141, 144
Patterson, George Geddie, 139
Paul, Jim, 281
Paul, William B., 141
Paypom Treaty, 114
Pickthall, Marjorie, 157
Pietsch, Tamson, 131, 153, 290
Popescul, Martel, 251, 266, 268
Public Archives of Canada, 35
Pyatt, J., 282

Quinn, Joanna, 319

race/racism (*see also* colonialism; imperialism): F. Boas and, 85n114; in history writing pre-1970, 180–1; and Indigenous peoples exclusion from juries, 261–2; revealed in commissions seeking justice, 338; in RSC papers, 162; RSC role in developing, 46, 69; in *R. v. Stanley* trial, 250–1, 252–4, 261; scientific, 40, 165; used to support imperialism, 73
Raddall, Thomas H., 132, 140–3, 144, 145, 150n62, 178n61
Rand, Silas T., 133
Ray, Arthur J., 185
Reade, John, 39, 171
reconciliation (*see also* Truth and Reconciliation Commission): and Brandon Residential School Cemeteries Project, 224; mobilization of universities toward, 310, 323–4; movement towards, 188; as part of TRC, 204; by RSC, 5–7, 11, 311–12, 319, 320–5; RSC's tokenistic move towards, 308–10; and Touchstones of Hope, 16
Redsky, Pete, 116, 122
Reid, John, 178n61
residential schools: and Brandon Indian school cemeteries, 211–15; and Brandon Residential School Cemeteries Project, 216–22; conditions at Brandon Indian Residential School, 207–11; D. C. Scott's responsibility for deaths at, 203–4; D. C. Scott's role in controlling, 4, 12–13, 113; deaths at, 13–14, 206–7; described as cultural genocide, 253; difficulty of Indigenous to speak of, 204; and *Indian Residential Schools Settlement Agreement*, 336–7; interest in knowing history of, 187; litigation for survivors, 185, 204; in P. Johnson's work, 101, 102; recommendations for search of missing children and graves, 223–4; reports of horrible conditions at, 14–15; sexual and physical abuse at, 13; and Tk'emlups Kamloops graves, 332–3; TRC calls to action on missing children from, 215; work of Missing Children Research Project on, 205, 206–7
Riddell, William R., 71, 85n107
Riel, Louis, 164, 287–9

Rifkin, Mark, 267–8
Roach, Kent, 259
Roche, William, 116
Rogin, Jillian, 255
Royal Canadian Academy of Arts, 299
Royal Commission on Aboriginal Peoples (RCAP), 183–4, 204
Royal Society of Canada (RSC) (*see also* Scott, Duncan Campbell): accomplishments, 62; A. MacMechan connection to, 131–2, 139; and avocational writers' impact on Mi'kmaw-settler interactions, 131, 132, 143–5; beginnings, 22–4, 26–7, 152, 174n8, 298–9; and Canada First members, 164–5; C. Blackstock encourages to implement TRC recommendations, 3, 12–16, 17n2; C. Blackstock's keynote address to, 4–5, 309–10, 338; and C. Hill-Tout, 167; and colonialism, 3, 4, 232, 276–8, 280, 291–2, 320–1; and contact between D. C. Scott and P. Johnson, 92, 94; creation of College of New Scholars, Artists and Scientists, 308, 315n56; D. C. Scott as president, 68, 89; and decolonization, 310–12, 324–5, 342, 343; difficulty securing permanent location, 42; earliest research of, 28; E. Pauline Johnson and, 39, 65, 178n60; Eurocentrism of, 300–1; as exclusionary body, 36–9, 73, 80n57, 156, 298, 300–1; fascination with Indigenous culture, 7, 33, 39–41, 159–63, 169, 171, 306–7; F. Boas work presented at, 167, 170, 284; feeling of inferiority about Canadian culture, 155–8; first annual meeting of, 26–8; how it has dealt with time and change, 44–5; imperialism of, 29, 46; inclusion of women, 54n89, 54n90; Indigenous scholars as members and performers at, 39, 81n57, 304, 307–8; induction of D. C. Scott, 62–5; initiatives and projects of, 31–4; international reach of, 282–3, 289–90; J. C. Schultz's address to, 164, 165–7; as keeper and creator of knowledge, 29, 73; lack of interest in Indigenous knowledge, 153, 158–9, 308; lobbies for national institutions, 33–6, 69, 154, 159, 280, 306; nation building of, 282, 283; objectives and mandate of, 4, 28, 62; and Parliament of Canada, 29, 30; paternalism towards Indigenous peoples, 165, 166–7; posts and honours for D. C. Scott, 59, 66, 68, 74–5; practicing extractive history, 280–1; problems with attendance and participation, 41–2; *Proceedings and Transactions,* 174n7; *Proceedings and Transactions* of, 21–2, 31–3, 42–4, 154–6, 159, 160, 174n9; process of inducting new members, 27–8, 50n32, 82n73; procurement of Indigenous artifacts, 280; racism of, 46, 69, 162; research into Indigenous folklore, 168–71, 177n55; role in genocide, 277;

royal and government ties of, 29–30, 154; serving function as institutional cultural capital, 290–2; sets bylaws, rules and regulations, 27–8; S. Jackson's views of, 331–2; split between French and English sections on Indigenous knowledge, 171–2, 173n3; structural violence of, 300–1; support of National Archives, 279–80; T. H. Raddall's induction, 132, 143; ties to academic societies, 30–1; ties to government, 29–30, 154, 302–4; ties to Great Britain, 29, 283; tie to US, 283; tokenistic change to reconciliation by, 308–10; and Truth and Reconciliation Task Force, 5–7, 11, 311–12, 319, 320–5; urged to educate members on D. C. Scott, 5, 16; view of Indigenous people, 24, 277, 278, 307; women excluded from, 37–9, 156, 178n60

Ruffo, Armand, 98

R. v. Stanley: all-white jury for, 261–2; bias in favour of defence in, 260; charges in, 255; context of racism and colonialism surrounding, 250–1, 252–4, 261; decision in, 250, 255–6, 275n88; defence builds up fear angle, 264–6; facts of the case, 256–9; failure of judge to warn jury of bias, 266–8; no consideration given for trauma of Indigenous witnesses, 262–4; response to Windsor Law's verdict on, 268–9; trial of, 255, 259–60; Windsor Law's reaction to verdict in, 250–1

R. v. Williams, 267

Saint-Aubin, Ambroise, 142
Sangster, Joan, 6
Sapir, Edward, 177n49, 283–6
Saunders, William, 301
Schultz, John C., 163–4, 165–7, 176n45
scientific racism, 40, 165
Scott, Duncan Campbell: background, 75n8; and Brandon Indian Residential School, 208; on Canadian academia, 157–8; career, 91; C. Blackstock's urging for RSC to educate members on, 5, 16; chronology of his writings on Indigenous people, 97–8, 104–5; critics difficulty in assessing literary work of, 81n66, 89–90; death, 75; description and personality of, 68; early years, 61, 76n8, 90; effect of his Indian Affairs work, 61–2; E. Sapir's contact with, 177n49, 285; fairness in judging him by standards of his time, 13, 15, 71–2; focus on assimilation of Indigenous in literary writings, 88; history of his contact with P. Johnson, 91–7; honorary degrees for, 68, 74–5, 82n83; how his writing responds to P. Johnson's, 98–104, 105; inaction over poor conditions at residential schools, 13–14, 15, 203–4; and inferiority of Canadian culture, 168, 171; key role in Canadian colonialism, 111, 124;

as knowledge shaper, 73; life of affluence of, 73–5; list of RSC posts held by, 3, 59, 66, 68; literary work of, 62, 63, 65–6, 71, 89, 106n8, 108n35; lobbies for bill to stop Indigenous raising money for sovereignty, 84n104; lobbies for National Museum, 159; overlapping of government and RSC work, 303; photos, 60, 67, 72, 93; poetry readings at RSC, 39; portrayal of Indigenous people, 69, 73, 83n90; possible Indigenous ancestors of, 76n9; power accrued from RSC president post, 68; pressures government for ethnology survey, 69–70; receives inventory of Indigenous objects, 175n30; role in control of residential schools, 4, 12–13, 113; role in Shoal Lake 40 dispossession, 113, 116–17, 120–1; RSC duties, 83n94; as RSC gatekeeper, 66, 177n49; RSC induction of, 30, 62–5; RSC presidential address in 1922, 155, 156, 157–8, 159; RSC's need to hold accountable, 5, 16, 338; S. Jackson's view of, 332, 333; slurring F. O. Loft, 70, 84n98; summary of government posts held by, 59, 75n2, 78n34; tragedy in life of, 87n127; view of P. Johnson, 94, 96; work on Six Nations Confederacy, 307; correspondence with A. MacMechan, 139–40

Scott, Elizabeth Duncan, 87n127
Scott, William, 61, 90
Selwyn, Alfred R. C., 23, 47n6

Shekon Neechie (website), 186, 199n33
Shoal Lake 40 First Nation, 112, 115–16, 118–23
Shortt, Adam, 64, 131, 137
Sifton, Clifford, 78n34
Simcoe, John G., 66, 69
Simpson, Audra, 293n7
Simpson, Leanne Betasamosake, 279
Sinclair, Murray, 184
Sioux Valley Dakota Nation, 211, 215, 216–22
Six Nations Confederacy, 70–1
Smith, Goldwin, 23–4, 48n11, 54n84
Smith, Keith, 115
Smithsonian Institute, 24, 53n65
Social Sciences and Humanities Research Council (SSHRC), 187
Spencer, Scott, 260, 261, 264, 265, 273n47, 275n88
Spivak, Gayatri, 276
Stanley, George F. G., 286–9, 290
Stanley, Gerald (see also *R. v. Stanley*): and decision in *R. v. Stanley*, 250; fined for gun ownership, 273n47; killing of Colten Boushie, 256–9; lawyer's use of bias to get him off, 267–8; testimony during trial, 259–60; use of fear of Indigenous in his defence, 264–6; Windsor Law's labelling a murderer, 269
Stanley, Leesa, 256, 257, 258, 259
Stanley, Sheldon, 256, 257, 258, 259, 267
Stark, Heidi, 254
statues, removal of historical, 187
Stoler, Ann, 276

Stonechild, Neil, 254
Strapp, Principal (Brandon Residential School), 210
Strathcona, Lord (Donald Smith), 30
structural violence, 300–1, 302–4
Sulte, Benjamin, 170
Supreme Court of Canada, 261, 262, 266–7
Swan, Angela, 240

Teit, James, 177n48, 177n49
Ternier, Rachelle, 265
Titley, E. B., 61, 71, 75n2, 113
Tk'emlups Kamloops Indian Residential School, 332–3
Todd, Alpheus, 29–30
Todd, Zoe, 280
totemism, 167–8
Touchstones of Hope, 16
Treaty 3, 114
Tri-Council policy statement, 322
Trudeau, Justin, 331
Truth and Reconciliation Commission of Canada (TRC): calls to action on missing children and burial information, 215; Cindy Blackstock's call for action on, 3, 4–5, 12–16, 17n2; complications of calls to action 74 to 76, 216–22; establishing crucial statistics on children's deaths at residential schools, 206–7; issues its *Calls to Action,* 3; launches Missing Children Research Project, 205; mandate, 336–7; as product of IRSSA, 204; recommendations for law schools, 234; release of final report, 336; and teaching of history, 184
Tupper, Charles, 42

universities: creation of non-denominational, 299–300, 312n7; decolonization of, 310, 342–3; exclusivity of, 301–2, 304; lack of Indigenous students at, 304–6; mobilization towards reconciliation of, 310, 323–4
University of Western Ontario, 299, 301–2

Vankoughnet, Lawrence, 78n34

Waite, Peter B., 179
Wallace, Robert C., 17n6
wampum, 239
Wereley, Ian, 68, 154, 278
Wesner, A. B., 282
Wet'suwet'en protest, 112, 123–4
Wilson, Alex, 242
Wilson, Alice, 54n89, 304
Wilson, Daniel, 23, 37, 48n10
Wilson-Raybould, Jody, 187
Windsor Law, 250–1, 268–9
Winks, Robin, 180
Winnipeg, City of, 114–15
Wintemberg, William J., 141
Wise, Sydney F., 179
Working Group on Missing Children and Unmarked Burials, 205
Wright, Ramsay, 46
Wrong, George M., 131
Wurtele, Catherine, 76n8
Wuttunee, Kiora, 256, 257, 258, 263

Yeigh, Frank, 91

Zizek, Slavoj, 250
Zoom conferencing, 326